The Regenerate Lyric
Theology and Innovation in American Poetry

In her book *The Regenerate Lyric*, Elisa New presents a major revision of the accepted historical account of Emerson as the source of the American poetic tradition. New challenges the majority opinion that Emerson not only overthrew New England religious orthodoxy but founded a poetic tradition that fundamentally renounced that orthodoxy in favor of a secular Romanticism. In the years between the Unitarian controversy of early to mid nineteenth century and the rise of Neo-Orthodoxy a century later, New argues, the very orthodoxy that Emerson pronounced moribund found new life and sanctuary in the unlikeliest of places: the American poem. She contends that Emerson's reinvention of religion as a species of poetry was tested and found wanting by the very poetic innovators Emerson addressed, and that a countertradition is evident in his major heirs – Whitman, Dickinson, Crane, Stevens, Frost, and Lowell. Emerson's own poetry failed to live up to his poetics and revealed instead an inherent paradox: the renewal of religion as, or in, poetic theory alienates religion from its life principle – theology – and disables the poem as well. Elisa New examines the poems in great detail, offering searching readings and concluding finally that "it is 'regeneracy' rather than 'originality' that is the American poet's modus operandi and native mandate."

CAMBRIDGE STUDIES IN AMERICAN LITERATURE AND CULTURE

Editor
ERIC SUNDQUIST, *University of California, Los Angeles*

Advisory Board
NINA BAYM, *University of Illinois, Champaign-Urbana*
SACVAN BERCOVITCH, *Harvard University*
ALBERT GELPI, *Stanford University*
MYRA JEHLEN, *University of Pennsylvania*
CAROLYN PORTER, *University of California, Berkeley*
ROBERT STEPTO, *Yale University*
TONY TANNER, *King's College, Cambridge University*

Continued on pages following the Index.

The Regenerate Lyric

Theology and Innovation in American Poetry

ELISA NEW

University of Pennsylvania

Published by the Press Syndicate of the University of Cambridge
The Pitt Building, Trumpington Street, Cambridge CB2 1RP
40 West 20th Street, New York, NY 10011–4211, USA
10 Stamford Road, Oakleigh, Victoria 3166, Australia

PS
310
R4
N49
1993

© Cambridge University Press 1993

First published 1993

Printed in Canada

Library of Congress Cataloging-in-Publication Data
New, Elisa.
The regenerate lyric : theology and innovation in American poetry
/ Elisa New.
p.   cm. – (Cambridge studies in American literature and
culture ; 64)
Includes bibliographical references.
ISBN 0-521-43021-6
1. Religious poetry, American – History and criticism.
2. Experimental poetry – United States – History and criticism.
3. American poetry – History and criticism – Theory, etc.   4. Emerson,
Ralph Waldo, 1803–1882 – Aesthetics.   5. Theology in literature.
6. God in literature.   I. Title.   II. Series.
PS310.R4N49   1993
811.009′382 – dc20   92-23412

A catalog record for this book is available from the British Library.

ISBN 0-521-43021-6 hardback

Contents

Contents

Acknowledgments

To have received encouragement for a study of theology and poetic form in a critical era so otherwise preoccupied has been more than a piece of good fortune. I have been privileged to have worked with scholars whose belief in the ultimate worthiness of literary study was firm, and to have come of age at two universities, Brandeis then Columbia, where the decoding of texts has not replaced the reading of books. To Allen Grossman, who taught me to read poems, I owe a debt not only of career but of vocation. His conviction as to the human service a poem – and its teaching – can perform has lent not only purpose but abiding joy to my work. Ann Douglas, the kind of mentor most graduate students only dream of, has been a model of scholarly passion and tenacity, and in recent years, a dear friend. I owe deep thanks to Andrew Delbanco for his incisive and witty guidance, and for the example he sets of intellectual probity and rhetorical excellence. And I am grateful to Jonathan Arac for his gentle persistence in asking the same question again and again. Joseph Mazzeo, Frank Kermode, Michael Riffaterre, Phyllis Trible, Hilene Flanzbaum, Peter Conn, Vicki Mahaffey, Rebecca Bushnell, and students in my various poetry seminars at Penn all made valuable contributions to the manuscript and to my faith in my work. Thomas Werge, who published a version of Chapter 5 in *Religion and Literature,* made crucial suggestions for its improvement. Eric Sundquist has been a scrupulous pilot and tactful editor; my readers and editors at Cambridge helped me immeasurably. In addition, Allison Bloch provided help with research, John R. Lennon aid with editing and manuscript preparation, and grants from the Memorial Foundation for Jewish Culture and the University of Pennsylvania Research Foundation gave me time I might have had to spend otherwise. Nor would that time have been mine without the help of Chanikul Chanukaroon, Terry and Ed McCulley, Debbie Lewis, and Denise Germont-Risser whose loving attention to my children, Yael and Orli, gave me freedom of mind and, thus, freedom to work. To all the above I am grateful, but to no one more than my husband, Fred Levine. Becoming an expert on subjects for which no Jewish boyhood is preparation, working on hundreds of pages – sometimes two or three times – and moving to where this manuscript has taken me, he has proven not only disinterested listener and tireless editor, but cherished intellectual friend.

Introduction

From Perry Miller's monumental investigations of the New England mind, scholars learned decades ago never to underestimate the staying power of even the most parochial of Puritan notions. It was Miller who first suggested that between the thought of Edwards and Emerson are complex, if vexed, affinities more salient and enduring than Emerson's liberal apostasy could efface. Miller's description of the "Errand into the Wilderness" extended the tenure of that errand's accomplishment well beyond the decline of Congregationalism, while studies of the next generation by Lowance, Brumm, and especially Bercovitch adumbrated, even as they complicated, Miller's conviction as to the flexible tenacity of Calvinist ideas, especially their uncanny capacity to thrive outside the realm of the sacred. More recently still, scholars as methodologically and temperamentally various as Barbara Packer, Ann Douglas, Lawrence Buell, and most visibly, Harold Bloom, have probed the shaping power of religious ideas on the developing culture and its tradition of letters.

But this reciprocity between the literary and religious worlds has implications – in particular, implications for the poem – that scholarship has left largely unexplored. When Harold Bloom writes that Emersonianism, far from being just another literary strain, is rather "The American Religion," a "religion," as he puts it, that becomes so by being "first . . . canonized as American literature" (*Ralph Waldo Emerson,* 99), he imputes to this literary faith a vigor sufficient to absorb and subsume theology without loss of metaphysical discipline to religion or generic integrity to literature. Such an assertion, although offered in Bloom's characteristic idiom of fresh surmise, is not in itself controversial. It is, indeed, consonant with a long-standing critical view of American poetry as prophecy; that is, as prospective speech whose chief object is a recovery of the newness that the Fall occluded. Putting Emerson at the head of a tradition of poetic agonists pursuing an "American Sublime,"

1

Bloom re-energizes and freshens, but does not substantially alter, what has been for many years the broadly accepted version of American poetic inheritance.

Two magisterial works of the last generation, Roy Harvey Pearce's *The Continuity of American Poetry* and Hyatt Waggoner's *American Poets, from the Puritans to the Present,* both claimed that the pulse of the American poem is Emersonian. Pearce argued in 1961 that the very Americanness of the American poem inheres in its capacity to remake the Fall of Man to its own advantage; the modernism that Emerson codified, Pearce contended, is the American condition. Waggoner argues even more explicitly, and in terms anticipating Bloom's, that only insofar as the poem strikes for originality does it "[pass] Emerson's test for the true American poem" (83). In Waggoner's version of the American Sublime, "nothing is known, nothing given, everything is discovered or created" (xvii). To date, many of the most powerful accounts of Emerson's role share the notion that Emerson's substitution of poetic inspiration for religious conversion is the deciding influence not only on the retreat of sectarian piety before the advance of civic religion (as religious historians such as Clebsch, Ahlstrom, and Marty join Bloom in affirming), but also on the development of our major poetic tradition.

The most important challenge to this now classic view of American poetic inheritance came from Yvor Winters fifty years ago. Winters's insight, that American poetry is finally not about linguistic power but about "human isolation in a foreign universe," assumes the ongoing influence of an experiential Calvinism not so easily dislodged by Unitarian, Transcendentalist or Romantic forces. Few have disputed Winters's intuition that the key to Hart Crane and Emily Dickinson is not Emerson but rather the seventeenth-century devotional lyric, and his observations about such poets as Very and Tuckerman have also been widely accepted and confirmed. Recognizing Crane for the most American of American poets, and linking Crane's recondite style to a strandedness of style emphatically un-Emersonian, Winters pursued a compelling line of argument that has not been forgotten. If its force is still acknowledged, however, its authority has been drastically undercut by Winters's own imperial, frequently vituperative, critical ways. Winters made no bones about calling Emerson a "fraud." His characteristically pugilistic titles (for instance, the title of his omnibus collection of essays, *In Defense of Reason*) show an indifference bordering on contempt for the very idea of critical disinterest. Finally, Winters's sensibility prevented his maverick case from gaining the authority of a critical countertradition. Thus, while Gelpi and Delbanco, Buell and Ahlstrom have continued (in Miller's stead) to insist that certain Augustinian habits of mind, and so certain kinds of literary patterning, are present and enduring in classic American literature, the special sanctuary given this strain of thought by the American poem has not received sustained treatment since Winters.

In this book I treat the classic American poem as the religious center of an already religiocentric literature, aiming thereby to complicate, and in some measure simply to refute, the by now classic argument for Emerson's preeminence. Winters's passion, although often impolitic, hewed close to the texts, and thus to a central truth about them. The poetics that Emerson invents to replace orthodoxy serves neither to quell nor even to defer the old American preoccupation with the End and the subject who experiences that End. In the decades after "The Divinity School Address" those intractable assumptions that the theologian Jonathan Edwards shared with the poet Edward Taylor pass out of the care of seminarians and into the care of poets. Emerson notwithstanding, the conviction that there is, in Karl Barth's words, an "infinite difference between Time and eternity" – God's Word and the poets' – goes underground in the American poem.

The book's argument is this: Growing up beside the mainstream tradition we call Emersonian was another tradition, call it anti-Emersonian, that articulated itself in terms Emerson did not fit us to recognize. Theological in character – at times nearly scholastic; at others, self-consciously heretical, as opposed to merely antinomian – this tradition represents the virtual abandonment of Emerson's poetics by the very poets he saw as his culture's new priests. Not only do these poets find language itself structurally resistant to that "transcendence" recent revisions of Matthiessen have pronounced all but defunct, they also find Emerson's tenet of deferral – what he called "transition" – equally inconsistent with the realization of the poem. Rather, Beginnings and Ends claim their interest and respect; they cannot do without the Judgment Day; they cannot imagine a world without shame; they cannot forget the prohibition against idols. Whitman, Dickinson, Crane, Lowell, and Frost write poems fruitfully exercised by all those appurtenances of the Logos Emerson forswore: purity and the Incarnation, idolatry and God's unnameability; awe, dread, and the lure of the Nations; sin, Doom, and the Fortunate Fall. Even as these poets try out the Emersonian "power" in the poems we have long called major, they interrogate that power in poems we neglect. In so doing, they inaugurate and sustain a poetic countertradition, giving sanctuary to the very theological praxis to which the Emersonian religion gave no quarter. In this poetic tradition, liberal enlightenment driven back on itself finds: mystery.

The coming chapters study how, in the years between the Unitarian controversy of the early to mid nineteenth century and the rise of Neo-Orthodoxy a century later, the theology that Emerson pronounced moribund finds new life and refuge in the unlikeliest of places: the American poem. Central to my argument is the claim that the American poetic tradition is not so unambiguously Emersonian as is assumed. Rather, Emerson's reinvention of religion as a species of poetry is tested and found wanting by the very poetic innovators to whom he addressed himself. What Emerson's own poetry bears out is a paradox: The substitution of a poetic theory for religion has the twinned effects of alienating religion from its life principle, theology, and disabling the poem as well. Much of this book is devoted to illustrating how such Calvinist ideas as fallenness, sin, idolatry, dread, the Atonement, the Chosen, and the Nations enter American poetry, and how that poetry, in turn, gives quarter and then direction to a whole new tradition of theological contemplation. Along the way the book also advances a theoretical argument, about the conditions under which poems thrive and those under which they do not. Describing Emerson's own failed accommodation of the poem to a "poetics," the book posits an essential antagonism between the lyric and indeterminacies of all kinds – Unitarian or poststructuralist – suggesting that whereas theory depends on what we currently call deferral, the American poem, sanctuary of an American theology, finds its purposes better served by Ends.

The book is divided into two parts. In the three chapters comprising Part I, I excavate the implications of Emersonianism. The first chapter theorizes the language of Emerson's "original relation," the second chapter historicizes this language and demonstrates its repulse of poetic voicings, and the third explores the applied Emersonianism of the one American poet, Wallace Stevens, most engaged with Emerson's premises. The chapters of Part II, by contrast, treat Whitman, Dickinson, Crane, Frost, and Lowell as poets of fallen temperament writing in a densely theological grain.

Chapter 1 lays the foundation for the studies of separate poets to follow. Beginning with the modern figure Robert Lowell, it traces the tradition of theological inquiry back to the poems of Edward Taylor. This foundational chapter sets up a basic tension between the fallen poetry of Edward Taylor and the unfallen poetics of Emerson. The chapters that follow endeavor to demonstrate the ways in which the theologically "unoriginal," or fallen, will prove more consonant with the development of the poem than the "original." On the other hand, the deferred choice of an indeterminate poetics has in the end the same effect *on the poem* as the old ideal of transcendental originality.

Chapter 2 treats Emerson as both theorist and poet, setting him in his Unitarian context and suggesting the fundamental affinity between a Unitarian and poststructuralist poetics. After establishing the parallel function Emerson serves in his own literary culture and ours, I closely examine a selection of Emerson's best and worst poems. These readings link Emerson's failure as a writer of poems to the very poetics that so distinguish his theory. They prepare the ground for consideration of the poets addressed in subsequent chapters.

The third chapter, on Stevens, shows the results of the Emersonian poetics in the hands of a poet more gifted than Emerson. This chapter skips the standard anthology pieces to peer rather at Stevens's strange, even freakish, poems of the mid-century years. Here I underscore the ways in which Stevens brings the Emersonian notions of originality, or unfallenness, to their logical conclusion in poems whose "savagery" is their armor against the Divine. Renouncing, in Emerson's footsteps, the patrimony of Adam and the tribe of Israel, Stevens writes a poetry of the Nations – not genteel but ritually Gentile, totemic of faith, and unconverted to shame. Stevens's bizarre literalization of the Emersonian "original relation" dramatizes certain consequences earlier poets had detected from the outset.

Opening the second part of the book, the fourth – and longest – chapter advances the case that Whitman stands, from the very first, 1855, edition of *Leaves of Grass,* in a more complex relationship with the Emersonian mandate than "Song of Myself" would suggest. Granting the Emersonian thrust of that poem, the chapter performs an excavation of Whitman's scripturally saturated and radically experimental "The Sleepers" in order to advance a frankly revisionist view of the structure and intent of *Leaves of Grass* as a whole. As Hyatt Waggoner noted, "the source from which Emerson felt completely estranged is Biblical" (654). The in-depth, nearly exegetical attention I give to "The Sleepers" is authorized by my sense that Whitman's a-Scriptural, Emersonian poem, "Song of Myself," depends on the scripturalism, indeed the legalism, of "The Sleepers." Rather in the same way that, as David Damrosch has observed, the Pentateuch subsumes narrative within law – the inceptional myth of Genesis not the setting for but rather set *within* the legal codes – Whitman's *Leaves of Grass* delineates a cosmological and theological organization that "Song of Myself" benefits from, but cannot, for all its mesmerizing power, be said to found. This chapter shows how, in "The Sleepers," Whitman returns to the very Scriptural universe Emerson had abandoned, harrowing – and so, in Emerson's stead, saving Americans from – the Puritan Hell, but not before reopening the book on matters liberals had hoped to put to rest: priestly conduct, impurity, Adamic shame, and especially Christ's Atonement. Laying bare Whitman's profound engagement with Levitical prohibitions, with the Pauline taxonomies of saved and damned, and especially with the Puritan literature of unprepared sleep, I aim principally to propose that the liberty the speaker of "Song of Myself" enjoys is not originary, but regenerate, wrested out of Whitman's engagement with an older law. Under the auspices of that law, "Song of Myself" can be born.

Chapter 5 explores Emily Dickinson's image of "circumference" as a theological limit, distinguishing such a limit from an Emersonian "transition" or the contemporary feminist "subversion." The negotiability of limits by power, or, an understanding of limits as emitting power – these are the axioms of Emersonian, but also of recent feminist, theory. I wish to complicate current feminist readings, which pronounce all limits in Dickinson as linguistically constructed (and so vulnerable to a poet's counterpressure), and simultaneously to complicate Emersonian readings which overemphasize Dickinson's faith in a poet's vision. In other words, whereas feminist and Emersonian readings of Dickinson's work emphasize her essential demolition of received forms, my interest is in Dickinson's much more chastened attraction to an unformed realm where she exercises little power to speak of. There, where "A Species stands Beyond," not only the forms of her culture, but the very forms of her poetic and female self-reliance are emptied of meaning. I thus describe the development in her poems of a religious attitude neither conventional nor antinomian, but rather intrepidly speculative and theological, meditative, and at times nearly mystical. Focusing on the tension between poetic seeing and that idolatry Reformed Christianity reviles, the chapter argues that the value Dickinson attaches to a blind and wandering language – as spiritual instrument – yields poems whose supernal difficulty has left them largely untreated in the critical literature. Finally, Dickinson's Emersonianism is of a drastically limited sort, more often curtailed and corrected than indulged.

Chapter 6, on Hart Crane, deepens the discussion of fallenness and limits pursued in Chapter 5. Detecting in Crane's recurring image of the "Hand of Fire" an overdetermined emblem of the fallen agony (it is, all at the same time, flaming sword of the angel guarding Eden, the Pauline sword that divides, and the outstretched hand of Edwards's fiery God), this chapter explores the religious psychology – of anxious dread, absurd humor, and fitful ecstasy – that structures poems from *White Buildings,* but especially *The Bridge.* I concentrate on doubt and ignorance as a condition of the fallen speaker, de-transcendentalizing Crane's work by employing, as I do in the Dickinson chapter, the same Kierkegaardian model of faith that will so engage Neo-Orthodox scholars in the 1940s. In Crane, the sinner whom Emerson had pardoned is ushered back into the canon, with dramatic effect on the poem as a form of the voice.

The book concludes with an epilogue that meditates on two poets, both of whom saw their careers crest as theology resurfaced in the work of the Niebuhrs and Tillich. Invoking in this epilogue Richard Niebuhr's *The Kingdom of God in America,* and noting especially Niebuhr's Kierkegaardian reading of Edwards as American theologian par excellence, these pages assert the continuity of thought Emersonianism may have interrupted, but which the poetic tradition has sustained. I thus call Niebuhr's conviction as to the instructive if irremediable gap between the subject and God an abiding preoccupation of the American poet who is more accurately heir to Edwards than Channing, to Taylor than Emerson. I conclude with readings of Robert Lowell, a poet solidly in Taylor's tradition, and Robert Frost, a severely chastened, or "experienced," Emersonian. The book loops back to its beginning with the claim that it is "regeneracy" rather than "originality" that is the American poet's modus operandi and native mandate.

The argument developed in the following chapters is cultural to the extent that I am interested in showing how a species of theological inquiry, once the exclusive purview of seminarians and the spiritually panicked, resituated itself in another cultural sphere. Chapter 2, for instance, combs the historical record to show how the highly literate Unitarianism that prepared Emerson's development as poetic theorist proved infertile ground for the poem's flourishing. Although making itself hospitable to poetry in theory and to poetry as theory, liberalism was nevertheless enormously indifferent to the requirements of the poem proper. The markedly theological character of these interwar poems – written between the Civil War and World War II – can be seen as part of a larger intellectual discontent with liberal religion that finally expressed itself in such watersheds as William James's critique of Emerson, Eliot's conversion to Anglo-Catholicism, the rise of the Neo-Orthodoxy I take up in the last chapter, and, of course, the career and influence of Perry Miller. Historically speaking, the tradition this book treats is not in the least eclectic. If the years between the 1840s and the 1940s see theological concerns driven underground in the American poem, on either side of the poetic century I chronicle is orthodoxy – unsublimated, voluble, and fighting for a foothold: Hopkins and other heirs of Edwards battling for suasion over the American soul well into Emerson's lifetime, and the Niebuhrs well into the productive primes of Stevens, Lowell, and Frost.

Poets, it is true, do not write in vacuums. Nevertheless, such historical framing as I here essay should not be understood as a prelude to an exercise in New Historicism or in that strain of cultural studies energized by the work of Foucault. There can be little doubt that the theoretical, cultural, and historicist turn of literary studies in the last twenty years has had salutary effects on our understanding of numerous American writers, nowhere proving its efficacy more than in the rediscovery of Emerson, as essayist, if not as poet. The example of Emerson merits for just this reason close and particular scrutiny precisely because his current rehabilitation as essayist has not helped him much as poet. One has to wonder why Emerson's poetic theory does not find its natural illustration in his poetic work. What, we may ask, does theory do that poems can't? Or, what do poems do that theory can't account for? To put it another way, how might the aims of a theoretical and of a poetic language be so different that a "poetics" as sophisticated as Emerson's could not help him write a better poem?

With such questions before us, one aim of this book is to ask where a poetics can go and where the poem, perhaps, can't; to explore in particular the limitations of the contemporary premium on openness and open form.

It is beginning to be noticed, for instance, how much of our theory is narrative theory. Reacting against New Critical hierarchies that took the poem as archgenre – Logos even – of the body of literature, contemporary theory is, not surprisingly, punctilious in withholding protection from the relics of a retrograde literary establishment. Further suspicion of the lyric as the luxury object of a patrician class has had the effect of cooling interest in ideas about poems proper, instead rendering to various theories now going under the name of "poetics" the attention poems once claimed.

This shift of attention from, in effect, *parole* to *langue* has proven undeniably fruitful as we have gone about describing the larger systemic forces that influence literary output and especially the shaping of American narratives. Many of the most notable critical works of the past decade have been those concerned to demonstrate how a skeptically based "poetics" can expedite understanding of, say, the discontent of American narratives with the freedom America actually offered. American novels that disbelieve themselves can join in a project of query that suspends all social givens, all political inequities: To understand a narrative as governed by "poetics" credits the way it problematizes the social order, holding in abeyance any precipitous claims to achievement of a perfect union.

But poems that disbelieve themselves can renounce the one power they have: call it voice. I would contend that even in the extreme case of a poet like Ashbery, it is the scattering of voice that gives the poem its ironic power, the odd wonder of a ventriloquized performance no one speaker owns that gives Ashbery his place in a tradition of lyric voicings. Whether the voice that utters the poem in fact owns itself, is individual, has some coherence outside the exigencies of the various systems that press on it – these are not easy questions to answer. Still, one can say with assurance that poems are written *as if* such coherence might obtain, as if the choice of a word, of *parole*, makes virtual the chooser; as if the record of a voice print not at all arbitrary but willed and designed gave the self, or the soul, some foothold not otherwise there. Poems cannot prove the existence of the integral self, but the lyric does not exist save where the existence of the speaking self is seriously entertained – as an article of faith, if not a foregone conclusion.

To contemplate certain American poems in particular, is to be thrust out of the theoretical universe we've come to know. Assumptions about, for example, the equation of literariness and an intrinsic skepticism of language are thrown into question when we acknowledge the fundamentally affirmative quality of these poems, as opposed to the negative – by which I mean antithetical rather than dolorous – and deterministic quality of our theoretical climate. Unconsoled by social truths, repelling skepticism, and resisting even the disenchantments of irony, the poems treated here are, to put it as simply as possible, religious. They are invested in structures which only a critic sure of her freedom from prejudice should venture to "deconstruct." Though enormously powerful, these poems are driven not so much by the Nietzschean will to power on which current theories rely as by what William James called "the will to believe." To read them in good faith does not require piety, but it does exact a certain suspension of disbelief, at least for the space of the poem.

One practical effect of this acknowledgment of belief rather than disbelief as operative and vital in the constitution of the poem is that the theological terms deployed here will often be the same ones our theory has disposed of with alacrity. It may seem obvious to some, for example, that what I will call God's unnameability resembles what Derrida calls the hegemony of the Logos, the absolute presence that Western, and specifically Christian, culture sanctifies at the expense of writing. This accounted for, such readers might parse, say, Edward Taylor's shame at writing as epigraph to Derrida's theory of graphemic denigration, and deem all this book a footnote to Derrida's *Of Grammatology*. Moreover, in days which have recently seen the Law of the Father routed by theorists concerned to expose dualism as a strategy of power, this book may seem to take an antiquarian, if not retrograde, interest in "binaries." Revising the work of Lacan and Foucault, feminist critics here and abroad have of late devoted themselves to showing that imbalances of power are as much fixed by the old Cartesian coordinates – of me and not-me, thought and being, signifier and signified – as by the explicitly guilty antinomies of male and female, reason and emotion, mind and body. Such theorists would, and do, claim that what a traditionally misogynist Christianity calls the Fall is no more than the loss of the Mother, transposed as myth. Following out this train of thought, the dividedness of human experience that Western metaphysics naturalizes as dualism is little more than a reaction formation, or patriarchal habit, which compulsively repeats, in order to master, the separation from this mother. After assigning Dickinson her due place of honor, such a criticism might enjoy noting that when Emerson seeks to overthrow the language of his Puritan fathers, he finds his best strategy in the polymorphous language Kristeva has called "semiotic," and that what Whitman in fact discovers in his revisionist reading of Leviticus is precisely the maternal figure the Mosaic and later the Christian cultures are established to repress. Finally, one might ask what historical ruptures conditioned this poetic interest in the Fall? Theorists who follow Foucault in seeing history as the force that names in order to institutionalize what it is already nostalgic for would not find it inexplicable that a modern, secular anomie should seek comfort in the Fall as metaphor.

The methodologies I have sketched above are different from each other in manifold ways, complex in their own right and not reduced without violence to analogues of one another. They may, nevertheless, be said to share one thing: a certain confidence that faith, or religious experience, is best described in terms alien to itself. Why? Because of faith's habit of concentrating power in a God who, as metaphor, shores up the power of other, material structures (the Patriarchy, the Law, the Truth) by lending these the prestige of the immaterial.

When a contingent structure is made divine there is surely warrant for deconstruction. This does not imply, however, that such warrant should hold reciprocally, that structures of divinity or faith require reduction to material designs. But one result of the poststructural reaction against illegitimate immaterializing of the contingent and material has been just this: a reactive materializing of the immaterial. To wit: God in the text is equated with the textual or actual orders he is suffered to prop; piety with love of dominance or domination; contemplation of Time to a denial of history. We run out of ways to credit poetries of faith with intrinsic sense or interest.

Thus, around the very issues of faith this book treats materialist analyses of various kinds can overstep the limits of their discipline, totalizing where other total explanations hold the field. I do not suggest that religious history is not as susceptible as any to the play of contending powers, but rather that around matters of the immaterial a single-minded search for material causes risks not merely tactlessness but also an odd parochialism. My primary interest in the coming pages is in the workings of poems, and particularly the ways in which an American poetic language is first infiltrated and ultimately transformed by the specific lexicon of American Calvinism. Its uses are manifold, but theory is characteristically unkind to poetic texture, absorbing that texture, as a matter of course, into its own cultural or heuristic matrices.

Nor, let me be clear, does the critical method that the recent theories have unseated serve poems much better. The New Criticism sealed the poem in the inertia of its rarity. Poetic stresses and tensions, caught in the object, allowed the critic his interval of admiration, but the poem, meanwhile, went rigid. As I understand the poems I treat here, they are neither iconic – divine artifacts of human genius – nor constructed by forces indifferent to them. Made of voice, they solicit ear. Made of timing, they distend time. The space they fill is a space of intimate concourse; the intention they realize, willed choice within limits.

Allowing, then, that all criticism is a kind of rewriting, and that no critic stands outside the circle of a hermeneutics of one kind or another, I endeavor a critical practice ultimately committed to the poem as voiced and experienced, not as object, but as movement across the page and mind. As the reader will soon enough notice, my readings are composed to *produce* the poem: dramaturgically. A kind of infusion – the suspension of the poem in a solution of clarifying prose – is my goal, rather than any kind of extraction, or taxonomic naming. I see the analysis of poems as rejuvenating art. In the end, not only the poem, but criticism of the poem as well, must depend on our will to believe in language's regenerating force.

PART I

1

An Original Relation: Taylor and Emerson

Near the end of Robert Lowell's last published volume, *Day by Day,* comes a poem, "Shifting Colors," that connects the late Lowell with the early Lowell, and indeed the most contemporary and worldly of American poetries with the earliest and most pious. The poem surprises. For if the young Robert Lowell had been exquisitely sensitive to *kairoi,* those metaphorical days when God's time bisects ours in a text – Genesis, Revelation, or the sermons of Edwards – the speaker of *Day by Day* seems, in contrast, wholly chastened by the daily round. Sharp-eyed, but doubtful of vision, incarcerated, but in the quotidian, not Hell, Lowell's speaker opens chary of any recuperable Beginnings – "Things changed to the names he gave them, / then lost their names"(3) – and bereft of that clarity shed by great Ends. Once, all his lyrics sought apocalypse as an act of faith. Now, a thin wistfulness stands in for faith, and a groping after last lines for Last Days. Overstocked with ends, Lowell's very table of contents courts a closure that will not come. The titles are plangent, repeating and repeating themselves – backward or forward the same – like the palindrome of the "day by day": "Last Walk," "Suicide," "Departure," "Burial," "Death of a Critic," "Endings" and – most poignant – "Our Afterlife I" followed by "Our Afterlife II."

Indeed, so resigned to repetition is this last book of Robert Lowell's, so inured to the Ecclesiast's wisdom – "There is no End to the piling up of books" – that we are hardly prepared when the timeserver's ennui deepens. Then, the day book of a man in the fall of his life becomes a book of Fallen Man. The speaker of the poem might as well be Michael Wigglesworth or Edward Taylor as Robert Lowell, for beneath his bemusement at outliving both Hiroshima and John Berryman, is the Puritan's prehensile certainty that any day might be the Day of Doom. And beneath this poetry, urbanely psychoanalytic, believing "art a way to get well," is the old rock pile of Christian exercise that called neurosis sin,

15

and cure redemption. The poet from whom we no longer expect regret returns, fretful, to Eden.

> I fish until the clouds turn blue,
> weary of self-torture, ready to paint
> lilacs or confuse a thousand leaves,
> as landscapists must.   (119)

Like Adam's, the poet's besetting grief is his separation from an essential unity. What was effortless is now work. What was unconscious is now conscious. The nature once continuous with his own nature is now only as continuous as solipsism makes it; its onetime fullness and sufficiency, now detached and artificial as "landscape." The affliction of a restless and agitated mimesis is to replete expression as original sin is to prelapsarian belonging. Then, understanding was innocent of death. Now, consciousness quickens where the senses tell us we end; feeble language and the body's obtrusive extent mark Adam's fall into knowledge and noticing. Not that either notices what it might; only what it must.

Lowell's "Shifting Colors" is a poem that invokes the Fall as what it feels like: unoriginality. Behind the speaker's blurred landscape are Whitman's fecund emblems, leaves and lilacs; and behind his weary fishing, Whitman's virile promise to remake the world, to write Genesis in the self's own seed. Drooping limp-lined, the speaker's "miscast trout-fly" parodies Whitman's spermatic optimism. But the problem of poetic repetition that Lowell – in an Emersonian funk – attaches to a flaccid manhood is only proximate, only a personalization of the larger problem the poet intuits: our failure to secure an "original relation" – to precursors, yes, but also to "the universe." For it is not just that poets are made out of other poets, poems cobbled out of other poems, but each word echoes what it is not, each utterance reminds us of the separation from what is: In a Fallen world, all writing is, as Derrida has it, supplemental. Observing, as Whitman did, his better and double in an "ageless big white horse" munching unself-consciously, the speaker mourns, "Poor measured neurotic man" – and concludes "Animals are more instinctive virtuosi."

Why poor? Why measured? Because only the human being, lacking the animal's unconscious grace, is consigned to fish "until the clouds turn blue." Aping a Creator who gave sky and water articulation with the magisterial Word, the poet fishes, troubling the face of the waters, anxious, driven, prolix. By the time, a few lines later, that he brashly exclaims, "But all nature is sundrunk with sex," we understand too well this pathetic fallacy for his own, so dazzled he cannot tell which reflects which – sea or sky? – which is "blue"? – sea or sky? – or his own mind, which, "sundrunk on sex" casts for its blue dreams in both.

As the speaker goes on, "How could man fail to notice, man the only pornographer among the animals?" we know his question is rhetorical. He could not fail to notice. He is the creature constituted by noticing, by dual consciousness, of me and not-me, of self and other, of word and thing. Born in that moment when Adam espied himself – his shame coincident with the birth of his consciousness – poetic vision is inseparable from this shame. All representation is, in Roland Barthes' words, embarrassed figuration.[1]

Two poems before the end of his career, what Lowell probes in the miasmic "Shifting Colors" is the unchanged state of affairs that makes the American poet of the mid-twentieth century as much Adam's heir as his forebears of three centuries earlier. The poem testifies to more, however, than simply the enduring impress of the Fall, and Calvinism, on the American poetic tradition. It is also an exemplary case of the phenomenon this book treats: an American poetry doing the work of an American theology, its language taking on the burden of dualism, and its speaker the old affects of Fallen Man: The poet's every trope echoes Adam's old tropism. Even as his poor language – always after, always outside – traces and retraces in its own ineffaceable structure the line of dualism, the poet suffers that line as self-division, playing Devil to his own Adam, eternally at, as it were, his own window. Just as Adamic desire marks the breach from unity, writing virtualizes and embodies limitation, traducing God's Creation in mere representation, desecrating divine ecstasis in what is, for Lowell, the pornography of objects.

At such a pass, the poet of "Shifting Colors" who goes on to cry, "I seek leave unimpassioned by my body" has left the quotidian for the deepest time, has left Ecclesiastes for Genesis. What he seeks is nothing less than to unwrite the Fall, to unwrite the theological fiat that made desire (a longing for union) and language (a longing for knowing) the twinned signs of our distance from what was. Searching for an original language, a language with, as Lowell puts it, "the directness that catches everything on the run and then expires," the poet would enter the world in some extratemporal way, recapture his innocence, shed his experience, and do all this in a world not projected by him, not haunted by him, free of him and his reflections: He would be original.

This was the task Emerson set the American poet as far back as 1836 when in "Nature" he asked, rhetorically, almost casually, "Why should we not enjoy an original relation to the universe?" The sentence represents Emerson's first, rhetorically mildest, challenge to the Calvinist doctrine he will face more pugilistically two years later in "The Divinity School Address." But its casualness should not disguise the dangerous invitation Emerson here offered an audience not unconvinced of man's innate depravity since Adam. Invoking an "original relation" achieved in pleasure rather than shame, Emerson lays down a mandate for a new theology gained through a new kind of poetry; for a spiritual satisfaction secured through a poetry outside time, exempt from the Fall's strictures. The coming pages will treat the failure of that mandate, and the paradoxical rediscovery of the Fall by a tradition of American poets unmoved by the man-centered Unitarianism Emerson brought to the very breaking point by codifying.

Nevertheless, if this book describes the development of an American poetic tradition eschewing Emerson's solutions, it is a tradition never straying far from Emerson's problems. Had Emerson found a way to liberate pleasure as a poetic principle God could approve, all our poetry since might be different. As it is, Robert Lowell's latter-day dolors are ironically predicted in Emerson's own hobbled idea of an originary speech. Both fail to free themselves from the set of problems, simultaneously poetic and religious, sustained by the earliest American poets.

Indeed, claims to the contrary notwithstanding, Emerson's work, like Lowell's, wears as its peculiarly American signature the constitutive fallenness that Edward Taylor knew. In this regard, Harold Bloom's assertion that the "American religion is Protestant without being Christian" (*Ralph Waldo Emerson,* 5), and that "the voice of an American poetry can be heard . . . not so much . . . in Taylor, who was a good English poet who happened to be living in America" (*American Poetry to 1914,* 299) exactly reverses the argument I will develop here. For Bloom, Taylor's verse of sin and incompletion is alien (or at least unnaturalized) with respect to that American Sublime he takes to be the American poet's normative mode. Taylor's fallen stringencies describe, for Bloom, Taylor's eccentricity, if not his un-Americanness. Consider the reverse. What Taylor's undiscovered corpus first established was the poetic utility of a sense of stain; in his work we discover how the weight of the Fall gives the poem both impress and moment, dimension and timing, depth and time. Taylor's poems thus predict what all Emerson's answerers come to know as well: the poetic weakness sustained by any notion of originality that does not allow for the finality of division. Eschewing originality, Taylor's poems instead strike for a state of renewal – a *regeneracy* – by which the lyric keeps faith with the Fall and so with the timbre of a mortal voice speaking in time. His poems, and the tradition of the regenerate lyric his poems anticipate, strike at the heart of the Emersonian Sublime.

Not that Emerson does not assist the project, acting in a certain way as his own nemesis. His sublimity is, all along, self-confuting, so much so that the tolerance, and even affection, he bears for struggle itself seems beside the point when Emerson's fairest hope, fulcrum of all his notions of power, is imperiled. Even allowing that Emerson's appetite for a good face-off of ideas – a "gnosis" in Bloom's parlance – was considerable, his "original relation" is not an assent to contradictoriness so much as it is a flare sent up out of such: name of a state lifted above the either/or. Exempt from the abrasions of gnostic combat, the phrase "original relation" is nothing if not logocentric. It wants the peace that precedeth understanding.

Yet, gesture as he does toward a reforged union with the All, Emerson's very query "Why should we not enjoy an original relation to the universe" fails, word by word, to express much but the opposite of such union. "Enjoyment" is troublesome enough, but I want to start with "original relation," for in this phrase is the crux of the problem Lowell inherits. Describing in its most obvious sense a relation unmediated by institutions or received ideas, in its depths, or more precisely, in the concourse set up between "original" and "relation," the phrase devours the very possibility of such an unmediated state. Like other such terms that fall into semantic illogic at junctures of Awe (the man/God, life out of death, the virgin birth, the Passion itself), "original relation" thwarts itself at the point of articulation, belonging to that class of words Freud called "antithetical." So dependent for significance on their opposites that they remain dual to their lexical roots, such "primal" words float up from prememories of some old, ineluctable fission.[2]

Not surprisingly, therefore, to be original in English is possible only in the most unoriginal of fashions: "Original" only entered the English language in 1309 as an adjective modifying – what else? – sin. On its own, sin precludes originality. A breach against a prior state, sin is constitutionally relational. Compounded of these two, the phrase "original sin" defies its own semantic coherence, paradoxically describing a burden each sinners own, but gotten, in fact, secondhand from Adam. The origin of death, Adam's sin was also, in ways important to us here, the death of originality.

To contemplate the truly original, as Emerson so assiduously endeavored in "Nature," is to imagine something prior to all relation, and to do so without recourse to temporal or spatial metaphor. The genuinely original recognizes nothing like priority, nothing like extension, having neither precedent nor fulfillment, neither size nor dimension. When God describes himself in Genesis with the tetragrammaton YHVH, root of all verbs to be, past, present, and future, he names Himself identical with Himself through time, never shadowing His own former self-presence in articulation; never, as Harold Bloom would have it, "belated." The Hebrew registers, in other words, not only time and space surfeited, and so superannuated, in Being. It also registers the way in which this surfeit makes Being impervious to that "relation" which cancels originality by regarding, or expressing it. Theologically speaking, relation is the condition of our dividedness from God. Temporally speaking, relation distinguishes past from present and so gives us history, Lowell's own "day by day." Linguistically, relation defines our capacity to name. The etiology of all three is a dividedness, a scarcity of the original, yearning for reparation.

The only originality to escape such relation is, in fact, an *ab*-originality from which Emerson maintains a curious and finally wary distance. On the one hand, his interest in words as "fossil poetry" hypothesizes a time before time when such artifacts as might be deemed simply archaic redeem themselves. Prehistory improves on mere history as a place without strata, without pecking order. Part of prehistory, the aboriginal is a reservoir of power somehow not cannibalizing the present as the past does. And yet this originality of the aboriginal, rather like the originality of relation, cannot manifest itself except through the rude offices of mediation. Poetry may have been written before time was, and yet its naissance is registered nowhere but in words, all marked with the tiny boneprints of time upon them.

What's more, the truly aboriginal, when Emerson dares to imagine it, is a force of inexpressiveness nearly unbearable to contemplate. "The Snow-storm," unformed and void till we "come see" it, possesses an aboriginal power that is simultaneously chaotic and apocalyptic: It has the yawning vacancy of the one – before Creation – and the implosive power of the other – after Creation has exhausted itself. Such originality is relieved only by our relation to it, which is to say, by its compromise. Like the whiteness of the whale, or like the pale fog where we last glimpse Arthur Gordon Pym, or like the "desert place" where Frost's speaker finds himself "too absent spirited to count," Emerson's imagined places of Beginning without mark are as likely to horrify as to free. Originality, imagined as a space prior to dimension, regathers to it the Mystery earlier Calvinists knew for one attribute of God's power: The aboriginal terrifies.

Emerson's phrase, in short, cannot even posit the new without dragging behind it the "rags and relics" of the old. The "original relation" is, ironically, almost indistinguishable from the original sin it would annul. Moreover, this is only the tip of the problem, literary and theological at the same time, that Emerson's fragile conception of the new exhumes.

Exhumes I say, because, of course, the problem of an "original relation" does not begin with Emerson. In our own time its best interpreter is Heidegger, who detheologized it. But long the property of mystics, the problem of the "original relation" finds its place in the more mystical interstices of Puritan literature, understood by no one better than Edward Taylor. His *Preparatory Meditations,* discovered too late for Emerson, may indicate for us all the impediments to poetic originality the Fall implies.[3]

To Emerson's query, cannily cast in a rhetoric brooking no reply, Taylor might have given vigorous reply. Why should we not enjoy an original relation to the universe? Simply because as sinners we are unoriginal. Ours is not to enjoy. To enjoy is to pursue a heightened self-consciousness we are explicitly programmed by shame to flee. Indeed, from the very launchpad of its penetrating prefix, en-joy not only springs toward a bliss sacrificed long ago in Adam's garden, but it also takes for granted a volition, or a Free Will, different indeed from the shame whose salient characteristic is to contradict the will. To be ashamed is to be subject to a selfhood one does not will, and so to rely, not on the power of the self, as Emerson would later adjure in "Self Reliance," but on God's pleasure, or his grace.

Further, if all genuine pleasure originates elsewhere, so all fitting speech belongs to the One who needs no speech but a Word. Coextensive with human unworthiness, language is the loose cannon of the Will. Too deft, too accomplished a language, as I will soon indicate, may bewitch, and so blaspheme, but in the normal run of things, words are simply embodiments of sin, redeemable only insofar as they mark the chasm between us and God.[4] Virtual waste products of the poet's struggle to escape the sinful self, words metonymize, in Taylor's work, man made a waste product to his own former virtue.

Yet the matter is more complex, for Taylor's language theory is no more idealist than its theorist is self-hating. Emblems of sinfulness, yes, but words are also paradoxical vehicles to grace. In their use, the poet finds an effective gestalt of regeneration. Make no mistake. Thoroughly orthodox in his eschewal of Works, Taylor nowhere intimates that one might write one's way to heaven. Still, in the *Meditations* words tamp down a route to that experience of sin from which salvation breaks. Look for a moment at a few lines from Taylor's much read Meditation 26:

> Unclean, unclean: my lord undone, all vile,
> Yea all defiled; what shall Thy servant do?
> Unfit for Thee; not fit for holy soil,
> Nor for communion of saints below.
> A bag of botches, lump of loathesomeness:
> Defiled by touch, by issue: Leproused flesh.

The lines may strike the modern ear as extravagantly self-punishing, even masochistic, but in context their excess is normative, and in a certain way profoundly freeing. They commit their speaker to an arduous exercise of self-examination impatient of all repression. Going squishy in "bag of botches," with its viscous and rotten "c" echoed in "touch," "issue," and "flesh," Taylor's words trace language back from the dignity, and distance, of denotation; they trace language back to sound exiting from the body. The pride of speech decomposes, as it were, back into tongue on palate, lobe on lobe. What the poet seeks here is the full experience of that degradation of the Logos in the corporeal (the Fall) which is mended in the Word made flesh (the Incarnation). Taking up the burden of shame in a language inextricably bound to body, Taylor makes language the register of his fallen state. Through his words he can not only accede to, but reexperience, the Adamic sin from which he issues. This is the experience prerequisite to saving grace. Shame, for this Puritan poet, is simultaneously the pivot of salvation and that on which all poems turn.

The whole problem of human articulation is only disclosed in full, however, when the poet tries to represent that which defies, and is defiled by, representation: God. How to express His originality in a secondary language, a language best suited to pointing out human inadequacy. "My rhymes do better suit my own dispraise," writes the poet at the exact midpoint of Meditation 22, "than tune forth Praise to thee." This is no coy disclaimer on Taylor's part. Rather, it is preamble to an object lesson in the snares awaiting human language, first among them the fearsome self-sufficiency of words. Steeped in sin, language knows how to pleasure itself: "Dispraise" is skilled at limning a world of dimension and texture.

To return to Meditation 22, note how thoroughly indeed the poet's "rhymes do suit," his very protestations of unworthiness embedded snugly in a language of apt, if homely, verisimilitude. With their colloquial precision – "My quaintest metaphors are ragged stuff / Making the sun seem like a mullipuff " – Taylor's words reach a level of poetic resolution, a virtuality, at odds with piety's more tenuous relation to Being. They too much please. As the poet goes on: "The sun grown wan; and angels palefaced shrink, / Before thy shine, which I besmear with ink," the effect is again double. "Making" metaphors, and "besmearing" ink, the poet's laboring praise is nearly excremental, the expenditure of imaginative effort thickened and corporealized by his own mortality, light itself rendered opaque by the human eye that catches it. And yet the words also "make" what Williams later called "contact," or what Frost means in "After Apple Picking" when he writes "My instep arch not only keeps the ache, / It keeps the pressure of a ladder round." In this pressure is the kind of pleasure that calls the Fall fortunate, man lucky to labor in a vineyard, hefting apples, filling a page. Cutting out an arc of work that holds the shape of a human presence, Taylor's lines begin in bodily subordination but gain poetic footing as they go. In this spell of poetic reverie, a kind of fallen attentiveness, the poet writes as if of this world, not merely consigned to live in it.[5]

God cuts no such swathe. The immanence of His Creation, its completeness, precludes such. He whose labor yielded Creation repels further predication, and holds aloof from that hacking which leaves its mark in a poem. Indeed, Taylor's God is precisely a kind of antilinguistic field, a force of Unnameability:

> This shining sky will fly away apace,
>   When Thy bright glory splits the same to make
> Thy majesty a pass, whose fairest face
>   Too foul a path is for Thy feet to take.

The lines anticipate the problem of Emerson's "original relation" inasmuch as they describe a Being sullied by articulation itself: the "path" God blazes is befouled in its very separation from Him. Not only does the act of imagination split divinity, violating that visage it would see face to face, but God Himself, projected in attributes, is an imposter, blasphemous double of His own indivisibility. What the anthropomorphism of the poem delineates, spatializing the intangible, is an edge where Being is travestied in knowing, an edge defined by consciousness and maintained by language. On this edge, labor marks the Fall from repose and sufficiency, and representation the distance from that Being which, out of Eden, does not need to know itself. By situating the evocation of the Unnameable in an eschatological future tense, "The Shining sun will fly away apace," Taylor would head off time, reflection, and all words too late for Being, and yet the increment remains: originality lost in relation.

Flush out the human stink, purge the poem of human metaphor, and the poet still darkens God's door with his speech. Further still, the lines to come dramatize an even more troublesome aspect of Taylor's poetic problem. If too fleshy a speech can shackle the poet in complacency and self-reliant worldliness, than a rarified, purified language risks worse. Ambitious praise is a slippery slope, and the poet's very aspiration to a language unstained by sin is under peril of blasphemy. Moses, who saw God face to face, is a type of Christ, but Moses' own presumption did not go unpunished. The pursuit of a knowledge of God beyond the ken of the sinner allies the poet with one who would be more than Moses, more than human. It allies him with Satan, or with the Faustian violator of God's privacy. "One glimpse," concludes Meditation 22,

> of Thy bright judgement day,
> And glory piercing through, like fiery darts,
> All devils, doth me make for grace to pray.
>   For filling grace had I ten thousand hearts,
>   I'd through ten hells to see Thy Judgment day,
>   Wouldst Thou but gild my soul with Thy bright ray.

Taylor intuits here that fitting praise may equally serve as the Tempter's converting ordinance. The poet's "desire," motivated as it is by piety and the greatest of deference, cannot in the end be distinguished from the rasher, cheaper desires that are the Devil's stock in trade. Indeed, the penultimate line of Meditation 22 as much suggests the poet's resignation to hell as his harrowing of it. The Christian desire for pure illumination that trades this life for eternal life is susceptible to parody in the Faustian hubris that bargains hell for judgment. Ironically, the human inadequacy, the poetic pitiableness, that mandates the poet's subordinately fleshy relation to God also serves as ballast against such weightless hyperbole. With God's Unnameability the foundation on which a Puritan poetics must rest, pleasure in the text can be idolatrous business.

To be sure, it is this very craving for a sight beyond the human prospect – for, if you will, Power – that is implicated and interrogated in the work of poets writing after Emerson. Again and again, Emerson's moment of supernal freedom, where the vision is seen through and the self goes transparent, is found wanting, not only wanting humility but also wanting weight.

Against this value of Power, Whitman, for instance, posits the value of things "in their places" with *place* functioning in his thought to suggest particular loci of meaning cohering within a ring of determinants. The space without coordinates, original in its own ether, is as likely to be a vacuum as a forcefield. Thus, in Whitman and the poets after him, the vantage point high above the earth and above contingency is frequently singled out for suspicion. The transcendental loge is hard to tell from the limbo Satan occupies. From Satan's vantage point, the attraction of originality is indistinguishable from the pull of the vacuum, and infinity is just another word for nothing. As Satan apostrophizes in Mark Twain's parody of Emersonian hope:

> Nothing exists: all is a dream. God – man – the world – the sun, the moon, the wilderness of stars – a dream, all a dream; they have no existence. Nothing exists except empty space and you. (Twain, 252)

Its due terror restored, Twain's piercingly literal reading of the Emersonian vision shows how too facile a transparency allies the seeker after meaning with the guarantors of meaninglessness. Subtract the conviction of human fallibility from the search for Infinity, and Infinity exacts no more discrimination than the nihilist's nothingness. Take away God's mystery and all values become one, as blasphemy finds names equally pronounceable or unpronounceable. Egotism – or a reduction of Being to what the eye can compass – exposes the idolatrous face of the Emersonian confidence, while Faustianism, or a bogus confidence in transvaluation, reveals the costs of excising the unique savior.

Blasphemy, egotism, solipsism, Faustianism, triviality – these are names of some very old syndromes one would not expect an originary poetics to harbor. But if all these thrive as live threats in the poetry of Emerson's heirs, as variant names for facile compensation, they drive American poems into crisis and accordingly back into the precincts of the poem. Indeed, what we may call the Emersonian interval plays its role in the education of the American poet to originality's impossibility, but also to the lyric's regeneration.

In Whitman, in Dickinson, in Crane, in Frost and in Lowell, and even in Stevens, sooner or later it comes: that moment when the poet – having wandered far for the sake of sight – draws back. What this pilgrim took for originality's locale (a place out "upon circumference," a place "Incognizable," or simply "new") is not so at all. Then Dickinson's wanderer, Crane's explorer, discover, dismaying, all they have imposed. How hackneyed is a Satan thinking himself alone!; how feckless an Adam, calling delirium unself-consciousness!; how shallow the Christian who mistakes the old Eden for a tropic undiscovered!

The Emersonian afflatus gives the American poet reach. It gives the poet an elasticity Thoreau called "extra-vagant." And yet the poet stretched beyond his limits or past her reach must, in the end, come back to his powerlessness, back to her purblindness. If vision is to be realized in a poem, that poem will depend on the knowledge that comes, as Crane puts it, "to each of us alone." With this, the Emersonian self-reliance is retuned in a lonelier key, resolving back into Augustine's, or Calvin's, more islanded solitude, the poet not creating so much as carrying the self, not inventing Eden so much as marking time outside it. His compensation is the poem. Whereas originality proper finds no register in the human voice, the sin that dogs it with relation is richly voiced.

Emerson struggled against this understanding the whole length of his career as a poet. His best poems, among which one should count "Hamatreya," unwittingly demonstrate the poetic efficacy of fallenness, even as they assert the philosophical or theoretic power of the new. "Hamatreya," crystallizing the difference between the two, cracks into two halves along the faultline of Emerson's misjudgment. In that poem, the object of the poet's disdain is the literate clod – the fallen man as complacent local – whose will affirms "I fancy these pure waters and the flags know me."

Suffering the fellow only so long, Emerson would counter the farmer's obtuse confidence with the wisdom of the Earth. Thus, the farmer's stolid and shortsighted perambulations are plunked out in an iambic meter meant to tire us. But the Earth is a metrical original, obeying no timing but her own. Fey, she cries: "Mine and yours / Mine not yours. / Earth endures; / Stars abide" – her ditty only four lines long before she hops another meter, cutting off an unexpected length of stanza: "Shine down in the old sea; / Old are the shores; / But where are the old men? / I who have seen much, / Such have I never seen."

The great irony and, I think, the poetic justice here, is that although the Earth Song may mock the farmer's pacing out his land and life and lines, may deem his incessant measurement provincial, narrow, grasping, may possess a knowledge he does not even know enough to miss, she cannot make a poem. She cannot sing as this humble Flint or Hosmer can, bound for his grave, yet marking off his lines as, Lowell might say, "landscapists must." The Earth's Song – transparent – cannot know itself, and so is voiceless. Hosmer cannot discern much beyond his time. But Hosmer sings.

In "Hamatreya" and a whole tradition of American poems, regeneracy garners lyric speech while the originality Emerson conceived must find another idiom, one finally, curiously, less parochial than the idiom of the poem. Emersonianism, as the coming chapter argues, builds a religion out of the notion of poetic license, but in so doing saps the poem of what makes it a poem: the limitation all licenses press. That the poem itself would require precisely what the Emersonian religion had abjured was a truth that Emerson, taxed by sore experience, learned too late to fill his own poetic days. But not too late for the poets who would follow. From Whitman down through Lowell, the Emerson that the American poet best hears is the poet Emerson knew he wasn't. That poet joins, in Emerson's stead, the file of days, or as Lowell has it, the "day By day" to live in time, and so, like Taylor, to trace and retrace the fissure where God gave Adam the obscure text of consciousness.

2

Poetics and the Poem: Emerson

No casuist, and famous in the popular mind for calling "a foolish consistency the hobgoblin of little minds," Emerson habitually supplies his own countertexts. Thus, in the same months that he was completing "The Poet" – the essay that completes the work of the "Divinity School Address" by transferring from priest to poet the calling of ministry – Emerson nevertheless wrote in his journal: " 'God,' 'Grace,' 'Prayer,' 'Heaven' and 'Hell' are those sacred words to which we still must return" (Whicher, 213). Among jottings toward a creed that abolishes all backward-glancing, Emerson's use of "return" is notable, interrupting but not diverting the current of his thought. His resolute, albeit stray, acknowledgment that the terms of a fixed orthodoxy had not yet exhausted their usefulness is instead left to be taken up by his poetic heirs. If all the quarter Emerson gives the old faith is compassed in the concession that he "is for preserving all those religious writings which were in the origins poetic, ecstatic expressions which the first user of did not know what he said" (213), the poets who follow him query in their work the existence of such poetic priority, and thus the possibility of what Emerson had earlier called "an original relation to the universe." Paradoxically, they return for their poetic sustenance not only to Heaven and Hell, to Prayer, God, and the Grace that Emerson's attenuated Unitarianism still allowed, but also to terms out of a Calvinist lexicon Unitarians less venturesome than Emerson had long since jettisoned. The coming chapters develop the idea that this lexicon, orphaned by Unitarianism and pronounced moribund by Emerson, finds new life and an adoptive home in the work of the very poets Emerson is said to stand for. That this would happen, Emerson, for all his prescience, did not predict.

Poetry, Emerson reasoned in the 1830s and 1840s, was the antithesis of orthodoxy. Capacious where orthodoxy was crabbed, inspiriting where orthodoxy sapped, poetry stood in something of the relationship to doctrine that the New Testament had to the Hebrew Bible, and in turn,

Protestantism to the Pope. With the Church dead of its own weight, it was the poet, learning from Nature, who would rebuild the sanctuary orthodoxy had despoiled. Hence, the technique of "The Divinity School Address" – but of "The Poet" as well – is to liberate divinity from the strictures of orthodoxy by mandating a new law on the same scale and expansiveness as the law of imagination. Describing a human spirit, freed from monstrous Incarnation and now securing its redemption through the heart's own expressiveness; envisioning ministers, released from dreary ritualism, and now at liberty to perfect their own representative souls; and mooting the grace/works debate by showing how the Calvinist introspection might now summon a spirit Adam the namer knew, if Adam ashamed did not – through a series of fiats, Emerson effected a crucial transfer of Divine power. What had been exclusively God's was now man's; what was once known only to God was now knowable through the agencies of a language. And with language given plenipotent, if not total power, Emerson could reclaim for the sons of Adam a faith in language's divine possibility. No more was the Divine beyond human speech, His grace beyond our ken. On the contrary. Now, when through arduous, imaginative search we found God, we would know Him like a native tongue. He would speak to us in our heart's own language, His very Revelation, as Sylvester Judd saw it, manifest as "cardiagraphy."

These are the essential, readily recognizable tenets of what we have come to call American Romanticism, or what Harold Bloom has called the American Religion, Emersonianism. There is no disputing the power of this creed. As generations of religious historians have shown, it has established itself on the firmest ground possible: the ground of popular assent and of national values. To reimagine an American poetry not at one with a faith of such public probity is difficult indeed, and harder still since our readings of canonized American figures have so long been organized under its auspices. The coming pages will describe a strain of theological inquiry so retrograde in Emerson's terms that key poems written in this strain receive, at best, the credit due the experimental, but more usually, the condescension accorded the minor. Emerson, on the other hand, invented a religion so powerful and ready to hand it could pass like the midday rush of congregants out of churches and the narrow precincts of poetic appreciation to find its place in a realm less parochial, less culturally minor, than either church or poem. There are almost no words for the national ethos that do not flash back, and with alienated majesty, Emerson's vision; conversely, there is almost no Emersonian inspiration that is not part of the common currency.[1]

Emersonianism, however, is neither strictly a faith nor solely a language, but rather a result of Emerson's project to convert neither to the other, but both to each. Writing that the American religion "cannot become American religion until it is first canonized as American literature" (*Emerson*, 99), Harold Bloom stops just short of assenting to Huck Finn's proposition – applied to victuals, but applicable to Twain's most Emersonian horror of religious purism – that. "things get mixed up, and the juice kind of swaps around, and the things go better." Although Bloom is right that it is the reciprocity of the religious and the literary that Emerson "established among us," it is important to note, with Huck, the disestablishment such reciprocity implies. For if Emerson invented a mode that made religion and poetry identical with each other, this very mode also made them alien to themselves.

In a certain way our own literary era has seen the relationship between these two separate alienations confirmed. In the aftermath of Derrida's toppling of the Logos, we witness the ascendancy of various poetics thriving independent of the poem itself, and, at the same time, the rediscovery and rehabilitation of Emerson. Emerson attracts our focused admiration, as opposed to our merely general appreciation, in large part for what we take to be his intuition about language's essentially resistant and unfixable character. It was, after all, Emerson who, in the 1840s, supervised the unseating of orthodox Grace and its replacement by a poetic grace, and it was Emerson who deposed the arid erudition and bogus prestige of the "thinker" for an ethos of productive "thinking." That the same Emerson was responsible for such limping compositions as "Humblebee," "Threnody," and "The World Soul" inconveniences but does not finally prevent his installation as poetic theorist par excellence. The inconsistency should give us pause, however, especially for the light it may throw on the current situation of the poem in literary studies. Given the strong affinities between Emerson's project and certain contemporary literary assumptions, understanding the rift dividing Emerson as poetic theorist from Emerson as poetic practitioner cannot help but lend us perspective on our own theoretical moment.

In this discussion, the key parallel to note is simply that the mid-nineteenth-century liberal religion, like the late twentieth-century theory, defines itself through an eschewal of Ends (interpretive finality, univocal meaning, universal truth) and a concomitant abolition of any origin prior to the knowledge of the signifier, or the human word. In both bodies of thought, Mystery is inevitably defrocked as a feint of mystification. Recall that the current term of indictment for a language of bogus authority is also the name of Christ – Logos or Word – and it will seem no accident that critics of the late 1980s should have rediscovered a mandate for current language theories in Emerson's sometimes quite local, sometimes quite parochial, assaults on sectarian opponents pledged to worship of Him. In essays that loosen all orthodox verities from their moorings we discern prototypes for our own poetics of baffled closure.

But just as Emerson's essays seem models of what theory can do when freed of origin and telos, his career also, paradoxically, dramatizes the loss of the poetic attendant on the renunciation of those same Ends that religion, like the poem, formalizes. If the poem going the way of the Logos is not a possibility that has yet received much attention, it should, for our theory – just as Emerson's theory – may be poetry's nemesis, with the poem as déclassé in the 1990s as Christ became in the 1840s among Emerson's enlightened Unitarian colleagues.

For some years now, the reaction against close reading as a priestly activity has made contemplation of the poem qua poem suspect as a nearly fundamentalist activity. Such contemplation, guilty of association with New Critics who also happened in great numbers to be religious ritualists, has attracted further suspicion for appearing to lend credence to such chimeras as the "humanist subject," the fallacy of "sincerity," or, that mannequin, the "unbiased" reader. Only through accommodation of the poem to an essentially narrative, and frequently materialist "poetics," does the pet genre of the New Critics survive the age of theory.[2] Reutilized, as Habermas might say, as script for the cultural closed captioning of female protest, or as emblem of the "dialogic" at work, or as anthem pitched against "hegemony," the poem is now understood to join in a cultural work that redeems it from the decorative. Allowed to throw its weight behind a project of resistance that rehabilitates it from a merely "humanist" self-absorption, the poem defers the ignominy and stigma Terry Eagleton prophesied when he wrote that "there may come a moment . . . when poetry has to be apologized for" (Eagleton, 17). Such apology cannot long be postponed, though, given the theoretical requirements now placed on the lyric's good faith. It is unlikely, in particular, that a "poetics" can preserve the poem, since a "poetics" earns the moniker only when it is pitched toward *langue* rather than *parole*. Militating against the autonomy of closed or specific utterance, and deposing the "I" in favor of the determinants producing such an I, a poetics is constituted to suspend and dissolve particular organizations of literary language – lyric utterances – in the solution of the theoretically iterable, the possible.

Let me propose, following the model of Taylor sketched out in the Introduction, that a great many American lyrics of the crucial, I would even say classic, period between the Unitarian controversy and the rise of Neo-Orthodoxy, pitch themselves against the merely iterable. Dragging *parole* out of *langue*, the poem chooses this word and not that one in the conviction that one word is truly more fitting than another, weightier, more likely to count. In other words, these poems I shall describe emerge from acts of a Jamesian holding-it-so, which is to say that their mood is not doubt but a wholly invested faith. Rather than gesture at their own constructedness, they seem bent instead on sinking the deepest foundations possible. Against the vertigo of what they do not know, these poems concentrate themselves; against the limitlessness of what they cannot control, they make the choice of form a principle of onto-logical gravity. It is the fashion to suspect acts of linguistic mastery as imperialist, or, at least, phallocentric. I would rather follow Gadamer and Kierkegaard, or, closer to home, William James and Bushnell behind him, to call such acts gravely playful, as children's highly organized games are playful, to consider them a means of offsetting, but also ex-periencing, that littleness Dickinson would describe when she calls her-self "A Speck upon a Ball": a means of Being in the world.[3]

Like the theology they absorb, these poems that concern me mediate what will not be deferred, displaced, or overthrown: they mediate death, or to use a more suggestive and flexible term: Ends. Whereas narrative – and American narratives in particular – may well be about the transac-tive flux of power relations, and so may participate either in the shoring up of illegitimate powers or in their displacement, a poetic language too hospitable to flux is likely to be decomposed by it. This is because in-determinacy is the morbid element it treads; it is the chaos the voice's thin scribble would make habitable. It is the element that Richard Nie-buhr, paraphrasing from Kierkegaard to explicate Edwards, character-ized when he described the soul "treading water with ten thousand fathoms beneath us" (Ahlstrom, 940).

We may say with Bloom, and Pearce and Waggoner before him, that Emerson's signal intellectual contribution of the 1840s is a divinization of the human word that makes permeable, or at least negotiable, the barrier between God and the human subject, and so, between an illimitable and a limited language. The poets who follow Emerson are left to test that contribution, to put in practice a poetic language as unlimited as God's.

By and large, though, they discover that the Emersonian permeability, or to use its theoretical correlative, "transition," is inhospitable to the lyric's poise or even to the lyric's coherence. It would surely be going too far to claim that only sin, or a recent showdown with Doom, produces poems; nevertheless, the poets I will treat find the "transition" Emerson offered in Doom's place a medium unlikely to float the lyric poem. Fur-ther still: Until Niebuhr's – and Neo-Orthodoxy's – rediscovery of Ed-wards and Calvinism in the 1940s, it is in the American poem that the very limitations Emerson forswore are not only sustained but given a form of their own. Calvinist limitation is more than given sanctuary – it is vernacularized – in American lyric poetry, with the poem's very raison d'etre becoming the projection of a voice, the shaping of the covenantal

sentence "Here I am" in the midst of utter insecurity.[4] The will to believe that the self speaking this sentence is not merely becoming but *is,*
albeit insignificantly, that the sound it releases will carry, is the will that
many post-Emersonian lyrics are made of. And whereas literary history – in particular, recent history – abounds with demonstrations of
things poems can do besides ground a voice (for instance, Ashbery's poems, which dislocate this voice), it is the lyric's status as a form of determination that gives Ashbery's experiment its occasion.

When I say, therefore, that the poems of a certain American poetic tradition are infused by what Karl Barth later calls the "infinite difference
between time and eternity" (Ahlstrom, 934), it should be clear that I am
describing these American poems as made of the very materials Emerson
held anathema to poetry. Genius of deferral, Emerson produced a body
of theory which, fusing time and eternity – or *parole* and *langue* –
collapsed figure and field. In suspending the stakes for which the lyric
plays, he devised a theory that would prove in its implications as resistant
to the lyric as it is to the Logos. Ceding both the uniqueness of Divinity
and the singularity of the poem, the new canon that Emerson conceives
spiritualizes neither God's Being nor ours, but rather, through language's
agency, a becoming we companionably share.

But a becoming what? To read reviews of the "Divinity School Address"
is to be made aware of the grip of just this question on the minds of Emerson's contemporaries. Though none at first knows why, all are united
in their suspicion of Emerson's confusion of the literary and theological,
dramatized by a stylistic extravagance verging on the vatic. The critical
agitation around Emerson's style is so marked that Theophilous Parsons,
responding to Andrews Norton's attack on Emerson in the *Boston Daily
Advertiser,* expresses noticeable pique at the strange predominance of aesthetic chatter in a rejoinder so crucial to the defense of Christendom
(Burkholder and Myerson, 35). And Parsons no doubt spoke for others
who expected Andrews Norton, Dexter Professor of Sacred Literature at
Harvard and appointed defender of Unitarian dignity, to make better use
of a polemical opportunity than a scattershot sally on Emerson's debt to
Carlyle. We might well wonder with Parsons why reviews of an address
so cavalier in its dismissal of hard-won Unitarian points should be so
little concerned with Emerson's doctrinal waywardness and so exercised
by his language of delectation.[5]

Rather than complain, for instance, of Emerson's characterization
of the Christian miracle as "monster," Norton devotes most of his review to lambasting Emerson's "incoherent rhapsody" (Burkholder
and Myerson, 34), to lamenting the ascendancy of stylists like Carlyle
and reviling the "vanity" that makes a man, in the name of Christian

teaching, break out in "obscure intimations" and "ambiguous words" (Burkholder and Myerson, 34) An anonymous reviewer in the *Quarterly Christian Spectator* launches his own salvo against Emerson by complaining in the first sentence of "the obscurity of style in this performance" (Burkholder and Myerson, 44). When Norton takes particular exception to Emerson's phrase that "religious sentiment is myrrh, and storax and chlorine and rosemary" (Burkholder and Myerson, 34) and the reviewer from the *Spectator* to Emerson's assertion that miracles "are not one with the 'blowing clover and the falling rain' " (Burkholder and Myerson, 46), the intuition in both cases is that Emerson is wielding style as a theological instrument.

However oblique in formulation, the concerns of Emerson's reviewers were well placed, were, in fact, right on the mark. What Emerson did in the "Divinity School Address" was to attempt a conversion of theology as a discipline. He sought to change the terms of theological debate, so making its tenets accountable to canons of taste, the judgments of its clerics measurable against those of poets. Not only are the embodiments of language for Emerson not sinful correlatives to our fallen state, but through them may be realized the birth of a new man unencumbered by sin. Such a one is self-starting. Confident that Christian satisfaction might be secured through the offices of poetic pleasure, and sanguine that God's Grace is literally a species of literary grace, he writes, "A true conversion, a true Christ, is now as always to be made by the reception of beautiful sentiments" (Whicher, 107). Both the Calvinist's shame at the Fall and even the Unitarian's simple diffidence before the priority of Creation are, in Emerson's radical formulation, made irrelevant. They are vanquished along with a Christ now attenuate in "beautiful sentiments." No wonder that at the end of his reply to Emerson Andrews Norton should scramble to batten down the terms of his discipline. "The words God, Religion, Christianity," he protests like a man in a gale, "have a definite meaning, well understood" (Burkholder and Myerson, 34).

If Norton recognizes Emerson's strategy, however, he does so too late. Emerson's assurance of God's compatibility with the human style was more than well prepared by that Unitarianism whose long awaited ascendancy it was Norton's good fortune to enjoy. The blurriness of these early fulminations against Emerson's innovation has much to do with the fact that Emerson's detractors are all themselves perched on Emerson's same slippery slope. Indeed, the "The Divinity School Address" is amply anticipated by the writings of a Unitarian mainstream confident not only in God's benevolence, but in his nameability, and so in the safe conduct of theology through humane letters.

Norton seems completely unaware of his own at least tacit acceptance of the very terms on which Emerson builds. For example, in the opening sentence of his critique of Emerson he wonders at the "strange state of things existing about us in the literary and religious world" (Burkholder and Myerson, 31), so taking for granted the shared interests, even mutual aid, of two disciplines whose fundamental discontinuity, if not antagonism, earlier American Christians knew well. His acceptance of this model is, however, quite explicable, considering the historical development of the preacher's role in America.

Once the jealous guardian of God's mystery, in just over a hundred years the typical preacher had evolved into broadcaster of His saving Word. For Taylor, remember, the role as professional functionary put a heightened focus on the Unnameability of the One whose glory it was his sacred task to transmit, God's peerless Word putting the minister's poor words, quite literally, to shame. This discontinuity served an important spiritual need, for from the sense of linguistic inadequacy, Taylor, as we saw, found an access route to his own sin. His *Meditations* document nothing so much as the religious efficacy of a discontinuity of human and divine language. By Norton's time, though, with the idea of innate depravity on the wane among liberal Christians, an antithetical language corresponding to the paradox of original sin was becoming an increasingly defunct thing, while challenges from revivalists made verbal reclusiveness bad religious policy.[6] Ministerial volubility became imperative to the survival of liberal Christianity: Once secreted like the Holy of Holies, God's news now circulated quarterly, if not weekly.[7] A consequence of all this, aside from the swelling membership of denominations and the proliferation of religious organs – each vying better to represent God's purpose in print – was the inevitable obsolescence of that axiomatic Unnameability Taylor had in mind when he wrote "Whether I speak or speechless stand, I spy, I fail thy Glory."

To read Unitarian literature from the thirty years leading up to Emerson's address is to observe God become slowly more accessible, more iterable, and Christianity increasingly instrumentalized to serve as the uncontradictory language God speaks through Christ – and man reads, as it were, in the original. Innate depravity, the Trinity, Christ's miracles, and his Atonement – all these depend on the mystery of a God whose purposes confute human understanding. A Unitarianism that would flourish must first, therefore, jettison the Unnameability of the tetragrammaton Taylor took for his sign of an inscrutable God.

The sermons of Unitarian prodigy Joseph Buckminster reflect this process, pledged as they are to the steady deemphasis of mystery, and vaunting the new conviction that God wrote the Good News of our salvation in a vernacular we all share. Compare, for example, Taylor's sense that God's very self-expression violates His Being, etching a path "whose fairest face / Too foul a path is for Thy feet to take" with Buckminster's chipper faith, as early as the first decade of the nineteenth century, in God as a great communicator. In a sermon entitled "The Practicableness of Christ's Example," all the old emphasis on Christ's recompense for our sins, all the mystery of his link – a unity, a Trinity? – with God, all our terror before his sacrifice and so before the God who exacts such sacrifice – all fall away. Christ, for Buckminster, is a model of conduct, clear-edged and imitable stencil for human behavior. To be a Christian is not to suffer the disjunctive agonies of sin and suffering, but the pleasure of analogy. Indeed, decrying the "symptoms of excessive sensibility which the evangelists, without disguise, ascribe to him" (Buckminster, 226), Buckminster offers a transparent Christ whose death's extremities will not be suffered to stand in the way of our identification. Offering not so much his life for our sins as his "practicable" example for our better imitation, Christ's function is to act as tenor of the living metaphor we activate and realize: "Everything about Christ is precept and practice . . . everything is suited to the precise wants of man in society" (Buckminster, 228). Dispensing with a doctrine of the unlike for a rhetoric of the like, thirty years before the "Divinity School Address" Buckminster lays groundwork for Emerson's explicit transmutation of theology into poetic theory.

A decade later, Buckminster's fledgling anthropocentrism, and his new confidence in the compatibility of our expression with God's will, is authorized in William Ellery Channing's famous Baltimore sermon of 1819, given at the ordination of Jared Sparks. Boldly championing the efficacy of human reason and unembarrassed to reject all those tenets of Christianity not explicitly "suited to men in society," Channing is remembered best for dispensing once and for all with that linchpin of Calvinism, original sin. Channing's multipurposed sermon can hardly be done justice in the space I have here, but I do want to note how much Channing's disparagement of doctrine depends on his conviction of its unintelligibility, the very unintelligibility Taylor, following Luther, found so persuasive an aid to faith. Writes Channing, "If God be wise, he cannot sport with the understandings of his creatures. An infinitely wise teacher who knows the precise extent of our minds . . . will surpass all other instructors in bringing down truth to our apprehension and in showing its loveliness and Harmony" (Channing, 370). Beyond instancing Channing's well established faith in human reason, and his unabashed Pelagianism, these words suggest a theological system not incompatible with standards we would call aesthetic. God's truth, rather than recoil from articulation, its own "fair face," as Taylor would have it, loses nothing, but rather gains, by disseminating itself in grace: in "loveliness and harmony."

A man of supernal verbal gifts, Channing is unique in acting not only as champion of God's expressiveness, but also in a certain way as His proxy. It is no exaggeration to say that American Unitarianism – before 1819 more a beleaguered umbrella coalition than a denomination – was born full grown out of the head of Channing. But in this birth, as Channing uneasily recognized, was the death knell of an older, much cherished, sense of mystery.[8] Ingesting and dissolving this mystery in his own rhetoric, Channing's pellucid exposition at the ordination of Jared Sparks establishes a new heuristic norm, seizing the high ground in a language whose symmetry and clarity vanquish not only nitpicking, logic chopping, and scholarly arcana, but also the possibility of a certain mystical impulse – Taylor's – which theological rigor can protect.

Arguing, to give a brief example, that it is to "cast dishonor upon the Creator" to believe that God would select some for salvation while letting others languish, Channing asserts that the doctrine tends

> to discourage the timid, to give excuses to the bad, to feed the vanity of the fanatical and to offer shelter to the bad feelings of the malignant. By shocking, as it does the fundamental principles of morality, and by exhibiting a severe and partial deity, it tends strongly to pervert the moral faculty, to form a gloomy, forbidding and servile religion, and to lead men to substitute censoriousness, bitterness and persecution for a tender and impartial charity. (Channing, 377)

Channing's impeccable clauses, with their timed swings of parallel structure and their adjectives in stately array, have the sound, even the authority of Proverbs, if not prophecy. No wonder the collected works of Channing took their place on so many New England shelves beside the Bible. For if Channing's speeches are circumspect not to usurp the place of Scripture, they are unabashed at setting a standard for its interpretation, positing a Providence which could hardly fall below the probity of such language. Before Channing's speech mere theology must kneel.

Most of all though, what Channing helps to engineer in his time is what we have learned, after Foucault, to call a shift of episteme: He renders speechless a theology of disjunctive unintelligibility while making prolific one of fluent mimesis. Whereas the Puritan found his overarching trope in the image of Adam's expulsion, Channing highlights the moment of metaphoric junction when God templated himself in man. His paradigm, explicated in the famous sermon "Likeness to God," leapfrogs back over the Fall to Genesis One to point out that we are made "in God's image." In 1848, ten years after the 1838 "Divinity School Address," Horace Bushnell would ascend the lectern at Harvard to call the Creation account a story; all prophecy, song; Christ, "God's last Metaphor," and the highest theology, a form of poetry. But ten years before

Emerson's Address Channing smoothed his way in his 1828 sermon "Likeness to God."

There Channing writes,

> Likeness to God is the true and only preparation for the enjoyment of the universe; in proportion as we approach and resemble the mind of God, we are brought into harmony with the creation; for in that proportion we possess the principles from which the universe sprung. (292)

Channing's displacement here of the breach of sin with the soul's similitudes seems almost a rough draft of Emerson's query: "Why should we not enjoy an original relation to the Universe?" Both unwrite the Fall. If Channing's man is, in Emerson's terms, still unoriginal – thrown vehicle to God's tenor – Channing nevertheless anticipates the Emerson who will find the model for a just relation to God in the joyous pursuit of resemblance. Emerson's last step, his identification of God's soul with man's, such that God recognizes, even reads Himself, in us, is one Channing scrupulously avoided. It is a step taken, though, in the work of the young Sylvester Judd, Hopkinsian Calvinist turned Unitarian minister turned novelist, and a figure whose career dramatizes the drastically eroded borders demarcating the "literary and theological worlds" in mid-nineteenth-century America.

Judd, who entered Harvard Divinity School four days before Emerson delivered his Divinity School Address, had already written his own declaration of independence from Calvinism in a journal entry he called "Cardiagraphy." Devoted to a soul's purge of original sin, "Cardiagraphy" posits an "original nature," prior to original sin, where man's power of inception is identical with God's, and Creation itself is a human prerogative. Just as God "looked down upon the works of his creation, the heavens, the earth, man, all living creatures, [and] pronounced them good . . . " Judd writes, "I now look upon the sun and moon and stars and find them adapted to good" (Hall, 87). Beyond proclaiming with Channing, then, that we are made in "God's image," Judd calls the human soul divine, uttering by fiat its own autogenesis.

Language had perhaps never held a place of more privilege in America, for Judd's theology of likeness exactly reverses Taylor's poetry of the Fall. In Taylor's formulation, the heart's words, muffled in sin, pulse far, far from the heart of God. What Judd finds in "Cardiagraphy," as the title tells, is God written literally on the human heart. Taylor's poetic theory called language ungainly and amputated: Linguistic inadequacy was a kind of useful phantom pain, marking human shame, but also marking the way back to a more integral membership in divinity. Judd's "original nature" phantomizes all Revelation not original to itself, trusting best the scripture written in the human breast. With this shift from a God secure in His own imperviousness to a God realized in the soul's glad garrulity, Unitarianism veers toward Romanticism, and a theology of the unsayable toward the fluency and confidence we call "transcendental."

Emerson's "Divinity School Address" codifies all the implicit hints of a new language theory gathering in Unitarian writing of the early nineteenth century. The slow evolution toward similitude that made Buckminster's Christ an imitable model, Channing's God a fashioner of images, and Judd's man, God's best Word, finds logical outlet in Emerson's mandate for a theology as a poetics. Or, for the Word's fresh harvest out of the fecundity of words. The aim of the sermon is nothing less than a renewal of Christianity through a rehabilitation of its language. This will involve a reissuance of the theologian's terms in a literary currency, but first it will require a scourge of theological clichés, among them the very elements constitutive of Christian faith.

The most irksome of these, and the one that most taxes Emerson, is Christ. Not that excesses of the Atonement had not long weighed on the minds of liberal Christians. Buckminster was only one of many who smelled in the popular enthusiasm for the Atonement the grisly sentiment that loves any public hanging.[9] And Buckminster's consequent emphasis on Christ's life over his death was, moreover, typical of a widespread liberal effort to replace hysterical reactivity with a historical sobriety authorized in high places. After all, the gospels themselves accorded considerably less attention to Christ's death than his ministry. But if Emerson's precursors had softpedaled the Atonement, and had sought a gentler Christology, they rarely went further than to call the Atonement bad history. Admirably served here by that famous cool so perplexing to his fellows, Emerson calls the suffering Christ: bad poetry.

Thus he writes, "The idioms of his language and the figures of his rhetoric have usurped the place of his truth; and Churches are built not on his principles but on his tropes." And with perfect sangfroid, "Christianity is become a Mythus." By trope Emerson means a calcified form of language without vitality, by "Mythus" a narrative that lives independent of the authenticating vernacular of the present. Imagining no spiritual horror more chilling than this verbal inertia, Emerson would free Christ from cliché, restoring to him an afflatus, or spirit, he deems the soul of the poetic. Down from the cross, Emerson's Christ is less evangelist than muse, informing "the divine bards" who "admonish that the gleams which flash across my mind are not mine, but God's; that they had the like, and were not disobedient to the divine vision." As Ur poet, Christ "serves thus and thus only" (Whicher, 107). And so, adjures Emerson, should his ministers. Indeed, the preacher who fully apprehends this service of Christ's would join the poetic tradition to which Christ belonged. Or, as Emerson told his nonplussed audience of fledgling ministers and their teachers, aghast in their seats, the true preacher, "enamored of this excellency becomes its priest or poet."

Emerson's "or" is revealing, for it sums up the verbal revolution he would carry down to the very particles of the language he inherits. As if seceded from a Calvinist syntax, Emerson's "or" is an agent of likeness infiltrating a system of bristling oppositions. Not only rocking the stability of those particular terms Norton defends – "God," "Religion," "Christianity" – it subverts as well a Christian ethos structurally founded not on "or" but on either/or. Calvinism, taking the expulsion from Eden, the Atonement, and the Last Judgment for its kairoi, legislates an economy of choices – death or eternal life, saved or damned, God's word or human palaver. One or the other and never both. By contrast, the spiritual "law" Emerson describes in the "Divinity School Address" recognizes no such economy, indeed fails to recognize that law is itself an economy, a system for the weighing of claims, or the adjudication of boundaries. Emerson's "law" is in fact indistinguishable from the metamorphoses of image whose nature it is to cross boundaries. When God's truth is the law of identity, the piety He exacts of those made in His image is: making in His image. Cheered by such, Emerson can write with insouciance, "so like, so unlike; many, yet one." And so in the course of his essay he can confer the fluidity of his new Law of laws upon not only those words "well understood" by Norton, but upon the locutions of the old Law as well. "High communion," "New revelation," "Fire on the altar" are all divested of any meaning not ultimately inclusive, all rehabilitated by a principle of infinite resource. This principle resembles more than a little that linguistic force we are accustomed to call the "free flow of signification."[10]

In this prolegomenon to a theology freed of the Logos Emerson seemed to promise that every man might find his Savior in the poet within, and a generous and graceful language take the place of God's grace, parsimoniously dispensed. Revelation, rather than being impeded by language, might be effected through language and the Fall itself fall away before a new, and truly great, awakening of words. With poetics and theology now swapping terms in porous heterogeneity, the poet, true spokesman for divinity, would be free to create anew rather than to kowtow to a prior Creation. If Adam stood between the Puritan poet and his originality, Emerson's new "priest or poet," disaffiliated from Adam and absolved of the Fall, could write his own unfettered Genesis, could set down, as Whitman would put it with characteristic humility, a "New American Bible" departing from the testament Emerson authored.

"There is, thankfully," writes Harold Bloom, "no Emersonian Church" (*Ralph Waldo Emerson*, 99). Beyond respecting Emerson's disestablishmentarianist spirit, Bloom's relief at our freedom from such an institution is palpable, indeed so palpable we might wonder what anxiety about the Emersonian it displaces. We have, of course, not far to look, since, if we have been spared Emerson's church, we are in uncomfortable possession of his liturgy: a corpus of poetic work not noted for its power to awaken.

With a few notable exceptions, Emerson's poems are unnervingly undistinguished. Beggared by comparison with the poems of contemporaries Whitman or Dickinson, Emerson's poems, once detached from the theories they illustrate, give less pleasure than the poems of Poe or Bryant, less courage than the poems of Whittier, less consolation than the poems of Longfellow. Measured strictly on their own terms they lack certain essential Emersonian components – will power, or that verbal adrenaline that so dynamizes his prose.

To be sure, to read the "Divinity School Address" as a piece of theoretical prose is be confirmed in the ways in which Emerson's flight from stale Christian forms makes him so important a figure for theorists of our own day. In the last ten years a number of distinguished books on Emerson have all challenged Matthiessen's disparagement of Emerson as failed organicist in order to describe an Emerson less interested in unity than fracture, less in resolution than dissolution, less in hypostatized mastery than in power's kinetic thriving on resistance. Bloom's and Cheyfitz's view of Emerson as filial agonist, Poirier's view of Emerson as master of a chafed but energized displacement, and such readings as those of Packer, Ellison, and Lopez, are all energized by the theoretical shift which, foregrounding hitherto eclipsed moments of crisis in Hegel, redefines Romanticism as one outgrowth of that same contest of forces Nietzsche described in the last century and Derrida and Foucault in ours.[11] It is fair to say in passing that sometimes poststructural enthusiasms for the Emersonian indeterminacy have softened the critical mind.[12] The desire to laud any piece of writing that shakes up the New Critical object can discourage a sufficiently critical perspective on those moments when Emerson, acting the Lyceum timeserver, resembles (far more than Nietzsche) his American cousin Timothy Dwight. As Lewis Leary once observed of Dwight's epic poems, Emerson's prose can gush prolific as a broken faucet. Then, indeterminacy is too generous a term for what needs to be acknowledged as simple prolixity. All this notwithstanding, it takes no special pleading to recognize essays like "Fate" and "Experience" for prose models of restless imaginative will.

To pursue this matter of Emerson's recent rehabilitation a bit further, Emerson seems, additionally, to have emerged as theorist for our time precisely because he is, in fact, a theorist not much interested in time, except as it is compensated by futurity, or – stilled geologically in "fossil poetry" – as it repays our critical interest in archaeologies. This indifference to any tense but the indefinite present (not now but any time) corresponds to Emerson's ambiguous, we might say posthumanistic, pronouns – the transpersonal "I" who is not Ralph and the "you" who is no ticketholder in the auditorium – and his habit of posing rhetorical questions. Such stylistic features enhance our sense of Emerson's magisterial understanding of an infinity of language no lecture can corral, no utterance represent, no subject, genius or not, comprehend. Moreover they go far in persuading that the old view of Emerson as "transcendentalist," pursuing a unitary all, must yield before the other Emerson: virtuoso of *différance,* poet of fracture, an Emerson, to borrow Lopez's coinage, "detranscendentalized."

Should we ignore a certain congruence between these two Emersons? Whereas the old Emerson pursues a unity always just out of reach, the new Emerson, skeptical of unity, pursues the ever regressing truth on the back of a signifier alternately giddy or grave – insatiate in "The Poet" and unpersuadable in "Fate" – either way, vagrant, or, to use Thoreau's term for the sensibility of the signifier, extravagant. What the transcendental mood shares with the detranscendentalized, or more precisely, poststructuralist mood, is a suspension of the lived hour, the imminent test, the crisis; what both flee is the Day of Doom and the One who suffers that doom. Emerson's forebears called this figure Christ, but he is just as accurately the poetic speaker. In his place is now installed the Emersonian scholar who, free of thoughts, gives himself over to thinking, just as the divine, free of Divinity, is given over to divining.

And the poet, free of the poem, to regarding that language from which poems come. There's the rub. Although an intellectual life freed from the *idée fixe* presumably suffers no threat to its vitality, and, one might argue, a religion purged of God still has its human and ethical repertoire of work, a "poetics" free of the poem is another matter. Allowing in advance certain signal exceptions that I have already noted (to wit, those postmodern poetries that explicitly doctrinalize an a-lyrical, a-personal, and finally theoretic poetic practice – Ashbery comes to mind, but so too do the Language Poets), I am proposing that the lyric is not very well adapted to deferred horizons, to temporal imprecision, to indeterminacy, for it is precisely a genre of determination.[13] Hewing out a time of its own, if you will a term, the poem replicates in its sound and shape what it feels like to live that term, determining its own contours from limits it discerns and internalizes.

Let me be quite clear here about the function of poetic closure as I see it, distinguishing "finish" as a quality of consumption, from the Finish, as in *finis*, or the End. One is a patina sealing the poem's rarity; the other is a force the poem reckons with. One garners to itself more human power than perhaps any human organization has coming; the other acknowledges in the simple, but terrible recognition of human mortality a power beyond. Thus, distinguishing the American poem I will describe is not its status as *objet d'art*, nor its rarity or superiority as edged thing, but rather the service it performs for a human voice. This voice would find its own longitude and latitude in the work of speech, feeling its own figure against the recess of ground. As I have challenged an Emersonian or poststructural indifference to closure as hostile to the poem, I mean also to modify a New Critical embrace of closure that internalizes as virtue what for the poets I describe is rather dire necessity: not the luxury of exclusiveness but the rock pile of singularity. Closure in this American tradition serves as belief's retaining wall, or, as a limit where the determinations of the poem and the undeterminable square off. As Kierkegaard has it, "The despair of possibility is due to the lack of necessity" (*Fear*, 168).

Necessity readmitted, the self marshals its energy for choices. In this contest all the power is on the other side, massed in its immensity against a voice struggling for scale. This means not language's and not its gender's, and not its social class's – but its own. The poem's intelligibility is no more guaranteed by the language it draws on than its particular crisis is alleviated by being shared. For unlike narrative – which is dialogic, mediating a range of social voices of varying power, none strictly separate from any of the others – the lyric, at least as Emerson's most formidable heirs conceived it, must believe that the sounds it makes are sounds it solely determines. We call this faith, voice. Without voice, the lyric is at best a challenge to itself and its own premises; at worst, in circumstances Emerson mistook for enabling ones, it is simply mute.

To achieve voice the lyric must put by becoming to be; *langue* for *parole;* what Kierkegaard would dismiss as an omnivorous "possibility" for "possibility become actual" (*Fear*, 169). Only by the exquisite, honing movement of verbal choice does the lyric poem emerge, made of these words and not others.[14] Along these lines, Robert Frost, both the most and least Emersonian of American poets, called poetry "the impossible undertaking we undertake." The phrase harvests a whole history of American poetic experiments to characterize the genre as one of limitations contested, linking its production to a set of values I now want to specify as Calvinist. The very structure of Frost's formulation recalls the typical cognitive inversions of Calvinist thought – dying to live, finding salvation in sin, performing good works in a world governed by grace. Thus, for example, in Frost's own poems "Rose Pogonias," "Stopping by Woods," and "Mowing," the imaginative enterprise – yielding such felicities as jewels, promises, or simple accuracy – is carried out in full knowledge of those obliterating forces that blunt all facets, nullify all pacts, efface all accuracy. Covenantal, the poems make a bargain the world has no obligation to keep. In Frost, the Emersonian "original relation" yields to what I call regeneracy; not newness, but the acknowledgment of impossibility undertaken, labor in the face of its utter undoing.

We might take one of Frost's greatest poems, "After Apple Picking," as alternative paradigm, and a most persuasive argument against his Concord teacher who would unwrite the Fall. Celebrating the heft of Being rather than either its "transcendence" or its "indeterminacy," the speaker "feels the pressure of a ladder round" as a linguistic embodiment, feels time's pressure in the very metrical foot. Indeed, in Frost, the very system of poetic stresses becomes a means of absorbing, organizing, and distributing the pressure of necessity. Whereas the prose of man thinking, prose of deferred origins and telos, "invite[s] men drenched in time to recover themselves and come out of time," poetry for Frost is specifically a means of assenting to time, an accommodation of being in time. It is a fallen genre.

The paradox of Emerson's career is that his failure as a poet derives from his brilliance as a theorist. Theory's raison d'être, somewhat like that of Unitarianism, is the impartial capacity to thrive and revive in power from all encounters, to make out of the narrow gate of the either/ or, the multiple access of the or. But when a poem disengages from a particular pressure and the particular identity withstanding that pressure, it can lose its reason to be. What for theory may be deemed "resistance," translates, for the poem, into something more like "strength in adversity," or the trumpet cry: "Courage." The lyric lapses into that inspirational mode whose signature, whether saluting nuptials or offering condolences, is never to lose, and so never to feel, its footing. Mimicking a genre intensely experiential and acutely perturbed, that of the lyric, the inspirational functions imperturbably, substituting fluency for urgency and technique for metrical pressure. Except on cue, its throat never catches, for it will always be sustained by the sheer abundance of words. Occasionally a poet, but more frequently an inspirationalist, by preserving the Spirit in poetry Emerson not only makes the spirit vitiate, but he also makes poetry gratuitous.[15]

Take a positive example. What distinguishes one of Emerson's finest poems, "The Snow-storm," is this pressure of necessity, given metaphor in the image of the "mad wind's night-work." The phrase itself is a virtual cross section of a fallen poetics whose art comes from work, but well before the last line – which returns us to a fallen beginning – the poem's first lines invoke an End – an apocalypse even – whose tumult mirrors the primordial Chaos:

> Announced by all the trumpets of the sky,
> Arrives the snow, and driving o'er the fields,
> Seems nowhere to alight; the whited air
> Hides hills and woods, the river and the heaven,
> And veils the farmhouse at the garden's end.

Opening with an image of the rent sky of Revelation heralded by trumpets, the poem collapses End into the Beginning, before Creation. Those inclined to read Frost's "Stopping by Woods" as only moderately threatening – sublime – are likely to read "The Snow-storm" as Emerson's prescription for a poetry copied from nature's gusty passion. Yet nature is not so much passionate, or sublime, in these lines as obliterating and formless, spirit of that void to which Creation gives order. "Driving o'er the fields," the snow is a force of indistinction. Its whiteness, the American hue of primal terror, hides hills and woods, rivers and heavens; its very pallor is the absence of genuine light. The snow that "seems nowhere to alight" strands the eye in a miasma of cancellation, a child's game of imagining a nothingness unshaped and unhued, with the pun on "alight" suggesting both the yawning marklessness of an untrodden place (what Frost later calls "the blanker whiteness of benighted snow") and absence of that Light which ushers in creation. Here is "originality" proper, relationless, unsurveyed, literally dreadful, the snow a soul-shaking force not of creativity but ghastly nothingness. What, then, transforms this chaos to "snow-storm"? to fierce artificer? What "furnishes" the drive of ice with "tile"?

Not the snow itself; its chaos is total, imagining nothing so unlike itself as domestic making. But those intimates, the "housemates," progeny of the Adamic couple, must have something to do with it. They exert, even in their repose, the counterpressure of creation: symmetrical, Promethean, complex: "Delayed, friends shut out, the housemates sit / Around the radiant fireplace, enclosed / In a tumultuous privacy of storm." The image of the house secure against gales, and the oxymoron at the close, "tumultuous privacy," together suggest the tensile resistance of some form, some making that is hardly the snow's own. To create this form is ultimately the craft of the poem, which projects an image of itself in the architectural enclosure of the house, but it is also the work of those housemates and of us, those summoned as the next stanza opens to "Come see."

"The Snow-storm" gains its power as a poem from its recognition of the formlessness that attends the truly original, and its embrace of a more compromised, temporally implicated species of creation. Call it a dualistic poem, but I would prefer to see it as situated at the juncture of two axes: time and work, with the second understood as the means by which humans dignify their fall into the first. To state what may be obvious, a snowstorm is a phenomenon of weather, and hence the most time-bound of makers. Like the human maker, it is a force whose "hours are numbered." If our lives are like grass, what we make is mutable like snow. Pressing in against the force of human making is Time itself which chills all fires, distorts all forms, which, as Frost puts it in his bleakest snowscape, "smothers all things in their lairs." As emblem of the time that both makes and unmakes us, the snowstorm is oxymoronic force of outline and baroque distortion, both wreathing and blurring human forms. When Frost, to recur to my favorite example, depicts in "After Apple Picking" apples magnified "stem to blossom end" through a pane of ice that finally drops and melts, the pane is imported from Emerson's workshop. The melting lens through which we glimpse apples, the snowstorm that unconceals human line – these are symbols of the poem itself impelled to speech before it is too late. Not deferral but Doom, the day imminent and cold, crystallizes both visions. It is against the utter failure of compensation that they find their peace, their repose, seizing not the originality that transcends relation but the regeneracy whose grounding is relation. And what fills the space of that relation is work.

For "The Snow-storm," if it is chilled by a Time to which it owes its crystallization, is also warmed by work: the snow's mad night-work, yes, but also that human day-work which the snow, rather than obliterate, "wreathes." The snowstorm less shames than lends the prestige of art to certain human structures that hold utter destruction at bay. "Curving his white bastions" around simple roofs, draping "wreathes" around coop or kennel, and crowning the "work" with a "tapering turret," the snowstorm sincerely flatters through "mimicry" not only itself, but also the human work it drapes. Giving this human labor its due, if the storm imparts its form "mockingly," what is mocked is hardly human pretension, or pride, but rather a failure of "astonishment" which does not duly honor form as it sees it, which "sighs" rather than quickening to "come see" the structures the snow only more sharply defines. Not only does "The Snow-storm" bid us contemplate the model of Nature's urgent art we can only, belatedly, "mimic in slow structures." It suggests as well the way forms appear only to the mind that takes the shaping of such forms for its night-work. That mind holds forms snow cannot begin to sustain. The last lines of the poem read like a palindrome, baffling our efforts to judge whose work is more imitable: ours "built in an age" – and to last – or the snowstorm's, which "leaves when the sun appears":

And when his hours are numbered, and the world
Is all his own, retiring, as he were not,
Leaves, when the sun appears, astonished Art,
To mimic in slow structures, stone by stone,
Built in an age, the mad wind's night-work,
The frolic architecture of the snow.

Itself mimicking – in the sense now of imitating rather than mocking – the human maker, the snowstorm holds sway over a world "all his own" in the most limited and Miltonic of senses. "[H]ours . . . numbered . . . ," he retires "as he were not" and his departure holds no imprint of his passing. Notice that "Leaves" is both verb and noun, both the "leaving" of departure and the leaf the leaving denudes. The phrase hints too at a nothing left, at the relative profligacy of the mad wind's night-work against the forms laid up "stone by stone." The lines read just the other way as well, as celebration of the snow's "frolic architecture" which makes of dour human work, play. Whose work wins the laurels, the true "wreathes"? Farmer's or snow's? the house or the storm? Finally only one work does it all; namely the poem that holds them both, making of the work all Time arrests a form of play, yet driven by that chill to renew muscular work that lasts. It is the End, the trumpeting blast of Apocalypse, that braces this poem to its task; its beginning is that End, with all its power wrought by a compression that does not originate with itself, and that is finally uncompensated.

"The Snow-storm," in its very excellence demonstrates why Emerson's poems of compensation, making up much of his poetic corpus, so disappoint. Deferring ends, skirting the very threats which give the poem its occasion, the stanzas of the compensated poem unroll smooth as cloth, with the speaker reduced to theory's deputy, simply flipping the bolt until it's done. As Frost puts it in "The Gift Outright," something that these poems withhold makes them weak.

This withholding of the self from the implications of poetic speech, particularly from the limitation of time the Fall implies, and from the labor of regeneracy to which the poem is committed, disables Emerson's whole poetic corpus. It is as though the very freedom – or skepticism – of the speaker proves his poetic exile, the very ubiquity, as it were, of compensation nullifying those perceptions that compensate the mortal ear. The lived sense of time, the pang of seized particular, the long arch of an ascent are a few of the poetic virtues Emerson's poems systematically resist.

"The Rhodora" is a good example of what I mean. Belonging to a tradition of American mutability poems which includes Freneau's "Wild Honeysuckle" and Bryant's "Fringed Gentian," the poem begins exquisitely. The first line, "In May, when sea-winds pierced our solitudes" has the stringed delicacy of need finding its own sweet timbre, while the line that follows, "I found the fresh Rhodora in the woods," specifies a particular human figure who finds because he looks. By the next line, though, the poem commences to sap itself. "Spreading" its "leafless blooms in a damp nook / To please the desert and the sluggish brook," the Rhodora loses its singularity: The very intimacy of its revelation is lost to the ubiquity of suitors. Only an ideal flower could "please" settings so far-flung as "desert" and "brook," while the coy muting of the opening's fervency in "pleases" blunts the urgency of a quest. As the poem goes on we watch in dismay as the imagist loveliness of "the purple petals fallen, in the pool," is traduced in the metrically ostentatious "Made the black water with their beauty gay." The detail to follow – "Here might the red bird come his plumes to cool/And court the flower that cheapens his array" seems not only gratuitous but self-reflexively so, with the bird's "cheapened array" reflecting back unfavorably on a speaker whose ardor is, after all, just heat, not passion but the tawdrier spring fever. From an almost painful localization of desire in the first lines, the poem has been steadily weaning itself from implication, parrying necessity by introducing elements that seem hypothetical, casual, or spatially or temporally discontinuous: the desert, the gentility of "please" and "court" and the rhetoric of inconsequence sealed by the red bird who "might" cool his plumes. All these subvert that ache of need the first lines established, replacing that need with fancy. The reasons for this temporal dissolve become altogether clear as we reach what we realize is the poem's peroration:

> Rhodora! If the sages ask thee why
> This charm is wasted on the earth and sky,
> Tell them, dear, that if eyes were made for seeing
> Then Beauty is its own excuse for being.
> Why thou wert there, O rival of the rose!
> I never thought to ask, I never knew:
> But in my simple ignorance, suppose,
> The self-same power that brought me there brought you.

Halfway through, this poem about desire driven to find springtime emblems for its own longing becomes a poem about the ontological status of beauty not seen, now engaging in theoretical language the whole problem of desire that has been the province of poets since Kant. Is beauty beauty when not seen? What is our relation to the objects under our gaze? To what extent is their beauty a projection of our desire? Provoking questions, these. Yet Emerson's answer forestalls the very reality testing such questions engender, that testing which connects such expansive poems as "The Prelude" with such exercises in minimalism as "The

Plain Sense of Things." In these poems, the problem of distinguishing between the hunger for a redemptive seeing – a contemplation that satisfies – and the claims of contemplated thing takes over, with the poem itself holding the shape of that dualist problematic as a movement of reverie – away and back; or discipline – conservation and release; or passage – summer to winter. Not least, this querulous movement of oscillation suggests a process of human growth, human change.[16] Emerson's lines preempt such reverie in a precocious over-familiarity. Thus, the "Rhodora" is not released to, but from, the reverie that yields understanding. The knowledge the first lines promise is thwarted in a line that does not answer desire but rather judges it unwarranted. Yearning snaps back on itself in aphorism preprepared. "Tell them, dear, that if eyes were made for seeing, / Then Beauty is its own excuse for being." Such lines as would intensify and virtualize the ripening of need never come. Instead, the poet suggests a simple design, a fit of mind and world engineered by a power so benevolent that the objects of our contemplation lose their strangeness, becoming "dear." Superintended by avuncular powers dispensing favors, the speaker and the Rhodora cozily share the assurance that "The selfsame powers that brought me here brought you."

In this last line, "Rhodora" crosses the line from a thin Romanticism to romanticization, from the transcendental to the inspirational, as the record of desire's implacable sharpness yields to a quicker kind of wish fulfillment. Beginning in a Tayloresque mode, with a speaker whose aloneness and whose need provide the chief impetus to the poem, it ends in Unitarian compensation, more mighty than the deus ex machina.

It will be useful for a moment to consider the difference between Emerson's "The Rhodora" and Frost's "Tree at My Window." "Tree at My Window" records the reverie of a dreamy speaker who, projecting his own consciousness on a tree beside his window, makes that tree a "window-tree" and his intimate, his "dear": "But let there never be curtain drawn," the speaker confides, "between you and me." Both poems insist on a certain intimate reciprocity between self and world, but to radically different ends. Emerson, unwilling to make vision dependent on what it sees, defends a hypostatized "seeing" – "Tell them, dear, that if eyes were made for seeing" – no more dependent on the object seen than that object depends on being seen – "Then Beauty is its own excuse for being." With subject and object made free agents, neither dependent on the other, the Rhodora needs not our contemplation, just as the speaker need not the Rhodora to see: His eyes were made for it. Compensation preempts the need for projection, and so the dualist mirage is handily circumvented. So, too, however, is the poem's occasion. Why follow the speaker in?

For the reader of Frost's poem the reason is amply clear. The hunger for reciprocity is much keener, the speaker and tree knit together by none but the speaker's projection. The relation of consciousness and world is hardly so egalitarian as in Emerson's poem. Now all the independence is on the tree's side and all the attraction on ours:

> But tree, I have seen you taken and tossed,
> And if you have seen me when I slept,
> You have seen me when I was taken and swept
> And all but lost.

Frost's speaker, who has lain awake to watch the tree, can only hypothesize wistfully that the tree has seen him. Compensation is part of our desire, not of the nature of things. Thus as Frost's poem ends, "Fate must have had imagination about her, when she put our two heads together," the poem's explicitly childish formulation comes to ironize the naiveté which seeks the easy compensation of "design," even as it strengthens our identification with the speaker who craves such symmetries. The speaker's credulous salute to a mythological mentor, Fate, underscores his isolation and need. We might say that Frost's poem cuts dualism some slack, interposes a little ease, but in such a way that marks ease as just that, the soul's holiday from its aloneness. Over the whole poem hangs the certainty that presently the speaker taking it easy shall indeed be "lost." Emerson's speaker is supervised by forces altogether more benevolent, and he remediates dualism through the offices of a power more providential than Providence, and less capricious than the gods. The philosophical points gained are canceled by the poetic loss, or specifically by the loss of what pulled us into the poem in the first place, that promise of a human need finding in verse its grain. The poem seems chimerical, its speaker not childlike or "unripe," as Wordsworth's speaker sometimes is, but childish, escapist. Disingenuously guileless, he who "never thought to ask, who never knew," enjoys a prelapsarian security, a protection from knowledge of his own projections, that is simply not credible. Poetic innocence, like originality, cannot be willed.

"Each and All" works in similar fashion to divest itself of poetic interest as it sacrifices a circumscribed but deeply felt human knowledge – Each – for a hypostatized All. The irony of its failure is that "Each and All" is Emerson's, the mentor's, rendering of that notion of interrelatedness his protegés Thoreau and Whitman bring to such high resolution in *Walden* and *Leaves of Grass*. In both of these texts, the relational matrix resists all general terms: The unspoken rule is that a monochromatic "All" must necessarily dull the variegated palate of "Each." When, for example, Thoreau describes the booming breakup of the pond in April he makes the "day the epitome of the year": The pond's thundering is associated with the dull thud of axe on tough ice even as this booming predicts the roar of the swollen cataract in spring. The prose in which the network is made manifest is so vascular, cilliated, and intricate that there is little chance of multiplicity ever resolving into unity. In Whitman, each discrete blade of a line depends on the whole field of waving lines for its true definition, while the whole field can only be seized in its discrete and local particles: pokeweed, mullien . . . Congressman, Cuff. To be quite clear, the point of this poetic vascularity is not any simple celebration of the "signifier," but rather the disciplining of poetic consciousness to feel its way with words, to depend on tactile variation and grade in the terrain for its voice. To sojourn, in Thoreau's terms, in the work of words, each word as if the last.

Along similar lines Emerson's poem makes its argument: that the very harmony a songbird offers is connected to his setting in "river and sky"; that the shells which, slicked with tides, are "fresh pearls," grow noisome once "home"; that the beauty of the "maid" depends on her setting in the "virgin train." Emerson's theoretic knowledge is impeccable, and so far the poem does not let us down. But then, the shoe drops in the "perfect whole." Predicting the current theory's ubiquitous trick of celebrating the "free play of signification" in language sufficiently generalized to skirt contradiction (but thereby, perhaps, making play itself a dreadfully standardized work), Emerson's "perfect whole" is oddly joyless. Whitman and Thoreau, keeping faith with the grain of the particular, know this bliss of interrelatedness to be fragile indeed, threatened by nothing so much as reified description of its own saturation. There must always be more than the total for the poetry to hold a sense of surfeit. Outside each phenomenon is the next phenomenon. Outside winter is spring; outside privacy, sociability; outside the poem itself, the poet, waiting for us, or for the next line.

This accretive and infinitely patient poetic, sketched out in Emerson's own extraordinary essay "Circles," conflicts in "Each and All" with a drive to be past knowing: to Know. "Nothing is fair or good alone," intones the Emersonian poet, echoing the Divine speaker who reasoned it was "not good for man to be alone," and so assuming a vantage point from which the very particulars the poem salutes inevitably blur. This vantage point impoverishes the poem. Even as Emerson's speaker goes through the Thoreauvian motions, chiding his callow speaker ready to call "Beauty unripe childhood's cheat" by resituating him in a landscape not tinctured by poetic will, that will, knowing too much for its own good, prevails: "Again I saw, Again I heard, / The rolling river, the morning bird – / Beauty through my senses stole; / I yielded myself to the perfect whole." Lapsing in the last line to a possessive and totalizing "All," this "all" stills the poetic movement that feels from joint to joint, raising the braillework of images as an act of faith in what Thoreau calls the "infinite extent of relations." Or, Revelation. Emerson's blinding paean to unity would seem to approximate such Revelation as God sees; but what God sees, in Huck Finn's words, is too "pesky regular." The "perfect whole" is somehow less exquisite, less persuasive than any bird or pearl, rendered its due language, might be. It is so because glimpsed through a lens not fitted to the human eye, but rather to the opera glass of a spectator Divine in the guise of theorist.

Once again I want to return to Frost's "After Apple Picking" for an alternative treatment of similar material. There, the closest the speaker comes to a "perfect whole" is, as I have said, a vision of apples appearing "stem to blossom end" after a great labor. Through a disc of ice whose mutability metonymizes time itself, the speaker is privy to a vision of fullness, repleteness, and plenitude, and yet his vantage point is never anything more than modest. Raised on a wooden ladder a few steps off the ground, he sees only what tired sight admits. Just so, his knowledge of his own place in Creation is only as comprehensive as the myth of the Fall will focus for him: It is a piece of apple picking, a good but partial harvest whose truth he cannot know except in the warmth of his own muscles, the ache behind his eyes.

Only one of Emerson's many agents of compensation, "All," has brothers in "The World Soul," "Brahma," and the spirit of "Hamatreya" who sings the "Earth Song." The problem with such figures is, again, not any lack of theoretic force. Indeed, all these Emersonian figures share a distinctly privileged theoretic vantage point: They lend the perspective of *langue* to the purblindness of *parole*. And yet, there is a decided inconsistency between a theoretic freedom from determination and the poetic need for such. As theorist, Emerson's very atemporality, founded in his resistance to Christian dogma, is his freedom. As poet it is his superfluity. The theorist who abjures ends in indefiniteness reveals the constructed nature of our notions of time, but the poet who does so is abdicating his genre. Theory may say, with Stein, there's no there there, but a poetry protesting there's no now now cannot sustain a poetic mandate; a lyric pitched at the meta-linguistic threatens our interest in its words.[17]

Only in the few poems that accede to fallenness does Emerson, as poet, escape this self-imposed superfluity, only when he cedes the God's eye view for evocations of a human need at ground level. My spatial terms are not accidental. The voice of Emerson's poems frequently issues from a place designedly unplaced, a place without dimension or extent. Like an enveloping nimbus of the transparent eyeball, such spaces elide inside and outside, sequence and perspective. Then, the lookout, the parapet, the latticed garden cohere as materializations of a pure suspension, of a vision not limited by its own extent. But also: a vision that, having evacuated its own outline, still tongues the empty socket, haunting the place where Adam, self-conscious, says "Here I am" and the sinner wakes in his own body. The privileges of God's eye view are increasingly qualified in Emerson's poetry by representations of a state where the new union of me and not-me does not so much defer the threat of not-me as strand a self now no self. Unfallenness comes to seem not so much freedom as weightlessness, the will of the speaker not so much untrammeled as simply depressurized, and innocence a merely myopic denial of knowing.

"Each and All," with its interest in perspective – "Little thinks in the field, yon red-cloaked clown / Of thee from the hilltop looking down. . . . Nor knowest thou what argument / thy life to thy neighbor's creed has lent" – is an object lesson in the poetic pallor of what one sees from God's, or a theorist's, loge. Emerson's greatest poem, "Days," to which I will turn in a moment, allegorizes just how limited is a poetic vision outside time. But a much earlier poem, "Grace," written in 1833 just after Emerson's resignation from Second Church in Boston, is enormously revealing. In this poem the very magnanimity of a free "Grace" that Emerson holds in 1843 to be sufficient replacement for the Atonement, already reveals its capacity to deprive a speaker of that outline fallenness paradoxically guarantees. Keep in mind the poetic ballast that sin gave Taylor's speaker while reading this poem of "grace" and its "parapet":

> How much, preventing God, how much I owe,
> To the defenses thou hast round me set:
> Example, custom, fear, occasion slow, –
> Thy scorned bondmen were my parapet.
> I dared not peep over this parapet
> To gauge with glance the roaring gulf below,
> The depths of sin to which I had descended,
> Had not these thee against myself defended.

As the record of the last days of a minister's belief, such a poem is not remarkable. Archly overstating "how much I owe," to a God whose creed is so transparently shored up by convention, the poem is prolegomenon to the spiritual autobiography of "Nature," and to the celebration of will in "Self Reliance." God's narrow solicitude may shield the speaker from untold sins, but of what use, the poem's uneasy tone queries, is such magnificent protection to one who, habituated to it, is unlikely to risk a "fall"? Further still, to look back at this poem from the vantage point of later essays is to feel no surprise that the "parapet" which here protects a speaker timorous of "the roaring gulf" also emasculates him.

Emerson's tack, often repeated, is to offer a feminized characterization of the irresolute self, describing his own faintheartedness as that of Rapunzel or an anemic Juliet.[18] And yet what I want to stress is not so much the gendering of God's protection, though this is well worth noting, but the way in which the chamber of access to the All, here called "Grace," is in this early poem ironically also space of exile, superiority of view not protecting the poet from spiritual triviality. Outside the fray one may see but not be, as Emerson reasons later in "Days," outside the day's progression one never finds true measure.

Just as the Unitarian "free grace" makes the preacher a spiritual lightweight, so too that grace converted to a poetic virtue deprives the poet of profile. The "parapet" of "Grace" – haven of the conventionally orthodox Emerson – is mirrored in the sequestered "pleached garden" of "Days," a poem which affords its speaker an independence from orthodoxy, yes, but little more determination than orthodoxy did. From this space of wide angled vision, the speaker may see all Time framed, and yet, as the poem dramatizes, the very God's eye view of time's parade the speaker enjoys is a grave poetic handicap.

> Daughters of Time, the hypocritic Days,
> Muffled and dumb, like barefoot dervishes,
> And marching single in an endless file,
> Bring diadems and fagots in their hands.
> To each they offer gifts after his will,
> Bread, kingdoms, stars, and sky that holds them all.
> I, in my pleachèd garden, watched the pomp,
> Forgot my morning wishes, hastily
> Took a few herbs and apples, and the Day,
> Turned and departed silent. I, too late,
> Under her solemn fillet saw the scorn.

These lines, Emerson's finest poetic achievement, are the acknowledgment of one who has too long seen time through the wrong side of the telescope, through deferral's rather than the End's aperture. Resettling itself in a poetic tradition of mortal urgency uncompensated, the poem grieves for vision wasted. Not only about the loss to life inattendance to time yields, it also grieves for the loss to poetry a negligence before time exacts.

The title of the poem suggests the lyric's proper context. "Days" is a kind of postmortem variant on the carpe diem pattern. It is a lyric regretfully looking back, elegiac and strangled, at work unaccomplished, at days "unseized." The poem's precursors are Herrick's "To the virgins, to Make Much of Time" and Marvell's "To His Coy Mistress." Transposing the drama of the urgent lover and reluctant mistress into the botched love affair of the speaker and time, Emerson retunes these lyrics in his own brilliantly metaphysical key. Whereas Herrick and Marvell give us an ardent, irrepressible lover urging a reticent mistress to consummate love while time allows, Emerson makes Time herself the mistress, not reticent but washing her hands of a speaker so cool to her charms. Consciousness of time produces in Herrick and Marvell the speaker's muscular resolution that, though he may not make the "sun stand still, yet . . . will make him run." This vigor, personified in the cocky brag of Marvell's speaker, is also a quality the verse enjoys. Emerson's speaker, by contrast, is not only passive, "watching" time's "pomp," but emasculate, diminished by what he withholds. Absent spirited, he "forgets" "his morning wishes"; precipitous, he "hastily" takes apples, while, dilatory, he retreats "too late" behind the lattice. The implicit lexicon of incontinent sexual timing, of passion premature or lagging, dramatizes the sterility of a failed engagement with Time. Nor does Emerson spare his speaker a theoretic justification, the cover of innocence, of "never knowing." By holding aloof from the liaison with days, the speaker maintains an overnice, wholly technical virginity that is only rationalized as innocence. His "pleachèd garden" is no bower of the ideal, raised above particulars, nor even a topos of language's multifoliate life beyond time. It is, rather, a preserve of the precious. There, closeted with his "few herbs and apples," the speaker languishes in fastidious isolation. Under cover of the "pleachèd," he is the Unitarian denying both Adam's fig leaf and Christ's crown of thorns. The irony is that in his woven garden he is left for a parody of both. Neither the dignity of great suffering nor the tragedy of fortunes reversed can make this garden an Eden or a Gethsemane. The garden, sequestering its scholar, affords its tenant the most tenuous possible kinship with those whose crisis he refuses. Like the garden, genteel rather than faithful, the poem too is gone the way of the crisis or – the Day of Doom – spurned.

Emerson's greatest poem, "Days" paradoxically achieves its success at the expense of Emerson's whole poetic corpus by acknowledging how enfeebled is a poetry not pledging its voice to the hazards of Time: a poetry not fallen. Just as religion "converted" to poetry is not poetry, neither does the American poetry Emerson would supervise thrive in his unfallen garden, for poems prosper in gardens of the Fall, limited by time and made out of timing; admitting impediments, yet holding the human shape. But the poetic failure that accompanies Emerson's eschewal of orthodoxy makes explicable the salutary effects of theology's recovery for the poets who follow him. To understand where Emersonianism breaks down is to gain access to larger tracts of poetic territory than we have so far compassed.

Although it is entirely reasonable to see many American poems as striking for an Emersonian sublimity, and so to see Whitman orbiting around the Emersonian self-reliance, Dickinson around the Emersonian "possibility," Crane around the Emersonian "utopianism," and Stevens around the Emersonian pursuit of "the new," such a view must exclude Whitman's studious, backward-looking Scripturalism and the emergence in his work of a fine grained exegetical Christology. It cannot account for Dickinson's subtle, nearly scholastic attempts to define the relationship of poetry to idolatry, nor for the spiritual psychology of faith and dread, awe and the demonic that Hart Crane's lyrics elaborate. Moreover, it cannot account for the way in which Stevens, genteel fabricator of that double to the Emersonian poet – Major Man – is also poet of Canaan. Not so much genteel as willfully Gentile, Stevens takes the Emersonian heterodoxy to its logical conclusion, setting against the comforts of Sunday morning not just a poet's priestcraft, but totem and facepaint, fleshpots and the Nations naked in the sun. Writing to the limits of Emerson's "original relation," a whole tradition of American poets reset their sights on lyric regeneracy, linguistically realized, theologically secured.

3

The Savage Source: Emerson and Stevens

> I am a transparent Eyeball.
> I am nothing. I see all.
>
> Emerson, "Nature"

> The poem is a nature created
> by the poet.
>
> Stevens, *Adagia*

One must have a mind of winter
To regard the frost and the boughs
Of the pine trees crusted with snow;

And have been cold a long time
To behold the junipers shagged with ice,
The spruces rough in the distant glitter

Of the January sun: and not to think
Of any misery in the sound of the wind,
In the sound of a few leaves,

Which is the sound of the land
Full of the same wind
That is blowing in the same bare place

For the listener, who listens in the snow,
And nothing himself, beholds
Nothing that is not there and the nothing that is.

One has to have known Wallace Stevens' great early poem "The Snow Man" a long time not to think of what it owes to Emerson. Long acquaintance with the poem strengthens one's sense of its stark and rare originality, even as, paradoxically, the poem's pursuit of a humanly estranged immediacy is familiarizing, its evocation of the new recalling an older evocation of the same. Stevens' poem, about a knowledge prior to reflection, is itself a reflection. It is a reprise – white-on-white – of the most famous sentence of "Nature"; it re-imagines the classic Emersonian moment of epiphany in a field of snow puddles.

At the same time, "The Snow Man" predicts the career of the only American poet to accept the literal requirements of Emersonian originality. Exercising the prerogatives of the new as no other American poet does, and concerned somehow to hold the Emersonian poetics in a poem of lyric shapelessness, Stevens takes Emerson as far as he will go. If, ultimately, Stevens' most important poems demonstrate the limits of the Emersonian faith, these limits are discerned through a radical internalization rather than an expulsion of Emerson's tenets. Stevens may be said to practice a poetry of "relation" dependent on and nourished by a more comprehensive and rigorous understanding of the "original" than Emerson ever achieved.

"The Snow Man," a poem that seeks a clean being unshaded by knowing, telescopes Stevens' Emersonianism, both as that Emersonianism is "possible, possible, possible" – and not. In the white of the snow, aboriginal color of beginnings, Stevens crystallizes the Emersonian dream of pellucid vision. Rewriting the episode of the transparent Eyeball – that epiphanic instant when, on a winter plain puddled with snow, the writer of "Nature" is purged of himself by cold drafts of being – Stevens names the philosophic conditions in which originality, or the utterly new, can cohere.

The key condition is abstractness, or a philosophic disinterest I called in the last chapter, theoretical. Such disinterest requires that the "eye" be divorced, in Poirier's terms, from the "I." It requires, moreover, that the mind or "me" that guides the eye be not itself, but, rather, be coextensive with an other, or "not-me," whose undifferentiated currents somehow pose no threat. Not seeing *for* someone, and not an organ compassing, or choosing, specific sights, the eye, so understood, is rather a channel of possible sightings. Consciousness, having neither mass, extent, nor integrality, is now a kind of linguistic palate, its blankness containing all possible colors but isolating none. As an organ of knowledge without need, such consciousness is exempt from that desire that preconditions knowledge in the human world.

Thus, the heroic "One" of the poem, it follows, is not one in the sense that we each are one, but rather in the sense that we all might be; "one" in the impersonal, generic sense that anyone – for the sake of argument – could be, but no one precisely would be for himself. The language of such a one is nonspecific, drawing *parole* up into *langue,* the said into the sayable: and without regretting the chance to choose, without regretting the time lost or the season unseized. But if "one" does not feel the scarcity – is not chilled by it or unmanned by it – this is because "one" is not a man, and certainly not a woman. One is not a person at all.

"One," a crystal compound of texture and syllables, is a snow man, an antic no-man, or a now man, or a "nothing that is / now man." The "is" that links the poem's end to its beginning, making the notion of an original whiteness depend on an eternal present that " 's' now" – elides time. Like the God who calls Himself YHVH (the Hebrew verb *to be,* conjugated past, present, and future) the poem's final "is" is not temporal, but transtemporal. It is a place of liaison, where a cognition freed of both spatial and temporal limitation can dwell, hearing and beholding, yet disencumbered by the senses.

Call it nonsense, if you like, that ties God to the Snow Man, but it is a nonsense of just that high philosophical seriousness that Stevens most enjoyed. The comical demeanor of no-man, the snow man, flows from an abstract newness that has nothing to lose, or, one might say, from the absolute originality that is God's primary attribute. His roly-poly contour formed of primary shapes, the Snow Man stylizes a certain imperturbability; not resistance or thick skin so much as the literal *sang froid* enjoyed by one who never dies. Thus, the pleasure the Snow Man offers is the astringent sight of matter not made morbid by relation, matter rendered free by perfect uselessness: matter that does not matter.

Setting the terms for a lyricism cut free from Adam and his squamous needs, this early poem from *Harmonium* is not a song, but an instrument; not a harmony, but an octave for harmonies. Iterable, but not uttered, it is an early instance of the poem Stevens writes again and again: the poem where transparency is composed as voluminous sound, where movement, hanging weightless, is only by the poem contained. In "The Snow Man" the Emersonian poetics gets lyric shape. "Transition," in this poem of a landscape shagged with ice, gets what Stevens calls "crunch."

Complexly enough, however, it is in acknowledging the futility of the selfsame theoretical knowledge that it pursues that the poem comes to matter as a poem. All its abstractness notwithstanding, "The Snow Man" is also a hauntingly eloquent poem of mutability, loss, and the constitution of the human. As such, the poem shows Stevens' early disinclination to be, as it were, "snowed" by any transcendental fantasy. The unlikeliness of a human knower ever attaining to the snow man's unknowingness is made apparent through the archly prescriptive, even orthodox list of "musts" and "nots." Moreover, the effort to gain a perspective not subject to exposure or alteration is rendered not only ironic but pathetic by our knowledge of what happens to snow men in the spring. Nature may be in us, but it is also against us: Our outlines are as crude and temporary as a snow man's silhouette. And since the pressure of change outside must exact responsive change inside, detachment is artificial and deferral, vain. In the end, the poem of man-made snow – in both the sense of theoretic dispassion (that is, man made of snow) and of nature synthesized by the poet (snow made by man) – foresees the dissolution of the Emersonian poetics in Stevens' own most important work. The nature made by the poet is, as all man-made things are, impermanent.

Like Emerson's own "The Snow-Storm" and "Days" – his two poems least hobbled by an abstract poetics – Stevens' greatest works allow Fate and the Fall of Man to melt our brave constructs. Even as "The Snow Man" strains to find the impersonal poetic medium – an "All" through which we might glimpse a Being not muddied by "Each" – the poem does so by invoking the particular life that suffers misery, that fears exposure, that repels the "circulation" of a Universal Being so out of touch with its human circulatory needs. The genius of the poem may lie in its invocation of a knowledge of Being in which the knowing self is present but not alive to the claims selves have. We may go even further in calling its finest technical achievement the imagination of a lyric voice detached from this loss of the self. And yet this very naturalization of change, of the Emersonian "transition," cannot purge the knower utterly. Where the poem is, there is always the mind bent over loss, the mind knowing cold, the mind naming it later. The poem never recoups this loss, but rather formalizes it. The poem cannot escape its own knowledge.

Perhaps for this reason Helen Vendler arrives at the term "posthumous" to describe Stevens' characteristic use of an oddly detached present tense.[1] When the present is posthumous, lost to itself – in reflection, in image – the Emperor of Ice Cream, celebrant of the present, hangs his harp on a tree to sing the songs of Adamic exile. Vendler portrays a Stevens like an Ecclesiastes, sage elegist of dualism, fundamentally urbane: essentially fallen. And indeed, in the major poems Stevens' more resplendently savage alter egos – dandy, snow man, clown – are shed for the wise man who observes "The absence of the imagination had itself to be imagined." The meditative poet harnesses his passion to an exquisitely calibrated sense of limitation. Idea gloves idea; "relation appears" (*Opus Posthumous*, 101); always the rat comes out to see, to be seen, to be seen being seen.

Certainly by the time of that most admired and famous of his poems, "Notes Toward a Supreme Fiction," it is clear that Stevens' pursuit of an Emersonian originality, free of Adam, is an endeavor now most drastically qualified. The qualification is already spelled out in the first two words of the poem's title – "Notes" and "Toward." Both allow the provisional, desirous, and necessarily tardy quality of our attendance on the absolute. Moreover, the movement of the poem itself is toward the fiction that all notes arrange, rather than to the Supreme Being beneath such fictions. The poem's final stanzas accede to the inventing mind and its impositions. Finally, Stevens' most important poems bear witness to the notion that originality can only be known through the offices of relation.

But how, Stevens nevertheless puzzles in poem after poem, is relation to be known? Consider this: relation cannot instruct relation since it is relation. Relation occludes rather than brings out relation. To make itself known, relation needs encounter with its diacritical cousin, its "cold copular." And that cousin is none other than: originality.

For Stevens, the Fall and the Fall's boon of "an occupation, an exercise, a work" ("Notes," 405) have themselves to be imagined. The very acknowledgment, stanzas earlier, that " . . . we live in a place / that is not our own and, much more, not ourselves" ("Notes," 383) is most meaningful when discovered and retrieved out of an understanding of that nothing that gives something extent; *it is originality that gives relation a field to shadow.* Just so, the poet's own mandate flows from his capacity to depict the world that is before the world is known or said. The poet must create his own necessity, as angelic mediator, by invoking the world without him and his words. In order to write poems tense with human need, he will write poems theoretically, as if he did not need to. In order to write words, as Vendler puts it, "chosen out of desire," he will write words vacant of such desire. A cultivated affectlessness is the field on which desire can be manifest. Thus, the dualist who allows in "Notes" that "Time will write them down" and that "Winter and Spring, cold copulars, embrace / And forth the particulars of rapture come," finds time and the seasons in a place knowing not knowing time or season. His poems of "relation" necessarily spring from a field of unbearable origins.

Stevens' corpus maps this field, though one would not know it given the scanty regard extended the many, many poems Stevens devotes to limning a radicalized and absolute Emersonian originality. Yet anyone who reads the *Collected Poems* poem by poem must be forcibly struck with how many titles there actually *are,* as opposed to the few one really knows. For every "Sunday Morning," for every "To the One of Fictive Music," there are, in fact, dozens of weird little poems resisting integration with the great Stevensian themes. Frequently attracting only such critical attention as elicits the label "gaiety," these poems, dismissed as "exercises" or as examples of the poet's athletic exoticism, comprise well over half of Stevens' poetic output.[2] Just to turn to that volume most studied – *Transport to Summer* – even there, the anthology pieces and outright masterpieces ("Esthetique du Mal," "Crude Foyer," "Notes

Toward a Supreme Fiction") are nearly submerged in a winking crust of bizarries with titles like "Poesie Arbrutie," "Jouga," and "Late Hymn from the Myrrh Mountain." Only a tradition of critical solicitude for the Major Man of "Notes" helps us to shake him loose from his gaudier, more enigmatic fellows: "gelid Januar," "So-and-So," "Ha-ee-me," and "Choracua" – not to mention the denizens of "Neversink," of "Schuylkill in mid-earth," and of "The Gardens of Acclimatization."

These odd poems with their strange titles and their motley circus characters are not exercises, however, and they are not, as Robert Frost once disparaged, bric-a-brac. They are, instead, the domain of that origin in which relation gestates. The poem that subtracts not only Son of Man but man himself, Adam, here attains to that original relation Emerson blueprinted but never quite built. The maker of such poems attains to that culture Whitman essayed but finally put by, of "nature without check with original energy."

I begin with an early poem, "Life is Motion":

> In Oklahoma,
> Bonnie and Josie,
> Dressed in calico,
> Danced around a stump.
> They cried,
> "Ohoyaho,
> Ohoo" . . .
> Celebrating the marriage
> Of flesh and air.   (*Collected Poems*, 83)

If one thing is clear about this poem it is that it aims for something more than acquainting us with two girls named Bonnie and Josie, residents of Oklahoma. Rather, Bonnie is Bonnie and Josie is Josie because they live in Oklahoma: Their names earn entrance to the poem as modulations on the orotund sound of the place. The "calico" they wear is there for the same reason. Calico is a fabric, after all, on which pattern itself may be said to square dance. Wearing calico, Bonnie and Josie wear their own dancing as well as the cleared field on which they do that dancing. But more, Bonnie and Josie's homespun "calico" (ocilac) is Okla, the poem's "home," in mirror image. "Folded over, turned around," as Stevens puts it in a later poem (*CP*, 487), the images all converge on their casual center like an inkblot opening on an arbitrary axis. Further still, that its arbitrariness may perplex is not only acknowledged by, but thematized in, the poem. The "stump" around which the poem organizes itself hints at, or at least acknowledges, the reader who might be "stumped"; or, in the argot of Oklahoma, what a "stumper" Bonnie and Josie pose the literal-minded reader. This stump, a more antic version of the jar in Tennessee, is part of the poem's fun. But it is a sign of its seriousness as well. Stevens' stump is the severed trunk of an older kind of poetic culture.

To get an even fuller appreciation of this arbitrariness of Bonnie and Josie, just compare their dance "around a stump" with the dance in the "East Coker" section of Eliot's *Four Quartets*:

> On a summer midnight, you can hear the music
> Of the weak pipe and the little drum
> And see them dancing around the bonfire
> The association of man and woman
> In daunsinge, signifying matrimonie –
> A dignified and commodious sacrament.
> Two and two, necessarye coniunction,
> Holding eche other by the hand or the arm
> Whiche betokeneth concorde. Round and round the fire
> Leaping through the flames, or joined in circles,
> Rustically solemn or in rustic laughter
> Lifting heavy feet in clumsy shoes
> Earth feet, loam feet, lifted in country mirth,
> Mirth of those long since under earth
> Nourishing the corn. Keeping time,
> Keeping the rhythm in their dancing
> As in their living in the living seasons
> The time of the seasons and the constellations
> The time of milking and the time of harvest
> The time of the coupling of man and woman
> And that of beasts. Feet rising and falling.
> Eating and drinking. Dung and death.

In both cases we have sacramental dances, yet the motion of Eliot's dancers is cognate with a larger, seasonal motion, and finally with the motion of Christian history. Stevens' dance, by contrast, defoliates such history. If, cavorting around their stump, Bonnie and Josie "celebrate" the "marriage / Of flesh and air," it is not as congregants of any kind. The "Ohoyaho" they utter belongs to no established ritual; it is instead transcription of their motion, just as Bonnie and Josie are crude materializations of an "Ohoyaho." They are as abstract as points on a geometric figure, or markings on a musical staff. It is as if the semantic meaning of this poem strains after, imitates the noise of vocables. Curling on its own sound, the poem asserts an autonomy not only at odds with a poem like Eliot's but radically unrelated to Stevens' own late penchant for fine discriminations. The poem is, to be plain, uncivilized. Or, better, it is "original."

In Stevens' poem "Life is Motion" the project Emerson outlined in "Nature" ("Why should we not enjoy an original relation to the universe?") is fulfilled in the most literal way. All reference, all depth, is closed by a Being pushed up on a flattened plane repelling denotation. In this way is Stevens most the heir to Emerson. As has long been noticed,

Stevens takes up Emerson's case against the old and shopworn, rejuvenates Emerson's poetic Namer in his Major Man, and assembles a lexicon of eclectica like fossils in a box: portentous, gnomic, and rare. For better or worse, he seems also to have inherited Emerson's penchant for rhetorical questions yielding to non sequiturs, Emerson's contradictory and attenuated ideas about community, and – it is no use denying – a philosophical attitude to evil verging on chill.

But chiefly Stevens follows Emerson in his belief in a Nature coextensive with the power of the poet. Like Emerson, he would rewrite the tale of the Edenic garden as a story without sin or falling, as a tale of an undiscovered tropics, unseen by God or by Christian man. Stevens' gardens are places no God supervises; his America is a place no Israel discovered. The vision that follows the Emersonian act of unimagining Adam and his progeny is one of man naked, unashamed, and ruling his own world. Anthropocentric and self-regarding in inverse relation as Adam and his tribe are theocentric and supervised, Stevens' garden exotics are denizens of their own domain, resplendent with the confidence they have nothing to hide. If, as I will show in Chapter 4, Whitman's effort to unwrite the Fall breaks down precisely at that moment when his speaker, shed of distinctness, helplessly reenacts the Adamic coming to consciousness in shame, Stevens begins at that moment, rehabilitating nakedness, or better, un-knowing it. Then the ineffaceable dialectic of shame and voyeurism that poets inherit from Adam can give way to a glad exhibitionism. The seer who was transparent eyeball is revived in the most vivid kind of human transparency, wholly uncloaked, wholly alive. Taken to its logical conclusion the Emersonian nature becomes a culture of salutary savagery.

A nearly interchangeable use of culture and nature is warranted here, but on grounds that need establishing. We may say that anthropology's geometric pugilists, culture and nature, are derived from theology's older couple, mortal man/punishing world. Like Emerson, Stevens seeks to thwart, or overleap, the abyss separating me and not-me. Thus, his tactic is to invent a culture that does not know it is rent from nature, an explicitly pre-Christian, and often comically pagan, culture of totems and idols, of dances and chants. There, among the natives, the poet as traveler will find an original relation he can be and not see. To understand a figure like Josie or Januar or Jouga aright is to understand the poet looking like an anthropologist on a world whose autotelic descriptions might give him shelter. It is a world such as that glimpsed by Lévi-Strauss when he set out to study the Caduveo.

The Caduveo, Lévi-Strauss explains in *Tristes Tropiques,* are a tribe of Brazilian Indians distinguished by two things: first, their belief in their godlike superiority – a literal "election" – and, second, their practice of an extravagant face and body painting. Rejecting any power greater than themselves, the Caduveo spurn sexual procreation and instead practice abortion and infanticide, maintaining the tribe by adoption rather than by a biological means they find abject. Their ornate face painting is consistent with such a system of family planning in one crucial respect. It utterly ignores the contours of the human face; it despises the face's natural "God given" lines. As the anthropologist describes:

> The painter improvises her design on the living model, with neither sketch nor prototype nor focal point to guide her. She ornaments the upper lip with a bow shaped motif finished off with a spiral at either end. Then she divides the face with a vertical line; this she occasionally cuts across horizontally. From this stage onwards the decorations proceed freely in arabesque, irrespective of the position of eyes, nose, cheeks, forehead and chin – as if, in fact, the artist were working on a single unbroken surface. Her compositions, perfectly balanced for all their asymmetry, can begin from any corner of the face and proceed without slip or hesitation to their final conclusion. (*Tristes Tropiques*, 166)

Sanchez-Labrador, a Jesuit who preceded Lévi-Strauss in recording the practices of the Caduveo, queries of this art form: "why this contempt for the Creator's activity; why should the natives insist on changing the look of the human face?" (Lévi-Strauss, *Tristes*, 170). His answer: "art for them is dangerously close to sin. . . . Each Eyiguayegui sees himself as an Atlas who bears, not only upon his hands and shoulders, but upon his whole body, the weight of a clumsily charted universe" (172). Or as Lévi-Strauss concludes, "this may explain the exceptional character of Caduveo art: that it makes it possible for man to refuse to be made in God's image" (172).

There is no better way to describe Stevens' "Life is Motion" and poems like it than to say that they refuse to be made in God's image. Throughout his career, Stevens wrote poems whose designs, like the designs of the Caduveo, "begin in any corner and proceed without hesitation to a final conclusion." These poems, often left to one side by critics reading Stevens through his final subtleties, exhibit a rawness verging on barbarism. Emerging from the "fortuitous," they pursue a wayward, antic, inhuman kind of design whose very asymmetry marks their theological resolve. What such poems have in common is a quality Stevens called "savagery," a quality he develops by recourse to concepts of nakedness, nudity, exposure. Finding analogue in the art of the Caduveo which negates by extravagant creation, these poems find synthesis and their peculiar dogma in the central poem from *Auroras of Autumn*: "Ordinary Evening in New Haven."

The following pages are devoted to tracing a snake path of "savagery" between poems more often studied. My aim is to describe a Stevensian savagery that culminates not in the superb "Notes Toward a Supreme Fiction" – product of what Stevens called his "imaginative period" – but in "Ordinary Evening in New Haven." The latter is a poem paradoxically born out of what Stevens learned from Simone Weil to call "decreation," or "a pass from the created to the uncreated" (*The Necessary Angel,* 175). Oblique, often humanly unintelligible, the poems treated in this chapter forge what should by now be familiar – Emerson's "original relation to the universe." Their technique is to stitch a life around a motion, around a chaos God has no hand in ordering.

In his seminal essay on Stevens and symbolism, Michel Benamou writes that Stevens "projects Adamic hopefulness."[3] The verb "project" is revealing. As Emerson himself knew when he wrote "our age is retrospective," only by projecting do we attain something new. Stevens is not the first American poet to be taxed by the formlessness of time and to project by spatializing. He is not the first to renegotiate the theological questions of our origins in a land only the poem can produce. But Stevens projects an austere and radical kind of pastoral. Where Whitman's poetry will interrogate the meaning of our nakedness and the knowledge nakedness enforces, Stevens conjures Edens where the logic of the Fall, preserved in language, is paganized by language. The shame by which we fell into vulnerability and divided speech becomes the nakedness by which we reclaim ourselves from God's image. Like the Caduveo, Stevens' savages fashion their own plates.

Still, as will become clear, if a poetry of extravagant nakedness can, in its way, secure the very freedom Emerson meant by the original relation, originality thus secured comes at a high price. Such originality yields a hermeticism, an a-significant preliteracy, an "aboriginality" Emerson never quite imagined. The very richness of Stevens' poems can put them outside comprehension, preempting the "pleasure" all poetry must give. Dressed, as Lévi-Strauss describes the Caduveo, like the court figures in packs of playing cards, these poems achieve a haughty dignity, a stern singularity yearning for the completion of the Fall's symmetries.

Such dignity does not come all at once. The poet who invents savagery begins in a cruder kind of opposition, in a well established American antinomianism. If Stevens' most accomplished Emersonian sallies scarcely acknowledge the Christian God, the early Stevens not only quarrels with God, he downright bickers. In this he is like Dickinson whose search for circumference began in skirmishing.[4] In Chapter 5 I will show that for Dickinson, the theological struggle to articulate "Heaven" and "eternity" is frequently worked out in the struggle to free words of Christian context, to loosen the grip of an overweening Christianity that seems always to get there before the poet. Dickinson's early use, for example, of the Jacob model – the model suggested in lines celebrating "the bewildered Gymnast" who "Found he had worsted God" – seeks outright confrontation with a tradition the poet would vanquish. And, as I shall argue, in lyrics like "The Bible is an antique volume / Written by faded men" (#1545), Dickinson shows her own gymnastic valor, but finally defeats herself by entering, as heretic, the very Christian figure she abhors. The gesture is not only ineffective iconoclasm, but it also makes for sterile poetry, inhibiting the poet's own theological imagination by locking her in a persona that has no flex. Thus Dickinson will write nostalgically of the "Columnar self / How ample to rely," but undercut such nostalgia with the caution that that "certainty" that with too much facility eyes its prize is attained only at some remove from "furthest Spirit – God" (#789). To seek, in Emerson's terms, an "original relation" to the universe requires use of original forms: Confrontation is a stance already owned by doctrinal Christianity; it will hence be replaced in Dickinson's theology by more "slant" attacks, by a poetic circuity.

Looking to "worst" God, Stevens, like Dickinson, discovers the futility of confrontational gestures in poems like "High Toned Old Christian Woman" where the "Madame" addressed is the target of the poet's *ad hominem* volleys. The poem is less an examination of Christian sanctimony than an indulgence of secular prejudice, its own high tone crippling the poet's claims to disinterest. Religious symbols lock and stoop to make a stepstool for poetry:

> Poetry is the supreme fiction, madame.
> Take the moral law and make a nave of it
> And from the nave build haunted heaven. Thus,
> The conscience is converted into palms,
> Like windy citherns hankering for hymns.   (*CP*, 59)

If the poem's tone is so inflated it finally becomes arch – as if to exaggerate its own pedantries – its argument, nevertheless, remains inadequate, descending as it does to trivialization, to disparaging "disaffected flagellants, well stuffed, / Smacking their muzzy bellies in parade." Similarly, in a later poem, "Blue Buildings in the Summer Air," the poet's truculent second guessing of Cotton Mather's heaven enjoys an advantage no polemicist deserves: an immobilized opponent.

> Cotton Mather died when I was a boy. The books
> He read, all day, all night, and all the nights
> Had got him nowhere . . .
>
> Look down, now, Cotton Mather from the blank.
> Was heaven where you thought?   (*CP*, 216)

Stevens takes advantage here of a sitting duck, baiting the Puritan everyone loves to hate. If the poet thinks he can haul in Christianity simply by harpooning its *enfant terrible,* Mather, and traducing its most vulnerable tenet, the heavenly reward, he is wrong. The faith is not so easily speared, and its attacker has good reason after such contests to retreat abashed. His "columnar" stance, like Dickinson's, only thwarts the poetics that would overthrow the whole Christian system and its heaven. As Dickinson does, Stevens will move beyond this stance. "Sunday Morning" shows the poet seeking a tactic more subtle and incisive than the heretical or "columnar" stance. In "Sunday Morning" Stevens drops the tendentiousness so apparent in the poems above to regroup, with the new terms he discovers becoming central to all his later work in the precincts of the Creator. The fulcrum of "Sunday Morning" is the idea of an Emersonian transformation, that transformation he later describes in "Auroras of Autumn" when he writes "Or is this another wriggling out of the egg, / Another image at the end of the cave, / Another bodiless for the bodies slough." In "Sunday Morning" Christianity is the "slough," the old form that must give way to the new. The point is, thus, not simply that a Sunday morning spent languorously over "coffee and oranges" is, as the poet of "To a High Toned Old Christian Woman" had it, better because less chimerical than the "imperishable bliss" orthodox religion offers. It is, rather more subtly, that old consolations naturally yield to new consolations.

Instead of defaming a heaven one would have to share with Cotton Mather or Madame, Stevens appeals to his interlocutor's love of beauty. His tactic is to link beauty with change. Thus he draws out of his reluctant addressee words which confirm his assertion that beauty lives in friction, trembles always on the cusp of things. His case gains weight as she admits to loving birds that "test the reality / Of misty fields, by their sweet questionings," of "evening, tipped / By the consummation of swallow's wings." For his part, he describes the sterility of a world of no change, where "rivers like our own . . . seek for seas / They never find, the same receding shores / That never touch with inarticulate pang." It is this "pang" of contact, the line where one state passes into another that the speaker loves and defends. The Emersonian "transition" gets no better defense than these lines. As the "Divinity School Address" made Christ a muse rather than an icon, here the divine is discovered in poetic apprehensions, and in languages' own fecund fastness.

Notice, however, that Stevens' own chosen form cannot keep pace with his argument. He writes in a tradition that, once again, locates him as infidel. Written as a dialogue of body and soul that lets flesh shed spirit rather than spirit flesh, the speaker's Sunday morning sermon against "divinity" and "imperishable bliss" only inverts the older Christian project of shedding body in favor of soul. Indeed, for all its thematics of change, the poem's contour is static. In tilting the dialogue for Flesh and against Spirit, Stevens would, but cannot quite, renew a long defunct theological option. Like Anne Bradstreet's corporeal hussy who baits her modest sister, Spirit, "Dost dream of things beyond the moon? / And dost thou hope to dwell there soon. . . . / Earth hathe more silver, pearls, and gold / Than eyes can see or hands can hold," Stevens appeals to our sense of the luxurious. His language has a vascular, bodied quality. Lingering over the pleasures of the flesh, evoking "Elations when the forest blooms; gusty emotions on wet roads on autumn nights," the language itself lives by a kind of felicitous friction, suggesting the durée of time lived through the body: "Sweet berries ripen in the wilderness. . . . Casual flocks of pigeons make / Ambiguous undulations as they sink / Downward to darkness, on extended wings."

On at least two counts, however, the lines above seem not to know how late they are. On the one hand, there is the fact that this voluptuous language belongs to the Other Side. It is the Devil's; to hypostatize it is to accede to the oldest of dupes. On the other hand, such language recalls Taylor's vivid evocations of what Frost comes to see in "To Earthward" and other places as the Fall's fringe benefit. Only a body cursed with mortality, with drastic difference from its world, knows that pleasurable pressure of space hugging the sinews. The mortal pleasure "Sunday Morning" celebrates is a version of the Fortunate Fall.

In short, both these perspectives on the meaning of flesh – the demonic and the fortunately fallen – are standards in a theological repertoire not nearly so impoverished as the polemicist claims. Flesh captains a minority party, either way, but not a new one. Like Dickinson wrestling God as a Jacob, the speaker of "Sunday Morning," simply by writing within an orthodox form, defeats himself: To enter such a form credulously is to enter already ironized, shadowed, as parody. The poet's "Shall the earth seem all of Paradise that we shall know?" recalls the Miltonic Satan whose metaphors are always derivative. Querying

> Is there no change of death in paradise?
> Does ripe fruit never fall? Or do the boughs
> Hang always heavy in that perfect sky,
> Unchanging yet so like our perishing earth,
> With rivers of our own that seek for seas
> They never find.

Stevens' speaker inverts the ordinary typological priority, claiming heaven made in earth's image, God in ours, He fiction to our Supreme Fictions. The trouble is, again, that this is the Devil's material, or, to put it in Stevens' own terms: This is the "necessary" angel defrocked, now archangel. If, as Emerson himself found it, "infidelity" is a false position, it is nevertheless one the poet who would seize God's prerogatives must know how to overstep. The seeker after the new is easily confused with God's nemesis and infernal revolutionary. Later on, I will show how Whitman, peering over his "sleepers," risks Satan's prurience, Dickinson, championing "circumference," his transparent pique, Crane, half in love with Faust and Poe, his ghoulishness. Like his precursors Stevens cannot cleanly sidestep Satan's sophistries. And so his poem is weakened by the antinomian posture, delegitimated by the precedent of the Devil who first spoke up for Flesh. The voice that was merely rebellious in "High Toned Old Christian Woman" is here more ambitious, but its ambition is shot through with the pathos of imitation, of secondariness, that impelled Milton's archangel to boast of making a "Heaven of Hell, a Hell of Heaven." In sum, by writing his dramatic dialogue in the form he does Stevens consigns his speaker to routine eviction as fallen angel, or in Bradstreet's terms, "unregenerate part." The reduction must be galling, and certainly we feel Stevens chafed by it, looking to write himself out of the Christian figure.

In stanza seven of "Sunday Morning" he endeavors to do so, supplying something entirely new to displace those Christian forms that are the "slough" of "Sunday Morning." These lines sketch out the savage paradigm:

> Supple and turbulent, a ring of men
> Shall chant in orgy on a summer morn
> Their boisterous devotion to the sun,
> Not as a god but as a god might be,
> Naked among them like a savage source.
> Their chant shall be a chant of paradise,
> Out of their blood, returning to the sky;
> And in their chant shall enter, voice by voice,
> The windy lake wherein their lord delights,
> The trees, like seraphim, the echoing hills,
> That choir among themselves long afterward.
> That shall know well the heavenly fellowship
> Of men that perish and of summer morn.
> And whence they come and whither they shall go
> The dew upon their feet shall manifest. (CP, 69)

To sue for the pleasures of the flesh is one thing. To found a new religion "of the sun" is quite another. In a poem so full of felicities that one doubts that any didacticism could bow its grace, this contrived stanza does. It strains our tolerance.

The chief trouble seems to be an inflated liturgical idiom. Encumbering his "supple circle" with archaisms like "whence" and "whither," summoning "the windy lake wherein their lord delights," the "heavenly fellowship," the "choir," the "seraphim," the poet forces us to squint at this savage source through a palimpsest of quasi-Christian honorifics. The corporeal quality we loved in earlier stanzas is gone. In its place is a baroque version of native unself-consciousness, a colonist's tapestried version of New World authenticity. Rococo confusion contradicts the "savage source" it encrusts.

But if all this heavenly paraphernalia seems counterproductive in a poem that would depose "Jove in the clouds," when we look more closely it becomes clear that what Stevens looks to pull off is a daring typological coup. His effort is to avoid Satanic confrontation and its threat of parody by absorbing all he would displace. This is Milton's strategy and the Miltonic stay against the blandishments of all that prior culture. Stevens simply flip-flops Milton's terms. Where Milton absorbs the Greek and the Hebrew into the Christian, Stevens would absorb Christianity into the "supple circle." In so doing he endeavors to alter his relation to metaphor. Unwilling to be vehicle to God's tenor, he would make God type to his fulfilling antitype, heaven and all its accoutrements prefigurations of his "supple circle." The problem is that the antitype is simply too narrow to absorb the monumental types. The inversion of metaphoric priority results in a poetic awkwardness typified by the severely hobbled line that gestures vaguely at a human divinity whose status the poet has yet to determine.[5]

For the meantime, then, the projection of the "savage" breaks off. The poem settles back into a more speculative and humble tone, "the porch of spirits lingering," and the lovely last ten lines which, as I have already said, evoke space parted by body, body hugged by space, a marriage of "flesh and air."

Although the seventh stanza of "Sunday Morning" is strained enough to curtail any definitive breakthrough, its ungainly lunge after the savage is a portent. It is a key to the disposition of later work. Not unimportant, it is also a stanza that shows us the aspiration of a poet who, as Helen Vendler describes, would marshal desire, but find no object adequate to that desire, who finds real "discrepancy between the irresistible yearnings of desire and the irreversible misery at its failure" (Vendler, *Words,* 21). In "Sunday Morning" we see Stevens threshing the "dump" of heaven's cultural heritage for terms adequate to the savagery he seeks. If he is to offer some theological insight that is new, if he is to spare his poetry diminishment by relation to such structures of adequacy, he must strike out on his own. This he realizes in "Man with the Blue Guitar" when he writes "That is this or that is that / But do not use the rotted names."

For a poet who must spatialize in order to project – and with Whitman, Dickinson, and Crane, Stevens is such a poet – new utterance needs new space. When, therefore, names rot they rot in rotted places; to refresh the poem is to find novel weather for it, new space. In terms I will go on to apply to Whitman, to Dickinson, to Crane, the poet who would have an "original relation" must wander. Thus "The Man with the Blue Guitar" continues:

> How should you walk in that space and know
> Nothing of the madness of space,
>
> Nothing of its jocular procreations?
> Throw the lights away. Nothing must stand
>
> Between you and the shapes you take
> When the crust of shape has been destroyed.   (*CP*, 183)

Stevens associates the "shapes you take" with a flight from the world mediated by Christian forms. If his "supple circle" is to find a home it will be a home not in heaven or the underground of heaven's imitation – dark domicile of the Devil – but a home carved in the "madness of space." Such madness is not easily found. Pursuing it, the poet must find his way out of a number of culs-de-sac whose "crust of shape" defrauds the savage "madness."

Three of these merit enumeration and then description. Call the first an anthropologist's Romanticism; the second, a decadent's surrealism; the third, an aboriginal's exhibitionism. In this last, Emerson's prelapsarian ideal will find its simultaneous realization and exhaustion. There, the "original relation" will find its standard bearers, and they, the insupportability of the newness they bear.

But the Romantic option with its long Christian background comes most easily to hand. From the Pentateuchal narratives on, the seeker who would apprehend Being has the best hope of doing so by shedding himself. It is a commonplace, both literary and theological, for this shedding to be expressed spatially, through an exercise of pilgrimage: The soul falls in behind the feet as the pilgrim obtains a truer relation with his Maker. Thus, by abandoning those norms – of habit, of association, of place – which obscure both the chaos of existence and its piercing verities, the Christian opens himself to an experience beyond appearances. The Romantic quest mimes this form. Through a purifying journey, the wanderer attains a summit from which he may surmise his identity with what he sees, his unity with Nature, and, in turn, its reliance on his vision.[6] The pilgrim as Romantic tears off civilization's blinders that he may become, as Emerson put it, a transparent eyeball.

In the *bildungsroman,* or secular pilgrimage, of Crispin, we observe the education of the poet through such Romantic perambulation. Crispin's name, just missing "Christian" by one trip of the tongue, establishes from the outset both his prehistory and the ironies of that prehistory. Just as Crispin is the most callow of secularists, a literal greenhorn whose supernaturalism peeps out from under his naturalism like a corner of native garb, "The Comedian as the Letter C" is a poem that broadens the self-reflexive comedy of "To a High Toned Old Christian Woman." It reveals the Romantic journey to be as little original as the pillorying of simple piety was. That the poet knows he is dealing with defunct matter in the "Comedian" is clear. He knows that the hunger for a Being purged of division is first translated by youth and credulity into Cartesian coordinates – "Adam is the father of Descartes" – and that these map Romantic patterns of quest. It is this knowledge – of the hunger of subjects for objects and of the forms of romance that allegorize that hunger – that yields the irony shadowing the whole poem and the alienation that comes to hang over the poet of gaiety. "Comedian as the Letter C" is the first of many poems to explore romantic illusions of engagement with the object and to find in those illusions an old piety.

In its way a Romantic tour de force, like all the best Romantic poems, the poem's very failure to afford Crispin a genuine "transcendence" is compensated by the demonstration it offers of the post-Kantian dead end. There is no knowledge we do not project; there is no Kublai Khan that does not flash back the same mundane poverty the speaker flees. The imagination is less discoverer than colonist, or tourist. Ever the self-deluding anthropologist, so mind draws feckless at the native pipe.

The poem begins gaily enough with Crispin setting out to commingle with the elements, to find a natural setting unmarked by culture. There, the self might train itself to be "native," might learn its "relation" to the universe. In an illuminating aphorism in the "Adagia" Stevens remarks "the poet must put the same degree of intentness into his poetry as, for example, a traveler into his travels" (*Opus Posthumous,* 161). The travel analogy is suggestive. Crispin's "philosophical" quest for the *ding an sich,* by realizing itself in travel, traverses those few increments that divide theology from anthropology. Indeed "Comedian as the Letter C" with its post-Christian hero, Crispin, is a poem whose lampoon of exotic journey designates anthropology a spatialized theology. Stevens' traveler is reminiscent of that prodigy of understanding Lévi-Strauss recalls himself to have invented as the anthropologist's persona. As Prodigal Son or gifted outcast, such an anthropologist lives in his exceptionalism, "psychologically speaking, an amputated man. . . . Anthropology . . . is one of the few true vocations; and the anthropologist may be aware of it within himself before he has been taught it" (Lévi-Strauss, 38). "Amputated" from his social milieu, such a pilgrim was uniquely capable of discovering an essential correspondence between his own mental structures and the structure of the world he studies. It takes an older Lévi-Strauss – kin, as we shall see, to the mature ironist of the "Comedian" – to reflect on the jejune optimism of his "crisper" self:

> Knowledge . . . consisted in the choice of subjects which were true – which coincided – that is to say – with properties of my own thought. Not at all, as the neo-Kantians claim, because my thought inevitably exerted a certain constraint upon the object of study; but rather because my thought was itself such an object. Being of this world, it partook of the same nature of that world. (59)[7]

Just so Stevens' Crispin would lose himself to find, "or enlarge," himself in the tropics:

> Stopping, on voyage, in a land of snakes,
> Found his vicissitudes had much enlarged
> His apprehension, made him intricate
> In moody rucks, and difficult and strange
> In all desires.   (CP, 31)

The search for perfect correspondence between the mind and nature, for the *ding an sich,* ironically only leads the poet-traveler back to the "land of snakes," to the scene of knowledge awakened by desire. Seeking innocence at the ends of the earth, he stumbles rather into the archaic landscape of guilt. In a chapter called "Crusoe Country" a sardonic Lévi-Strauss retraces his own dispiriting passage from ingenuous confidence to disgust as explorer turns exploiter, his very vision transforming and defrauding what is before him. Jeffrey Mehlman points out that Lévi-Strauss's innocent landscape is modeled precisely on the classic Fall narrative.[8] His paradise is an Eden, not discovered but recollected by a mind that can wander no further than Genesis Two:

> Trees grew in every direction, with flowers in full bloom across waterfalls. It was difficult to tell whether the river's main purpose was to irrigate the astonishing garden, or whether it would be quite simply overwhelmed by the multiplicity of plants and fauna which had arrogated to themselves not merely the vertical dimension, but all space's dimensions now that the ordinary distinctions between earth and water had been abolished. One could not longer say, "Here is the river," or "Here is the bank"; rather was there a labyrinth of bouquets kept ever fresh by the running water, with earth burgeoning on the crest of the waves. (323)

The passage recalls Milton's description of Eden as a place of no differentiation, of a profusion beyond words. Stevens' "tropics" share this quality: "such an earth / So thick with sides and jagged lops of green, / So intertwined with serpent kin encoiled / Among the purple tufts, the scarlet crowns." Fleeing God's old orders of knowledge, the pilgrim wanders into His garden. The tropics entice in an old way, and, as the presence of the serpent indicates, the knower and namer is doomed in an old way, too.

If irony suffuses both texts, it is because both are Fall narratives; both are unwitting accounts of knowledge haunting the scene of lost innocence. The romantic attempt to discover the "structures of the human mind" by circumspectly guarding against "imposing," instead "discovers" the old myth which founded its distance from such structures in the first place. In efforts to see the sun again with an "ignorant eye," to see it in the "idea of it," the pilgrim projects a landscape that he knows too well. To sojourn for a time as a "rainy man in a rainy place" is finally to remain distant from "innocence" by surveying it, as subject to object. It is to learn that the mind cannot tolerate its own innocence.

Thus, romantic optimism yields to alienation, nausea, or to what was all along, in religious parlance, an escapist despair. The anthropologist laments, "and yet this experience which began with such high hopes, left me with a feeling of emptiness" (*Tristes*, 326). Desire, interest, enthusiasm are dissipated in satiation, in possession, in knowledge itself.

> What I will not be deceived by . . . is the album in full color. Now that the Indian's marks have been destroyed, these albums have taken their place. Perhaps our readers hope, by the intermediacy of these color plates to take on something of the Indian's charms. (*Tristes*, 43)

Exactly so, Crispin's quest dead ends in the "colony," in the poem as verdant travelogue. The fecund imagination, like the anthropologist's insight, resolves into salad.

> Was he to bray this in profoundest brass
> Arointing his dreams with fugal requiems?
> Was he to company vastest things defunct
> With a blubber of tom toms harrowing the sky?   (*CP*, 41)

Fascination with the exotic as an escape from the traditional past does no more than translate laterally: We are back at the metaphoric virtuosity of "A High Toned Old Christian Woman" with its "squiggling palms." To seek self-renewal in foreign air is to yield not only to alienation but, worse, to a dilettantish tourism. And that is the peril under which much of Stevens' poetry labors: peril of an idolatry investing too much in objects of the imagination which, in turn, prove mere trash. The "locale" is quickly domesticated. The speaker, now just another local, withers like the "warty gourd" of "Monocle de Mon Oncle." So Crispin ends a sub-urbanite in the tropics:

> Because he built a cabin who once planned
> Loquacious columns by the ructive sea,
> Because he turned to salad beds again.

When Lévi-Strauss writes "Travel and travelers are two things I loathe" (17) in the opening of *Tristes Tropiques,* he paraphrases and characterizes the particular post-Romantic ennui of "Comedian as the Letter C." Stevens' remark in the "Adagia," "the time will come when poems like Paradise will seem very triste contraptions" (*Opus Posthumous,* 167), serves equally well as epigraph to Lévi-Strauss's *Tristes Tropiques.* In both texts, travel spatializes the desire for a union of subject and object. Both poet and anthropologist come to loathe the shipwreck of this desire in the "Nice Shady Home." Both shun that colony presided over by the has-been Crispin, "beginning with green brag, / Concluding fadedly," the same has-been Emerson himself predicted when he wrote in "Self Reliance": "travelling is a fool's paradise." Not by pilgrimage will a fool feel his way back to the savage source. Self and other remain at arm's length. At best, the Romantic quest only carves more deeply the longing for an innocent time; at worst, Romantic vision appropriates the savage to its own narrow purposes.

This tristesse of travel, however, serves to impel Stevens' experiments with a more self-reliant genre, a genre not so indebted to God's *topoi* as Romanticism. Thus, in numerous poems he reaches for the "savage" through the offices of the surreal. If the natural world is always owned by God, its penetration always delivering us back to Eden, then Nature itself must be renounced. Stevens' surrealism attempts, accordingly, to bypass Nature, with the poet acting as surveyor of an invented locale. A good example of such a locale is that scoped out in "Dance of the Macabre Mice":

> In the land of turkeys in turkey weather
> At the base of the statue, we go round and round.
> What a beautiful history, beautiful surprise!
> Monsieur is on horseback. The horse is covered with
>   mice.
>
> This dance has no name. It is a hungry dance.
> We dance it out to the tip of Monsieur's sword
> Reading the lordly language of the inscription,
> Which is like zithers and tambourines combined.
>
> The Founder of the State. Whoever founded
> A state that was free, in the dead of winter, from mice?
> What a beautiful tableau tinted and towering
> The arm of bronze outstretched against all evil!   (*CP,* 123)

Instead of the tropical wilds of the "Comedian," distant but never out of reach of the Divine Cartographer, this poem delivers us into the fabulous "land of the turkeys." At first this state seems even more mysterious, more abstract than Josie and Bonnie's "Oklahoma." Yet closer scrutiny must lead to some disenchantment. What seemed so "original" is only the familiar distorted.

How, indeed, could we have missed the landmarks of this place as little novel as a grade school bulletin board, not fresh, but charming with a skillless primitiveness? "Turkey weather" is – what else? Thanksgiving weather. The time is late November in a city where a monument is covered with whirling leaves. Transmogrified by a surreal eye, the leaves become the swarming mice which make this poem "macabre." With these images once in place, the homily comes into focus. The dance is "hungry," and the mice, ravenous, gnaw the outstretched arm of a Founder who stints to provide in the "dead of winter." The same Stevens who abhors aesthetic stasis castigates a State so rigid, a hagiography so stolid, it cannot accommodate the needs of starving mice. Moreover, the pieties of this "State" are as inert as an inscription in stone: the "sound of zithers and tambourines combined" mocks Republican sanctities. "Monsieur" with his sword "outstretched against all evil" (symbol of change personified as a Revolutionary) is now the figure of greatest evil – of the refusal to change. In larger terms, the irony of the poem flows against any ossified thing, any "State," eaten away by agents of change. Like the Verrocchio statue in "Noble Rider and The Sound of Words" the courtly Monsieur has outlived his usefulness. He now must fall subject to the devouring and "macabre" hunger of change. The poem recalls America's founding as, at the same time, it enjoins a renewed spirit of intrepid venture. Such venture, the poem reveals, has fallen on depressed times.

Without too much trouble I have organized a tidy allegory out of materials that seemed at first inchoate, inaccessible, even bizarre. The ostensible savagery of the poem lies like a thin film on a Stevensian truism ("It must change"). The poem is less the product of the fortuity on which the genuinely new depends than of a kind of thick linguistic impasto. When Stevens writes in the *Adagia,* "The essential fault of Surrealism is that it invents without discovering. . . . to make a clam play an accordion is to invent not to discover" (177), he might indeed have been thinking of this poem. He goes on: "the observation of the unconscious, so far as it can be observed, should reveal things of which we have previously been unconscious, not the familiar things of which we have been conscious plus imagination." A good example of a poem "plus imagination," "The Dance of the Macabre Mice" simply projects the doctrine of "The Noble Rider and the Sound of Words" through a watery lens.

Thus what at first has the aspect of savagery – of reality stripped of prior consciousness – is really the opposite: reality seen through the hyperconscious contrivance of the surreal. Another example of this comes in "Forces, the Will and the Weather." The poem would situate us in a savage place, a place of antic weather created solely by the poet:

> It was at the time, the place, of nougats,
> There the dogwoods, the white ones and the pink
>   ones
> Bloomed in sheets, as they bloom, and the girl,
> A pink girl took a white dog walking.   (*CP*, 228)

No special dexterity is required to peel back the nougats. The poet's prestidigitations have made them metaphors for the dogwoods, and their color composes a painterly scene of child and dog. Not that there is anything in particular to dislike about this poem, or those like it. It is accomplished, luscious, hypnotically satisfying to the eye. Yet the surreal produces poetry imposed and not discovered; secondary, not savage. Its gaudiness drapes the familiar. It lapses into the decorative. In such poems Stevens puts surrealism into overdrive, as if by pressing gaudiness to its limit one might shake the familiar.

Turn then to "Bantams in Pine Woods," the poem that begins famously: "Chieftain Iffucan of Azcan in caftan / Of tan with henna hackle halt! / Damned universal cock, as if the sun / was blackamoor to bear your blazing tail." Paraphrased, the poem reduces to a familiar Stevensian maxim. Its job is to indict the corpulent poet as Ego ("fat fat fat fat") who treats the sun as his slave. Indentured to himself, this poet is unaware of the resplendent reality that surrounds him, of those "Appalachian tangs" that put his "henna hackles" to shame.

To thus gloss the poem is not, however, to have plumbed its particular effectiveness. What makes "Bantams in Pine Woods" memorable is not the homily about poetry it offers, but instead, the way its language runs away from just that homily. What distinguishes this poem is its strenuous sound, the stuttering "ans" and "c's," the trochaic syncopation of the blank verse line. The poem's familiar meaning staggers under its sound, yet it is the sound we rest our faith in. Married to a staple homily. "Bantams in Pine Woods" is an experiment with savagery, a poem that goes halfway. Not yet weaned from sense, it is literally half-cocked. In this same vein, and manifesting the same divided resolve, is another rooster poem. The poem is "Country Words." It begins:

> I sang a canto in a canton
> Cunning-coo, O, cuckoo cock
> In a canton of Belshazzar
> To Belshazzar, putrid rock,

> Pillar of a putrid people,
> Underneath a willow there
> I stood and sang and filled the air.   (*CP*, 207)

The stanza readily boils down to a surreal fable of the cock as poet. Sounding the alarm with his song, this singer crows the downfall of Belshazzar whose stinking and moribund kingdom (putrid rock) links him with the "Founder" of "Dance of the Macabre Mice" and the massive Chieftain "fat fat fat fat"; links him with, in other words, all Noble Riders who outlive their usefulness. This is the gist of the poem. Yet the interest of the stanza is not in its gist, not in the aesthetic doctrine it disseminates and that the following stanzas rather predictably reinforce. What makes these lines memorable is that autonomy of language that sets a fecund sexual diction – "Cunning-coo, O, cuckoo cock" – against the scripturally austere language associated with Belshazzar – "Pillar," "willow," "filled," "rock."

My discussion so far leaves implicit two Stevensian habits that are better made explicit. There is, on the one hand, that Stevensian habit of the homiletic. As homileticist, Stevens supplies his readers readily applicable maxims on the function of poetry in the modern world. The critical tradition has well served this Stevens, accommodating poem after poem to this or that Stevensian doctrine so that even Stevens' most puzzling, most nonsensical lines find explication under the rubric "gaiety."

But Stevens is better than a good explainer. Lines like "Chieftain Iffucan of Azcan in caftan" do more than introduce the inauthentic figure of the poet in a Stevensian aesthetics. The line literally curls upon its own sound. Resisting the exploitation of homiletic function, it seems to strain for a virtual nakedness that would free the poet from his podium, free experience from explanation.

Shrewd critics of Stevens have not missed the ways in which the poet employs various stopgap measures to thwart this homiletic tendency. A first is to couple a syntax of explanation with a content that flouts explanation. The semantic meaning of the words subverts the syntax. For example: "Let the place of the solitaires / Be a place of perpetual indulation." By crowding declarative rhetoric with riotous and extravagant objects Stevens ironizes rhetoric itself. A second technique that Stevens often deploys is to subvert his propositions by giving them provisional titles. Resisting doctrine, Stevens offers instead "abstracts," "notes," "preludes."[9] Still, both of these techniques have a certain pedantry about them. Like surrealism they are hyperconscious rather than unconscious, knowing rather than artless. Predicated on a reader's prior apprehension of his gist, such methods give Stevens a bit of slack, while still tethering the poem to a diacrisis which permits revision but not invention. Irony is no solution either; it only intensifies the exteriority of the subject bending over a meaning he has imposed.

By the time of *Parts of a World* – Stevens' strangest and least read book – he has come to think of this explanatory mode and its mitigating countermodes as a kind of tyranny, albeit self-administered. In "The Latest Freed Man" he dreams of what it would be like "To be without a description of to be, / for a moment on rising, at the edge of the bed, to be." What the poet is after is not merely the exotic but the as yet uncreated, the unfallen, or at least the unchosen. He flees the repetitions of perception, of thought scurrying between the eye and the landscape, of us and it. *Parts of a World* would, instead, draw the expressive or reflective subject into the object. Romantic affect would be purged in favor of a comic effect. And so the stakes of the surreal are raised immeasurably as well, since the artificer now has no power of expression outside the object. Rather than reflect on experience, mimetically, the Stevensian speaker now becomes the naked object of reflection. There is no escape route into a gist.

This new movement will drive poems to a state of what Benamou calls "absence made visible," or what Stevens calls "decreation."[10] In the terms Emerson gave us, this would be a state of true originality, when self-consciousness yields, when light floods opacity. The hero of the poem is a knower uncreating the subjective mechanism by which he knows, or, in terms I have used before, unwriting the testimony of his own consciousness to the Fall. This hero is paradoxically bodied yet impersonal, abstract. In the late "Primitive Like an Orb" Stevens sketches this by now familiar figure:

> . . . an abstraction given head,
> A giant on the horizon, given arms,
> A massive body and long legs, stretched out
> A definition with an illustration, not
> Too exactly labeled.   (*CP*, 443)

This giant, an "abstraction given head," is a simulacrum of the savage. The event precipitating his birth is an involution of subjectivity. Describing Lévi-Strauss's response to "the impossibility of significantly knowing the otherness of others," Jeffrey Mehlman suggests that Lévi-Strauss "delineated a third domain neither self nor other . . . but the system of communicative relations by which both are necessarily constituted and in which they are alienated." In this way, "he comes to terms with the unconscious structure he shares with them: with his otherness to himself" (Mehlman, 17). What Stevens develops in *Parts of a World* is a figure analogously other to itself, a figure introjecting consciousness. We see this introjection commence in "Prelude to Objects" (another gloss on Emerson's transparent eyeball) where the self, or what we might call the ego, becomes transparent, shone through by objects it once beheld:

> If, while he lives, he hears himself
> Sounded in music, if the sun,
> Stormer, is the color of a self
> As certainly as night is the color
> Of a self, if, without sentiment,
> He is what he hears and sees and if,
> Without pathos, he feels what he hears
> And sees, being nothing otherwise,
> Having nothing otherwise, he has not
> To go to the Louvre to behold himself.   (CP, 194)

In this poem we see Adam as a figure of density and self-consciousness mooted by a subtraction of those affective or emotional determinants which give consciousness person.[11] Sense of self, sense of separateness, desire from union, apathy – all those factors that make knowledge more than a purely cognitive function, those factors that condition the human craving to know – these Stevens eliminates by subtracting "sentiment" and "pathos." This accomplished, he may contemplate a creation which, "being nothing otherwise, / having nothing otherwise" needs no projection of itself to perceive itself, is free of mind and its images, is other to itself and sufficient:

> To change nature, not merely to change ideas,
> To escape from the body, so to feel
> Those feelings that the body balks,
> The feelings of the natures round us here:
> As a boat feels when it cuts blue water.   (CP, 234)

These lines record a drive to render consciousness as pure sensation, to transcend the mind by bodying it. Thus the protagonist of "Phosphor Reading by his Own Light" disappears in order to appear writ "green." Subject becomes object.

> It is difficult to read. The page is dark.
> Yet he knows what it is that he expects.
>
> The page is blank or a frame without glass
> Or a glass that is empty when he looks.
>
> The greenness of night lies on the page and goes
> Down deeply in the empty glass . . .
>
> Look, realist, not knowing what you expect.
> The green falls on you as you look,

Falls on and makes and gives, even a speech
And you think that that is what you expect,

That elemental parent, the green night,
Teaching a fusky alphabet.   (*CP*, 267)

We are very far here from Crispin who journeyed to feel new. "Phosphor" is no pilgrim, indeed no person. Rather, he is an "abstraction given head." Incarnated out of very light by which he is, paradoxically, dematerialized, in this reciprocal cancellation is his "nakedness." The radiant light which saw – now is seen. The lamp of perception that "phosphor" evokes is now turned inside out. And just as what he sees goes empty, "the frame without a glass / Or a glass that is empty when he looks," he, on the other hand, fills up with "green."

In "Phosphor Reading by his Own Light" imagination no longer finds words to mediate between us and the world. Language no longer mediates, period. It is perhaps most accurate to say that we mediate; we are the images language casts, the letters its fusky alphabet shapes. Having thus renounced mediation, Stevens begins to spell out, in terms similar to those Lévi-Strauss applied to the Caduveo, a nakedness signaling refusal to be made in God's image, a paradoxically "gaudy" nakedness whose images free them from, rather than bind them to, a relation to Him.

Michel Benamou describes this nakedness as "that quality of the object and of man which abolishes the irradiating difference between the circle and the center" (Pearce, 116). Dickinson, as we will see, abolishes this "irradiating" difference by going "blind." Her sojourns on the circle become a means of losing the self the circle and center conspire to stabilize. Stevens' terms are analogous, but he obviates the self by straying inward from the circle, confounding outside by asserting an inside which, lacking the vision of the circle, no longer knows itself. In "Extracts From Addresses to the Academy of Fine Ideas" Stevens describes a nakedness that collapses the ring formed in "Sunday Morning" into a center which is the self. When, as Benamou goes on, "perception is participation . . . then there is an organic relationship between the circle of appearances and the center of the self" (Pearce, 115). The vision from the periphery turns in upon itself. It is the absence of self-knowledge, not the privilege of its possession, that rewards "Adamic hopefulness":

Where is that summer warm enough to walk
Among the lascivious poisons, clean of them,
And in what covert may we, naked, be
Beyond the knowledge of nakedness, as part
Of reality, beyond the knowledge of what
Is real, part of a land beyond the mind?   (*CP*, 252)

By now Stevens has jettisoned polemics, Romanticism, and surrealism to engage a theological bona fide: the relationship of knowledge to nakedness. Notice, in the lines "And in what covert may we, naked, be / Beyond the knowledge of nakedness," now "covert" – space of a world crouched under concealment – functions as its own antithesis. If the "covert" is the place where a fallen Adam and Eve conceal their nakedness, it serves here rather to stand for the nakedness that does not know to hide: but only to be. This pure being in a world of appearances is by necessity "covert" inasmuch as it is a state secreted, unrevealed. Where thought is governed by dualistic knowledge, by the eye bending over the naked thing, this gazeless nakedness will only come into being in "a land beyond the mind." "Montrachet-le-Jardin," an Emersonian exercise in the mood of Laforgue, recaps the passage to this land as a liberation from the old gods and from a desiccated Romanticism. Stuck in a tired pseudo-Coleridgean diction whose thumping rhymes secure irony through monotony

> A little while of Terra Paradise
> I dreamed, of autumn rivers, silvas green,
> Of sanctimonious mountains high in snow

the poet arrives at the fertility of abstraction:

> . . . The cataracts
> As facts fall like rejuvenating rain,
> Fall down through nakedness to nakedness,
> To the auroral creature musing in the mind.   (CP, 263)

This creature is the bodied mind, emptied out by a "fusky" language, venturing out of its covert. "Auroral," it emerges two poems later in "Metamorphosis," a poem of mind bodied in language, of syllables released to autonomous transformations, to change. "Metamorphosis" begins auspiciously:

> Yillow, yillow, yillow
> Old worm, my pretty quirk,
> How the wind spells out
> Sep - tem - ber. . . .
>
> Summer is in bones.
> Cock-robin's at Caracas.
> Make o, make o, make o,
> Oto - otu - bre.   (CP, 265)

These nonsense syllables attain the abstractness, the savagery, Stevens seeks. Although the submerged subject of the poem may be Keatsian – the transition from summer to fall – its language corrects the tender-

voiced subjectivity that would chronicle seasonal passage as a passage of
the self. The Keatsian affect is all gone. Instead, the movement from season to season is literally spelled out by the wind of a language that is
deathless because indefinite. No pathos uses this language: Rather language uses the human voice, or *langue* the convenience of *parole*. In place
of the conventional description of the autumn leaves and sky, we get
"yillow, yillow, yillow," an off-tint of yellow signaled by one letter.
September, the "pretty worm," slides out of summer syllable by syllable
(Sep-tem-ber), and the passage to a season summer finds unpronounceable is recited out of a primer, "Oto-otu-bre." The vicissitudes of the seasons have been abstracted into phonics, as the vista of migratory birds is
clipped to a mnemonic: "Cock-robin's at Caracas." Death does not register on the human plane; the only death is the death of a syllable, a letter,
as "Otu" replaces "oto." The Emersonian poetics is realized in a verbal
action uninhibited by the exigencies of voice.

Another characteristic poem in this mode appears in *Transport to Sum-*
mer shortly after the sublime imaginings of "Notes Toward a Supreme
Fiction." The poem, already brooding toward *Auroras of Autumn,* is
called "The Countryman":

> Swatara, Swatara, black river,
> Descending, out of the cap of midnight,
> Toward the cape at which
> You enter the swarthy sea,
>
> Swatara, Swatara, heavy the hills
> Are, hanging above you, as you move,
> Move blackly and without crystal.
> A countryman walks beside you.
>
> He broods of neither cap nor cape,
> But only of your swarthy motion,
> But always of the swarthy water,
> Of which Swatara is the breathing,
>
> The name. He does not speak beside you.
> He is there because he wants to be
> And because being there in the heavy hills
> Among the moving of the water –
>
> Being there is being in a place,
> As of a character everywhere,
> The place of a swarthy presence moving,
> Slowly, to the look of a swarthy name.   (*CP*, 428)

"Swatara," with its swaying and swarthy sound, controls everything that
goes on in this poem. The "countryman" is not a man living on the
banks of Swatara, but a figure engendered by "Swatara" as Bonnie and

Josie spring full formed out of Oklahoma. The linguistic is an attribute, a force of the physical world, not its medium, not its "crystal." And the beings born of this linguistic force do not use but rather present or wear the images that now thrive in the place they are. Stevens yields up reflection to exhibition. There is no human eye, and no divine eye, bending over this nakedness, but only, as Heidegger might put it, Being unconcealing itself, only, as Emerson dreamt, the "original" in language revealed.

Such poems are closer to the center of Stevens' poetics than has yet been acknowledged. These "savage utterances" are nothing less than the fulfillment of a promise awkwardly made in "Sunday Morning," but made good in the ensuing years. The problem with such poems is a problem Stevens acknowledges in his statement of the *Adagia* that "(f)or most life is an affair of people . . . but for me it is an affair of places": unintelligibility. Poems like "Metamorphosis" enforce a hermeticism that dooms them to obsolescence rather more quickly than even Stevens might be ready to accept. Their self-sufficiency defines their unreadability; one has to have written them to like them. One has to have, in the vernacular, been there. Even having been there, one fears that no one else was. If Stevens brings the Emersonian self-reliance to its natural realization, he also draws out the implications of that idea: a privacy without person, a poetry of studied and literal apathy.

For in order to unwrite the Fall, Stevens has unwritten the fallen. Writing an "Ode to Autumn" that empties out the human mortality autumn's changes traditionally metaphorize, writing of a "countryman" who has no existence but that generated by place, Stevens writes human experience into a strange and harlequin kind of corner. Such poems put us in mind of the asexual practices of the Caduveo: The beings who flit through these poems are, as it were, adopted rather than conceived. Refusing God's image they refuse human lineament as well.

This is the acute point toward which Stevens' experiments in originality are inflected, the headland toward which any absolute notion of originality surges. Such figures as "Swatara" and the "pretty quirk" act out the enigmatic "myth before the myth began" that Stevens mentions in "Notes Toward a Supreme Fiction." Beginning fresh, with a Word, Stevens radicalizes Emerson by conceiving a "relation" not expressive of man or woman, but cohering in the absence of the human. His relation is enjoyed, but not by us. It is original, but not so "we" know it. Neither Christ nor Adam mediates, or gives meaning, to an experience of language that wholly encases the word in flesh and flesh in the word.

Stevens' a-personalism dramatizes the consequences implicit in rejecting the patrimony of Adam. Against, say, the intense and uncompromisable voicing that characterizes Crane's speakers – each, as we will see,

constituted by "the world that comes to each of us alone" – Stevens'
speakers are oddly voiceless; or, perhaps, better, they seem: voiced over.
It is as though the Emersonian rhetorician who pronounced from above
"Nothing is good or fair alone" had entered the level voice. Now affect
is gratuitous; there are no days to regret, for the world is all in us, or, in
the vivid words more truly us than any lack of them. As I will show,
Crane's speaker knows himself constituted by the very lack, as does
Dickinson's. And for all his sometime faith in autogenesis, in the fecun-
dity of words, Whitman too allows the truth dejection tells, allows a
muteness as much us as volubility. By and large, all the above heirs of
Emerson reject any idea of change that is not also an idea of mutability.
They resist any scheme of variation that does not give full register to
loss, regret, hope. They reject that most Emersonian tenet spelled out in
"Notes Toward a Supreme Fiction" – "It must be abstract" – reattach-
ing to the Emersonian "transition" a sense of human crisis, of annihilation and of dread.

I have proposed that Stevens' chief difference from other American
poets who follow Emerson lies in his elision of the person. And I have
linked that elision to a way in which language is made a kind of sixth
sense, a faculty of austere theoretic design, which, like the designs of
the Caduveo, takes its singular nobility from being literally man-made.
The chief faculty of the human in both cases is the creative gift, but,
crucially, a creativity that equates the world's perfectibility with its
own, rather than a creativity that knows Divine Creation ever and always
to mock its own. If all that stands in the way of this design is the de-
signer, his impositions, the task is to find a Nature the poet can make
without contrivance, a natural design not "gaudy" but "plain." This
pursuit of the plain Stevens explores in "Ordinary Evening in New Haven." Dedicated to a nakedness bright with imagination, yet free of intention, "Ordinary Evening" telescopes Stevens' entire search for savage
unself-consciousness.

The opening lines, "The eyes plain version is a thing apart / the vul-
gate of experience," adumbrate Stevens' search for the state antithetical
to that pursued in "Notes Toward a Supreme Fiction." What he is after
is "the commonplace and ugly" (Doggett and Buttel, 299), yet here, as
so often, the celebrant, Stevens, proffers this ugliness like a gift. His tone
is evangelical. Plainness saves:

> The plainness of plain things is savagery . . .
>   . . . Plain men in plain
>   towns
> Are not precise about the appeasement they need.

> They only know a savage assuagement cries
> With a savage voice; and in that cry they hear
> Themselves transposed, muted and comforted
> In a savage and subtle and simple harmony,   (*CP*, 467)

These lines are Stevens' mature revision of the "supple and turbulent" circle of "Sunday Morning" and they are certainly more credible. By designating the "plain town" as his savage venue, Stevens overcomes the contrived quality that marred the seventh stanza of "Sunday Morning," yet still he explains too much, too incompletely. We do not know why we should be "muted and comforted" by this "plainness." The very potency of the plain is lost, as earlier, in a certain discursive prosiness. What Stevens circles incessantly around in "Ordinary Evening in New Haven" is not an exoticism or ritualism but a native singularity, a savagery of the person, local to our blood. He struggles to capture some moment where the plain will reveal its uniqueness, in which we may glimpse – in a *"trouvaille"* – the originality of ordinary space beyond the need to defoliate Eden or to craft an ersatz heaven. He knows that the key is in some fusion with the object that will collapse circle into center. His alter ego, Professor Eucalyptus (a figure incarnated – like Bonnie and Josie, and like Phosphor – out of the greenness of imagination) knows well "not to look beyond the object." Rather,

> He seeks
> God in the object itself, without much choice.
> It is a choice of the commodious adjective
> For what he sees, it comes in the end to that:
>
> The description that makes it divinity, still speech
> As it touches the point of reverberation – not grim
> Reality but reality grimly seen
>
> And spoken in a paradisal parlance new.   (*CP*, 475)

Eucalyptus is, alas, a professor precisely because of such pedantries. He has theory well in hand, but explanation runs away from him. His advance toward the "plain" is frustrate. Discursive where it would be consummately "poetic," the savage has difficulty warming up to itself. The mind that would seize savagery for its own instead flounders again and again in "knowledge," in the "and yet, and yet, and yet." What the poet gets is more language, more trash, or bric-a-brac, when what he wants is to wear an origin like his own skin. Even after purging the problematic personae from the poem, Cotton Mather and his scarcely secular romantic cousin, Crispin; even after purging quester, religious innovator, ephebe, and spiritual anthropologist – all impediments in a quest for a place beyond knowledge – the discursiveness persists, describing, doubling back and back on itself. Then, finally, the savage breaks through:

> The instinct for heaven had its counterpart:
> The instinct for earth, for New Haven, for his room,
> The gay tournamonde as of a single world
>
> In which he is and as and is are one.   (*CP*, 476)

To understand the special difference of "Ordinary Evening" just compare this line to the parallel apostrophe of "Notes Toward a Supreme Fiction": "I have not but I am and as I am I am." There, the speaker, meditating on the subjectivity of the Major Man, utters a line sublime in its Romantic power, yet suffused with the utterance of the older Supreme Being who said to Moses "I am that I am." "Ordinary Evening" rejects the "I," purging the poem of self for a "he" who is abstract: no one. The subject or pilgrim here enters the object of study, the man in New Haven, heaven. In its very unsayableness, the line "In which he is and as and is are one" marks the place of poetry, or culture naturalizing itself. Declaring itself uncreated thing, the poem is willing to be minimal in order to be self-engendered.

I noted earlier that the price of this savagery will be a certain vulnerability to the absurd; the "simple seeing" of the "ignorant eye" has as a consequence the sacrifice of ironic control or distance. Savagery in New Haven, the absurdity of it, yields to a piercing kind of exposure. The passage from talky anthropology to "moving with the objects" costs the poet not only a describing power, but a "concealing power." If Romantic seeing was voyeuristic, the subject decked out as object is nakedly vivid.[12] Stevens' subject is eroticized, exposed:

> The objects tingle and the spectator moves
> With the objects. But the spectator also moves
> With lesser things, with things exteriorized
>
> Out of rigid realists. It is as if
> Men turning into things, as comedy,
> Stood dressed in antic symbols, to display
>
> The truth about themselves, having lost, as things
> The power to conceal they had as men.   (*CP*, 470)

The dignity of the discursive, of the "imposed," is here contrasted with the nakedness of "men turning into things, as comedy." To lose "the power to conceal they had as men" is to achieve a nakedness wholly original, but not quite human. In "Things of August" Stevens meditates further on the externalization of the subject we see in "Ordinary Evening in New Haven":

> The thinker as reader reads what has been written.
> He wears the words he reads to look upon
> Within his being,

> A crown within him of crispest diamonds,
> A reddened garment falling to his feet,
> A hand of light to turn the page,   (CP, 492)

The self, absorbed into the text of the world, or materializing as text, is vivid with a color and light that abstract him. No longer recognizably human, he is agent or conduit of originality. The very newness of his "relation" to the universe defines his inhumanity.

> The world? The inhuman as human? That which
>   thinks not,
> Feels not, resembling thought, resembling feeling?
> It habituates him to the invisible,
> By its faculty of the exceptional,
>
> The faculty of ellipses and deviations
> In which he exists but never as himself.   (CP, 493)

What is it to exist but not as oneself? What does it mean to so exist in New Haven? The pathos attaching to such efforts should not be missed. We are at the very extremity here of the Emersonian "self-reliance" as it is achieved, paradoxically, in a theoretical suspension of "self." In purging "Ordinary Evening in New Haven" of intention or desire, invoking "men turning into things, as comedy" the poet delivers us back to a beginning of things, before we fell into separation and into the language through which we communicate human aloneness. Section 19 of "Ordinary Evening" finds us in a place wholly consecrated to itself, scrolling back like a Scripture to give its own genesis:

> A century in which everything was part
>
> Of that century and of its aspect, a personage,
> A man who was the axis of his time,
> An image that begot its infantines,
> Imaginary poles whose intelligence
> Streamed over chaos their civilities

Through an elimination of the inquiring subject Stevens has arrived at a theogony of the savage: The imaginary pole begetting images replaces the monolithic Absolute in whose image we shuddered. At the center is a new poet, an Ecclesiastes not rehabilitated to serve God, but doggedly peeling back vanity after vanity, image after image, to offer the text of an unintelligible redemption. The wise man sheds his knowledge, mandating a relation undreamed of, "something new under the sun."

> . . . A figure like Ecclesiast
> Rugged and luminous, chants in the dark
> A text that is an answer, although obscure.   (CP, 479)

The "obscurity" is crucial, for it points to the way that Stevens' savage sites, sacraments of a kind, are stripped of communal, consolatory function. In Emerson's stead, Stevens offers in such poems a way to "sift things" for oneself, to be "self-reliant," and by so doing to shrug off the "slough" of creed, tradition, and God's overbearing Book. The nature in which the earlier poet read God is literally "displaced" by places God does not see. Such places created by the poet are sprung up around the "swarthy names" he "discovers."

But displaced as well as that faculty of sympathy whose assent confers intelligibility, that agrees to call these texts readable and not merely writable. And if such poems present us, as readers, with difficulty, the requirements of the savage tax the poet as well. To achieve a savage originality is to shoulder the burden of not only reading but writing the text. And the text is nothing less than the whole world. In "Things of August" Stevens writes:

> A new text of the world
> A scribble of fret and fear and fate
> From a bravura of the mind,
> A courage of the eye,
>
> In which, for all the breathings
> From the edge of night,
> And for all the white voices
> That were rosen once,
>
> The meanings are our own –
>
> . . .
>
> A text of intelligent men
> At the centre of the unintelligible
> As in a hermitage, for us to think,
> Writing and reading the rigid inscription.   (*CP*, 493)

When the "meanings are our own," the freedom of "men chanting in orgy" must be understood as a freedom of heavy obligation. The figure like an Ecclesiast, in order to constitute Being, no longer reads God's Book but writes, in the midst of the unintelligible, the Book of the world. This major man gains freedom from dogma only by shackling himself to an awesome task – in the triangle composed of God, man, and language he must not only inscribe himself everywhere, but inscribe himself as savage, unintelligible.[13] The achievement of the "perfect whole," as Emerson had it, cannot sustain the paltry articulations of any "each." The weight borne by such mediation is the weight of the whole world, the same weight pathetically, heroically carried by the Caduveo covering their bodies with "star-shaped motifs." Occupant of a "hermitage," the poet, splendidly decked out, escutcheoned like a Caduveo warrior, pays the price of isolation in order to escape the onus of being named. "We may now understand," writes Lévi-Strauss, "why the Caduveo style strikes us as a subtler variant of that which we employ in our playing cards" (174).

> Each of our card designs corresponds to a twofold necessity and must assume a double function. It must be an independent object, and it must serve for the dialogue – or the duel – in which two partners meet face to face. It must also play the role which is assigned to each card in its capacity as a member of the pack in the game as a whole. Its vocation is a complicated one, therefore, and it must satisfy the demands of more than one sort – symmetrical where its functions are concerned, asymmetrical where its role is in question. (176)

It is this asymmetricality in the midst of symmetry that Stevens' savage poems reveal. By achieving the asymmetricality of the savage, they live, like court cards, in the dignity of their own autonomy. Vivid and acute, they are, in the terms of "Ordinary Evening in New Haven," "transfixing by being purely what is." They map the originality against which relation is defined; they discover the insupportability of the original and the sterility of the abstract.

In the end, the very singularity that they achieve cries out for change. The asymmetry of the savage yields to the symmetries of imagination. Nakedness uncreated falls back on an older nakedness, back into the world of concealment, dualism, of human loneliness relieved by the marriage of opposites. Thus in "Notes Toward a Supreme Fiction" the desire that Stevens' poems of savagery so hold at bay is readmitted. Words chosen out of desire have their place, for they restore the poem to an expressiveness an absolute Emersonianism must preclude:

> Winter and spring, cold copulars, embrace
> And forth the particulars of rapture come . . .
>
> And North and South are an intrinsic couple
> And sun and rain a plural, like two lovers.   (CP, 392)

And so on. Out of this fecundity of imagination, the savage, surfeited, revolts, imposing autonomy on diacrisis. In the moment of the savage, division is suspended, held at bay. Writing of the dualism which "recurs over and over again like a hall of mirrors" in Caduveo society, Lévi-Strauss notes how, in the moment of Caduveo creation, dualism recedes:

> These antitheses are glimpsed after the creative process, and they have a static character. The dynamic of art – the way, i.e., in which the motifs are imagined and carried out – cuts across this fundamental duality at every level. The primary themes, initially disarticulated, are later

blended into secondary themes which establish a sort of provisional unity among fragments borrowed from their predecessors, and these in turn are juxtaposed in such a way that the original unity reappears, as if as the result of a conjuring trick. (174)

In Stevens' savage moments of decreation he achieves this fundamental dignity of "disarticulation." Men "dressed in antic symbols to display the truth about themselves" seize the "savage source" of "Sunday Morning." In this antic moment, resplendently original, the Emersonian poetics sojourns in the poem. Then, theory occupies a form of intention, and language uses speech not to say but to unsay; to wrest a reprieve from that dualism that is the condition of Wallace Stevens' poetry, and of all poetry exiled from God's garden.

PART II

PART VI

4

Crossing Leviticus: Whitman

O then! Let the secure World drowned in its sensual pleasures, and sunk into a deep sleep of carnal security; that flatter themselves by saying, The Evil Day is far off; wake out of sleep; and as you are hastening unto the coming day of God; O look out sharp.

New England's Lamentations, 1734

One can well imagine the bemusement of those sundry acquaintances with whom the unexceptional Walter Whitman of the early 1840s shared plans for his "great and ponderous" book, but hindsight allows us the pleasure of reflecting just how amply the 1855 edition of *Leaves of Grass* justified not only Whitman's wildest boasts but also Emerson's highest hopes. A combination, as Emerson famously put it, of the "Bhagvat Gita and the New York *Herald Tribune,*" the first *Leaves of Grass* brimmed with that salvific confidence Emerson had sketched out in his 1838 "Divinity School Address" while its creator seemed to have both the large scope and common touch Emerson went on, in 1846, to call characteristic of "the Poet." Emerson's approbation no doubt helped sustain Whitman's ambition in the years that followed the release of the 1855 edition, emboldening the poet – whose work Emerson had found revelatory – to conceive a function for his book larger than any yet imagined by an American. In a diary entry of 1857, Whitman recognizes his first edition as just that, fascicle of a testament more ponderous still than a simple book:

> The Great Construction of the New Bible. Not to be diverted from the principle object – the main life work – the three hundred and sixty five. (*Notes*, 57)

Hefting its gargantuan ambition, the note has all the muscle and rousting pitch of the Big Top that had so stamped the first *Leaves of Grass*. A note, after all, from Whitman's personal binder, the passage's tone of resolute self-exhortation recalls something of that striving to do good that had motivated Mather's *Bonifacius*, but another ancestor is the Franklinian diarist who turned boosterism inward, letting, as it were, no grass grow under his feet. The phrase "Great Construction" itself, minted in the poster-ad argot of engineering marvels or of the Greatest Show on Earth, demonstrates afresh just how impossible it is to take the phrenology parlor out of Whitman. It also reveals, though, with what seriousness Whitman understood the vigilance exacted of one who would write a New American Bible. Not to be reduced to mere camp-meeting hyperbole, the phrase "three hundred and sixty five" is especially resonant, reflecting Whitman's understanding of the revision of the Christian time line his work had inaugurated, his ushering in of a new day superseding the *kairoi* of Fall, Atonement, and Judgment.[1] Such a day Emerson had never conceived.

Not that Whitman's new revelation, *Leaves of Grass,* does not conform in some considerable measure to Emersonian specifications. Casting off the "rags and relics of the past," and stripping down literally naked, from the opening lines Whitman's speaker makes literal the transparency Emerson had, though more modestly, called for in the memorable image of the "transparent eyeball." "Song of Myself," the steady burning center of a bush-green volume, moves, moreover, so auspiciously toward achieving Emerson's "original relation" that Emerson's famous salutation "I greet you at the beginning of a great career" seems an anticlimax in a letter that stops just short of recording Moses' wonder: "I rubbed my eyes a little," Emerson confesses, "to see if this sunbeam were no illusion." With the sheer brio of his self-reliance – "I celebrate myself and sing myself" – with his faith in an unmediated Revelation – "You shall not take things second hand, nor look through the eyes of the dead, nor feed on the specters in books. . . . / You shall listen to all sides and filter them from yourself" (*Leaves,* 30) – with his embrace of nature and his eschewal of poetic jingling in favor of a "meter making argument," the Whitman of "Song of Myself" harnesses the religious audacity of Emerson's "priest or poet" to a sprightly lyric gift. Not surprisingly, then, it is the Emersonian Whitman, the Whitman of "Song of Myself," who has by and large been institutionalized. R. W. B. Lewis made the classic case for this most Emersonian Whitman when, in *The American Adam,* he suggested that Whitman's originality flowed from a faith in the power of language cognate with Emerson's. Essaying the autonomous genesis of a new kind of man in a new kind of language, "Song of Myself," as Lewis argued, displays an impulse, rightly called Adamic, to recreate the world out of words (Lewis, *The American Adam,* 41–53). More recently, Paul Zweig ascribed Whitman's mysterious emergence from mediocrity to the converting power of language itself. Something like the way that God, as the Talmud recounts, looked into the Torah and then made the world, Zweig's Whitman models himself by hearkening to the dictates of his own Scripture. Between them, Lewis and Zweig compass the mainstream view of a Whitman who maneuvers unconstricted within the poetic theology Emerson lays down in the "Divinity School Address": a Whitman whose theology adumbrates Emerson's.[2] Bloom's Whitmanian sublime, a revision of the Emersonian sublime, depends on this mainstream consensus.

"Song of Myself" tends to support this view, but it is only one poem in the original 1855 edition of *Leaves of Grass,* and far from Whitman's most theologically searching work. Although hardly wasted on a work of such beauty, the attention lavished on this most Emersonian of Whitman's poems diverts our attention from a stranger, more apocryphal Whitman, the Whitman who even as he composed the ebullient "Song of Myself" – a masterpiece of evangelism – was committed as well to formulating the very doctrine of his New American Bible, to laying down its Law. The poem devoted to this Law is "The Sleepers."

If "Song of Myself" is justly called Whitman's Genesis, Emersonian in its drive toward aboriginal beginnings, "The Sleepers" is his Leviticus and Deuteronomy. Only by penetrating the simple shimmer of myth to devise a New Law, and anointing a Savior to uphold it, can Whitman hope to give his Bible the "comprehensiveness" it needs. Thus, the lambent energy of "Song of Myself" is, from the earliest editions, tested by the archaeological depth and striated density of "The Sleepers," a poem whose engagement with Christian history and Christian poetry lends "Song of Myself" its very good faith. To understand the place of "Song of Myself" in the larger context of *Leaves of Grass* is to fathom just how decidedly its prophetic reach depends on a retrospection Whitman's mentor not only did not authorize, but outright discouraged.

Emerson's discouragement of Whitman's sexual frankness was no doubt informed by a shrewd and even market-wise appraisal of just how much light a purblind American public would stand. Emerson knew the prudery of the American public, perhaps by sharing it, and he probably did not want to see Whitman's long-term impact traded off for short-lived shock value. The flouting of Victorian mores would have to go. Unquestionably, some of the passages Emerson urged Whitman to expunge from the 1860 edition stood to offend Americans of tastes considerably narrower than Emerson's own. Yet the cuts Emerson proposed do more than pare prurient excrescences or gratuitous exhibitionism from the manuscript; they rather gouge into the very structure of Whitman's vision.[3] Many years later, recalling his rejection in 1860 of Emerson's prudent counsel, Whitman insisted "I have not lived to regret my Emerson no," explaining, "If I had cut the sex out, I may as well have cut everything out" (Kaplan, 249). Even allowing for Whitman's testiness at Emerson's cooled affections, such remarks bring into the open a conviction Whitman had had, by that time, years to develop. Emerson's appreciation of his work, for all its good faith, was partial indeed. Precisely that part of the work Emerson deemed unbecoming to the poet, most bereft of enduring poetic value, Whitman regarded as most valuable.

The section of *Leaves of Grass* over which the two famously quarreled on the Boston Common sheds light on the precise character of this "everything" Emerson left out. One might surmise that this sheaf of poems, tellingly called "Children of Adam," troubled more than Emerson's sense of propriety: It must have offended his faith as well. Beginning "To the garden the world anew ascending / Potent mates, daughters, sons, preluding," and concluding, "Be not afraid of my body," Whitman's "Children of Adam" restores density and influence not only to that naked physiognomy Emerson would rather drape, but also to an Adamic progenitor all Emerson's passion had gone toward toppling. Whitman's unabashedly genealogical language is not merely uncouth in pointing out the sexuality linking generation to generation. It is also, in Emersonian terms, theologically retrograde, reinstating an ancient determinism which shifted the burden of sin onto the shoulders of innocents down the generations. Emerson had quite self-consciously orphaned the children of Adam – for their own good and for the greater good of poetry. The disaffiliation from Adam was meant to secure a specific poetic benefit: the liberation of language from that morbidity of denotation coextensive with human sin. The unpleasant fleshiness, that dead weight of language that so plagues Taylor as fallen poet is for Emerson but symptom of an orthodox inertia the new revelation may discard; or, better, the new poet preempt.

These terms "discard" and "preempt" should suggest just how hard and implacable were the obstacles looming in Emerson's way; just how plaguey and tenacious was this corporeal Adam with which he contended; just how taxed the poet who would do without him. Earlier I suggested that Emerson's "original relation" amounts to an unwitting reiteration of the very notion of original sin that he is bent on discarding: The phrase invokes an immediacy, or purity, that representational language must traduce. The poet accepting the patrimony of Adam will find his language as compromised as any language since Adam. Thus, Emerson's ideal poet creates himself without recourse to the mold of Adam. Emerson's notion of originality requires a poet outside the differential, a figure ubiquitous and deathless because out of time. "Sacred history," he insists, "attests that the birth of a poet is the principal event

in Chronology" and "poetry was all written before time was." Enjoying
a naissance prior to time, and so prior to the Fall which ushered time
into the world with its attendant sin, Emerson's poet would rescue time
from itself.

It is hardly indelicate to point out that such is the Savior's job. The
telescoping and comprehension of time is the task charged to the Christ
who is "first and last." In more ways than one Emerson's poet is Christlike, and not simply in the figurative sense. In point of fact, a figurative
savior who "secularized," and thereby superannuated, Christ by a kind
of typological completion would more creditably serve Emerson's sup-
posed purposes than the spotless Redeemer he actually produces. Emerson's poet is a lamb of God. Not only fallen notions of time but
especially fallen notions of purity and impurity attach to the figure
whose integrality with himself should repel such attachments, but who
rather gains resolution in Emerson's thought in the old, stark chiar-
oscuro of the fallen palette. It might have been the Fall's sublime apol-
ogist, Milton, who said, "The sublime vision comes to the pure and
simple soul in a clean and chaste body," but it is instead Emerson, glean-
ing his poet's job description from *Hebrews,* where Christ is described as
the fulfillment of Leviticus, as "ideal high priest . . . holy, innocent, and
uncontaminated." No catalogue of the snares besetting the seer poet
could dramatize better a vision of a world despoiled – and so requiring
repair – than this anxious appeal to spotlessness. The impurity jettisoned
from Emerson's poet is, in effect, structurally identical with the increment of "relation" denied in the phrase "original relation." Neither escapes a Christian metaphysic, and both suggest a fall-back position that
is essentially sin-based, taxonomizing clean and unclean with all the energy expended by upholders of the earlier Law.

Emerson surpasses all his Calvinist forebears in a fastidiousness whose
signal expression is the rejection of the Christ he calls "Monster." If Taylor's attitude to flesh was singularly unrepressed, this is not least because
his Calvinism converges on a figure of suffering flesh, a Passion. Emerson, by denying the efficacy of Christ's suffering and instead focusing
on His power to inspire, dismantles, as the last chapter showed, the chief
obstacle between liberal soul and its bliss. But with this progress comes
a regress. To deemphasize the agony of Christ is to clear the way for optimism in God's benevolence, but it is also to lose a certain heuristic hold
on corporeality that Calvinism offers. The post–Unitarian progressivism
paradoxically returns pain, suffering, and the body to a kind of pre-
Christian and archaic "Fate" which visits earthquakes and suffering upon
us inexplicably.[4]

Moreover, the occlusion of Christ as Sufferer – and the suspension of
absolute Ends such an occlusion suggests – affects, as I showed in Chap-

ter 2, Emerson's very prose style. This point bears a bit more explication, for Whitman's revision of Emerson addresses just that tendency of the Emersonian language to disembody itself, making of the poem, poetics. Just as there is something vagrant about Emerson's poet, a figure driven, as it were, out of flesh, there is something insubstantial about a poetics so much on the run from corporeal realizations, from Incarnation. Many critics have noted the unmistakable forgettableness of Emerson's essays, their tendency to resist the iconic so successfully that they dissolve just behind the reading eye.[5] It is as though the very differentiated structure of a paragraph casting its shadow on the mind virtualizes dualism. Resisting dimension itself, Emerson develops a kind of writing that does not mark its time in space, that is the opposite of architectonic – or, as any undergraduate will attest, the opposite of memorable. Call this freedom or the free flow of signification if you like, but such a description appears to gainsay what in other lights seems simple mortification, or, fear of the End. Emerson's unmatched theoretical powers, his invention of multiple notions of American freedom, and his invention of a distinctly defetishized speech are all related to his obtuseness around the grosser human needs, an obtuseness that makes his rhetorical pronouncements as a rule abstract, not infrequently rarefied, and sometimes downright precious. Taylor's "leproused flesh" he will not touch, and there is much else Emerson finds indigestible.

Digestion is the right word here, since what Whitman has in abundance is maw. Like Ezekiel, who swallowed the whole dry scroll of God's Scripture, relearning the savor of the Law for a generation in exile, Whitman may be said to gulp down the very dry wafer Emerson refuses. Or, to invoke a parallel closer to hand, that other massive Scripture of the 1850s, *Moby-Dick,* Whitman's New Bible may be said to absorb without incorporating an older scripturalism.

Melville's resistance to Emersonianism in *Moby-Dick* informs that work's structure in ways that may shed light on Whitman's analogous resistance in "The Sleepers." Setting opacity and a comprehensive differentiation against the Emersonian transparency, Whitman's poem is a kind of "Cetology" – syncretic, rather than synthetic, and in this way very much like *Moby-Dick,* which fragments "theological" unity in the punning substitution of a "cetological" hash. In both Melville and Whitman, textual heterogeneity is no threat to the spirit. With Melville's text shattering the unity of Beginnings in a sheaf of "Abstracts," and Whitman's New American Bible made subject to the fresh starts of revision, scripture's historicity is reconciled with its enduring truth. Indeed, the outcome that theologians of both liberal and orthodox bent most feared from the Scientific Bible criticism – the irretrievable seepage of the potent Word (ethical, on the one hand, doctrinal on the other) into the tissue of documents – becomes in Whitman's work, as in Melville's, a saving article of faith. In the text itself – domain of the letter and of history and of flesh – the sacred is renewed, as the sea renews itself, or as grass does. Documentary tangibility is the form of the Law.

Whitman thus presents to the critic, now acting as exegete, the paradox of a textual body which, though not reducible to what bulges inside it, is yet nourished and enriched by what its stomach holds. Moreover, without jettisoning the "rags and relics" of the past, this new text thrives. Its time is not clogged by complication of history; its inceptions are not dulled by reflection or mimesis. Like Melville's whale of a book, harboring in its great bulk an illimitable number of mental and material things (blubber and oil, Melville's reading and maritime politics, Shakespeare and Carlyle, and ethnicities distinctly differentiated), "The Sleepers" calls attention to the weight of an ineffaceable materiality, or corporeality, whose spiritual potency has nothing to do with transparency. Flesh need not be saved from itself. Flesh is the safe harbor of spirit.

Even further, covered thickly with writing, the "leaves" of "The Sleepers," like Melville's "Bible Leaves," resist the tyranny of a Word, and so, accordingly, the transcendent office of Him who comprehends all words in His silent flesh. In Whitman's poem, Christ himself is freed from the lonely task of being all words in One. Multiplying the sacrament by itself, desanctifying the swallowing in a larger swallowing, the poem offers passage not to one Word alone, but to many words; it blesses not Christ's anguish alone but the anguish Christ bears for the world. The consuming spectacle of God's Chosen One killed is itself consumed by a poem that would cannibalize less by swallowing more.

At this very same pass Emerson had resolved to swallow not at all. For the generations before Emerson, whose own break with organized religion came, not incidentally, because he could neither, as it were, swallow nor administer the swallowing, the sacrament of the Last Supper had absorbed the prophet's task, with the body of Christ superseding, or embodying, all the nourishment of the old Law. But determined as he was to displace inherited sin with self-taught seeing, and the boon of grace with an energetic self-reliance, Emerson promulgated a law that had perforce to avert its (transparent) eye from that suffering Body whose density, vulnerability, and final expendability manifests how decidedly unfree we are, how determinate our possibilities, how limited our knowledge.

It is not only out of a more liberal sexual frankness that Whitman restores to the body its full weight and dimension, but also out of a considerable theological perspicacity. In the glancing nimbleness of the Emerson style Whitman must have intuited a disembodying impulse not transcending but fleeing physical virtuality, and so, in Emerson's resistance to any structure enclosing and so framing itself in space, a repression of the way that consciousness, enveloped in body and made frail by knowledge, is never free of its own weight and mass, never finds a balance that death's gravity does not upset. Whitman's simple reassertion of a spatial matrix Emerson cannot afford, his lifelong respect for things "in their places," has a theological resonance surpassing its simple capacity to soothe. This deference before the way space sculpts the object is characteristic of the Whitmanian theology that springs up in the interstices of Emerson's thought, filling in what Emerson "left out."

The verity that Emerson, as poet, acknowledges only in his best poem, the rueful "Days," and that the ricochet of idealism and stoicism in his essays bears out, is something Whitman knows and applies in "The Sleepers." The Christian *kairoi* are not so easily dismissed, for the uncertainties they address are neither so arcane nor so archaic as the broadsides of the Unitarian controversy would indicate. In jettisoning the Exile, the Law, the Passion, the Judgment – each with its own fair quotient of impurity – a Unitarian metaphysic dedicated to our union with the universe impoverishes itself of symbolic solutions to the problem of our rending from that world. Sequestered in his "pleached garden," the Emersonian poet is never free of the hard and divisive facts of death that Christian myths of rending would account for and for which Puritan poems of judgment are preparation. On the contrary, cordoned off, stripped of Christian reference, and so also, of the power of ritual comfort, these facts inevitably surface in Emerson's work. Now called "Experience" and now "Fate," their threat is only enhanced by a mechanism that coils tight and hoards them. The gesture that informs Emerson's entire bifurcated canon is a repulse of the Fall, the menace of which is only intensified since it is wrenched free of the "comprehensive" theology that would allow for its circulation.

Seeking this comprehensiveness leads Whitman to redefine his relationship to Emerson. By reconsidering the Emersonian confidence in autonomous creation Whitman finds his own Adamic speaker of "Song of Myself" an untested fellow of hortatory, but limited actual power. Further, by exploring that class of experience Emerson quarantines under the rubric of Fate, Whitman discovers the formidable cultural and spiritual power of the suffering Christ whom Emerson had summarily jettisoned. Last, by probing the Emersonian sufficiency, or compensation, Whitman is recalled to the last and first bar of our unhappiness: Shame. The emergence of the Emersonian poet marks the end of a Unitarian trajectory prospective and increasingly secular. Whitman's trajectory is, by contrast, recursive, not shedding but rather harrowing orthodoxy in pursuit of its own consoling word. And the poem committed to the devo-

lution of this Emersonian evolution, the poem in which Whitman treats
Emerson more as nemesis than mentor, is "The Sleepers."

Of all the poems included in the first, 1855, edition of *Leaves of Grass,*
we may surmise that it was the fourth poem, "The Sleepers," at which
refined sensibilities most took umbrage. More risqué than "Song of Myself," itself occupied quite enough with armpits and "milky jettings" to
alarm readers used to the edifications of William Cullen Bryant, "The
Sleepers" introduces a woman who "rolls herself" upon her lover as
"upon a bed," suggests with some but not sufficient indirection the
"wild flapping . . . joy" of homosexual courtship, and develops a tableau of adolescent masturbation not lacking in pornographic impact. Fly-
ing in the face of nineteenth-century American mores, and, it is safe to
guess, Emerson's own taste, "The Sleepers" is not merely scandalous; it
is theologically rending. From its earliest version, "The Sleepers" traces
the largely unconscious, nocturnal wanderings of a seer through a visionary topography whose landmarks are spiritual stations and whose inhab-
itants are souls on trial. This nightscape, indeed, preserves links with the
nether worlds of Homer, Dante, and Milton. Its closer precedents, however, are to be found in the sermonic literature of the First and Second
Great Awakenings, and in such American nightscapes as Wigglesworth's
"Day of Doom" and Mather's "Midnight Watch." These texts find in
sleep and sleepers metaphors for unregeneracy.[6] The scriptural point of
departure for all such texts is the First Letter to the Thessalonians where
Paul adjures:

> So then let us not sleep, as others do, but let us keep awake and be so-
> ber. For those who sleep, sleep at night, and those who get drunk are
> drunk at night. But since we belong to the day, let us be sober.

In the best known American poem of unregenerate sleep, the locus clas-
sicus "Day of Doom," Whitman's Puritan precursor Michael Wigglesworth had sent the disembodied voice of an unimpeachable orthodoxy
over the somnolent. The poem sounded the alarum of apocalypse to all
who would be saved.[7] Its voice urged wakefulness and clean hands, recalling the errant soul to tend to its own redemption.

Neither disembodied, nor unimpeachable, the voice reciting Whitman's
poem does not waken but rather rocks the cradle in which its souls, somnolent, lie, finally climbing into the cradle to "sleep close with the other
sleepers . . . to become the other sleepers." As little as his sinners rouse
to save themselves, just so little do they tend to the orthodox hygiene:
Their hands are unclean. "Hand in hand," adulterate from the start,
Whitman's sleepers mingle promiscuously – unredeemed with redeemed,
sinners with innocents, dead with living – as apparently unconcerned as

their ministering savior about the salvation of their single souls. As we will see, this solitary but integral soul, apotheosized in the figure of the solitary Christ, will be abandoned too, as Whitman seeks to alter the very structure of a faith based on waking individual travail, replacing that travail with a heterogeneous and corporate sleep.

Consecrated to finding its way through orthodoxy, by its last lines "The Sleepers" will have answered the question Emerson posed. There, rather than claiming the freedom *from* the Fall that Emerson had asked why we might not enjoy, the poem has claimed its freedom *in* the Fall. In these lines, the soul, brought home from wandering, now "comes from its embowered garden and looks pleasantly on itself and encloses the world." Complete in itself, and drawing the garden around it, this soul is not exiled but "embowered," and not shamed but blessed by a body of which it is happily self-conscious. Shame recedes as the poet assures, "Perfect and clean the genitals previously jetting, and perfect and clean the womb cohering." The poem ends with a statement of faith, sanguine of ends as of beginnings:

> Why should I be afraid to trust myself to you?
> I am not afraid. . . . I have been well brought forward
>   by you;
> I love the rich running day, but I do not desert her in
>   whom I lay so long,
> I know not how I came of you, and I know not where I
>   go with you . . . but I know that I came well and shall go
>   well.   (*Leaves of Grass,* Bridgeman, 77)

The lines have the ring of doxology, of praise to a being to whom all praise is due, but note how different from that of "Song of Myself" is the creed they offer. Acknowledging something outside the consciousness of that giant of "Song of Myself" who, ubiquitous, upstaged both the enigma of Beginnings – "I celebrate myself and sing myself / And what I assume you shall assume" – and the terror of Ends – "I stop somewhere waiting for you" – these lines credit a mystery prior to poetic creation. Call this Mystery, birth.

Here is the exact point of inflection; here is the junction where Whitman parts company with Emerson, for here Whitman's theology wrests virtue out of that same necessity that worries Emerson's thought to the end. To wit: Whitman's version of human regeneracy is identical with Emerson's version of human fallenness. His regeneracy is achieved precisely in "relation." As if folding, vaginally, on the seam of the Fall, Whitman's doxology superimposes Creation and Birth, Eden and Exile, fallen and unfallen, naturalizing division through sheer repetition, and dissolving garden and cross in webwork of crossings. Juncture becomes network becomes tissue becomes flow. Moreover, the horror of the inchoate Creation, of the literally unfallen, of the *aboriginal*, that haunts Emerson is recuperated by Whitman as a febrile and primordial Chaos the poet counters God in calling good.[8] Dogged by problems of division and death his language cannot escape, Emerson remains to the end stalked by sin and stalled by Fate, both contravening his sense of an original and originary purity. Whitman's theological innovation or, it might be said, his apostasy, is to deem it *oneness that kills*, unity a grief only dualism cures. Thus he posits an origin itself lobed and split – literally a relation – and out of this he births an Adamic figure not one of a kind but one of a brood, and then a Christ saved by this brood: liberated from paying the cost on their heads.

Consider now just how well designed is such a revisionist notion to undergird the project of a New American Bible. For if division is a mechanism of Creation itself, and thus no catastrophe but rather "beautiful," then the shock waves of that catastrophe – Sin, Law, Atonement, and Judgment – are rendered benign. Taylor's shame at a human excremetiousness unbefitting God's unity is mooted by a theory that cosmologizes this exteriority. It eases shame through a rehabilitation of the human appetite for cleaving now naturalized in a cleft world. This obtaining, Whitman's new theology may also be seen to rouse the incipient pleasure of the text buried in Emerson's query as to why we should not "enjoy" an original relation. With division restored to its "place," made a force of attraction rather than repulsion, homecoming rather than exile, fusion rather than purity, and mimesis rather than immediacy, his theology can find, as a matter of course, room for the Female, for a language which is by its nature dual, and for a kind of history distributed in sequence rather than contracting in eternal, vertical *kairoi*. Such a theology will, consequently, find its best minister, and so its chosen poet, in a figure not pure and set off, but polymorphously perverse. *Imitatio Christi* no longer decrees that we be made one in the body of Christ, with all existence a test and striving after the one wakeful moment of salvation. Now, he mimics us. He "sleeps" with us. Saving himself by entering us, he is complete only in our multiplicity. He comes into himself only through return to that field where the singular blade – its frailty the cost of its definition – is redeemed to its comprehensive vigor as: grass.

Contaminate, divided, and decidedly carnal, this priest, in the coming pages, travels the universe of the "Sleepers" like a multiexposed image of the Christian savior. Just so, in the course of the "The Sleepers," Whitman renders inarticulate all those rituals by which Christian culture stigmatizes dualism. On a backdrop of normative division they lose, as it were, definition. Spelling out the Law of Whitman's "New American Bible," "The Sleepers" is the poem that rescues Christ from Atonement by overthrowing his dominion. Saved by Adam himself, a child of Adam, Christ is once again a mother's child, passing into our "rest." In Whitman's poem, the "Great Awakening" passes, and Christ himself finds new life among us as a "sleeper."

In a moment I will begin to describe Whitman's contaminate savior and to survey the new Creation over which he presides, but not before specifying the literary alias of that Christ figure Whitman's savior topples and the literary genre corresponding to that orthodoxy Whitman's scripturalism contravenes. The figure is the dying hero; the form, the elegy.

A hallmark of virtually all Christian thought, and especially of Reformed theology, is the idea that death is the omnisignificant prooftext. Death is the punishment of the Fall, and mortality the line drawn between us and an "original relation." This line, traced first by the angel with the flaming sword who guards the gates of Eden, is enforced by the taxonomies, boundaries, and limits of the Law, and then suffered by a savior whose mediate role both bridges and illuminates the absolute heterogeneity of God and human existence. The Fall is a great divide: we are on one side, God and immortality on the other. Theological meaning is articulated in a line, the boundary, the either/or that distinguishes us from God, quick from dead, wakeful souls from sinning sleepers.

The elegy templates this Christian commonplace, for at its center suffers a giant suspended between us and divinity, a hero whose fate is both better and worse than ours. The elegy frames, encircles, and inflames the distance between subject and object, me and not-me, recapitulating that dualism of the Fall. The central metaphysical problem troubling Christian modes of elegy – of which "Lycidas" probably stands as high watermark – is not so much the repulse of subject and object as their fusion in death as sentient subject becomes mere matter.

The elegy is thereby charged with making exquisite what in life is simply unbearable, first, by visiting death on someone else while letting us watch, but second, and more important, by framing a protracted and protected interval wherein the subject realizes the full measure of his individual definition. He draws majestically up into himself just at the moment that the forces that beleaguer his definition gather for the kill. When, with complexly mingled pain and pleasure, the subject witnesses the death in art of another subject, we participate in a cathartic repetition that performs, as Peter Sacks has shown, the work of mourning, with "work" suggesting both hard psychic labor and circumscription of that labor in the quarantine of the literary object (*The English Elegy*, x). It is not hard to see how the form of the Christian elegy is turned on the same sword as that held by Eden's angel. When the death that appalls encroaches on life, the taxonomies and taboos we set up to hold death at bay are those of Law. Both ritual and the rule-bound closures of the elegy are parallel phenomena, each addressing the same problem, death's robbery of our human definition. Christ's task, and the task of all his elegiac aliases, is to die the good death, so marking the line, acting the boundary, embodying and so absorbing in the flaming sword of his own agony the Law of loss the Fall spells out.[9]

As I have already intimated, the theological ambition of the "The Sleepers" is to fashion a new way to absorb such loss not contingent on sacrifice, and specifically not modeled on the suffering of Christ. Working backward from his new Christology the poet will unscroll a faith comprehensive and promising peace. Thus he builds his poem around the Passion, around an elegy inset and polished to a high degree of beauty, but denied the theological affirmation of closure. Neither first nor last, Whitman's Christ floats in the eschatological middle of his poem. He is part of death's history, rather than herald of its teleology.

Let me therefore commence my reading of "The Sleepers" not at the beginning, but rather at the poem's inflamed center where Whitman sets up the Christian tableau his poem would overcome. Section 3 of "The Sleepers" introduces precisely such a "Monster" as Emerson described and as Whitman later replicates in the nearly parodic "O, Captain! My Captain!" The hero is a victim of sacrifice, a "giant" whose drowning evokes all the grief and despair to which art and religion give their separate but related comforts. The form of this almost perfectly freestanding poem is that of the elegy; the "swimmer" is a Lycidas whose death we cannot change but can only witness. The text throughout is from the 1855 edition.

> I see a beautiful gigantic swimmer swimming naked
>   through the eddies of the sea,
> His brown hair lies close and even to his head . . . he
>   strikes out with courageous arms . . . he urges himself
>   with his legs.
> I see his white body . . . I see his undaunted eyes;
> I hate the swift running eddies that would dash him
>   headforemost on the rocks.
>
> What are you doing you ruffianly red-trickled waves?
> Will you kill the courageous giant? Will you kill him in
>   the prime of his middle age?
>
> Steady and long he struggles;
> He is baffled and banged and bruised . . . he holds out
>   while his strength holds out,
> The slapping eddies are spotted with his blood . . . they
>   bear him away . . . they roll him and swing him and
>   turn him;

> His beautiful body is borne in the circling eddies . . . it is
>   continually bruised on rocks,
> Swiftly and out of sight is borne the brave corpse.

Whitman's "beautiful gigantic swimmer" is situated at that nexus where elegy – the spectacle of a man overtaken by forces stronger than his will – and the Passion converge. The effective force of the passage follows on the reduction of the courageous agent of strength and great will to a soulless piece of flesh battered by rocks, to carrion. The topic is archetypal, evoking that desperation which is one of the most powerful incitements to poetry we know: So long as the hero's death is framed in a poem, we may watch with cathartic relief. Moreover, through the mechanism of closure, the cordon of ritual or poetry, the horrible gains beauty, the abomination becomes Passion.

To specify a bit more, we observe that the chief tension in the lines stretches between the handwringing subjectivity of the witness and the sheer objecthood of that which he views. For it is not only the swimmer's, but the speaker's own subjectivity that is under attack by the "ruffianly red-trickled waves." The punishing force of nature, of what Emerson called the not-me, makes war on the consciousness of the witness; objects weigh heavily unresponsive to the hopeful buoyancy of the speaking voice. What the speaker sees with his pellucid "I see" is a "beautiful gigantic swimmer swimming naked," a phrase already leaded with a sink line, its polysyllabic cadence slowed, impeded by the doubling of "swimmer" and "swimming." And the speaker is likewise at war with those "swift running eddies" whose force only underscores his, as well as the swimmer's, helplessness. Dashing against his "I see," and "I hate" are the brutal and punishing waves: "they/bear him away . . . they roll him and swing him and/turn him:/His beautiful body is . . . continually bruised on the rocks."

Note, too, how the very verb tense of the whole passage, the simple present, lends its own peculiar inevitability – the inevitability of timelessness – to the incident.[10] The death of the swimmer is not historical, that is, relativized by the massive precedents of our mutability; it is rather part of a repetitive mythic time, the no-time of an eternal Passion setting up reverberations with other moments in no-time: with the death of Lycidas, of Christ. Further, if the poetic form defrauds or defeats time, that defeat is clearly at the expense of the historical, actual swimmer (as, say, Lycidas' eternity is gained at the expense of Edward King). The poignancy of this elegy – as with all elegies – flows from how the endurance of the swimmer's beauty is made possible only by the sacrifice of the swimmer's life.

Nor should the "beauty" of the swimmer be overlooked. His is a special kind of beauty, that beauty of the ultimate offering whose "perfection," in Georges Bataille's phrase, "gives point to the full brutality of death" (144). The swimmer's is a beauty etched, outlined, by the particularly limpid language applied to its evocation. Bataille's description of sacrifice as erotic observes in particular a certain hyperefficiency of objectification in the sacrificial episode. The classic language of the sacrificial scene does its work best when it falls away behind the sculptural mass of the sacrificed object, draping invisibly around and behind the object deeply shadowed, conserving its light. The language Whitman deploys here is language we might recognize as quintessentially fallen. It is language of a consciousness altogether separate from that which it sees; it is language that underscores its own mimesis, whose very clarity suggests its distance, its separateness, from the event it apprehends. Although such distance, maintained by "plate glassy" language, is in other poems by Whitman celebrated for its "divine" superiority over the more rococo and sentimental verbiage of the time, it is language here suffering, though exquisitely, for that "plate glassy" vantage point.[11] Apprehending under this particular slide not the botanical specimens of "pokeweed and mullion" but a death it can only "wring its hands" watching, this is language whose otherwise vaunted subjectivity is now uncomfortably concentrated. As if backed up, subjectivity bends back on itself, enforcing the aloneness of the speaker as a congested and uncomfortably acute consciousness: The vulnerability the speaker describes is his own, that of all who must die.

Such helplessness of language is the normative mode in fallen texts. It is the helplessness that hunts for a style, tragic or "answerable," to justify the ways of God to man, to explain our fate, or, following Job, to shake the fist at God – only to be chided not to "darken wisdom with false counsel." In "The Sleepers," Section 3, we see how the ignorance of a speaker before death, the impasse of a subject apprehending the reduction to dead flesh of another subject, generates out of one closural structure the sacred and the beautiful. Even as the sacrificial thing is, technically speaking, an abomination, quarantine by the rituals of closure purges it of contaminating influence, lends it incontestable grace. The region of sacrifice purifies death of its universality, of its historical ubiquity; the sacrifice keeps biological mortality at bay. Sacrifice is, as such, the supreme gesture of control, subduing the death that takes us all by taking only one. And representation of this sacrifice depends, as the Law itself does, on order, on logic; discomfort may "interpose a little ease," in Milton's terms, by tracing and retracing the beautiful fissure between us and the world in a pellucid language we call mimetic, or classic.

It is this sacrifice and its corresponding classicism that Whitman undoes in "The Sleepers" – undoes by freeing the hostage, the "beautiful gigantic swimmer." As I will show later, he goes on to combat this moment in "When Lilacs Last in the Dooryard Bloom'd." Eschewing sacrifice, Whitman's tactic in "The Sleepers" is to offer an alternative to the classic agony. Whitman will write a poem in which his sacrificial hero goes AWOL. Circulating in the culture and so eliding the line between one and many, this savior brings News not of eternal life but rather news of death's continuum. Only such a death kills death as we know it, leveling Golgotha, effacing the rift the Cross marks.

It is important to note at the outset that this is no mere optimism Whitman offers, no liberalism. The sentimentalist will lose as much as he gains: Freedom from the Passion is also an exemption from Eternal life. Christ also takes with him the mimetic clarity: We wonder what's what, threats loom abroad. For once this rift is blurred, the result is a disorder and a confusion that nonetheless generates alternatives to the taxonomy of the Bible and to the "beauty" of the unique sacrifice at its center; that posits a new theology and a new aesthetic. In his creation of a savior not pure and set apart but contaminate, intimate, and "ill-assorted," Whitman gives us utterance profoundly ambiguous and yet, he will prove, curative. Wandering outside the elegiac closure and traversing the Holy of Holies, his speaker proclaims an inclusive "religion" that promises to elide all distinctions. As he writes in another note of the 1850s:

> "Leaves of Grass" – Bible of the New Religion. Founding a New American religion (? no religion), that is comprehensive enough to include all the doctrines and sects, and give them all their places, and chances, each after its kind. (*Notes*, 55)[12]

Now we can begin at the beginning, reading "The Sleepers" as a poem that, harrowing the Passion and the elegy that sustains it, would yet convert the reader to a new faith whose most salient innovation is to offer peace but no security. Mazy indeed is the path of this faith, and suspect indeed its herald. The poet of "Song of Myself" usurps God's prospect, but the voice opening the "The Sleepers" issues from a vantage point altogether more discomfiting. The poem begins unstably:

> I wander all night in my vision,
> Stepping with light feet . . . swiftly and noiselessly stepping
>   and stopping,
> Bending with open eyes over the shut eyes of sleepers;
> Wandering and confused . . . lost to myself . . .
>   ill-assorted . . . contradictory,
> Pausing and gazing and bending and stopping.

From its opening lines, the poem sustains an ambiguous relationship with orthodox notions of the Holy, commencing first by amending the idea of vision itself – and then the idea of the visionary. Both the vision and the visionary lack a certain coherence. Visions are traditionally offered by prophets who, though perhaps reluctant, learn with some dispatch the new way God has mapped for them. One thinks of Moses protesting his lack of a smooth tongue; Amos, his prophetic pedigree; Jeremiah crying out, "Ah Lord God! behold I cannot speak / for I am a child"; or Jonah, stowing away in the hold off Tarsis. Following along into early Christian history and beyond, there is the doubting disciple, the Saul who goes blind on the way to Damascus before he can truly "see" as Paul; the Augustinian rover whose eyes finally clear for a vision of God's city; and then the literary apotheosis of the type in the figure of Milton who fears his lack of light unsuits him "to justify the ways of God to man." All such prophets are ultimately transported from their own nebulous vision into possession of God's vision, with spiritual entropy or bewilderment characteristically giving way to apprehension of significant moral regions, thickly edged. Divinity articulates itself in spatial terms. The circle within which Moses removes his shoes, the Niniveh that takes exactly three days to circumnavigate – by means of such bounded and significant spaces God, a great cartographer, expresses his will to the visionary. Thus Milton represents in *Paradise Lost* a world pared into regions separately reserved for saved and damned:

> Such eternal justice had prepared
> For those rebellious, here their prison ordained
> In utter darkness, and their portion set
> As far removed from God and light of Heaven
> As from the center thrice to the utmost pole. (I: 70–4)

If the story of the Expulsion (Genesis 3) draws the first, and primary boundary, this boundary is codified by Moses in the Law. His task in the narrative sections of the Pentateuch is the deliverance of Israel into a holy and separate land; his job as legislator is to constitute a community with the map of holiness drawn on it. The Law mandates, in effect, how a people might be organized like a land, with an inside and outside, the boundaries of ritual delineating territories of permitted and forbidden exercise, and so echoing those described by Adam's first breach.

In such an allusive context there is little question that the first wandering steps of the speaker of "The Sleepers" stray off the straight and narrow path of righteousness. Paul Zweig notes how Whitman's precursor in this traversal of Christian space is Blake (Zweig 150) and indeed Harold Bloom's evocative discussion of Blake's "London," beginning "I wander," might just as well refer to Whitman's poem beginning with the same "I wander." Bloom notes:

> Blake begins: "I wander through each chartered street," and so we begin also, with that wandering and that chartering, in order to define that "I." Is it an Ezekiel like prophet, or someone whose role and function are altogether different? To "wander" is to have no destination and no purpose. A Biblical prophet may wander when he is cast out into the desert, when his voice is a voice in the wilderness, but he does not wander when he goes through the midst of the city, through the midst of Jerusalem the City of God. (Bloom, *Poetry and Repression*, 37)

Such "wandering" is simply not in the repertoire of the visionary commanded, like Ezekiel, to act as God's mouthpiece. Indeed, to wander thus indiscriminately is to survey space traditionally claimed by the one who violates, corrupts God's regions, specifically that Devil "wandering to and fro in the earth," gaining his insight not from God, but catch-as-catch-can, by his own resources. In her work on Levitical taboos, Mary Douglas specifies such wandering as an explicit challenge to the external structure of Law: "External symbolism" she writes, "upholds the explicit social structure and internal, unformed psychic powers threaten it from non-structure."[13] To be sure, as Douglas notes, one name for this unforming agency is Satan, administrator of mazy ways, though Whitman's intent here is not, I think, simply to sign on with the Devil's party. His wanderer is not so much straying from the Right as discovering its native grain. During the period when the first drafts of *Leaves of Grass* were taking shape, Whitman wrote:

> I say that if once the conventional distinctions were dispelled from our eyes we should see just as much. I do not expect to dispel them by arguing against them, I sweep them away by advancing to a new level of development where they fail of themselves. (*Notes*, 55)

As guileless as Whitman's housecleaning metaphors sound, we would be mistaken to underestimate his sweep. The "distinctions" the poet would "sweep . . . away" are those inscribed on the community itself, those distinctions which, in Levitical culture, divide pure from impure, or, closer to home, regenerate from unregenerate through the mechanism of "justification." The very idea of the Visible Saint, relative of Emerson's poet, derives from the injunction of the Levitical priest, "Be holy for I am holy," with holiness itself meaning "set apart," or discrete. Holiness, or *kadesh*, in Hebrew is often coupled with *tahor*, or "pure," and *shalem*, or "complete." Holiness itself is, in Biblical culture, based on those "distinctions" Whitman shuns: on differentiation, logic, on the separation of things into discrete classes.

Accordingly, Whitman's first step in his purge of the "distinctions" is to abolish such distinctions in his speaker. Declaring himself of mixed category, he is ambiguous to a degree well beyond that allowed by "Song

of Myself ": "Do I contradict myself? / Very well then I contradict myself." "Lost to myself . . . / ill assorted . . . contradictory," the poet asks
us to accept a visionary not merely eccentric but beyond the pale: ex-
communicate. We have only to compare Whitman's embrace of the
"contradictory" with Milton's famous pursuit of a fitting moral consistency, to look further back in Christian history to the figure of the saint
and yet further back to the priest of Leviticus to see how unorthodox
such status is. Compare, for instance, Whitman's "ill-assorted" speaker
with the priest of the Pentateuch who purifies himself, donning white
robes (8:1) that he may . . . "put difference between the holy and the
common, between the unclean and the clean . . . that [he] may teach the
children all the statutes which the Lord has spoken" (Leviticus 10:10–11).
This priest, specifically commanded to be "holy," or "set off " from his
people, is further enjoined not to "let the hair of his head go loose, nor
rend his clothes, neither shall he go in to any dead body, nor defile himself for his father, or for his mother" (Leviticus 21:10–11). Among all
men, the priest must "take a wife in her virginity." Priests are warned:
"whosoever he be of all your seed throughout your generations, that ap-
proacheth unto the holy things, which the children of Israel hallow unto
the Lord, having his uncleanness upon him, that soul shall be cut off
from my presence" (Leviticus 22:3). The priest's hair, his beard, his nails,
his very bodily secretions are consecrated to that abstract pattern of Law
he "sets down in a book."

By contrast, Whitman's piebald minister is categorically unholy, not
only not "set apart," but already from the opening lines merging where
he must not merge – and, what's more, "setting down in a book" a
record of mergings it is the very function of the Book to proscribe. "Lost
to himself," he courts both sexual abandon and death, the two states
most rigidly held off by Levitical proscription. "Ill assorted," he flies in
the face of what the culture of purity explicitly "assorts" for God's sake
and under His Authority. Secreting the secreted, he reveals not light but
darkness and so throws into crisis the very idea of Revelation. In the lines
immediately following his wandering, the ill assorted speaker sets about
a revision of the world in His own image by eliding the boundaries Mosaic culture constitutes. He begins with the utmost delicacy:

> How solemn they look there, stretched and still
> How quiet they breathe, the little children in their
>   cradles.

Observe the cunning breach of the normative taxonomy. "Stretched and
still," the children at first seem corpses. "Cradles" may shunt aside the
phantom word "coffins," but the assurance comes too late for the reader's complete peace of mind. Whitman deploys this kind of legerdemain

throughout the poem with the effect of obviating the line between living and dead. The poem continues:

> The wretched features of ennuyees, the white features of
>   corpses, the livid faces of drunkards, the sick gray
>   faces of onanists,
> The gashed bodies on battlefields, the insane in their
>   strong-doored rooms, the sacred idiots,
> The newborn emerging from gates and the dying emerging
>   from gates,
> The night pervades them and enfolds them.

In this catalogue, all the chief categories of Levitical abomination are systematically fronted by a poet not "arguing" but sweeping through "on the way to a new level of development." The "ill assorted" speaker offers a vision not arbitrarily ill assorted, but Scripturally ill assorted, in explicit revolt against the Levitical code that the Christian either/or absorbs.

Since I want to reserve discussion of the category heading this litany, let me begin by taking up "the white faces of corpses." The entity against which the entire taxonomy guards, the corpse is the most toxic object the Law knows. The laws surrounding the exclusion of corpses stake all on circumstance: "Whosoever toucheth the dead, even any man's dead body, shall be unclean seven days. . . . Whosoever touches the dead and not purify himself – he hath defiled the tabernacle of the Lord – that soul shall be cut off from Israel" (Numbers 19:13). Next in line are the "drunkards" with their "livid faces." Although the drunkard is only deemed to violate Levitical ordinance if he happens to be a priest – "Drink no wine or strong drink" (Leviticus 10:9) – drunkenness is associated throughout Scripture with sexual abominations. Drunkenness is roundly condemned in the narrative sections of the Scripture. We remember from First Thessalonians that drunkenness is Paul's metaphor for the soul's unprepared sleep. In Leviticus, Nadab and Abihu are killed by God for violating the sanctity of the Holy of Holies when under the influence of drink, and before them there is the prototype in Noah, whose drunkenness led him to "uncover his nakedness," so incurring the guilt of that sexual impurity which, not by coincidence, comes next on Whitman's list. Reading later sections of the poem we will see how drunkenness is Whitman's metaphor for the very sexual profligacy the Law proscribes, spilled semen becoming "liquor." For now, we should not be surprised that next in line is the "sick gray [faced] onanist" whose sexual license the Law summarily bans. "When a man has an issue from his flesh it is unclean" (Leviticus 15:2). And the penultimate case is the "gashed body" whose mutilation puts it in that class of objects contaminating to all that is pure and holy:

> A man that hath a blemish, whatsoever man he be a blind man or a
> lame, or he that hath anything maimed, or anything too long, or a man
> that is broken-footed, or broken handed, or crook backed or a dwarf,
> that hath his eye overspread, or is scabbed, or scurvy, or hath his stones
> crushed . . . he hath a blemish, he shall not come nigh to offer the
> bread of the Lord. (Leviticus 21:18–21)

To return to the two groups bracketing the catalogue – the "insane"
and the "ennuyees" – their challenge to the structure of Levitical precept
is more formidable still. The "ennuyee," Whitman's agent of sloth, up-
sets the primary ordinance of the Fall – to labor – and so threatens the
law of the Expulsion, transgressing the line that severed us from Eden in
the first place. The insane, on the other hand, are paradigms of that ambiguity the Law cannot abide, their possession by internal powers so
drawing out the Law to bring the strongest forces of quarantine to bear
in "strong-doored rooms." Finally, the catalogue closes with a couplet,
praising "The newborn emerging from gates and the dying emerging /
from gates."

Key symbols in a poem that would revise our reading of Divine space,
these "gates" merit the closest scrutiny. The repetition ("the newborn
emerging from gates, and the dying emerging from gates") secures for
this image a comprehensive power that is Whitman's gnomic answer to
the splittings of the Fall. Orthodoxy rigorously enforces the heterogeneity of these two gates, differentiating between the birth canal – bloody
portal to the fallen world – and the gate of heaven – whose crossing cancels our corporeality. Whitman, on the other hand, intuits – and then ex-
ploits – the ways in which the distinction between the two, though
rigidly guarded by Law, is never entirely maintained. I have said that sacrifice, the gate to sanctified death, depends on the almost erotic perfection of the victim if it is to satisfy the living. Conversely, in the "little
death" of sex we attain, if only briefly, that unity or "original relation"
that is a premonition of Heaven. The Law may be said complexly to in-
dulge the very resemblances it would forestall, sublimating attraction in
antithesis: Whitman restores the attraction. Suggesting the essentially
vaginal contour of both canals, the poem finds its access route to an
"original relation" in a sexual and, we might note, specifically female,
fecundity. The factored "gate" puts a new spin on the creedal statement
"in my End is My Beginning" by making death the womb to which the
poet returns. The poem ends: "Not you will yield forth the dawn again
more surely than / you will yield me forth again, / Not the womb yields
the babe in its time more surely than / I shall be yielded from you in
my time."

It perhaps hardly needs saying that Whitman's sacralization of the vaginal canal has implications for a religious system devised to stigma-
tize women. I would, however, emphasize less the social consciousness

that makes Whitman feminize his new theology than his more absolute faith in a true theology's essentially female origin. Whitman's Mother is not only a social but also a cosmological being. Set against the God of distinctions, her companion symbol of the "gate" is implicit corrective to God's divisive and revolving sword which bars the entrance to Eden. Readers of the Mosaic Law know that it is the sword which enforces the Law with the penalty of *karet,* a cutting off which echoes the exile from Eden. Likewise, it is this sword which, described in Hebrews as "living and active, sharper than any sword, piercing to the division of soul and spirit," is entrusted to the priest who is "holy, blameless, unstained, and separated from sinners." If both images, gate and sword, are metonymies for the primal fissure that leaves us separate from the world we travel, the sword is a honed boundary – but the gate is a *valve.* The sword is an edge; the gate is a passage. As passage this gate boasts the salutary function of giving way, of opening as well as closing. This expansive capacity makes it marvelously efficient for a poet whose interest is the demolition of a system that sizes up souls, allowing only those fitting to cross its boundaries, or, to cite Hebrews, to "enter his rest." Unlike the sword, the gate has no such limitations, adapting itself rather to the size of those who pass through. As Whitman writes in another note, "bring in the idea of the Mother – the idea of the mother with numerous children; all, great and small, old and young, equal in her eyes" (*Notes and Fragments,* 59).

The literally essentialist implications of Whitman's figure of the Mother bear a few more words of comment. Whitman's reading of Scripture is stamped all over with the intuition, borne out by Biblical scholarship, that it is explicitly to combat maternal powers that the taxonomies of Leviticus (and, before them, the logic of Genesis) are set in motion. Thus Julia Kristeva's influential argument – that the Law represents a recoil from the *abject* products, or metonymies, of the body, of which menstrual blood is the paradigm (Kristeva, 101–2) – only elaborates on certain commonplaces of that scholarship. Umberto Cassuto, for one, argued thirty years ago that the opening chapters of Genesis, hardly naive, are rather latter-day polemics against Near Eastern Creation narratives unweaned from female flesh. The taxonomy of Leviticus, in these terms, is an elaboration of the simpler grid of Genesis where *tehom,* or "Chaos," becomes a principle under the sway of the Creator, replacing the Babylonian "Tiamat," the feminine autonomous goddess (Cassuto, 8). This named female power is replaced by a generic, and so anonymous, disorder that God will order with impunity. All is controlled by this God who drives asunder the unholy couplings of land and sea, earth and sky, who abominates mixing itself as the trademark of the mythological. The recoil from mixing, mandated in Genesis, and codified in the catalogues of Leviticus, is ubiquitous when trouble is afoot. The whore of Babylon, lasciviously riding her seven-headed and horned beast, inherits the stigma placed on all those of mixed character from Hosea on; all those who, ill assorted and "contradictory," create not according to law but by the impulse of tissue and blood; emerge not by grace but by the Mother's body.[14] At this juncture, the reader psychoanalytically disposed may well be tempted to observe that this God who divides land from sea – creating the world as a gaping fissure over which he hovers – resembles not a little the infantile subject who wishes nothing more than to return from whence he came, and who repeats in order to control. Read in this spirit, God is a human, and patriarchal, projection, and theology but an extrapolation from a wish that begins in the psyche rather than in the cosmos. The Divine power is a projection and model for a kind of mastery that male culture craves.[15] To draw such an inference, however, would be, I think, to take Whitman's ecumenicism too far, for the thrust of his New American Bible is not to rationalize by secular means, not to offer a precocious psychology that cuts the Christian God down to size. It is rather to find a new faith capacious enough to absorb the old faith. Less ironist than mystic, Whitman's point in his image of the gates is not to reduce the Creation to a displaced myth of human birth, but rather to give that birth foundational, theological weight.

Indeed, these "gates" through which we emerge and exit are justly called *emanations*. Pitched at far more than the subversion of "binaries," Whitman's "gates" have a mystical or visionary character, authorized no less than Ezekiel's chariot or Joshua's trumpets to *reveal* and to herald a world behind culture, behind appearance, a world available only to transports of faith. Nevertheless, as they sheathe and blunt God's "two-edged sword" – that which cuts and severs, separates and judges – they also have a social work to perform. They forestall our reading of Whitman's nightworld as a misfit orphanage for the unwanted and outcast. As in the prophetic books, mysticism serves the highest social ends. All sleep alike, all are blessed equally:

> The married couple sleep calmly in their bed, he with his
>   palm on the hip of the wife, and she with her palm
>   on the hip of her husband,
> The sisters sleep loving side by side in their bed,

the perfect and imperfect, the guilty and the innocent:

> The blind sleep, and the deaf and dumb sleep,
> The prisoner sleeps well in the prison . . . the runaway
>   son sleeps,

The murderer that is to be hung the next day . . . how does he
sleep?
And the murdered person . . . how does he sleep?[16]

All those subject to the constructs of "distinction," of the external law
of the dividing sword, are here blessed by a peripatetic, autonomous seer
whose very power to bless, to replace the Law with Love, should recall
another so empowered: should recall Christ. As Christ completed and
superseded the Law with a feminine Love, so with love Whitman's seer
will complete and supersede Christ.

I stand with drooping eyes by the worst-suffering and
restless,
I pass my hands soothingly to and fro a few inches from
them;
The restless sink in their beds . . . they fitfully sleep.

The earth recedes from me into the night,
I saw that it was beautiful . . . and I see that what is not
the earth is beautiful.

I go from bedside to bedside . . . I sleep close with the
other sleepers, each in turn;
I dream in my dream all the dreams of the other dreamers,
And I become the other dreamers.

Surveying now the whole vista of the Law, the speaker fuses with that
Savior whose living mission was to overturn, in charity, the Law's stern
covenant. Recall at this point that Emerson's poet was Christlike as well.
Whitman's savior, however, sustains a key difference: the difference impurity makes.

True, the tender eyes drawn down with pity; the soothing, unhesitant
hands; the sermonic mounting in space; the beatitudes tumbling; the
balm of the vicarious – all these are Christ's. And yet something jars.
The difference between this visionary and Christ is simply that of set-
offness. Our speaker, absorbing into himself the "sleep" of others, makes
Christ's motions, but the gestures have a baroque prolongation, a man-
nered accuracy that hints at imitation, or even parody. Whitman's Christ
in his very vicariousness seems double exposed. If he is the healing
Christ, he is also the gospel writer's "unclean spirit" who, "gone out of
a man . . . passes though waterless ways seeking rest . . . and then he
goes and brings seven other souls more evil than himself and they enter
and dwell there" (Luke 11:24–26). Like that tainted figure, this savior's
ministering vision, his glance that penetrates all, is not free of prurience.
The speaker who now goes "bending with open eyes," who goes "from
bedside to bedside," sleeping "close with the other sleepers, each in

turn / until the earth recedes from him into the night" recalls Milton's voyeur archangel and Christ's nemesis, who watched "from the utmost orb of this frail world," hovering over the cohabiting Adam and Eve with voyeuristic pleasure. Wandering outside the parameters of the Law, the poet who would find some relation to his world free of shame's divisive consciousness risks imitating that Satan who is, simply: shameful. Indeed, as will become clear in the coming pages, this double exposure of Christ and the Wandering Satan is endemic in American poetry, posing problems not only for Whitman, but for Dickinson, for Crane, and for Stevens as well. The Christ model is a tricky one, embroiling the poet in a grasping after absolutes, after a certain inviolate autonomy that is simply blasphemous. And the time for blasphemy in Whitman's poem is ripening. For now, suffice it to say that Whitman courts this confusion between Christ and unclean spirit, superimposing them to suggest certain affinities he will tease out later.

Passing his hands "to and fro" over the sleepers, the speaker's gesture is a caress, calculated to incite rather than quell sensation. The scriptural Christ transcended the purifying rituals of the priests by collapsing in his own person the distinction between pure and impure. He vanquished impure physicality in an excess of physicality; dying for the sins of the mortal, Christ brought immortality, and the corporeality of the sinners is canceled in the ultimate corporeal suffering of the Savior. Whitman's savior of sleepers, by contrast, rather than drawing the sinners' corporeal sleep into his more eternal sleep, so rescuing the soul from the body by drawing men's souls to his transubstantiated body, seems instead to release his soul into *their* bodies. Cohabiting with sinners, Whitman's revisionist Christ serves as imitable model of the rewards of impurity. Sanctifying the very processes of the body that Leviticus and, in turn, the human sacrifice, interrupt, Whitman's speaker abandons the fine outline of swimmer and savior: There is nothing to prevent his undoing.

Having broken down, in the first lines of the poem, the knit of relations that holds the culture of sacrifice together, the poet begins at this point to break down the style such a culture mandates. This is the answerable style of the elegy. By scrambling this style Whitman will make good his most radical claims for *Leaves of Grass*. Blodgett and Bradley, calling "The Sleepers" the only "surrealist" (*Leaves,* 424) poem of the nineteenth century, summarize the critical consensus as to its originality, a view first offered in Bucke's characterization of the poem as "a representation of the mind during sleep," later in Gay Wilson Allen's characterization of it as a "fantasia of the unconscious," and most recently, in Waskow's discussion of it as "monodrama" and Erkkila's as an "innovative exploration of the dream state."

To note a certain proto-Freudian quality to "The Sleepers" does no harm, I suppose, unless it assumes that the dream state can only open inward, into the world of the unconscious. On the contrary, dreams and dreaming have a salient role in prophetic traditions where the dream gives access to much more than the interiority of the dreamer.

In a culture crediting the veracity of dream visions, the dream is an authorized route into that truer world the dreamer is charged with making believable to his congregation. The dream for a figure like, say, Michael Wigglesworth, is sleep's very redemption. Washing sleep with light, the dream is a form of wakefulness lending coherence to perilous unseeing. In these terms, the hallucinatory language of "The Sleepers" seems less firmly connected to the automatic writing experiments of Breton, or to Freudian secondary process, than to visions of these older sorts. Its decidedly extrapersonal aims, and not least its central place in Whitman's plan for a New Bible, link "The Sleepers" rather more closely with the sometimes perfervid urgencies of Taylor or Wiggleworth or Edwards. For such poets, the dream's linguistic distortions and disproportions reveal a congregation gone bleary with sloth, or a world shrinking under God's rage. Whitman's tack is a normalization of this Puritan gargoyling. He will, in effect, reverse figure and field, rehabilitating the sinner at whom God points his accusatory sword by showing him a victim of wrong rather than "right" reason: a figment of superstition. Against a poem like "God's Determinations," with its choruses of the damned; or Wigglesworth's "Day of Doom," with its God's-eye view of a world squamous and inchoate; or "Sinners in the Hands of An Angry God," with its images of vertigo and slippage, Whitman's poem is not surreal but determinedly real. Restoring to proportion what the mechanism of division made horrific, it inoculates the fallen against terror by dosing them with the very death they defer.

Once this mechanism is dismantled, once these deferrals come due, the framing edge or boundary that maintains serene and classic diction of the elegiac spectacle collapses too. And when we lose the edge between the spectacle and the spectator, between the act of vision and the object of vision – between, in essence, subject and object – we are paradoxically free of Christian authority and exempt from the protection that Faith affords the sinner. The poem is no longer a by-product, an artifact of the mimetic process, but something much more comprehensive, what Stevens will call a "text of the world," a Scripture, indeed a New Bible. The poetic subject now has both a new power and, as we shall see, a new vulnerability. With his seeing no longer exiled from his Being, the subject's contact with the world is enhanced, made original, albeit in the way Christ's was original. To be the Word – sacred in oneself, bridging Adamic distance in one's own Being, contracting Christian history in one's own history – is to reassume the burden Christ took on. It is to be exposed naked in the flesh to shame and death. Autotelic, Whitman's Word made Flesh will finally converge on the shame of a speaker unprotected by subjective distance, now object of his own sight. This transfiguration of poetic word to Flesh, seeing to Being, that closes the gap of the Fall is a mystical union whose bliss cannot entirely defer Agony, but whose Agony is also crossed by bliss. If Christ's penetration into the world's body is emblemized in the crossed swords of the crucifix – unique juncture where the one who is cut off now bears away death – this speaker's penetration is copulative, indiscriminate, and the places of crossing are multiple:

> I am a dance. . . . Play up there! The fit is whirling me fast.
> I am the everlaughing . . . it is new moon and twilight,
> I see the hiding of douceurs . . . I see nimble ghosts
>   whichever way I look,
> Cache and cache again deep in the ground and sea, and
>   where it is neither ground or sea.

In these lines, it is as if "The Sleepers" begins again; the separate visionary whose subjectivity hung above the objects of his surveillance is now absorbed into those objects. "Lost to himself," he now "becomes" the dreams of the other dreamers; his vision of them is absorbed by them, by their nighttime visions. "I am a dance" claims an immediacy, a simultaneity of being and knowing, hitherto inaccessible to the consciousness wandering "all night in [its] vision."[17] Through this evenly stressed spondaic declaration the speaker, entering the sinning community as savior, so enters the enclosure of his vision, breaking the mimetic framing edge that objectifies, sets off, the work of art. The consciousness that now registers is of a kind that external modes of perception – God's divisive logic – cannot reach. Now disabused of the fallen world, Whitman's language is at this point under considerable pressure to pursue a kind of fluidity that the objectified language of the fallen world is relatively helpless to attain; the poem responds to this pressure by unwriting itself as a poem, by finding metaphors in language for the dissolution of discursive language itself, seeking in these metaphors a new medium which to be and to say cohabit.

> . . . Play up there! The fit is whirling me fast!

Music – a medium neither physical nor intellectual, both of mind and body, of the physical world and yet not confined by that world – is agent of this redemptive reciprocity.[18] In these lines, as in Part 5 of "Song of Myself," where the poet's "valved voice" described a circle of body and soul joined mysteriously in sexual union, music serves the visionary consciousness as a kind of eroticized medium of conductivity. In "Song of Myself" this medium, as much the body's as the soul's, enveloped God's creation, language, and its fissures as the speaker created himself in a sexual humming. Likewise, in these lines of "The Sleepers," music replaces discursive speech as instrument of God's creation. Creation is here not a matter of mind, not the reflective act of one "hovering over the face of the waters . . . to make man in his image," but now an utterly erotic, polymorphously perverse process. Where God created the world, surveying his work from above and declaring it "good," this poet does not survey: He cavorts. His creation is less an act of reflection than, let us say, of *dalliance,* of a play which is not a violation of, but rather a submission to, the law of his being. He comes into himself only by coming into the other. In a parody of Christian sacrifice, here a profligate sexual generosity consolidates self. Surrendering to play, the poet utters this suspicious declaration:

> . . . The fit is whirling me fast.

"Fit" is a discomforting word, a word that makes literal to an uncomfortable degree Emerson's notions with respect to the "enjoyment" the "original relation" might bestow. Although this fit has its religious associations – one thinks of the fits of Saul or of Jeremiah – its power is, again, from the Other Side. We are not permitted here to forget the speaker's relation to the outcast figures of lines 7 to 10. We think of the "sexual fits" of the onanist, the fits of the "insane" kept in strong-doored rooms, the "seizural fits" tabooed by Leviticus. And indeed we should think of these outcast figures, and of our visionary's increasingly explicit links with them. His rotation on his own axis is specifically the movement whose chaos undoes the lines of Law. If the dualist model is epitomized in the image of God surveying the world – His mirror – in a text whose strangeness to us is the back side of its complete transparency to Him, this poem posits a corkscrewing penetration that confounds the orthodox image of Creation.[19]

"Fit," all the same, is richer than we have noted yet. Whereas the fit's spasmodic connotations conjure the disordered abandon of a speaker "lost to himself," "fit" also suggests a constitutive securing of the self, as in, a good fit. Body and soul, whirled together without distinction, are sealed by "fast." Ending line 32 with a fixative stress, this "fast" suggests an integrative counterpull to the disintegrative direction of the fit. Indeed "fast" is typical of Whitman's procedure in these lines, a procedure that plays in the interstices, or "gates," of intelligibility, putting in use a new kind of poetic language. This language derives its power from the very dissolution of the distinctions that preserve, at the same time, our grammar and our bewildered distance from the world we live in: our fallenness. Crossing back and forth over the blade of the divisive sword, the poem tugs at the hem of coherence itself, as if to unravel both the figure and the language that suits him. The literal unspooling of these lines mimes the undoing, the unfashioning of a hero woven, as it were, into the cultural fabric.

This literal revolution wraps fallen language back around itself, baffling the division of Fall in disoriented circling. We should beware not to connect too hastily this vortical language, or its peripatetic inventor, with the Satanic, or Romantic revolutionary. Even though, as the coming pages will make clear, Whitman's Christ and Lucifer share, in certain ways, one ministry, the point is not, to paraphrase Melville, the saying of "no, in thunder," not the simple inversion of religious value that is the signature of Milton's Satan. What is sought is rather a substratum beneath negation, and so a language that would root out the power of the Devil's negativity.

In the current vernacular, this would be a language no power governs: language neither of the master nor of the slave. Thus, it will be worthwhile to digress, for a moment, to take up questions of current theoretical concern. Whitman's language, ineluctably poetic, illuminates the problem a theoretical language has with itself when it stands to reach that very vantage point on the diacritical – beyond the binary – that it necessarily pursues. Pulling a differential language into its vortex, confounding the denotative and overmastering function of language, Whitman's "fit" may be said to posit that same world that Foucault, in an uncharacteristic but intriguingly theosophical mood, calls "scintillating and constantly affirmed . . . a world without that serpentine 'no' that bites into fruits and lodges their contradictions at their cores" (Foucault, *Language, Countermemory*, 37). Neither fracturing, imitative, nor negative, Whitman's lines would free language from power itself.

> I see the hiding of douceurs . . . I see nimble ghosts
>   whichever way I look,
> Cache and cache again deep in the ground and sea,

An abstract French noun suggesting sweetness, "douceur" is here animated to mean something like agents, even elves, of sweetness. Quickened allegorically, these elusive pleasures now dodge and dart, and the "nimble ghosts" that follow are configurations of a language whose boundaries are more fluid than we think, a language rolling on the tongue, freed of meaning. "Cache" blurs the line between subject and object that binary assumptions are held to construct. A noun, again French (here Whitman's often-mocked polylingualism seems part of the same impulse to elide boundaries, including national ones), meaning secret place, "cache" is given the instrumental power of a transitive verb.

As "cache" creates its own depth in "deep," blurring a grammatical boundary, so the setting for the whole experiment is that liminal cusp, the sea line erased, elided. The lexical education Whitman would deliver here, an education into the interstices of language, mimes the other lesson the speaker urges: a passing, as through gates, those precincts of the Holy that divide subjects from objects through ritual; that leave the quick watching the dead protected only by the closural structure of the elegy. A new transitive verbal power now acts to realize itself. In a language unfamiliar to any nineteenth-century American poetry, "The Sleepers" breaks down those conventions of language which enforce not only the conventional niceties of Victorian America but the distinctions that underlie the whole taxonomy of Creation, showing holy and profane antithetically related to one root, all division authorized in the relatedness of the original. Or in, if you will, its sin.

The linguistic felicity sketched above is the all the heaven afforded the poet who would skirt the discursive language which oppresses "originality" with the instruments of representation. This is, as we have said, Emerson's problem, but it is also a problem engaging our theory whose vision of a language unimpeded by power relations and released to a pure subversion is – paradoxically – only achieved in the abandonment of theory. The marked lyricism, or as it is more recently termed, the essentialism, of this theory is explained by the recognition that a language that would earn subversive credentials must do without the dignity of a denotation that is oppositional and so power based. The theorist's approach to such a language thus resonates curiously with the mystical soundings of a poet like Taylor. That is because the problem of a nonrepresentative speech, and the dream of the Unnameable, leads inevitably back to Eden with its barred door. When, for instance, Bataille and Foucault struggle to conceive of a language no longer exacting submission and calling that submission truth, their theoretical enterprise must at a certain point retune itself in a theological key.[20] The infinite resource of a purely diacritical language now borrows the lexicon of another kind of infinity, as the salutary "silence" of a language realizing its own utterly conventional, and thus insubstantial moorings, is thrown on nothing so much as: Awe. Arriving at that same place that Whitman's speaker reached when, "losing himself," he entered the bodies of other sleepers, that place where traversal of certain boundaries forces language to start again, Bataille writes:

> If transgression became the foundation stone of philosophy . . . silent contemplation would have to be substituted for language. *This is the contemplation of being at the pinnacle of being.* Language has by no means vanished. How should one reach the heights if language did not point

the way: but descriptive language becomes meaningless at the decisive instant when the stirrings of transgression itself are taken over from the discursive account of transgression, and one supreme moment follows these successive apparitions. (275)

Note the phrase "supreme moment" as it reveals Bataille himself struggling with the impossibility of nonrepresentational language, lapsing at the end into a makeshift philosophical esperanto that must mediate between the idea of the atemporal – Infinity – and the necessarily successive nature of language itself. Relativist theories can indeed begin fretting when the antiontological position to which they are pledged keeps company off-hours with such essentialist notions as the "supreme moment," when, somehow, the very thought that authorized the ouster of the Logos finds itself at the feet of the Infinite. Edward Taylor would have known this border land for God's country and felt at home in his bewilderment. Bataille, discovering the impasse as if for the first time, is caught in an essentialism for which his theory is not precisely prepared. His "supreme moment," the very moment following "successive apparitions," transposes a problem of representation – the problem of what to call language no longer reflecting *on* the world – into temporal terms. We might recall Taylor's lines, "This shining sun will fly away apace / When Thy Great Glory splits the same to make Thy Majesty a Pass." They employed a temporal metaphor to describe "Being at the pinnacle of Being," a being undivided by predication, just as Bataille's "successive" substitutes for "mimetic" in an inevitably "discursive" account of a hypothetical language neither successive nor discursive. Foucault, glossing Bataille's struggle here, sheds light on a limitation not only Bataille's, but that of theory in general: its blind spot around Ends:

> Bataille's language . . . continually breaks down at the center of its space, exposing in its nakedness, in the inertia of its ecstasy, a visible and insistent subject who tried to keep language at arm's length but who now finds himself thrown by it, exhausted, upon the sands of what we can no longer say. (40)

One might observe that the foregoing is itself less theory than poetry. Foucault's point, one he makes good incidentally, through his own commitment to a lyrical, even ludic, prose style, is that Bataille's best chance for the expression he seeks lies the way of an implicated rather than an empirical speech that would "keep language at arm's length." For by now the theorist, speechless, has reached the limits of his theoretical position, finding only in silence a space free of language's jockeying power plays; only in the utter renunciation of the instrument, power.

We must ask how far are we here from faith? How far from a vision that calls Being only accessible to the self stripped down to itself, a self whose prototype hid in a garden? It is now fair to observe, returning to Whitman and his "fit," that the *poem* knows and thrives on what a *poetics* must discover, abashed, about itself. Whitman knew all along from his Christian forebears that the access route to originality, if it opens at all, opens only to the lyrical, or "naked" and implicated subject thrown upon his own irreducible self. Foucault calls this figure "visible and insistent" to point out the conspicuousness, the opaque virtuality, of him who bars the mouth of silence. Whitman calls him by his older name, name of the Ur-subject: Adam. The effort to swallow all words and so swallow difference converges back on the swallower, the one whose own shadow marks the first difference that all the splittings of gender and language follow. The distinction between this subject and the Adamic sinner of an orthodox Puritanism is not discernible: The "inertia of ecstasy" is a fig leaf, but Being is beneath. Essentialism does not contradict the current theory but is rather its most predictable of outcomes. The most skeptical of theories, when it seeks an abolition of denotation, must relax its supervisory vigilance. Then, its questions – mystical, groping, poetic – issue from a figure caught and exposed, ego-free and ecstatic: unconscious.

Or, if you will, sleeping among "sleepers." It would be hard to overstate the theological importance of the title of this, Whitman's most theologically committed poem, first called "Sleep Chasings," then "Night Poem," and finally in 1871, "The Sleepers." By means of a title Whitman's theology weighs in and takes measure of a whole divisive system the bipolar metaphors of sleep and waking support. The term "Great Awakening" has become so idiomatic we scarce remember that it, too, is a metaphor – just as we no longer recall that the function of a "revival" is to rouse the somnolent – and that both emerge from a Reformed theology that followed the Pauline epistles in finding the best metaphor for unregeneracy in Sleep. Recall once more that Michael Wigglesworth's runaway bestseller of the seventeenth century, "Day of Doom," is a gloss of Luke and Thessalonians, letting fall the full weight of God's judgment not on atheists and deniers so much as on unregenerate nappers. Just so, Cotton Mather in his *Midnight Cry* bade sinners put by all "corporal sleeping" to "Awake unto the time of the end." And, to cite a last example, Mary Rowlandson, in her *Captivity Narrative,* understood King Philip's marauding braves for the deputies of Judgment, executing God's cruel wake-up call. The cusp between day and night marks the path of God's sword, which slices and sorts regenerate from unregenerate along a horizon crisply distinguished. When sleepers are sinners, then it is the open-eyed struggle, the vigilant striving, the *tensing* of consciousness to full sense of itself, that redeems. Sinners must wake to the fact that they live alone with themselves.

Whitman's sleepers, on the other hand, live in consort. Moreover, the fact that Whitman's ecstatic speaker is not singular but double exposed – not only prince of light (Christ thrown forward) but agent of darkness – describes to the fullest degree the poem's theological "comprehensiveness." In the following lines of the poem, Christ, Satan, and the sinner over whom they contend find their "places" in a scripture that makes room for all, the poem swallowing up the very sword of Reformed theology in a great thrumming, valvular movement. The Adamic shame, the struggle between Christ and Lucifer, and the Crucifixion itself, come, in the ensuing lines, to seem mere symptoms of a theology in spasm, Christian time itself knotted and gripped by *kairoi* the poet-savior will relax. If these *kairoi* are but bad dreams, knots of clenched time the world's long response relaxes, it follows that the soul Calvin and Edwards described should be mooted as well, freed from the solitude that kills.

The innovation of Whitman's ministry is to redeem the wakened sinner by restoring him to a sanctified realm. Whitman would loosen the soul from the iron fist of sin, obviating the definition of the one in the all, and so, necessarily, grounding salvation somewhere other than in the sharply individuated, excruciatingly singular moment of the Atonement. Whereas Christ gave succor by freeing spirit of body, canceling all bodily suffering in the rigor of his own, Whitman exempts him from this rigor and exempts us from so unbalanced a debt, restoring Christ himself to the arms of a mother from whom orthodoxy perforce withholds him. Just so, he saves that sinner whose salvation depends on an experience of Christ's vicarious sacrifice. The poet's mission is to find some form whose accommodation of the End soothes better than the spectacle of a naked man, hung, bruised and crucified; to give us deeper comfort than the anesthetic thrill of Christ's agony.

What he conceives in "The Sleepers" is a simple inversion of that sacred time narrowing to one point. The pyramidal surge that gathered a phalanx of sinners behind the exact apex of the Atonement is driven back on itself. Once we were made one in the body of Christ. Now he is made many in us, his purity and set-off-ness, his hyperconsciousness, diffused in a vision of union. With this occlusion of Christ comes as well the occlusion of his demonic double: lonely Satan hurled from heaven. Likewise go their domains. The Miltonic heaven and hell, realms traced over God's Levitical map, are no longer maintained to receive the sinner. The razor-wired gate between is transmogrified to valve, and the sword of Hebrews that divides, awakening the slumberers to regret their somnolence, is in "The Sleepers" buried to its hilt, its divisive point diffused in a kind of pleasure. Now the guilty and sinless are indistinguishable in their passings in and out: Fallen fission lapses gently back into a pre-Creational coition.

I mean to exclude none of the associations this sword swallowing implies: virtuosity, healing, or sexual congress. In passages that link adolescent masturbation with homosexuality with a view of female sexuality not excluding aggression, Whitman baffles the accusatory, acute, and accurate sword of the Lord, preempting the excision of clean from unclean, blurring angles of guilt or sin, universalizing a loss of self not sinful but normative, and all through the agencies of a savior who is oxymoronic: an angelic demon, a sacred Lucifer, a princely slave.

This savior is of an "ill assorted" character I can now more explicitly specify. Not only, as earlier pages showed, conflating categories of Levitical purity, Whitman now also confutes the Pauline – and Emersonian – purity which distinguished Satan from Christ, savior from tempter. In the passages to follow, this opposition is revealed to be a fetish, or, more precisely, a *tropism*. I use the term in its several senses. First, to invoke an exegetical method inaugurated in the time of Calvin that reads religious history by fixed tropes; second, to characterize a metaphysics of reactive attraction and repulse (codified in Levitical taboo); and finally, to suggest a certain sexual unfreedom pleasuring itself in reactive exaggerations of power and powerlessness: in sadomasochism.

Whitman's extraordinary analysis of, and assault on, such tropism begins in a passage that works to destabilize the singularity of both Christ or Satan as representative models of discrete, set-off spiritual agents, either pure or impure. This passage is rather dedicated to showing the indiscriminacy from which we issue, and so, the incoherence in which we dwell. It experiments with calling the discrete self but a sojourn, a day trip of the sleeping self whose multiple character reveals our true being. Whitman's passage on the woman of the night emphasizes the artificial or at least contingent nature of integral selfhood:

> I am she who adorned herself and folded her hair
>   expectantly,
> My truant lover has come and it is dark.
>
> Double yourself and receive me darkness,
> Receive me and my lover too . . . he will not let me go
>   without him.
>
> I roll myself upon you as upon a bed . . . I resign myself
>   to the dusk.
>
> He whom I call answers me and takes the place of my
>   lover,
> He rises with me silently from the bed.
>
> Darkness you are gentler than my lover . . . his flesh was
>   sweaty and panting,
> I feel the hot moisture yet that he left me.

My hands are spread forth . . . I pass them in all
  directions,
I would sound up the shadowy shore to which you are
  journeying.
Be careful, darkness . . . already, what was it touched me?
I thought my lover had gone . . . else darkness and he are
  one,
I hear the heart-beat . . . I follow . . . I fade away.

From the opening couplet, the lines elide ideas of personhood and of
the singular responsible soul. We are very far in these lines from the Miltonic hierarchy: "he for God only; she for God in him." The woman of
the passage is both passive and active, "folding her hair expectantly," and
then rather like the speaker of Dickinson's "Wild nights" who would
"Moor tonight – in thee!" rolling herself "upon [him] as upon a bed."
By way of the fantasy the night affords, the woman, shrugging off the
constraints of a male lover who "will not let me go without him," ejects
her passivity and gains her lover's power. The object of her desire receives
her. The law established in Genesis to govern proper sexual relationship
is summarily overthrown.

But further, "Passing [her] hands in all directions," the woman, liberated as autonomous sexual agent, takes up the role of the one who, earlier, "Passed his hands soothingly." In her gesture, Christ's soothing
touch gains the specificity of sexual caress, and gains as well a liberty not
detached from pleasure. Through her, Whitman begins to demonstrate
the ministering power of an unregulated sexuality, and provisionally
then, we may say that Whitman finds his new Christ in a woman. But
only provisionally, for by and by she proves hard to locate in the panoply
of sexual actors the passage crowds. Besides the woman and her lover,
there is a "you" initially identified with the night, then designated as
"He" and then misplaced as the speaker recurs to the use of "you." The
multiplication of lovers suggests not a vulgar sexual party (though such
parties exist in Whitman – I will take them up shortly) but instead the
proliferation of identities sexuality permits, each person harboring a
"brood" of sexual orientations housed for convention's sake in one body.
Not, then, simply slipping the bonds of a patriarchal hierarchy which in-
stalls signifier over signified (word over thing, as Adam over Eve, as
God over man), the lines rehabilitate the reputations of the fallen woman
of Hosea and the Whore of Babylon, giving the lie to priestly and Pauline
definitions of holiness as discrete. The discrete and coherent identity of
the self is, through them, revealed as a mere legalism, a restraining order
on the multiple self that registers not only in the psyche but in the cosmos. One way to describe such a passage is to say Whitman performs
here a precocious psychoanalysis that retrieves the multiplicity of selves

from a regimented unity of self as a form of therapy. Another way, though, and one closer to the theological spirit of the poem, is to call Whitman's work pastoral: The poet offers a theological description of human *complexity* that is not censorious. A figure of "gates" allied with the Chaotic death mother to whom all sinners return, the woman in this passage reminds us of the rest we may claim outside the boundaried self.

Not stinting to give this rest its fullest explication, the end of the passage, "I follow / I fade away" renounces a certain hope in the restoration of the individual in death, in the reawakening of the sinner, good as new. Whitman's sleepers "unclothed" are never afforded the coherence of integral personhood. Losing self, they lose as well their link with Adam, prototype of individuated soul.

Finally, to undo Adam's excruciating self-knowledge – his disjunct and alienated vantage point on the world – will necessitate decreating Adam. Thus, the reciprocity that allows Whitman to call sin a mere agency of play, restoring to sexuality a transformational power, also exacts a new theory of loss. The curse of death, and the virtuality of the mortal body whose corruption is so close to the heart of Taylor's poetry, is still to be reckoned with. For in a fallen world there is nothing so fearsome as that loss of self the body's emissions portend.

Thus, the next lines bring us into the precincts of Adam and his anxieties; the very prosody, tight-strung, leaps forward in trochaic bursts. Out of a laving chaos, the speaker now suffers in self-consciousness and shame the culture's first, ever repeated nightmare – Adam's:

> O hotcheeked and blushing! O foolish hectic!
> O for pity's sake, no one must see me now! . . . my clothes
>   were stolen while I was abed,
> Now I am thrust forth, where shall I run?
>
> Pier that I saw dimly last night when I looked from the
>   windows
> Pier out from the main, let me catch myself with you and
>   stay . . . I will not chafe you;
> I feel ashamed to go naked about the world,
> And am curious to know where my feet stand . . . and what
>   is this flooding me, childhood or manhood . . . and the
>   hunger that crosses the bridge between.

The passage reveals, we should say at the outset, that perspicacity and intuition that Freud credited the poets with having all along. Its rendering of adolescent ambivalence in an image – the pier – that is both place of maturational crossing and tumescent emblem of physical humiliation, is a tour de force of condensation.[21] In addition, it traces the travails of the psyche back to the birth of consciousness in shame, rendering the experience of shame in a manner phylogenic, archetypal. The boy is Adam; his adolescence is metaphor for the gestation of the species. Adam's uncomfortable knowledge of corporeal extent – of the self's vulnerable separateness from the world – is magnified in dream fragments of a world pieced and subdivided: Dualism becomes geography.

Most of all, though, we should linger over the vision the passage offers of body islanded and exposed. The frailty and guilt concentrated in the image of the tumescent "pier" should remind us of the affective feel of that state of hyperconsciousness Taylor simply called original sin. Whitman is at the very source of Levitical taxonomy. His tableau of the boy freighted with body illustrates that burden of knowledge Christianity remedies in the Atonement: in the death of a "middle aged" figure the flood carries off, finally, to his death.

If the "beautiful gigantic swimmer" passage offers just this Atonement, its limpid classicism offering all the relief from taint that taxonomy – or more literally, scapegoating – affords, here such relief is put off. Rather than save this Adam with his Christ, the poet defers such salvation. The boy's nocturnal emission is dissociated from sin and released back into the primordial: The figure of Adam himself loses distinction. The division of the Fall itself falls and all other divisions with it. We are back now where Chaos broods, where it is unformed and void; the poet's language is aboriginal:

> The cloth laps a first sweet eating and drinking,
> Laps life-swelling yolks . . . laps ear of rose corn, milky
>   and just ripened:
> The white teeth stay and the boss tooth advances in
>   darkness,
> And liquor is spilled on lips and bosoms by touching
>   glasses, and the best liquor afterwards.

Discursivity is now renounced in favor of an associative immediacy that cryptically juxtaposes prolific sexuality with alcohol, orgasm with drunkenness. Images of a verdant fertility – of the phallic ear of corn that is as well source of liquor – link the two. Resigning any claim on mimetic clarity, this language enjoys a hallucinatory moment of reverie in which human sexual shame is canceled in the restoration of sexuality to an inchoate, value-neutral kind of overflow. The spilling of seed for other than procreative purposes is naturalized in analogues to corn, to yolks, and to the fragrant liquor of celebration. And again, although it is useful to see the lines as precociously psychoanalytic (tracing shame back to repression, revealing an obstreperous Id beneath the tense and guilty soliloquy), nevertheless, "shame," like "sleep," is alive with theological nuances that the simple dyad of ego and id doesn't illuminate. The ethos of vigilant introspection that made the Puritans, as Adrienne Rich once called them, "the most self-conscious people who ever lived," institutionalizes the moment of shameful awakening; only through such awakening does the sinner earn Christ's rest, a rest that he earned for us when he endured Adam's nerve-strung ignominy as his own nerve-ignited agony.

The question Whitman's lines beg here is this: Will our debt be so easily canceled? For a moment it seems so, as the lines unwrite the Fall, vaulting Christian history in a return to the prelapsarian. Where self-consciousness sees a shamed stripling, unsheathed penis in hand, the poem sees a simple ear of corn. Innate depravity is ceded to the benignly "natural."

But the facility, the fundamental unseriousness, of such a solution, is given away by a certain disingenuousness of metaphor. Corn, indeed! the skeptic fumes. The reader has every right to ask whether these lines aren't rather ludicrously evasive, concealing Whitman's own homoerotic fantasies in nonincriminating vegetable code. Paul Zweig, more than patient with Whitman's gaucheries in general, is not at all intemperate when he calls these lines "gibberish," taking issue with what he takes to be a euphemistic impulse that would substitute cloth for vagina (or foreskin), teeth for the advance of sexual members (Zweig, 246). There is, to be sure, a way in which the lines seem not only evasive but downright coy, the poet heightening the furtive atmosphere, the sly suggestiveness, by arranging the drapery so cunningly.

In addition, critics of Whitman will recognize in these lines the same uncomfortable prurience – less erotic than pornographic – that vexes key passages of *Leaves of Grass*. The fact is that with such passages before us no amount of wishful rationalization will dispel the impression that what we read is someone else's guilty masturbation fantasy, which is fundamentally different from reading an analysis of a masturbation fantasy, and additionally problematic if what we seek in Whitman is the sexual water-drinker who knows all erotic practices to be health giving. Such sections as 28 from "Song of Myself," which present "prurient provokers stiffening my limbs . . . Behaving licentious toward me . . . Depriving me of my best for a purpose," are only by the most wishful of thinking, comfortable. Such anxieties as revealed by "No consideration, no regard for my draining strength or my anger, / Fetching the rest of the herd around to enjoy them a while . . . They have left me helpless to a red marauder, they all come to the headland to witness and assist against me" resist readings that would deflect all that is wrong with this sex act onto Victorian small-mindedness. No, something is amiss here with sex.

I want to propose that this prurience, which makes us, along the way, complicit, has a function beyond simple titillation of the poet or his readers. The repeated descriptions of voyeurism, the recurrent scene of a nearly sadistic mastery, and especially the recurrent orgy fantasy in which a subject is made pet or sexual slave of a gang of "bosses" – all these are vitally connected to the scene of the "beautiful gigantic swimmer." Indeed, in these passages we may discern an analysis *of* Adamic, carnal knowledge not cured but rather exacerbated by the guilt offering, Christ.

Before outlining this analysis, one should mention that the poet has much to gain by literally naturalizing his own sexual behavior, finding a place for homosexual practices outside the Levitical system that abhors them (Leviticus 18:22). One might speculate that just as Christ transcended the law, the poet's portrayal of Christ as homosexual hero would transcend that same law.[22] Complicating this typological model, though, is the fact that Whitman's Christ appears not so much as savior of a fully spiritualized sex as a figure crucified by sex. He stands at the center, more precisely, of a body of imagery connecting the sexual domination of the one by the many with the Christology of orthodox teaching.[23] He is raped, he is enslaved, he is crucified; he is sexual victim, slave, and figure of God's greatness mutilated. That he is all of these at once – and dispenser of a saving word – makes him enigmatic indeed.

The triple exposure of these figures remains one of the abiding mysteries of *Leaves of Grass* as a whole, but also one of the keys to Whitman's early brilliance and late decline. In "The Sleepers" Whitman goes further than anywhere else toward clarifying the precise relationship of three figures – the slave, the homosexual victim, and the Christ – who form a loose trinity in his work. In this poem, they fuse in the figure of the "beautiful gigantic swimmer" who is three figures in one: a paradigm of naked manly beauty displayed to a witness helpless with love, a colossal Christ whose giantism is templated in the synthesis of Christ and Lucifer in the "Now Lucifer Was not Dead" section, and, finally, in that section, a slave. As white giant becomes black giant, the swimmer's bulk is now the bulk of the slave whose grievance is too immense to be contained. This figure, a swollen and outraged version of the black "picturesque giant" watched and "loved" in "Song of Myself," synthesizes both the beauty and power, but also the unacknowledged will to mastery and claim to justice of that figure. Like Christ, he is one who absorbs debt and wrong even as he exemplifies manly beauty.

To cut through some of this complexity, suppose that the lexicon of master and slave governing homoerotic love in "The Sleepers" and indeed throughout *Leaves of Grass* is borrowed from the debtor's economy of the Atonement. Not that the poet doesn't gain a certain advantage when he casts himself in homosexual tableaux as a Christ set upon by the mob. Not only lending a sacral quality to adventures otherwise licentious, such projection has an exculpatory benefit. Self-characterized as simple martyr to the desire of others, the speaker is then not responsible for what marauders do to him. Along these lines, one might find grounds for acquittal of the marauders themselves; frenzied, "they know not what they do." And yet, casuistical, such a construction of homosexual love is belied even as it is courted by the lines. Martyrdom is a pose inadequate to explain the pleasure that pain summons in these scenes: a pleasure not merely guilty but somehow grievously driven to unpleasure. The point is not that the poet judges homosexual love itself sinful or even shameful, or even transgressive.[24] Better to say he sees it transgressed, altered from without, obeying rhythms not its own: prey to tropism. Indeed, rather than give homosexual practice the sanction one offers either the "natural" or the "helpless," Whitman's sexual tableaux – framed again and again in imagery of the Passion – register the poet's judgment of the pathological disequilibrium, or fetish, that Atonement iconography teaches believers in its power. Christian sacrifice gives instruction in the erotics of punishment.

This indebtedness of sexual cruelty to the Christian Passion is to be found in Whitman's earliest treatments of the Christ figure as a beautiful boy, sold for his flesh. His early poem, "Blood-Money" reads: "Of Olden time, when it came to pass / The beautiful god, Jesus, should finish his work on Earth, / Then went Judas, and sold the divine youth, / And took pay for his body." Here the conventional indictment of Judas anticipates the larger indictment "The Sleepers" will lay down: that delivered against a God who takes Jesus as pay. By the time of "The Sleepers" it is the God of Reformed Christianity who is slaver and procurer. It is He and not Judas who puts flesh on the block, and His system that generates scapegoats for the sake of its continuance. "Blood-Money" is a paradigm lending perspective to two of the most perplexing sections of the 1855 "Sleepers," sections lifted up out of the dreamwork and raised, as it were, on a hill like Golgotha. Out of the soothing regions of sleep – where soul flows into soul – there is yet this surging, aggressive pulse. There is yet this atrophy of concourse in fixed, punitive roles:

> Well do they do their jobs, these journeymen divine,
> Only from me can they hide nothing and would not if
> they could;
> I reckon I am their boss, and they make me a pet besides,
> And surround me, and lead me and run ahead when I walk,
> And lift their cunning covers and signify me with stretched
> arms and resume the way;

> Onward we move, a gay gang of blackguards with
> mirthshouting music and wildflapping pennants of joy.

The speaker's martyrdom, or passivity, is affectation. It is obvious that his demurrals are an incitement to violation rather than a genuine defense against it. Equally vague is the exact character of this group in so intimate a relationship with the speaker. Beginning virtually angelic, as "journeymen divine," by the end they are a "gay gang of blackguards." They seem at the same time a company of faithful, known to their very hearts by the speaker from whom they "hide nothing," and the mob at Calvary, hounding the bewildered speaker by leading and running ahead as he walks. Moreover, as their boss and pet both, the speaker seems a very parody, a doubled gargoyle even, of Christ the Law and Christ the Lamb – parodically passive.

The parody, albeit grotesque, is precisely the point here, as is the sadomasochistic imagery that lends a certain queasy and lurid Gothicism to the whole scene. This passage, heralding the Passion of the beautiful gigantic swimmer, borrows the language of Calvary to distill a terror admixed with titillation, to suggest a thrill not separate from the pornographic that the scene of Crucifixion incites: Poe rather than Emerson seems the guardian spirit.[25]

In these terms the homosexual guilt that critics tend, although regretfully, to find in such passages, has a more interesting function than has yet been noticed. It is not simply that Whitman suffuses his homosexual disclosures with Christian imagery in order to borrow Christ's martyred helplessness, or, even to suggest that his own guilt merits punishment, though both of these may obtain. He implies in effect a covert homoeroticism in the Crucifixion itself, a certain simultaneous satisfaction and murder of homoerotic desire in the spectacle of the "divine youth." Later, in the punishment of the "Handsome Sailor," Billy Budd, Melville will attach a similar meaning to the spectacle. Even as these "wildflapping pennants of joy" suggest a kind of phallic Fourth of July, the emphasis here is on the frenzy that unifies the mob. The passage is energized by parallels between the "abomination" of homosexual dominance and that scene of torment wholly sanctified by Christian tradition. The passage is, in short, committed to anatomizing how Christian spectacle magnetizes the prurience of the Devil's seeing. The very cunning of the demonic, the cunning of the snake of Genesis, and Satan's cunning in *Paradise Lost* are not self-starting, but related to the Christ, the exhibition of whose "person" Whitman now joins Emerson in querying.

Satan needs reintroduction here, for after raising the obvious question of whether homosexuality be infernal or divine, we still face an inveterate confusion around the angelic or demonic character of the "gang," and specifically, the problem of determining to whose company the speaker belongs. Is he, to invoke now the third arm of the trinity, master or slave? Is he a victim, Christ hooted by a mob demon-possessed, or, is he of the "gay gang" of rousters which he does seem, at least by the end, to join? How can he be both Christ and Lucifer? How indeed, except if they are one, both singular hostages to debts not their own. Excised from the poem, the so-called "Black Lucifer" passage suggests nothing less than Christ's symbiotic relationship with Lucifer, their interchangeable function in a theology based tropically on attraction and repulse. And on a slavery the Christian God authorizes.

> Now Lucifer was not dead . . . or if he was I am his
>   sorrowful terrible heir;
> I have been wronged . . . I am oppressed . . . I hate him
>   that oppresses me,
> I will either destroy him, or he shall release me.
> Damn him! how he does defile me,
> How he informs against my brother and sister and takes
>   pay for their blood,
> How he laughs when I look down the bend after the
>   steamboat that carries away my woman
>
> Now the vast dusk bulk that is the whale's bulk . . . it
>   seems mine,
> Warily, sportsman! Though I lie so sleepy and sluggish,
>   my tap is death.

It is sometimes noted that in this passage Whitman expresses his conviction as to the consequences of chattel slavery by giving the black man the Promethean pedigree of the Romantic Satan (Asselineau, 38; Erkkila, 123). The presence of the "steamboat" is strong evidence that the "Black Lucifer" is Whitman's ennobling portrait of the avenging hellhound Southerners feared, the great beast who will rear up to destroy those who sported with him. Still, this reading excises aspects of Lucifer's imperial character; makes him in the injustice served him a tracing of Christ. Sufferer out of the ranks of the meek, informed against, and bled for silver, the slave is a Christlike figure wronged. But more important, he is also a figure of the Christ who, as victim of punishment, yet ushered punishment into the world. Not only as slave, but as slaver, Christ plays foreman to a system of values devolving on a pleasurable act of torture.

From Edwards on, and especially in the decades before the Civil War that saw the ascendancy of a man-centered Unitarianism over a Christ-centered orthodoxy, debates around the Christ's mission focused precisely on this aspect of punishment as model. The orthodox scholars from whom Emerson and others parted company saw Christ's sacrifice not just as sacrifice, but punishment for Adam's crime, his "expiation" functioning to cure mankind of Adam's sin, and the scene of the crucifixion trope of release. What Whitman detects – as Emerson did before him – is the tropism of the scene, the way in which the spectacle hardly quarantines itself, but rather breeds inflamed forms twisting into its light. Christ is hung helpless, his sanctity depending on the Satanic mocker who must kill him again and again; on the gaze which must fix his beautiful body in gospel or elegy. If Christ and Lucifer blur, assuming each other's roles in repetitive and compulsive scenes of sexual torture, it is because both are bloated emblems of a theology whose techniques of mastering death only enslave men to death, with "gigantic" Christ and "vast" Lucifer acting collaborators in a false consciousness, pawns in a slave economy. Christ's vigilant passivity is met, symbiotically, by the Devil's vigilant and predatory cruelty, but both the passivity and the cruelty are institutionalized by the scene. A culture that arranges its system of value around a scene of torture replicates that scene in its economic, its sexual, and its linguistic relations: in slavery, in the fetish of sexual dominance – and in literary forms whose most exquisite instant is the moment of the kill, when the swimmer is tossed bloody before a witness watching in thrilled horror.

The lexicon of debt and payment, and the very iconography of Christ hung in chains are symptoms, Whitman's poem reveals, of a systemic disequilibrium which always holds someone slave: The scapegoated Christ is liberated only when we, buying back our sins, enter his thralldom, so assenting to our powerlessness. This either/or which makes Christ our slave or slaver springs up, malignant, in images distributed over the poem, images coined out of a dualistic, frequently Manichean language, which pit the frailty of the subject against forces of a demonic and magnified power. Thus the waves in the "beautiful gigantic swimmer" sequence are "ruffianly" and in the journeyman divine sequence the celebrants are "blackguards," with the subject always half in love with the torturer pitted against him. When helplessness is thus deified, the swimmer is always ambivalently suspended, grotesquely torn between hypertrophied "boss and pet," master and mastered: between a power demonic and a passivity abject. An analysis of the profane, Whitman's poem suggests that "evil" and "impurity" are by-products of the sacred, not intrinsically but reactively malign. One might say that this invocation of the massive "whale's bulk" describes the vengeful return of the repressed. But it is also an image that connects the power of Leviathan, God's example to Job of unexplainable terror, to the hygiene of Leviticus, disciplining and containing both "fluke" and "pier" in the discharged scapegoat bent under impurity: the Christ bleeding from his wounds.

In these terms, Whitman's "guilty" tableaux of homosexual domination gather a new symbolic power behind them, inasmuch as he is implicated by them. As Christ wore flesh, Whitman's sexuality wears a Christian ideology of punishment by which its erstwhile naturalness is constrained. Just as the teaching of Jesus accompanies the wordless fact of his sacrifice, the poet's sermons are sealed by his absolute mediatorial function. Having abandoned mimesis, and especially the usual distance of a telling subject from described object – the distance that washes the object with light while leaving the subject opaque – the speaker has created a kind of vision that wraps back around him as well. The consequences here are far-reaching. As we have seen, it is not simply that the biographical Walter Whitman reveals in "The Sleepers" his own unconventional sexuality – this would not merit elaborating at such length. In his absorption, however, into the "sleep" of the other dreamers, in his release of ego into the bodies of others, the poet puts at risk something much more fundamental: his own authority as author, as God-like creator of a New American Bible. The privilege of the inscrutable God who sees us all, the omniscient eye whose text points both to a world we find opaque and He, in His opaqueness, finds transparent, is abandoned, and the actualization of the visionary's mediating role is complete. Like Ezekiel who swallowed the scripture, or Christ who became it, he is the text, read through. He is the body blackguards carry off. The vulnerability of this Author, his "Revelation," has never been so literal, so acute; the stakes of the text, never perhaps so high.

If Emerson and his Unitarian colleagues also forswore Christ, preserving the teaching but not the "cultism" of the sacrificial crisis, Whitman's scripture is best described as preserving the kerygmatic teaching of the salvific vision (overthrowing the sacrificial crisis) but without stanching the flow of blood. Whitman's own testament "completes" the Unitarian testament of deathless compensation with a vision of death's very compensation. Thus his "days" yield to night as Emerson's never did; his savior to impurity as Emerson's cannot. The whale's spout is topped off with death, and Lucifer, fallen star of the West, descends his western course not to reign over the dead, but to decompose. Sexuality necessarily wastes itself. The "liquor" spilled, the youth and semen spent, yield to the Levitical uncleanness:

> I descend my western course . . . my sinews are flaccid,
> Perfume and youth course through me, and I am their
> wake.

In Taylor the soul cut off from its God finds its best analogue in that "bag of botches" of the body: in "touch, in issue, leproused flesh." When Whitman asserts in these lines, not "I leave my wake" but "I am their wake," his strategy is to sacralize the very substances orthodoxy reviled. Discharges, leprous excrescences, all the functions of the body that hitherto violated the Holy of Holies are to be restored, made whole and free of taint. By the final lines of the poem, the human valvework, purged of clot, is synechdoche for the muscular gates of the cosmos itself whose quiescent function belies death's terror.

> The sweatings and fevers stop . . . the throat that was
>   unsound is sound . . . the lungs of the consumptive are
>   resumed . . . the poor distressed head is free,
> The joints of the rheumatic move as smoothly as ever, and
>   smoother than ever.
> Stiflings and passages open, the paralyzed become
>   supple,
> The swelled and convulsed and congested awake to
>   themselves in condition
> They pass the invigoration of the night and the chemistry
>   of the night and awake.

This peace that passeth understanding comes to be, not by a slaying of death or through the barter of death in Christ, but by a waking to death and night. Death is that passage, that gate, through which sinner and saved pass as one. The coming lines represent Whitman's final assault on "distinctions," an assault that will take its death with its sexuality, allowing that the end of the Emersonian enjoyment is extinction. The speaker does not withhold himself from wastage. With sex and death – the curses Adam brought on the world – made normative, the prospects for Christian sacrifice change. The Passion is quelled as individual loss is diffused in the unstanched flow. Christ's very blood is now washed, now redeemed, by the blood of a multitude whose deaths redeem his agony. His unique suffering is effaced in the stately passage of the life cycle.

> It is my face yellow and wrinkled instead of the old
>   woman's.
> I sit low in a strawbottom chair and carefully darn my
>   grandson's stockings.
> It is I too . . . the sleepless widow looking out on the
>   winter midnight,
> I see the sparkle of sunshine on the icy and pallid earth.

The trajectory from sexuality to the very extremities of biological life could not be more clearly traced. Finally made utterly passive, deprived of locomotion, the old woman serves the youth. She is low to the ground and to that earth to which she will return. She lives at the limits of the vital closed space where her grandson's life goes on. And yet no honed sword separates youth from age, her yellow hair from his vigor. Just so the widow crosses the very fireline of death to offer an insight Christian hyperconsciousness will not allow:

> A shroud I see – and I am the shroud . . . I wrap a body
> and lie in the coffin;
> It is dark here underground . . . it is not evil or pain here
> . . . it is blank here, for reasons.

Insisting that it is not "evil and pain here," but blank "for reasons," Whitman's poetic theology delivers us from a vision of death as Adam's curse to a vision of death as part of the initial creation, prelapsarian. Closer and closer the poem moves us to the tabooed object, and closer and closer to the corpse, the immutable repulsive fact of mortality from which all limits protect us.

In the words of the poem more indebted to "The Sleepers" than any other poem in the corpus, death is "sane and sacred." As the coming pages will show, this widow of "The Sleepers" who follows her husband to the grave has good news to give the mourner of Whitman's late great poem, "When Lilacs Last in the Dooryard Bloom'd." That later poem, I think, owes its vision to the theology of "The Sleepers," which lets a "courageous swimmer" of "middle age" die a better death than Christ's. As Whitman writes elsewhere of the Lincoln mourned in that poem: "The soldier drops, sinks like a wave, but the ranks of the ocean pass eternally on." Fortified with the wisdom of "The Sleepers," the widowed poet grieving for his president knows better than to worship one above all. His president, like the beautiful gigantic swimmer, will find his place alongside sleepers.

Among the cruder dependencies, "mendicant and sycophantic," that Emerson catalogues in "Self Reliance," he nonetheless reserves space for self-imitation, one of conformity's subtler strains. Describing the want of self-reliance that recycles itself, Emerson gives insight into the problems faced by any seer who would disseminate a vision by its nature unique, and, in particular, into the dilemma Whitman faced in the years after writing the first Leaves of Grass. How, indeed, to make of theology Good News? Emerson's description of the man who "once he has acted or spoken with eclat . . . is a committed person, watched by the sympathy or the hatred of hundreds," exactly describes the Whitman declaiming his worst poem year after year to audiences who congregated expressly to hear that poem. The first edition of Leaves of Grass, with its flourishes of gold scrolling on a leaf-green cover, aptly represents the poet whose "long foreground," as Emerson noted, was as obscure as his book was dazzling: "I rubbed my eyes a little to see if this sunbeam were no illusion." But the sunbeam image also portends an already retrospective

Whitman, a poet whose energy, almost from the start, was deflected into broadcasting the radiant productivity of a ten-year period. In his own words, Whitman never regained "the afflatus he had in writing the first *Leaves of Grass*" (Blodgett and Bradley, vxvii): between 1855 and 1865 he wrote virtually all the poems we most admire. He devoted the years between 1865 and his death in 1892 to augmenting, revising, and advertising *Leaves of Grass,* and to lecturing, a cultural spokesman and sometime visage on cigar boxes, to modeling the robust figure who produced it.

In *Leaves of Grass,* the fault line runs invisibly between two poems of 1865, both inspired by the death of Lincoln. The first is arguably Whitman's greatest work, "When Lilacs Last in the Dooryard Bloom'd"; the second, "O Captain! My Captain!," is the stump piece he recited for the next thirty years. The first is a poem of fine-grained theological determination, a poem that does no less than reconceive the elegy and the role of its suffering hero. The second is a piece of tinny evangelism. The difference between them is predicted in "The Sleepers."

"O Captain! My Captain!" is a work dedicated to what Poe had called a singular "effect." One of Whitman's shorter poems, "O Captain! My Captain!" less develops than envelops us in its doleful iterations. The last stanza suffices to represent the whole:

> My Captain does not answer, his lips are pale and still,
> My father does not feel my arm, he has no pulse nor will,
> The ship is anchor'd safe and sound, its voyage closed and
>   done,
> From fearful trip the victor ship comes in with object won;
>   Exult O shores, and ring O bells!
>   But I with mournful tread,
>   Walk the deck my Captain lies,
>   Fallen cold and dead.

All dénouement, the stanza extracts the maximum sentiment from the spectacle of the fallen hero. Its trochaic rhythms blow us inexorably, line by line, to the gasping Captain whose ship, as it were, has finally come in. Neither does the metaphor of the Captain strain our interpretive resources. Leader, chief, or as the poem fills in, "Father," the "Captain" is transparently that martyr hero, or Christ, to whom all pathos is due. The thumping closure of the last line – "Fallen cold and dead" – reassures any who might doubt that this is indeed a genuine poem, yet its literary status is not exclusive. Binding poet and listener in a fraternity of loss, it scarifies like a sermon, mesmerizes like a hymn. Exactly calibrated to the temper of his auditors, "O Captain! My Captain!" is typical of that mid-century American Christianity that was making out of theology a kind of holography, attenuating the mystery of death in pure sensation (Douglas, *Feminization,* 143–96). Which is to say that it is a poem that documents Whitman's compromise with the power of the "beautiful gigantic swimmer."

When Whitman ruefully confessed to wishing he had never written "O Captain! My Captain!" (Blodgett and Bradley, 337), he must have been thinking of that earlier poem, the poem written out of "afflatus," whose theological touch was as deft as this poem's was heavy-handed, and whose sufferer offered a revelation more comprehensive and less wrenching than the calculated thump of Captain hitting deck. For the ten years before Lincoln's death, Whitman had worked on deposing precisely the Christian martyr to whom "O Captain! My Captain!" does obeisance. To understand, therefore, the difference between "O Captain! My Captain!" and the strange, often inaccessible, work that precedes it is to apprehend the rigorous challenge Whitman set his readers in the early work. It is also to recognize precisely what he gave up for the sake of being "absorbed" by them. The early Whitman writes a poetry resisting the very religious sensationalism to which "O Captain! My Captain!" finally falls prey: a poetry that mandates a riskier, and less defensive relation to death and its mysteries.

Recall that the doomed seafarer of "The Sleepers," far from holding the stage, instead sinks out of sight in the middle of the poem, denied both the closural privilege and the thematic omnivorousness of the Captain's thumping death. The episode of the "beautiful, gigantic swimmer" floats like an island, serene preserve of a renounced literary option, in the turbid experiment of "The Sleepers." After this section, the speaker of "The Sleepers" departs the atemporal world of the elegy, the domain of the Savior and the typology of his death to return us to the communal world. The archetypal setting, the frieze of Part 3, is yielded to a more dimensional, historically textured setting. The lost hero is not lost alone, but lost in battle, among others.

> I turn but do not extricate myself;
> Confused . . . a pastreading . . . another, but with
>   darkness yet.
>
> The beach is cut by the razory icewind . . . the wreck-guns
>   sound,
> The tempest lulls and the moon comes floundering through
>   the drifts.
>
> I look where the ship helplessly heads end on . . . I hear
>   the burst as she strikes . . . I hear the howls of dismay
>   . . . they grow fainter and fainter.
>
> I cannot aid with my wringing fingers;
> I can but rush to the surf and let it drench me and freeze
>   upon me.

> I search with the crowd . . . not one of the company is
> washed to us alive;
> In the morning I help pick up the dead and lay them in
> rows in a barn.

In these lines we leave that elegiac space no time can violate for a time of "pastreading." Call the difference between the two that between a myth of vertical singularity – the myth of the Christ – and a chronicle of horizontal repeatability – an endless if reiterated tale of human mortality. Myth chooses the one swimmer, the one Lycidas, the one Lincoln. Around this figure it elaborates a cultural event whose classic beauty mandates its very unreproduceability. The hero dies alone situated in a time with depth but no duration. His dying exempts us from ours. Chronicle restores us, on the other hand, to a cycle of days whose meaning is distributed over time and over individuals: to grass and our lives that are like grass. The "rows" of dead in the barn can always absorb one more; the "crowd" searching in the freezing surf is just as disarticulated as the "company" washed up on the beach; "turning," the speaker "[does] not extricate [himself]."

We may profit at this juncture by looking again at the jotted note of Whitman's with which this chapter began. There, signaling his intention to write a "New American Bible," the poet goes on rather mysteriously to invoke "the three hundred and sixty five." The phrase suggests a certain correspondence between *Leaves of Grass,* the "New Bible," and the days of a year, intimating that we are in the province of a Scripture with a new view of time to advance. This time is to be distinguished from the time of, say, the Gospel of John, collapsing beginnings in ends. And it should also be distinguished from typological time, based on the essential simultaneity of then and now, history made but a veil over eternity. The contraction to one mythic event, a stressed yet sanctified moment binding the beginnings and ends of days, is precisely what Whitman's calendar would loosen.[26] His "three hundred sixty five" points rather to a cycle of years, to human time measured in human increments: consecutive, equally significant, paratactic. Tugging against the omnisignificant radiance of the one event, the one day of the "beautiful gigantic swimmer," are the "three hundred and sixty five." The poet's spatial metaphor for this kind of time, here as elsewhere, is the homely shoreline where land and sea meet, where the dead wash up. This line, susceptible to tides and change, breaks the closed circle, the vortex, into which the swimmer disappeared, "swiftly and out of sight."

This difference between the two kinds of time represented in Part 3 and Part 4 of "The Sleepers" merits underscoring since the distinction proves of great value when we go about interpreting other, later, poems from the Whitman corpus. The tension between the solitary hero whose death absorbs the deaths of all – the Christ figure, the savior – and the dead boy who is one among many, is a tension brought into particular relief in Whitman's treatments of Lincoln. Late in his career, as I noted, his impulse to liberate American prejudice is upstaged by his impulse to attain intimacy with a public whose favorite encore was "O Captain! my Captain!" Accordingly, we should not be surprised that the late Whitman will enstate Lincoln in an old frieze, giving his death a Christological singularity. Thus, in a lecture Whitman delivers in 1879, Lincoln is back-lit with the same lambency as the "beautiful gigantic swimmer." His death supplies a timeless definition to the meaning of American life; its meanings narrow to one End:

> I repeat it – the great deaths of the race – the dramatic deaths of every nationality – are its most important inheritance value – . . . Why if the old Greeks had this man, what trilogies of plays – what epics would have been made out of him? How the rhapsodies would have recited him. . . . Dear to the muse – thrice dear to Nationality – to the whole human race precious to the union – precious to Democracy – unspeak-ably and forever precious – their first great Martyr chief. (*Complete Prose Works*, 315)

Compare this rhapsody, synthesizing Christological cliché, national insecurity, and contemporary bombast, with Whitman's note in *Specimen Days,* entered in the mid-sixties. Steeled with the wisdom of "The Sleep-ers," the entry in *Specimen Days* repels hagiography to fill in history, giv-ing the bas-relief of Lincoln a depth of context it needs. The singularity of the dead hero is now ceded to praise of "Unionism"; in Union's ef-facing wave the martyr finds his best monument:

> Unionism, in its truest and amplest sense, formed the hard-pan of his character. These he sealed with his life. The tragic splendor of his death, purging, illuminating all, throws round his form, his head, an aureole that will remain and will grow brighter throughout time, while history lives and love of country lasts. By many has this Union been helped; but if one man, one name, must be picked out, he most of all, is the con-servator of it, to the future. He was assassinated, but the Union was not assassinated – one falls and the other falls. The soldier drops, sinks like a wave, but the ranks of the ocean pass eternally on. Death does its work, obliterates a hundred, a thousand, – President, general, captain, private – but the Nation is immortal. (*Complete Prose Works,* 69)

The final emphasis in this later tribute, even allowing for a certain an-gelism of language, is on Lincoln's participation, not his exceptionalism. It is not singularity, not the uniqueness of Lincoln's death for the Union that the poet emphasizes, but the Union of death which binds us all. Nor should we rest at noting the passage's resolute "democratic" force. Not only democratic, the lines are theologically heterodox, drawing power from that same effacement of the Cross in multiple crossings that was the chief work of "The Sleepers." Allen Grossman has called Whitman the "ideologist of union as happiness," going on to suggest how in Whitman's work this idea of union is lent a comprehensive and total power.[27] Grossman's observation corrects a critical tendency to restrict Whitman's stress on "Union" to the political, to suppose that Whitman is merely choosing sides: the side of Union, say, against that of Secession.

On the contrary, this "Union" comes to have the same nearly mystical status in Whitman's work of the mid-1860s as "gates" does in the earlier work. "Union," for Whitman, is what Crane later calls an "Incognizable Word." In the 1850s, "distinctions" between saved and fallen, mortal life and the death, are obviated by the erotic union of the poet passing through "gates"; in the 1860s it is "union" that gives passage. This key word speaks to every impulse in the Whitman corpus. Expressing linguistic, political, sexual, and national mergings whose common outcome is the Union in death – with the concomitant fusion and collapse of the singular soul – this "Union" is the theological realization of Whitman's apprenticeship to "mergings" in "The Sleepers." From the "merging" learned in "The Sleepers" emerges a principle of final rest, of final sleep in the later poem, rocking North and South in a shared death embrace. Whereas the Christian tradition from which he departs mandates the division of living from dead, going on to give finer and finer articulation to that division, Whitman will offer a Union that merges life with death. This Union, absorbing all experience, serves as totalizing Authority, replacing the authority of the God who divides, but also supervising the gruesome vivisection of the War between States. The capacious power of "Union" is that of "gates" only now given historical application. Whitman's abstract theology of "The Sleepers" does what a mature theology must – find the proper relation between *chronos* and *kairos,* history and eternity. That Whitman's greatest poem of the sixties, "When Lilacs Last in the Dooryard Bloom'd" adapts *kairos* to *chronos,* eternity to history – inverting the norm – is presaged by "The Sleepers." In that poem of ten years earlier Whitman found a form to accommodate a death multiplied yet not trivialized, a historiography to accommodate his new sense of Endings.

If we look briefly at the kind of history that commences in Part 5 of "The Sleepers," we see the poem take an abrupt turn. Just as the early section of "The Sleepers" effectively saved Christ, lifted the price from his head, by delivering him from uniqueness back into indistinction, Whitman's treatment of the historical hero is informed by interrogation of the vicarious role of this hero, of his function as savior. If anyone needs succor in this section devoted to Washington, it is Washington, healed by his troops. In lines that juxtapose Washington's defeat at Brooklyn with a cameo of an itinerant squaw, we see the poet honing a historic technique that would afford the singular Captain some surcease from his mythic function. Breaking with tradition, Whitman removes Washington from the sacred frieze where triumphantly, heroically, he crosses the Delaware as if alone, his very rowers blocked by his magnificent knees. Now, standing not outside the human community, but "crossing" into and among them, Washington is freed from stasis and its burdens. Standing "inside the lines," he seeks faith among those who traditionally invest faith in him. He weeps.

> Now of the old war days . . . the defeat at Brooklyn;
> Washington stands inside the lines . . . he stands on the
>   entrenched hills amid a crowd of officers,
> His face is cold and damp . . . he cannot repress the
>   weeping drops . . . he lifts the glass perpetually to his
>   eyes . . . the color is blanched from his cheeks,
> He sees the slaughter of the southern braves confided to
>   him by their parents.

> The officers speechless and slow draw near in their turns,
> The chief encircles their necks with his arm and kisses
>   them on the cheek,
> He kisses lightly the wet cheeks one after another . . . he
>   shakes hands and bids goodbye to the army.

What stands out is the relentless intimacy of the episode, and especially its structural reversal of expectation: the way in which it furloughs the chief from his salvific task. One might compare these lines with a contemporary account – say Bancroft's – to see just how poor it is in the etched majesty of the contemporary historical remembrance.[28] Washington's damp face; the death of the "southern braves" confided to the great general "by their parents"; the explicit inversion of all the flourishes of the Hegelian history that would recast Christ in the martial garb of a historical Spirit – all of Whitman's details go against a certain historical grain. Even more striking, though, is the following episode where this history, intimate, yet still inexorably public, is in turn yielded to a more anonymous, more intimate kind of chronicle. Linking the two sections is Whitman's subtle use of the word "braves." Not only a synonym for American troops, "braves" suggestively elides divisions between American and American Indian in the same way that he will later mourn soldiers of North and South together. Moreover, just as the boys Walt Whitman nursed in the wards of Washington enter history only in the letters he wrote to their parents, in the bits of conversation in his "Specimen Days", so the memorable beauty of the "squaw" is entrusted to a history random, quotidian. If such an observation accords with the cur-

rent view of Whitman as the most democratic of our poets, canon re-
constructor and cultural historian in his own time, the commonplace
misses something else: the reinvestment of faith not in saviors but in
those saved, not in those who Awaken but in "sleepers." The eye is
drawn not to the Mount but to the valleys, not to Golgotha, but to the
village where grace comes from unexpected quarters: a craftswoman
footloose as Jesus the carpenter, unlikely as Jesus the Jew. Myth yields to
ministry; resurrection to a simple teaching.

> Now I tell what my mother told me today as we sat at
>   dinner together,
> Of when she was a nearly grown girl living home with
>   her parents on the old homestead.
> A red squaw came one breakfastime to the old homestead,
> On her back she carried a bundle of rushes for
>   rushbottoming chairs;
> Her hair straight shiny coarse black and profuse
>   half enveloped her face,
> Her step was free and elastic . . . her voice sounded
>   exquisitely as she spoke
> My mother looked in delight and amazement at the
>   stranger,
> She looked at the beauty of her tallborne face and full and
>   pliant limbs,
> The more she looked upon her she loved her,

Not only does this oral history of the squaw correct the public history of
ritualized moments bound between the covers of books, but the experience of conversion the passage chronicles shifts the center of theological
gravity from a Grace dispensed from on high – and once – to a graceful-
ness one might enjoy tomorrow. I am not saying that this passage is literally a veiled scene of Annunciation, but rather that the implication of
Whitman's theology is a historicization of religion. The eclipse of the
Captain's spiritual high drama makes room for tableaux more deferential
to historical texture. This obtaining, however, it would not be irrelevant
to query in this connection whether Whitman's theological historicism is
not, in the end, consonant with the aims of the Unitarian mainstream:
soft-pedaling Christ's Atonement and highlighting his teaching. Like the
Unitarians, and like Emerson himself, Whitman would indeed deflect attention from the Monstrous Christ for the sake of the congregation
Christ served. Moreover, like liberal ministers, preternaturally sensitive
to history, Whitman's eye is keenest in reporting what happens.

We might locate the difference between Whitman and these colleagues,
however, in what they are equipped to describe as happening. I have said

that the Unitarian Christology commits an inferential error when it scants the affective centrality of the human experiences to which orthodoxy's extravagant symbology corresponds. With its emphasis on a human possibility indexed to the Divine Benevolence, it ends up more repressive in certain ways than the Calvinism whose morbidities it shunned. The Unitarian optimism is especially hamstrung where human turpitude and historical catastrophe beg the questions of God's benevolent presence. Subtracting Hell, Unitarianism marginalizes sacrifice as aberrational; subtracting the Atonement, it sacrifices the lexicon that describes the soul wrung with suffering, the Crisis of Ends. In short, how can Unitarianism account for the ghastliness of the Civil War? To portray history in extremis, without resorting to the fetish of an apocalyptic language, thus falls to the poet. Whitman's struggle to find a theology that does not blaspheme before history accounts for the most striking and important lines in "When Lilacs Last in the Dooryard Bloom'd" – an elegy not for the one but for the many, or for the One as redeemed by the many. In these lines, the poet, not content to remember Lincoln as "great Martyr Chief," remembers him rather as part of that wave of Union, as part of a congregation of dead "inside the lines" together:

> (Nor for you, for one alone,
> Blossoms and branches green to coffins all I bring,
> For fresh as the morning, thus would I chant a song for
>   you O sane and sacred death.

> All over bouquets of roses,
> O death, I cover you over with roses and early lilies,
> But mostly and now the lilac that blooms the first,
> Copious I break, I break the sprigs from the bushes,
> With loaded arms I come, pouring for you,
> For you and the coffins of all of you O death.)

To appreciate the power of these lines we should not forget for a moment that they are written within the elegiac form. That form invented and perfected the agonized cry of the witness for the singular martyr ("For Lycidas is dead, dead ere his prime, / Young Lycidas! And hath not left his peer"). Whitman's elegy renounces the sacral object in the very form that serves that sacral object, renounces the one victim whose perfection "gives point to the full brutality of death." Without that victim, death – no longer encircled by convention, and by the closure that hones death's brutality – is not mad and profane, but "sane and sacred."

The key word in the above passage is, as has been long noticed, "all." Not to one coffin but, "to coffins all" the poet brings his floral tributes. This is an interesting inversion of the Miltonic strategy: The disparagement of pastoral solace we see in "Lycidas," where the floral gifts are put away for the paltry "little ease" they offer, is turned on its head. The speaker's flowers – perennial, belonging to a spring "ever recurring," belonging to the renewal and history of the "three hundred and sixty five" – are wholly sufficient. It is the singular object of vicarious suffering whose adequacy falls short. Our cathartic relation of distance from the representative Martyr, Hero or Christ figure, is thus supplanted by a different kind of relation, a Union that restores the One to the many rather than the many to the one.

> And I saw askant the armies,
> I saw as in noiseless dreams hundreds of battle-flags,
> Borne though the smoke of the battles and pierc'd with
>   missiles I saw them,
> And carried hither and yon through the smoke, and torn
>   and bloody,
> I saw battle corpses, myriads of them,
> And the white skeletons of young men, I saw them,
> I saw the debris and debris of all the slain soldiers of the
>   war,
> But I saw they were not as was thought,
> They themselves were fully at rest, they suffer'd not.

In these lines history attains to its full theological significance, without, however, losing any of its virtuality. Note how all the horror of history and the awful repetitiveness of death is suffered in the plaintive iteration of "debris and debris"; in the flags "pierced," "torn," and "bloody" which seem the very tissue of soldiers also pierced; and in the skeletons "piled up." No liberal optimism softens the poet's evocation of suffering here, but neither is his vision suffered to tip into typology. This is no Golgotha the speaker sees, but an American battlefield. There is no martyr chief to stanch the bloodiness of the scene in his completing sacrifice. Rather, through "myriads," he passes to his own rest. Released from the rigor mortis of the Passion, his death throes yield to rest among those whose sleep is blessed, for it is "not as was thought." The sword that rends and divides, however cruelly it pierces, is of this world; it does not penetrate the world of the spirit. There, not only visible saint, not only ritually pure, not only redeemed, but *all* pass into "rest." If the orthodox Christ and his elegiac doubles die, and so slay death, Whitman's death subsumes the Christ, burying his divisive sword in the scabbard it came from, the vaginal gate which admits all to Her rest. As in "The Sleepers," this death is a Mother, an eroticized female presence entering the poem with her many children to bless the union of life with death:

> Dark mother always gliding near with soft feet,
> Have none chanted for thee a chant of fullest welcome?
> Then I chant it for thee, I glorify thee above all,
> I bring thee a song that when thou must indeed come, come
>   unfalteringly
> Approach strong deliveress,
> When it is so, when thou hast taken them I joyously sing the
>   dead
> Lost in the loving floating ocean of thee
> Laved in the flood of thy bliss O Death.

"When Lilacs Last in the Dooryard Bloom'd" brings into full flower the vision of Union conceived in "The Sleepers." Only in that earlier poem does Whitman achieve the theological vantage point that could see life released to death, and singularity to indistinction. As "The Sleepers" ends

> I will duly pass the day O my mother and duly return to
>   you;
> Not you will yield forth the dawn again more surely than
>   you will yield forth me again;
> Not the womb yield the babe in its time more surely than
>   I shall be yielded from you in my time.

so, too, "When Lilacs Last" ends, not in the waking vigilance and agonized witness of "O Captain! My Captain!" – evangelical simulacrum of the static Passion – but in the "dusk and dim." In this redeemed nightworld Whitman's theology finds its grounding, death coming like "companions . . . as holding the hands of companions." Thus, the consciousness of sin that found life sane and sacred, sex and death impure and despoiling, is overthrown with the Christ who marked their disjuncture. So, too, is the Emersonian dualism remediated by a lyric regeneracy whose very Beginning is through the gate of its End, whose innovation is not originality but rather the relation Adam made articulate for the sake of Christ.

5

Beyond Circumference: Dickinson

"They shut me up in Prose" begins Emily Dickinson's poem #613, " . . . Because they liked me 'still' – ." For all her assurances in the lines following, that, had they seen her "Brain – go round – / They might as well have lodged a Bird / For Treason – in the Pound," neither popular nor critical accounts have taken adequate measure of just how much freedom Emily Dickinson thought she had, and what kind. Instead, myth and scholarship together have portrayed a Dickinson hemmed in on all sides: generally confined by an age that liked its poems – as its women – pale and prosaic; specifically constrained by a father whose claustrophobic Calvinism made him her model for God the Father.

Indeed, Dickinson's protestations notwithstanding, recent work has institutionalized what was hitherto folklore by assigning Dickinson her highest place of honor in the contemporary pantheon of incarcerated female poets. An exemplary case of the dungeoned but undaunted, Dickinson joins Bradstreet as American matriarch of a heterodox women's faith in themselves. Her famous difficulty thus serves to illustrate the problem of patriarchal language, and all her open gestures are ironic. Wise to the stultifying conventions of a male speech repressing through reason, Dickinson, the argument follows, finds in poetic indeterminacy and the dissolution of a stable semantics a female *lingua franca;* breathing space. Behind the most thoroughgoing feminist work on Dickinson of the last decade or so – Margaret Homan's *Women Writers and Poetic Identity,* Suzanne Juhasz's *Feminist Critics Read Emily Dickinson,* and the book that inaugurated the eighties, Gilbert and Gubar's massively influential *Madwoman in the Attic* – is the assumption that gender not only constructs the limitations of the woman poet, but that it also defines her responses to that limitation. All the countermoves made available to Dickinson seem to devolve on gender identification.[1]

Packing all the drama of a prison tale with its concomitant great escape, this formula is nevertheless wrong for a poet of Dickinson's range:

on the one hand, too deterministic; on the other – paradoxically – too Romantic. Or, to take in both poles of the paradox, too Emersonian. It is not often enough noted that Emerson's axiom of strength-as-resistance has been absorbed and deployed by a whole generation of feminist critics building on the Bloomian paradigms of Gilbert and Gubar. The notion that voice coheres in acts of opposition, that poetic language crystallizes its differentness under pressure of, in diacritical tension with, a normative cultural discourse is an Emersonian idea that Bloom made applicable to a wide canon of Romantic texts. Its essence: that the poem lights up from within the structure of a struggle with the father (a struggle naturally more fierce when the ephebe is a woman); or in its historicist, Foucauldian version, that it lights up from within hegemony's complexly faceted patterns.

In the wake of the postseventies internationalization of theory, credit for such ideas is frequently tendered to Foucault, who is understood to have updated and advanced a Nietszchean formulation of broad intellectual purchase as well as hardy heuristic efficacy. But we should not forget, and indeed Bloom is right to remind us, that the understanding of individual power as burnished rather than vanquished by resistant force is codified in America by Emerson. In Emerson the superimposition of possibility on determinacy, or freedom on fate, produces the heuristic category of *resistance,* or, in Bloom's terms, *agon.* This resistance that Emerson described, whether characterizing a thematics of disenchantment with the status quo (religious, social, or political), or more theoretically, a frictive use of language against the grain, enjoys enormous current prestige. As I have already argued, Emerson patriates the deconstructive turn; he rejuvenates that old gray organ, the American Mind.

And yet. Despite the tremendous appeal and potentially total power of a theory that describes language as diacritically chafed – unmaking, silencing, disassembling itself always – when we come to a poet like Dickinson, any oppositional stance must contend at the last with the poignant absence of an answering pressure. In Dickinson opposition is a luxury of our interpretive infirmity, and Romantic contention – whether female or poetic or both at the same time – a pastime risking idolatry. Truth is finally too recondite, too strange, to reveal itself pugilistically. Divinity manifests itself as surprise; it does not meet the eye nor the muscle nor the word. It does not stoop to resist.

The ultimate door against which Dickinson leans is the door of the Void, with the result that, at least in the largest context of her complete poems, subversion is more often an exercise than an end, or, as Ann Douglas once put it, a stunt: carried off with breathtaking aplomb, but deferring the ultimate risk. The flexing of voice, the fronting of social stricture, the tilt to subversion, the will learning its power – these are the ubiquitous gestures of the work-a-day Dickinson. Subversion is her daily round. Quite possibly for another poet, a poet unconvinced of any power beyond constructed earthly ones, subversion may equal out to self-making, and, linguistic invention to world-remaking. But for a poet who presses boundaries precisely to find that place where God marks his domain as the absence of the humanly intelligible – for such a one, resistance is ultimately to be shunned for being too prosaic. Resistance is quotidian and, therefore, often subject to cliché; it is characterological and, therefore, running before mood; it finds abundant occasions, but is, therefore, also frequently facile. Keenness and dynamite, voice and vision may serve well at the center, but as Dickinson puts it, "[her] business is circumference." There, the poet cultivates bluntness and abnegation, blind sight and dumb tongues; she practices, in essence, an emptying of the articulate self for the sake of discerning the Other who needs not a Word.

Thus, as compelling as madwoman in the attic theories are – and in context, as persuasive – their self-sufficiency and self-consistency insure as well their parochialism. In feminist scholarship this is manifest as an almost willful insulation from Dickinson's considerable sense of the liberty afforded her to pursue both satisfactions and disquietudes other than those offered by female community. Natural history surely provided one such satisfaction, as did, apparently, her systematic – almost taxonomic – study of the emotions. But preeminent was that afforded by an arduous and lifelong pursuit of a speech fitting to God, a pursuit supported by Dickinson's firm confidence in what Robert Alter calls elsewhere "the autonomy of the spiritual realm in historical experience" (Alter, Defenses, 80). To subordinate this realm to gender politics, or to antinomianism of any stripe, is to miss not only the ways in which Dickinson's work is saturated by the terms of a Christianity whose male triumphalism she only sometimes notes, but also the way in which she pursues a species of theological thinking characteristically extracultural, metaphysical, and, at its most practiced, virtually mystical. Too exclusive a focus on the gender issue is especially mistaken when it leads us to miss how Dickinson revives Taylor's interest in divine Unnameability, and so – as religious thinker – stands outside her transcendental times. Ushering back into American poetry the Puritan's concern for the warping of Revelation by blunt and corrupt human senses, Dickinson takes up anew a problem Emerson thought he'd solved. The problem is idolatry; the way she finds round it, humility.

As I showed in Chapter 2, Emerson, emboldened by the Unitarian celebration of man's "likeness to God," put little stock in humility. More to his liking was the spiritual alacrity of "boys sure of their dinner," or, among divines, the confidence enjoyed by those whose sermons claim

Christ for a living Muse. Emerson's work demonstrates how in oppression we may find the will's opportunity. Thus, that humility should find a place of privilege in Dickinson stands to discomfit critics of the whole range of agonistic loyalties. Valuing subversion more highly than contemplation and dissent more highly than rapture, the contemporary critic invested in Dickinson as saboteur may well be dismayed to find that Dickinson's stance is not always so reassuringly and unequivocally antinomian as in the much quoted, and early, poem 49, "I never lost as much but twice":

> I never lost as much but twice,
> And that was in the sod.
> Twice I have stood a beggar
> Before the door of God!
>
> Angels – twice descending
> Reimbursed my store –
> Burglar! Banker – Father!
> I am poor once more!

Such a poem has enjoyed much recent popularity. The poem suggests a speaker who, in the privacy of her own poem, has precious little love to spare for the cabal of male Elders who control access to grace; for her own father's pretensions to Divinity; or indeed, for God as the Father Himself. The covenant theology of Dickinson's New England is reduced in the poem to a fairly straightforward system of quids pro quo, with God a genteel, socially protected mogul who swindles the down-and-out of their due. Not only failing in Christian charity but also something of a lout, this figure is perfectly cast as chair, or captain, of that patriarchal industry which, dedicated to the beggary of women, takes cover in a Christianity by disseminating humility as a means of control. With such a God in the Christian boardroom, it is easy to reduce, say, "He fumbles at your soul" – a poem describing an experience of God Anne Hutchinson might have recognized – to a poem of God's molestation, or to read "The Bible is an antique volume" as Dickinson's final word on scriptural authority, and all the poet's moments of incoherence as object lessons in the impossibility of a patriarchal language for a woman poet. And, although it is undoubtedly true that Dickinson, like her contemporary Fanny Fern, is skilled at deploying a sharp-tongued and glancing irony against the idols of her culture, the poem above is not so much iconoclastic as pugnacious; its genre not so much analysis as agitprop. Dickinson's more considered excursions into theology refrain from playing God's politics quite this fast and loose.

As do the best feminist critics of Dickinson's work. These critics pass over such poems as #49 to notice rather how Dickinson's interrogation of the very structures of language – those "binaries" that support a division of the discourse into (male) signifier over (female) signified – can disrupt the Christian hierarchy of Adam superior. Following Irigaray, Margaret Homans' reading of another early poem, "The Daisy follows soft the sun," perspicaciously detects the perspectival trick that swells the humble "Daisy" to equal stature with the male sun by the poem's end.

> The Daisy follows soft the sun –
> And when his golden walk is done –
> Sits shyly at his feet –
> He – waking – finds the flower there –
> Wherefore – Marauder – art thou here?
> Because, Sir, love is sweet!
>
> We are the Flower – Thou the Sun!
> Forgive us, if as days decline –
> We nearer steal to Thee!
> Enamoured of the parting West –
> The peace – the flight – the Amethyst –
> Night's possibility!

Homans' deft argument is that even as Dickinson begins with a conventional binary structure – small domestic woman is to imposing, brilliant man as Daisy is to Sun – the inequality is revealed, by the end of the poem, to be merely a matter of perspective. The daisy's very name describes her covert contention with the sun: As "day's eye," his double, she is also his metaphoric vehicle, and so, as signifier, mastering term. To be sure, by the end of the poem, the sun, the day's eye, sunk behind the horizon is mere penumbra around the flower. As political allegory, the poem seems to counsel a female staying power that, if it waits out its day, will achieve parity with man. The sweep of vision the Daisy achieves is identified with a rapturous kind of transport, or "flight," outstripping the fixed, hard brilliance of the sun, and "Night's possibility" opens up to a wider experience, perhaps sexual, that the fixity of the sun cannot admit. The poem dramatizes how a little poetic resource goes far toward eclipsing that "He" who keeps the daisy at his feet (Juhasz 118–19).

What Homans' analysis neglects, however, is the way in which this poem allusively situates itself in an old tradition that takes the sun for the Son; its illumination for his Revelation outstripping natural light; his place in the heavens fixed not by convention, or perspective, but by God. One might recall in this context the ways in which Anne Bradstreet's encomiums to her husband as "Sun" forestall idolatry by ceding this identification to a larger concept of Sun and a more mysterious one. The poet's longing for "Sweet Sol" in the figure of Simon Bradstreet is by the end of the poem yielded for a love surpassing hierarchy, as all worship based on crude diagrams of the high and low is yielded up in Bradstreet's work. Christianity indubitably suggests the relationship of man to woman as model of that of God to man, but the metaphor, when not understood as provisional, is simply idolatrous. It is thus not Bradstreet's anti-Christian apostasy but rather her orthodoxy that can dispense with comparison of Simon to the sun as sun-worship.

Homans' restriction of the sun, by contrast, to a simple species of the male obscures possibilities the poem's allusive texture suggests, leaving itself open to an anthropocentrism, even idolatry, that the critic may not recognize but Dickinson surely would. In addition, by implying that the humility of Daisy is a pose, Homans must neglect how the very exaltation of the last lines ("Enamoured of the parting West," etc.) is prepared by the lines "Forgive us, if as days decline / We nearer steal to thee." Here the speaker's diffidence, far from pose, seems rather the normative gesture of a Christian humility, the "declining days" an eschatological reference. The line "We nearer steal to thee" matches beat by beat, and almost quite word by word, that line from the hymnal of great glory glimpsed: "Nearer my God to Thee." The humility that Daisy practices here may not so much degrade the speaker – or protect her by a feint – as *prepare* her for a vision, for a "possibility" more complex than the simple gorgeousness of "Amethyst." And the eclipse of the sun at the poem's end may well indicate not so much the victory of the emboldened Daisy, as the reticence of Revelation before an imagination so enpurpled with Romance. Just as the poet approaches face to face, the sun slips beyond the horizon. Just as Taylor's God shrank from his own "fair face," so here too sun/Son eludes the visionary straining to see what mortal eyes cannot.

Homans' reading exemplifies how even the most astute accounts of Dickinson's poetry can unduly limit her when they consider the binariness of gender her abiding problem. Perhaps the most persuasive measure of Dickinson's reach as a feminist is the way in which, in a poem like "The Daisy follows soft the Sun" gender typing is so clearly hypostatized, or cartoonishly crayoned round, that it outgrows itself. Writing against the grain of a theological culture increasingly rationalizing itself according to Victorian convention, Dickinson's theological lyrics find in a mystical contemplation of the Divine a point outside the genteel exercise of Christianity, a point on what I will go on to call "circumference." Like the bird of #613 who "has but to will / And easy as a Star / Abolish his Captivity," Dickinson is a charter member of Whitman's wandering company, seeking, as Whitman does, a complex engagement with the Holy liberated from all those inert predications – Burglar, Banker, Father – a God worthy of her faith must shed.

Why be surprised? Not only the poet whose breathy evocation of "wild nights" has had critics for the last one hundred years goose chasing the paramour of the "bride of quietness," Dickinson is also the girl who remained seated at Mount Holyoke when all the other girls "stood" to declare their desire to be Christians (Sewall, 360). Dickinson's "wayward" verse, in mentor Higginson's words, drove her as early as the 1850s to ally herself with the angel who "worsted God." A straying to the edges of the permissible is not only characteristic of Dickinson but so self-consciously conceived that it earns its own place in her unique poetic taxonomy: The space to which both God's questions and the Devil's answers lay claim is called "Circumference." Thus, in some 1862 correspondence with Mrs. Josiah Holland, Dickinson writes, "The Bible dealt with the centre, not with the circumference" (Sewall, 622). And in a famous letter of approximately the same period to Thomas Wentworth Higginson, she claims "My business is circumference" (Sewall, 566).

This is all the theoretical description we have of an antinomy that will structure numerous poems from what is acknowledged as Dickinson's most stressed but also most fertile period, the period of the late 1850s and early 1860s when her writing shows what Sewall calls "increasing frequency of mature" if sometimes "distraught religious gropings" (465). Either for their distraughtness or their maturity – I incline toward the maturity – Dickinson's poems of this period show what is often a nearly insuperable difficulty. This is a difficulty only exacerbated by the problem of accurately dating the poems from this or any period of Dickinson's career. Without such accuracy one cannot with any certainty trace a development from difficult to more transparent poems, or vice versa. Yet there is much to be gained by sorting the poems in order to detect, if not patterns of chronological development, then at least specific dynamics; to chart, if not a line, then an ellipse on which the poet's work on a given theme may be said to circulate. "Centre" and "circumference" form such an ellipse, and their relationship in the poems of Dickinson's most fertile period provides a key to understanding her religious thought.

Not to say that this relationship is an easy one. Albert Gelpi, in *Emily Dickinson: The Mind of the Poet,* fronted it over twenty-five years ago, arguing in two juxtaposed chapters that "centre" and "circumference" map Dickinson's pursuit of an ecstasy of sublime centering, with "Awe [uniting] within itself the extremes of consciousness" (Gelpi, 126). Though Gelpi is certain that Dickinson is a poet who, as he puts it, sees "New Englandly," she is also for him the poet who proves, as Perry Miller had argued, the Emersonianism latent in Edwards' cosmologies: Center encircles circumference in the seeing self. One of Dickinson's most acute critics of the 1980s, Sharon Cameron, has made the parallel case, informed by deconstructive theory, that Dickinson's poetry is dependent on "an absent or invisible order that is invoked as 'Immortality' or alluded to as Centre" (Cameron, 1). Citing the theologian Dietrich Bonhoeffer's insight that the tree of life was in the "midst of the garden" and thus that "Man's limit is in the middle of existence," Cameron argues that the "desire for knowledge is the desire for possession of one's own center") (195). And Denis Donoghue makes a similar point when, discussing Dickinson, he invokes Antonio Machado's assertion, "When the poet doubts that the centre of the universe is his own soul, his spirit . . . wanders in a world of objects" (Donoghue, 113).

Cameron, whose interest is, as she puts it, "unabashedly theoretical" (23), is learning here not only from Bonhoeffer but also, among others, from Derrida. His categories of Christian metaphysics enable her to discover in Dickinson's use of "centre" a logocentric desire for an original founding truth. Donoghue's less explicitly theoretical remark is nourished withal by similar suppositions: The project is, for Donoghue, that of a displaced religion, or in M. H. Abrams' classic term, a "natural supernaturalism." In this view, what Dickinson pursues is a transcendental order, a truth that would organize the "chaos" of perceptions; the "tree at the center of the garden" is now the pastoral retreat of the poet's own mind. Both Donoghue and Cameron take as axiomatic that Dickinson seeks a kind of timeless transcendental signified, achieved through a linguistic wrestling through and past phenomena. Or, to restate the issue in the terms of the American influences to which Dickinson, through Emerson, was subject, Dickinson's "centre" is an expression of the Kantian hypostatized ideal. This makes her a kind of Transcendentalist, which is another way of saying: an Emersonian.

I mean here to raise questions about this line of reading, specifically about Dickinson's pursuit of an elusive centre. Although it is true that for Dickinson the centre is lost, one questions whether Dickinson's poetics can be said to flow from a desire for any centre, logocentric, matrifocal, or what have you. So much of her greatest poetry happens on its innovations, its originality, when furthest from its own center. Dickinson's "soul," if you will, is, in such poetry, situated not at the center but, much more riskily, on the circumference. The poet's apprehension of what Emerson called an "original relation to the universe" (Whicher, 21) is attained in a region dangerously far from the conventional "origin," the tree of life in the garden. It is gained at more peril in a region not only outside the walls of the conventional paradise, and even outside the sanctum of the Romantic self, but outside the poet's own competence, the boundaries of her religious experience, and, the verse conventions that experience habitually employs. One senses from reading not only the letters to Mrs. Holland and Higginson but so many of Dickinson's poems that the center is not so much absent as renounced; the logos not so much inaccessible as inadmissible; that Dickinson would write if not beyond, then athwart the quest for absolute knowledge, yet would write thus without consigning herself to the nihilism of the Devils' realm.

In this evasive movement comes Dickinson's discovery of a third alternative to both Romanticism and nihilism. The alternative is that of a theologically answerable doubt. Constitutive element in the faith of such American precursors as Edwards and Taylor, this doubt's ablest theorist is Kierkegaard, whose vocabulary contains terms for the mediate states of anticipation and dread, longing and uncertainty, that are Dickinson's staple fare.

Kierkegaard therefore occupies considerable space in the following pages. He is perhaps the unique case of a religious thinker whose answer to a dogmatic Christianity is a lyrical Christianity. Kierkegaard deems language not only the fitting locus for a theological speculation, but the medium best expressing the problematics of a faith that the reductions of reason and philosophical system defraud. Liberated from System, Kierkegaard's Christian is substantially alone, discharged to imagine God's limitlessness of his own. Understanding language as the medium in which spiritual crisis registers, and the agonistic interval as emitting knowledge of our absurd dependence rather than our incipient power, Kierkegaard has no true American coeval, as, say, Nietzsche has Emerson. What he has, instead, are guarantors of his lyrical theology in Dickinson and Crane, and perhaps in Frost and Lowell as well. Hence, on the one hand, his work adumbrates the Christianity of queasy precariousness that Taylor and Jonathan Edwards knew: a Christianity that reattaches to Emerson's self-reliance its due quotient of solitary terror. His work gives us tools to grasp the way that Dickinson's thought (and later Crane's) repels the transcendental alternative at the peril of losing, first center, then identity, and finally all coherence whatever.

On the other hand, and additionally, Kierkegaard's writing – with its distinctive and self-conscious preference for lyrical over logical or theoretical argument – functions in my overall argument to mediate and suggest the close affinities of theology to poetry. In the work of the poets, as Kierkegaard knew, is revealed the essential lyricism of faith itself; the poems of Dickinson and Crane demonstrate how essentially hospitable is the lyric poem to theological speculation. Recall that in earlier chapters I posited a fundamental antagonism between the determination of the poem and theories founded on resistance to Ends. In this chapter and the one following I will discuss the obverse phenomenon: the clarification and even realization of theological meaning held in a lyric suspension. Poems can imagine, in Kierkegaard's terms, not only the aesthetic contours of faith, but its internal timbre. They can do more than know Abraham's faith. They can know what it is to be Abraham. Poems can give form to a species of faith inexpressible in discursive philosophy.

Characteristically, such faith is quite simply no longer able to conceive God sanguinely, as essentially "centered," or, in terms that Emerson borrows, in "Circles," from Augustine: "God is a circle whose center was everywhere and its circumference nowhere" (Whicher, 168). In Emerson, Augustine's awed but signally disoriented faith before the Divine immensity is transformed into a trope of adequacy, even of compensation. A different, older kind of Augustinian, Dickinson is cognizant that, "if man is to receive any true knowledge about the Unknown [God] he must be made to know that it is unlike him, absolutely unlike him" (Kierkegaard, *Fragments*, 36). Dickinson intuits this in one of the first poems of her theological maturity. Scorning the human center as a weather vane that changes with every wind, Dickinson's poem #501 sets a theology confident that God's center guarantees ours against a theology enjoying no such guarantees:

> This World is not Conclusion.
> A Species stands Beyond –
> Invisible, as Music –
> But positive, as Sound –
> It beckons, and it baffles –
> Philosophy – don't know –
> And through a Riddle, at the Last –
> Sagacity, must go.

The progress of Dickinson's images is toward a kind of whiteout of all those human compassings by which the Unknown is organized for the sake of human apprehension. Thus, music's stabilization in the black and white of notation, and even its suspension in the ear or the air for the interval of the playing, is destabilized by "invisible" while its existence is assured in "positive." That the world to which she points exists is affirmed more rather than less true by its ineffability. The synesthetic baffling of the aural in "invisible" suggests the way music belongs not to eye or ear or heart or mind but to some realm in between all these: ultimately "positive" as sound, it outwits the detection of any one sensor. With the substitution of "positive" for "invisible," the poet educates us to an insensate knowledge, habituates us to belief in a substratum athwart the senses. The Being whose center is everywhere and His circumference nowhere partakes of this same paradoxically weightless ubiquity. Without discernible contour, He nevertheless exists, the proof of His existence strengthened rather than weakened by that indiscernibility.

Accordingly, the quality of mentation that faith exacts falls outside the realm of simple concentration. Just as music's power mysteriously issues from regions notation cannot encompass, so too does understanding. The poet consigns Reason – Lockean, Unitarian, or any kind enjoyed by "scholars" – to a lesser place in the order of things than the riddle. The riddle, a form of both humor and the deepest gravity, is mediately positioned between mystery and cogitation, engaging both but cracked by neither. The stricture of "riddle," through which "sagacity must go," recalls the eye of the needle through which camels are hard put to pass, and also the "straight gate" of Paul's admonitions. Dickinson's appeals to illogic resonate here with the inversions of the Beatitudes, and with that particularly Calvinist inheritance: the redemption promised only to the One who will sacrifice all. For Dickinson, as for Kierkegaard, the very nature of religious experience requires that we yield up our sense of God as centered in our world, yield up the knit of "Reason" that makes God's order explicable through Revelation. Replacing the "centre," then, is the "unknown," a limit distinctly outside the boundaries of what we can grasp. As Kierkegaard describes this limit:

> The paradoxical passion of the Reason thus comes repeatedly into collision with the unknown, which does indeed exist, but is unknown, and insofar does not exist. The Reason cannot advance beyond this point, and yet it cannot refrain in its paradoxicalness from arriving at this limit and occupying itself therewith. . . . But what then is the unknown. . . . To say that it is the unknown because it cannot be known, it could not be expressed, does not satisfy the demands of passion, though it correctly interprets the unknown as a limit; but a limit is precisely a torment for the passion, though it also serves as an incitement. (*Fragments*, 35)

Kierkegaard here displaces God from the center of the world, severing the identity between human reason and God, the identity on which Emerson's transcendental confidence and all Romanticism depends. Rather than sharing with man a center, God encounters man on a "limit" which is of a character necessarily veiled or unknown and which does not submit to human knowledge, human organization. "For how could the Reason be able to understand that which is absolutely different from itself?" (37) Kierkegaard goes on to query. As it was Edwards', this is Dickinson's precise question. On this very "limit," a limit traced round in Dickinson's poetics by circumference, she comes to situate her encounter with God. Indeed, the desire for center dead-ends in Dickinson's work as she comes to see first the center and then the circumference *that centers* as forms that successively substitute the certainty of doctrine for the hard questions God asks, and then the blasphemy of the Devil's "nots" for doubt. If center substitutes poetic hubris, static self-reliance, and finally, idolatry for these hard questions, circumference can ally the poet with Satan himself. Thus circumference and center are successively displaced in Dickinson's work by a "limit" beyond circumference, a limit represented in spatial metaphors of disorientation. Apprehension of this limit generates some of Dickinson's most original yet least described poetic language, language that seeks God through evisceration of centered systems of reference. According to this understanding, Dickinson is less an Emersonian idealist – an American Kantian or Romantic – seeking center through pursuit of her poetic persona, than she is the most confirmed kind of Protestant, everywhere apprehending her own "limit," finding in each Emersonian circle of adequacy but another center to be dissolved.

Written from a sense of human limitation that does not hope to see God face to face, Dickinson's poems turn their gaze on that area marginalized by Emerson as "Fate" and by Kant before him as the "phenomenal." In Kierkegaard's terms, what Dickinson pursues is a "faith" subject to all the hard exigencies of existence, subject to all those conditions of ignorance and painful doubt under which religious life is lived. Subject in particular to an ontology that is God's and so inscrutable, and to an epistemology that is human and so unreliable, Dickinson strays further and further from center, from Reason and thus from the stylistic unity that preserves our sense of center. Her sojourns on the limit traced by circumference yield poems that chronicle in "feet" increasingly hobbled and "blind" the wanderings of the poet as disoriented theologian who affirms God's knowledge through her own lack thereof. All the Paradise gained, all the center, all the Eternity, is gained in the "merciful mirage" of doubt by a poet who, indeed, "wanders bewildered among the world of objects."

But this is perhaps to anticipate. For Dickinson is as capable as the most giddy of transcendentalists of writing poems of heady optimism, poems of a renewed and purified Christianity. This we see in a famous poem that does double duty as both religious and poetic manifesto. Written around 1862, "I dwell in possibility" promises all in one leap the simultaneous ventilation of both poetry and religion. The poem, conceived as a kind of Temple, admits on all sides a "possibility" suffused with the psalmist's confidence and grace:

> I dwell in Possibility –
> A fairer House than Prose –
> More numerous of Windows –
> Superior – for Doors –
>
> Of Chambers as the Cedars –
> Impregnable of Eye –
> And for an Everlasting Roof
> The Gambrels of the Sky –
>
> Of Visitors – the fairest –
> For Occupation – This –
> The spreading wide my narrow Hands
> To gather Paradise –   (657)

If it is difficult here to tell whether a religious poem borrows a poet's self-reflexive metaphors or the reverse, that is because Dickinson is a poet, who, to paraphrase Frost, makes a vocation of her "occupation."[2] In this poem priest and poet share one bill. The poetry is not subordinate to God's purpose as it was, say, with Taylor, whose poems "jarred and jagged" beside the sublimity of a Creation human art could only travesty.[3] Rather, Dickinson boldly asserts by superimposition the equality of the "vocation" and "occupation": one, the poetry that betters prose, the other, the "gathering in" of paradise. The ambition of the enterprise should not be lost in the breeziness of the poem. In these lines Dickinson lays out not only the promise of poetic innovation that her work will fulfill, a wrenching of the poem away from the prose dictions that afford available paraphrase, but also the promise of an alternative, more commodious theology than that to which American poetry is used. "Possibility" implies both a poetic and a theological movement. By spreading "wide her narrow hands" the poet will gather in a redemption neither guaranteed nor made particularly available by her forebears' faith, a redemption whose paradoxes will deepen and compound.

Not surprisingly, though, Dickinson, like her compatriots Emerson and Whitman, would at first seize this redemption by dispensing with all the "rags and relics" of the past. The task is that of housecleaning: To erect the new requires bringing down the old; to build her "Cedar" roof the poet must tear down God's sturdy house.[4] Far from embarking on a pilgrimage of taxing spiritual inquiry – or paradox – the poet chooses in numerous poems simply, stalwartly, to plant her two rebellious feet. Predicting in such poems the bald God-baiting of Stevens' "Sunday Morning," Dickinson's speakers, with little vacillation and in no uncertain terms, take up the gauntlet against God and for man. The poet thus glories is an early poem (#59) to recount how "A little east of Eden" the "bewildered gymnast" Jacob "worsted God." In these early poems, the limber speaker is often as not a Jacoblike combatant of a God from whom, in what Harold Bloom might call an agonistic encounter, she wrests her very identity:

> I had some things that I called mine –
> And God, that he called his,
> Till, recently a rival Claim
> Disturbed these amities.   (116)[5]

In many of the late poems the poet's rancor has deepened; God is derided in the poem on the sacrifice of Isaac (1317) as a petty tyrant who "Flattered by Obeisance . . . demurred." Dickinson's summary indictment of the whole Bible and her defiant championing of the pagan alternative in Orpheus – figure of the Stevensian Noble Rider – is well known:

The Bible is an antique Volume –
Written by faded Men
At the suggestion of Holy Spectres –
Subjects – Bethlehem –
Eden –the ancient Homestead –
Satan – The Brigadier –
Judas – the Great Defaulter –
David – the Troubadour –
Sin – a distinguished Precipice
Others must resist –
Boys that "believe" are very lonesome –
Other boys are "lost" –
Had but the Tale a warbling Teller –
All the Boys would come –
Orpheus' sermon captivated –
It did not condemn –   (1545)

This hard boil of the Bible, its authority defamed in "Holy Spectres,"
its characters shrunk to captions or tics, offers some clue to what Dickinson means when she writes that the Bible is all "centre." One can't
help feeling, however, that the poet has an easy time of it here. The tactic is reductive, prosaic. What she sets up in such cut-out, flimsy personae as "Satan – the Brigadier" and "David – the Troubadour" are straw
men too readily knocked flat. And having knocked them flat, the poet is
free to suggest her own alternative, a theological life at sea, beyond the
charge of "faded men." There she may enjoy the glorious independence
of "circumference."

She staked her Feathers – Gained an Arc
Debated – Rose again –
This time – beyond the estimate
Of Envy, or of Men –

And now, among Circumference –
Her steady Boat be seen
At home – among the Billows – As
The Bough where she was born –   (798)

Here at last Dickinson arrives at the positive, offering "circumference"
to replace the narrower Biblical "centre," that tree of life guarded by the
"envy of Men." The poet who "Rose again" is on something of a saving
mission; the posture is Christlike; a new self-reliant redemption is at
hand, and yet there is still something wrong. The little bird at home protests a bit coyly, domesticates a bit much. One wonders what purpose
circumference serves if it is reduced with such facility to a sparrow's
feathered nest? And even as this poem would tend to decimate critical

claims that circumference is simply the anteroom, or negative state, of "centre," the tone here is so markedly off that one scarcely wants to claim the poem.[6] Dickinson's maverick pose is too crude, the circumference she champions now the soapbox of a false bravado, the platform for a poet who spreads wide her narrow hands to narrow the world. The problem, in short, is one of bad faith.

Look, for example, at Dickinson's choice of pronoun. The poet whose preferred pronoun is always "I" has here displaced herself in a "she." There is much precedent for this in Dickinson's work, and the precedent helps us read the poem better. The tactic is the same as that of "She dealt her pretty words like Blades" (479), a poem about the destructive power of words whose pronoun absolves the poet of responsibility for lacerating language. It is also that deployed by "My life had stood – a Loaded Gun" (754), a poem of such explosive threat that the poet, initially self-identified as "I," must finally distribute her gunpowder among a small cast of allegorical characters who act out her explosive drama at a safe remove. Dickinson writes her famous "Master" letters, letters of extraordinary vulnerability and passion, over the signature "Daisy"; her most unfeminine experiments in aggression under the signature of "boy." Here ("She staked her Feathers") she experiments with a displaced persona who would live beyond the religious pale, absolutely beyond the censure of "men." The persona is one for whom she bears limited responsibility, a disembodied "debater" taking potshots from an all too cozy stable "Bough."

Notice, too, that not only the debater but even her opponents are in camouflage, concealed in a nursery rhyme.[7] Thus, the "feathers . . . staked" barely conceal the "Fathers" risked by a poet who has perhaps lost the heaven of her forebears for the cold comforts of a "circumference" she too heartily claims to find commodious. The "Arc" of this circumference barely covers the "ark" of an autonomous Noah or of a covenant the poet irreverently steers to sea. And the "bough" the feathered speaker cites is a double entendre: It is the destination of a free bird, a diminutive Christ, whose autonomous "Rise" sheds the Fall of these "fathers"; and it is a deformation of that older "bowing" obeisance – humble, obsequious – the poet scorns. Dickinson is here toying with, nearly flouting, a whole system of religious etiquette, and yet if the tone is too blithe, we should note that the possible consequences of an embrace of "circumference" are quite grave. The risk buffered by the puns and double entendres is the risk of an exposure, an exile against which the speaker quite understandably defends.

For the transfer of security from the center to the circumference is one shadowed by other doomed displacements. The poem's tone is vulnerable to charges of a stunning narcissism; the construction of an alternative ark or Law erected in opposition to the established Ark or Law is a perilous undertaking. To bring down the Temple, to hew the cedars of one's own Temple, to posit alternative paradisal space to that designated by God is dangerous, Devilish work. It is work anticipated by Milton's fallen archangel whose own experience with challenging his Father brought him to survey from a kind of "circumference," from "the utmost Orb / Of this frail world" the paradise he violates, corrupts. For a poet to construct an alternative heaven is, on the other hand, to imitate the idolatries of Mammon who counsels Milton's fallen angels to seek "our own good from ourselves" and so build safe in the knowledge, "Nor want we skill or art, from whence to raise magnificence."

"Nor wants" this poet "skill or art." Yet to so employ her art is to take up positions already articulated by Christian culture, positions of false Messiah or counterfeit Christ; heretic, idol worshipper, Devil. Dickinson's challenge, like Whitman's before her, will be to accomplish something new without sinning in the old ways; her task will be to sin, originally, or by implication, to find regeneration's lyric spring. This will require the kind of hard theological scrutiny the fey synthesizer of "I dwell in possibility" did not perhaps bargain on, a kind of self-scrutiny Dickinson learns only by writing poems like "I staked my feathers." This scrutiny leads her to question and then systematically cancel her own premises, premise by premise, verity by verity, center by center, and finally circumference by circumference until she has reached what we might call the negative way of "possibility," a possibility refigured as doubt, attained not by hope or belief but by hard wandering. The Emersonian thrust of self-reliance will give way to a surrender to Edwardsean instability. The combative homiletic of "I staked" will be replaced by what Kierkegaard called a teleological suspension, a kind of negation that rejects universal, transcendental categories – so narrowly skirting the Devil's denials – to pursue its "Fairer house than prose." In the process, all lineaments of the conventional House – the struts of a prosaic theology, the strictures of an orthodox poetry – are whited out, and the Temple, the Poetry, the Paradise are reached by a poet who has wandered and wandered blind.

The suspension is dramatized in a key poem that questions the movement toward easy certainties, the overhasty constitution of fraudulent oppositional centers – self-reliance itself. In this poem Dickinson casts an ironic eye on the "columnar," or situated, self:[8]

> On a Columnar self –
> How ample to rely
> In Tumult – or Extremity –
> How good the Certainty

That Lever cannot pry –
And Wedge cannot divide
Conviction – that Granitic Base –
Though None be on our Side –

Suffice Us – for a Crowd –
Ourself – and Rectitude –
And that Assembly – not far off
From furthest Spirit – God –   (789)

The ambiguity of these lines has to do with the status of the maverick
figure who would face public opinion, secure in her own "granitic" convictions. The revelation the poem comes to is that the maverick may well
escape the tumult of bad opinion only in the grave, only when among
"that Assembly not – far off / From furthest spirit – God." Thus, these
are double lines, lines that both claim and shrink from the privileges of
the columnar self in an extremely complicated way: now claiming them
as a stay against the pressures of an unsympathetic society; now ironizing
them in words like "granitic," suggesting just how much the rigidity of
opposition resembles the rigidity of doctrine; now finally recoiling from
the realm whose boundaries the poet is loathe to cross. Dickinson is
wedged in this poem between the idols of the marketplace and the very
tomb. And if there is a touch of melodrama, of a grave haunting, that
reminds us of Poe and the literary necrophilia that pervades nineteenth-
century sentimental literature, there is as well a first apprehension of that
transgressive space of death it is the fate of circumference's champion to
invade.[9] There is a deepening of the Christ posture, a deepening akin to
Whitman's experiments with Christology which take him down to the
land of the dead at the peril of his self-coherence, as Christ goes down at
the peril of his.[10] The poet who used her diminutive voice in "I staked
my feathers" to "rise again" encounters here the descent that inverts the
rise, the sacrifice that blunts the hubris of the One set apart.

Yet Christ is not the only precursor here. The precedents are so traditional that, again, Milton's Satan writes the code of the "columnar"
principle: "The mind is its own place, and in itself / Can make a Heaven
of Hell, a Hell of Heaven." The backbone of the columnar self is imitation, the doubling of what is spurned, and to this very doubling, Dickinson, imitating Christ, has fallen prey. Another perhaps even closer
precursor than Milton's Satan is the Faust whom Kierkegaard describes
precisely as imitator of Christ in *The Concept of Dread*. Not incidentally,
it is this very Faust whom Hart Crane, after Dickinson, will rehabilitate
as a figure of human limitation, as he will offer a portrait of Poe as unregenerate Faust. Faust's precise sin, for Kierkegaard, is his renunciation
of limitation, the fact that he is not willing to "attire himself in himself"
(*Fear and Trembling*, 209). The test Faust fails is doing without the dis-

placements of a "columnar stance" or pronoun, without the security of a self-description, or justification, however antinomian: "Faith is this paradox; and the individual absolutely cannot make himself intelligible to anybody" (Kierkegaard, *Fear*, 81).

This Kierkegaardian paradox of the individual increasingly preoccupies Dickinson. The shrugging off of human limitation in the region of the dead, Faust's gambit – and Poe's – is an outré but not original gesture. Calvinism precedes the poet here: The Paradise beyond the grave is not only already crisscrossed with theological definitions, but with definitions supplied by the orthodoxy the poet would escape. Dickinson is caught in a profound religious fix – to oppose Puritan forms is yet to enter the Christian arena. Antinomies, the structure of Puritan discourse, belong to "the assembly"; thus by speaking in antinomies the poet enters, and enters with her script already written, the universal religious figure it seems her explicit aim to subvert. Escaping the antinomies she only flees into a Christian death already envisioned by orthodox convention. In that convention's terms, she is lost, strayed, a sinner. Between death, the community, and God, the poet struggles.

The search for "circumference," or a theological position with whose aid the poet might encircle, or compass between "her narrow hands – Paradise," must cut itself off without pose, imitation, without the comforts of Emersonian authorization. The quest is becoming distinctly oxymoronic, for the poet who would spread "wide her narrow hands" to apprehend God must search for the "limit" – which is God – by finding first her own limit, knowing both limits, insofar as they are genuine, to be "unknown," unrecognizable. What she seeks first is a simultaneous frustration of the "supernatural" pilgrim and his "natural" equivalent, the Romantic seeker. And yet if she would shrug off the persona or questing agent, she would preserve the quest itself. What must be dissolved is the framing consciousness that interposes its own doubled, and hence Devilish, image between its desire and that which it seeks. Flight from this heresy, from an agonistic or finally Emersonian selfhood, will advance Dickinson's progress toward God. The poet's struggle with this selfhood, her struggle to advance beyond it, brings her to a most paradoxical encounter, an encounter which even as it doubts the Self must by means of that Self go on. In Kierkegaard the paradox is expressed thus:

> The Reason cannot negate itself absolutely, but uses itself for the purpose, and thus conceives only such unlikeness within itself as it can conceive by means of itself; it cannot absolutely transcend itself, and hence conceive only such superiority over itself as it can conceive by means of itself. (Kierkegaard, *Fragments*, 35)

Dickinson's genius is to spatialize this paradox: A language of disorientation figures the search for a desubstantialized self; the language of wandering replaces the earlier language of a braggadocio "circumference," ossified in iconoclastic pose or tableau.

> Escaping backward to perceive
> The Sea upon our place –
> Escaping forward, to confront
> His glittering Embrace –
>
> Retreating up, a Billow's height
> Retreating blinded down
> Our undermining feet to meet
> Instructs to the Divine.   (867)

Along with both the assertive "I" of maverick opposition and the "she" of coy displacement, the poet here gives up the image of the sea as a region of stabilizing circumference. She who had Emersonian confidence in her own powers of possibility, in her journeying spiritual feet as in her poetic feet, is now full of doubt. The feet are now "undermining." The sea as metaphor for that region of circumference has been stripped of its encircling buoyancy. The Whitmanesque surrogate savior who "rose" to walk on the water of her own self-presentation has here yielded to the persona of the poet as escapee moving in a vertigo of "forward and backward," paradoxically rising and falling. The poet is no longer centering her "circumference," hardening in "granitic" certainties the conditions of her exile. No longer confined by, or borrowing the privileges of, self-reliance, she has, in Kierkegaard's terms, "let go":

> As long as I keep my hold on the proof, i.e. continue to demonstrate, the existence does not come out, if for no other reason than that I am engaged in proving it. . . . But this act of letting go is surely again something; it is indeed a contribution of mine . . . this little moment, brief as it may be – it need not be long, for it is a *leap*. (Kierkegaard, *Fragments*, 33)

In the poem above, hearkening to "Instructs to the Divine," Dickinson has let her grip go. But if the gesture of renunciation has its solaces – and we hear them in the measured closure of the last line – it also holds its terrors. Thus, #414, " 'Twas Like a Maelstrom, with a Notch," anatomizes the affective state of letting go, offering an Edwardsean demonstration of how the leap of faith is experienced, how it *feels* to the religious subject. It feels like a graphically literal reprise of the Fall. Given metaphor by that interval before sleep when consciousness trips and the waking self grapples for foothold, dread is that state felt by a religious subject who, hazarding the Unknown, cannot know with any certainty just what " 'twas."

'Twas like a Maelstrom, with a notch,
That nearer, every Day,
Kept narrowing its boiling Wheel
Until the Agony

Toyed Coolly with the final inch
Of your delirious hem –
And you dropt, lost,
When something broke –
And let you from a Dream –

The "narrowing" wheel of the maelstrom terrifies most precisely because there is no way of telling where its center is in relation to the circumference's "hem"; no way of seeing just where the self meets the
world except by inferring their imminent collision throughout the portent of anticipatory dread. Here is Emerson's God of compensatory circles returned to His true Augustinian orbit. His motion is not matched to
ours: only the dizzy see. In the uncanny unpredictability of the experience is its best religious affirmation. By the end of the poem, where the
speaker does not know "Which anguish was the utterest – then – / To
Perish, or to Live" we know the choice to be but structural support.
What is key is rather the anxious self, circling the constructs that choice
forces. The choice, the either/or, is, as in Edwards' sermons, only the
point of departure for a harrowing simulation through sensate metaphors
of our true spiritual instability. For the religious subject, the telos of
death is efficient catalyst for an experience. Death or life are only words
until the choices, and the chasm between them, are fully felt as a drop in
the stomach. What we learn from a poem like #414 is the salutary spiritual benefit dread can yield, "sagacity's" purgative evacuation for the
sake of a riddle experientially apprehended. Spiritual authenticity depends not on certitude but on strandedness.

Similarly, in another poem loosening its grip on center, we hear the
same queasy accents admixed of accomplishment and terror. Circumference is no safe harbor. In contemporary argot it is a place of black holes,
of nothingness virtualized and yawning. Thus #378 ventures far out
where music yields to sound and sound to mere slippery contour. Metaphors of sight and sound lack the elasticity, the simple relevance, to
cover what the poet finds.

I saw no Way – The Heavens were stitched –
I felt the Columns close –
The Earth reversed her Hemispheres –
I touched the Universe –

And back it slid – and I alone –
A Speck upon a Ball –
Went out upon Circumference –
Beyond the Dip of Bell –

Sharon Cameron, allowing that the language of this poem is "giddy with
disorientation . . . haunted by the terrible space of the venture," yet insists that #378 is "flung out into the reaches of the unknown in the apparent hope that it might civilize what it finds there" (*Lyric Time*, 9).
Cameron has the poet colonizing circumference with center, the "supernatural" with the "natural," imprinting the Emersonian "not-me" with
the "me." Clearly this is a pivotal poem for the "me" and the "not-me,"
the poetic self and the unknown, but one may observe here the converse
of Cameron's imperialism of center. The "civilization" of center is recalled only in nostalgia; the vision to which the poem attains is far beyond that Romanticism which saves by templating itself.

This is, we might note, the kind of poem that defies its period; it is
hardly a nineteenth-century poem at all. Its nearly surreal quality makes
us want to call it modern, or existential, but the isolation its images render is the Calvinist's normative state. To set #378 in its century is to see
the impulse to a Kantian idealism, a ranking of the noumenal reaches –
what Crane will later call a "threshing of the heights" – troubled,
checked, by a certain older anxiety, even dread.[11] The image "Dip of
Bell" is one that seems simultaneously celebrating its arrival at a kind of
religious outpost, a place where bells herald an arrival, and, making that
outpost metaphor for its distance from religious security. It is this double, reflexive movement, one we should recognize as essentially pious,
that delivers Dickinson into the only "originality" she will find, that invented by Adam.

The poem cannot escape a certain dread. Perched out so far from the
earth, she who feels the "columns close" is all too conscious of the sin of
knowledge that drove her from center in the first place. In Kierkegaard's
uncannily apt terms, "Dread is the dizziness of freedom which occurs when the spirit would posit the synthesis, and freedom then gazes
down into its own possibility, grasping at finiteness to sustain itself"
(*Dread*, 55). This state in which, as Kierkegaard puts it, "freedom
swoons," characteristically tempers heightened knowledge with a sense
of sin or transgression; in its very freedom, its very sense of "possibility,"
it is a recapitulation of the Fall. And to compound this discomfort, the
poet as dreading subject is not only ever more conscious of her ambiguous relationship to God, but she is also acutely aware that her distance
strands her, shrinks her to "A Speck," isolates her from human commerce. The comforts of that commerce, denied in the poem where "circumference" was a "steady boat," are not denied here. The rarefied
knowledge the leap yields is made ever the more poignant by the distance
from "home" it enforces. The discomfiture suffered by the self who arrives at "circumference" derives not only from the intensified confrontation with sin, but also from the loneliness in which this confrontation
is endured.

Perhaps it is such discomfort that suggests Dickinson's exploration of an alternative to the Jacob model, her identification with a Biblical model whose position on the circumference measures his fallenness before God, but also his isolation from the "Assembly" or "tribe." This new model reflects on the poet's own perplexed and triangulated stance between God and the community. Thus, in the figure of Moses exiled from Canaan, a figure virtually beyond the "Dip of Bell," Dickinson finds, intersecting, the pull of center, and the counterattraction of circumference. Center, depicted in this poem as Moses' Promised Land – object of his wanderings and justification of his antagonistic relationship to the community – is that cherished entity the poet commiserates with Moses for losing. Thus the poem begins:

> It always felt to me – a wrong
> To that Old Moses – done
> To let him see – the Canaan –
> Without the entering –

and ends thus:

> Upon the Broad Possession
> 'Twas little – But titled Him – to see –
> Old Man on Nebo! Late as this –
> My justice bleeds – for Thee!   (597)

Initially we might recognize in these lines Dickinson's old "columnar self" back at baiting God, griping against a Deity whose treatment of Moses is arbitrary and unfair. Indeed other lines in the poem suggest this. The poet as wrestler – or better, debater – makes her points with punctilious skill:

> In point of injury –
>
> Surpasses sharper stated –
> Of Stephen – or of Paul –
> For these – were only put to death –
> While God's adroiter will
>
> On Moses – seemed to fasten
> With tantalizing Play
> As Boy – should deal with lesser Boy –
> To prove ability.

The indictment seems clear: Dickinson's sympathies are with Moses and against God. The next lines seem to wrap up her case. There, she transfers the blame Moses suffered back onto the real culprits, the tribes, confiding that if the judgment had been hers, it would have been Israel excluded rather than Moses, grand in his "Penteteuchal Robes."

The fault – was doubtless Israel's –
Myself – had banned the Tribes –
And ushered Grand Old Moses
In Pentateuchal Robes.

And yet something jars in this reinstatement of Moses, robes and all. There is something nearly meretricious about "Grand Old Moses" in his regalia, something too easy about the facility with which the poet not only bars entry to the immigrant Israelites but also, to read the line another way, bans them from consideration, instead lavishing attention on a "representative man." The ambiguity of the lines suggests a new element in Dickinson's typology of circumference. What the poet intuits is a fresh threat to the integrity of faith. This threat is the lure of spiritual heroism, the creation of what Kierkegaard might call the "tragic hero," a figure whose symbolic conductivity allows the sinner vicarious redemption from her own sins, the less glamorous sins of the faithless Israel. Again the temptation to the speaker is that of displacement, the temptation not to "attire oneself in oneself." And again, Kierkegaard explains: "The true knight of faith is always in absolute isolation, the false knight is sectarian. This sectarianism is an attempt to leap away from the narrow path of the paradox and become a tragic hero at a cheap price" (*Fear*, 89). What Dickinson guards against in this poem is the temptation to fill the void felt by the loss of self with a hagiography – a cheap celebrity or Christ cult – that would at once columnize the hero and pardon the assembly for whose foibles he suffers. Circumspectly, and with a shrewd cancellation of her own premises, she ironizes Moses himself by calling attention to the "Pentateuchal Robes," forcing herself to see through the costumery of pathos, or tragedy, that would distort her own interpretation of Moses' exclusion, a mechanism providing easier solace than contemplation of the anonymous tribes. Dickinson will not suffer the Emersonian rehabilitation of anguished exile to representative man.

We will shortly see Dickinson's integration of herself among these tribes as anonymous wanderer, but here let us simply note how a kind of acidic doubt eats away at the impulse to "identify" with a hero, to displace or concentrate religious sentiment in an icon. This is the Jacob poem subjected to new tests, to a consciousness that refuses both the Devil's perambulation and adulation of a man dressed in Christological robes. What is severed at the roots here, in effect, is the whole Lycidas tradition Whitman dismantled. But if what Whitman targeted was the duplicitous cure of catharsis, Dickinson takes aim, on the other hand, at the Romanticization of the spurned hero. Not only Christ as buoyant hero "risen" at the center, but also Christ in the type of tempted Moses, driven to the circumference without succor – is refused.

The progress of such refusals is relentless. Dickinson's resolve has an almost muscular aspect, her theological program flexed and lean, martial and unsparing. Eschewing the hardened "granitic," or objectified "centre" as idolatrous, the martyrology or Faustian imitations of "circumference" as similar travesties, she becomes the very definition of a Christian soldier. To plumb what Dickinson would plumb will require simultaneous sacrifice not only of center but also of the circumference that centers.

So commences the final phase of Dickinson's search for an objectless spiritual state, a Paradise with no center, with no "gems."[12] Her rigor, both theological and poetic, is unstinting. The aesthetic of the ascetic, an aesthetic that renounces Moses' persona while preserving his plight, renouncing the hero's magnetic agony while preserving his hard quest, will rely on revelation of a new kind. This revelation will permit the visionary apprehension, if not, as we shall see, sight, beyond a circumference that would fix, limit, or "centre" itself in its own however commodious forms. To invent circumference is to have comprehended it, finished it, and so to rest in it. To see beyond circumference, however, is to exceed what circumference would limit or "Engross" – Finity:

> Time feels so vast that were it not
> For an Eternity –
> I fear me this Circumference
> Engross my Finity –
>
> To His exclusion, who prepare
> By Processes of Size
> For the Stupendous Vision
> Of His diameters –   (802)

This poem presents a number of problems; it is the characteristically difficult work of Dickinson's most mature theological period of 1858–64. Its attempt is to render more theoretical the discontinuity between God's instruments and ours that was the subject of a considerably easier poem, #287. In that poem, a sequenced series of riddles yields finally to a vision of God not as Deist Watchmaker, but as maker of Time for whom all watches are baubles.

> A Clock stopped –
> Not the Mantel's –
> Geneva's farthest skill
> Can't put the puppet bowing –
> That just now dangled still –
>
> An awe came on the Trinket!
> The Figures hunched, with pain –
> Then quivered out of Decimals –
> Into Degreeless Noon –

It will not stir for Doctors –
This Pendulum of snow –
The Shopman importunes it –
While cool – concernless No –

Nods from the Gilded pointers –
Nods from the Seconds slim –
Decades of Arrogance between
The Dial Life –
And Him.   (287)

Here Dickinson writes a kind of Augustinian primer, a catechismic guessing game, out of household materials. The clock that stops is gradually devalued over the first stanza to suggest the worth of the human body before God. Thus, "Puppet" suggests its dependence on the divine puppeteer, while "trinket" disabuses us of any self-flattery. If made in His image, we are beaten thin indeed: We are not God, or even as Emerson puts it, "part and parcel of God," but, rather, mere gauds of the Creation. More subtle than Switzerland's master watchmakers, and subtler still than that Christian mechanic of Geneva, Calvin, God is utterly outside the machinations of science or even the science of Him. Once dead, the human mechanism is beyond any help science might contrive through "doctors"; beyond also the quid pro quo of works the "shopman importunes"; and beyond all species of human measurement. The very calculations of theology, and especially the theologian's second guessing of God's Time line in organizing types or "figures," are mooted. In the same way that man in the image of God is made the limpest of bangles, the figure is dehusked. "[Quivering] out of Decimals / Into Degreeless Noon," the figure is stripped of all but Awe, its place on God's superordinate clock unsecured, its former Being reduced to the sheerest of nominalisms: the scribble of the decimal. At the exact midpoint of the poem the soul stands shadowless in the light of noon, the place of white on white and our extinction. The pendulum of snow, invisible and cold, is as obscure as God's time, and as comfortless.

Dickinson's drive in this poem is to wean a childish theology from its accustomed toys, to describe a discontinuity of the human and the Divine nearly geometric in its austerity. Between the "dial life" of human time as we understand it and the towering "Him" who looms at the end of the poem is a chasm our sagacity only clutters. The "gilded pointers" have thus an elegant double function. Not free of a certain pathetic glitter, they are emblems of the meretricious persistence of the mediating term in our descriptions of the Divine glory. Reduce and reduce as piety may, our understanding of God still depends on feeble predication: the glint of a narrow pointer, the sweep of a "second slim." At the same time, though, the seignorial "nod" of the "pointers" and of the "seconds slim" does suggest a certain divine elegance. God's attentions, transcend-

ing noblesse oblige, are suave. Like Edwards', like Taylor's, and like Kierkegaard's God, Dickinson's God will not stoop to conquer.

I have called "A Clock stopped" a primer poem because I think it performs precisely that function, as algebra to the advanced calculus of a
poem like "Time feels so vast." Keeping in mind, then, the relatively
simple lesson of "A Clock stopped" we can turn again to that poem. It
is a work that would make good Dickinson's oxymoronic project of
"spreading wide the narrow," or of finding God's limit by locating
the limits of one's own reason. On the one hand, the poem seems simply
to be about the eclipse of the finite self by Eternity, about the kind of
dread felt by a subject who has renounced the claims of a secure center. Accordingly, if we read "Finity" as the object of the verb "Engross,"
the poem is about the preservation of psychic boundaries, about the
strain placed on the integrity of self by the requirements of eternity;
about what Kierkegaard, in terms parallel to Dickinson's, calls, as we
have already seen, "grasping at Finity." Following this reading, the
speaker of the poem is simply battening down her hatches against a kind
of ballooning Circumference that threatens columnar steadiness, equilib-
rium, "Finity."

This reading is thwarted by the final lines of the poem, however. For
if we look ahead we find the "Stupendous Vision / Of his diameters," a
vision surely impossible to a poet of such jealously guarded soul, to a
poet so fixated on preserving her own center. Indeed, the issue of fixa-
tion, of center, is the pivot on which the poem turns. Let us suppose this
time that what the poet "fears" is that Circumference will be engrossed
by the poet's own Finity. Reading thus, we see an "engrossing," or fixa-
tion, of Circumference by "Finity." What Dickinson probes is precisely
the idol-making power of the mind, its tendency to formally fix, or
compass, time within the parameters of its own limitation.

And let us be sure not to forget that this is a poem about *time,* one that
begins "Time feels so vast." Circumference is here Dickinson's spatial
metaphor for that "Time" whose increments are nodes where God and
man meet, but in a false relation, a relation determined by human finity
or human Reason. As Kierkegaard writes on "Time" in *The Concept of
Dread:* "no moment is a present, and in the same sense there is neither
past present or future. If one thinks it possible to maintain this division,
it is because we spatialize a moment, and thereby the infinite progression
is brought to a standstill, and that is because one introduces a visual
representation, visualizing Time instead of thinking it" (77). "Circumference" in the above poem is Dickinson's spatialization of something
so temporally vast that to be conceived it must be visualized: yet in
this visualization of the invisible is the thing defrauded. Circumference
and Eternity, hitherto believed beyond "Finity," wider, more commodi-

ous, more replete with "possibility," are now reduced, narrowed, "Engrossed," by the "Finity" of the poet's eye.

Thus we need to read "To His exclusion" of the next stanza as an acceptance of God's exclusion, and of a kind of epistemological exile. The resolution is now to enter on an uncharted spiritual exercise of unknown form and so undetermined telos. "Exclusion," in fact, only increases the hardship endured in that region beyond the "Dip of Bell," for the isolation is now dual: The poet is cut off from both intelligibility to man and intelligence of God. In this phrase, "To His Exclusion," a whole history of Dickinson's renunciations culminates. As the narcissism of "centre," "finity," and finally even "circumference," were yielded; as the personae – Jacob, Moses, the Devil – were renounced, now the poet resigns herself to a simultaneous anonymity among the "tribes." In a later chapter we will see Hart Crane join similar company, establishing a fellowship with hobos rather than heroes, Chaplinesque clowns rather than visionary victims. Dickinson stands thus at the head of a tradition. Pronouncing "To His exclusion," she signals an acquiescence to a theological existence beyond the solace of stabilizing vision or any absolute understanding of God.

This prolegomenon to a poetics of doubt resembles in no small way Kierkegaard's "dialectical lyric" on Abraham's travail: the "Stupendous Vision" of "his Diameters" is a vision only gained by an "infinitely resigned" believer who cuts herself off from her finity, and thus from her own powers of vision or sight, who accepts a circumference she cannot grasp conceptually. There is an almost mathematical venturesomeness about this kind of theological movement, or faith, that must, forsaking imitation, make its own postulates, its own map, but which makes that map wholly aware that it radically differs from God's, that the terrain sketched is certain to be terrain crisscrossed with sin. For again, as this poetry is acutely aware, the very Fall determines the distance the map would traverse. Sin yields a spatialized time whose increments mark our remoteness from God.

The poems informed by such intense resignation, particularly by a Puritan resignation of the vision of the eye, are among Dickinson's least understood, and yet most ambitious; poems that take on the burden of spiritual exercise beyond the limits of circumference. Stripped, vertiginous texts, these poems commit themselves to theological ventures which systematically deprive the speaker of deliverance, telos, and so of organizing images. The proper confrontation of God in poetry, that problem that taxed and so subdued earlier Puritan poets, is here exacerbated by a straying, and so heretical poetry which, nevertheless, in remarkably orthodox ways, takes mediation, its enabling images, for idolatry; which records both the invention of the image and the renunciation of image. The rigor of the poetry derives from its steadily widening sense of what is image or idol, in its discovery of the "columnar" in its own widest conceptions. The search for an uncompromising piety, a piety that deifies nothing of its own mental process leads a poet now aware of the reciprocally constricting possibilities of both center and circumference to renounce, for example, her own favorite, "Eternity."

> You constituted Time –
> I deemed Eternity
> A Revelation of Yourself –
> 'Twas therefore Deity
>
> The Absolute – removed
> The Relative away –
> That I unto Himself adjust
> My slow idolatry –   (765)

The poem opens with a face-off – the poet "wrestling" God over definitions, not as in Jacob's case for a name, but for the angel's right to name. We begin with a safe enough proposition – that God created Time – and yet by the second line the poem is already at risk. Deem[ing] "Eternity / A Revelation of Yourself," the poet has already committed idolatry. Revelation, Eternity, and now even Time are subverted by that "Deem" which locates every statement about God within the poet's own repertoire of constructs. "Deity," yielded by the poet's now uncomfortably facile logic, is only another in the series. To preempt God by deeming or naming him "Eternal" is to freeze or petrify Eternity: such activity "deifies" and is thus guilty of the "idolatry" with which the poem ends.

Much lies, of course, between the "Deity" of the fourth line and the "idolatry" of the eighth. The relationship between these two terms depends on the even more perplexed relationship of "Absolute" and "Relative" in the second stanza. The difficulty is with assigning value to the two terms, for "removed" and "away" are modifiers that squint like a strabismus. "Removed" indicates, perhaps, banished; "away," exiled. Since we might naturally expect the "Absolute" to suffer a happier fate than the poet's idolatrous "relative," we are perplexed as to why the "relative" and the "Absolute" are dispensed with equal dispatch, why both are lost to the poet as theological possibilities.

The answer to this puzzle is the same as the answer to the earlier question about center and circumference, where circumference came to "centre" itself. By the poet's activity of deeming is the "Absolute" leveled to the status of the "relative." Whereas the poet may stratify by class, God's proportion reduces all human knowledge to equivalences.[13] One may thus hazard that as ontological categories, categories belonging to God's vision, both the "Absolute" and "relative" are here affirmed even as they are resigned; as epistemological, or heuristic categories, on the other hand, they are banished. In a paradoxical, contradictory syntax that confounds binary opposition, the poet affirms God's absoluteness and her own relativity while at the same time acknowledging the reduction, or idolatry, of her terms even as she posits them. The Derridean critic might describe this as writing under "erasure," the poem canceling its own premises even as it writes those premises. Better to call it, following Kierkegaard, "absurd," to suggest a crucial difference, one flowing from the degree of good faith required by the enterprise. Behind Derrida's erasures is the Nietzschean skepticism that answers Kantian faith with the death of Him who Knows, God, the only epistemological arbiter. The self-cancellations of Derridean language are thus those of a language discovering its own autonomy, its freedom from a transcendental signified. What drives Dickinson, on the other hand, is an impulse wholly different, an impulse not skeptical and thus invested in a relative, or differential, view of language, but one rather acutely aware of the incompleteness of human understanding. Our understanding is relative, but God's is not. So by naming or "deeming," the speaker turns God's ontology of unity to idolatrous duplicity. Her very description of the absolute must falsify God's absolutes in order to reveal, to utter, itself.

There is a relentless kind of multiplication at work that Dickinson cannot escape, a multiplication well known to her Puritan American precursor, Edward Taylor, whose Devil's chief trick in "God's Determinations" was a relentless division into categories. The structures of the mind are themselves idolatrous, defrauding the unity they would describe: absolute "one" becomes relative "two" – and then two becomes four. The negotiation of theological categories in poetry does not admit of any relation to God but that of parody. Deification, or epistemological replication, freezes the poetry's sublimest speculations. Thus, in the above poem, the implicit, oppositional, Jacob model is refused; the poet or trickster who narrows God's hands in order to widen her own is thwarted. Yet the problem lingers. "Eternity," that indivisibility to which the poet aspires, is itself necessarily limited by the poet's finite relation to God's ontological absoluteness. It must be relinquished, as anything on which the poet might set her eye, any "gem" out of Revelations, must be relinquished. The poet of an earlier poem of "circumference" who could "see no way" has now not only yielded hope of the way, but also hope of seeing. The only way is the way unseen, the way stumbled upon, and stumbled upon not by a maverick or a hero in "Pentateuchal Robes" but by an invisible, anonymous member of the tribes, infinitely resigned to earn no recognition: Thus:

From Blank to Blank –
A Threadless Way
I pushed Mechanic feet –
To stop – or perish – or advance –
Alike indifferent –

If end I gained
It ends beyond
Indefinite disclosed –
I shut my eyes – and groped as well
'Twas lighter – to be Blind –   (761)

It is instructive to compare this poem's self-referentiality – its double reference to both a religious and a poetic exodus – with the similarly reflexive "I dwell in Possibility," the first poem read here. "From Blank to Blank" actualizes such possibility in terms the poet had not, we suspect, anticipated. The sheltering architecture of "I dwell" is dissolved. The poetry – and here the link between the poetic and spiritual project is forged in the pun on "blank" and on "mechanic feet" which refer both to prosodic bewilderment and hard spiritual journey – holds real wilderness terrors. The feet wander, literally, in a kind of desert. Dickinson has by now, we should note, reinstated herself among the "tribes," the earlier spurned wanderers not dignified by the "Pentateuchal robes" of Moses as tragic hero. The poet, an "infinitely resigned" faithful wanderer, carries on a spiritual quest that is in every respect absurd. The teleology of "Paradise," an "end," is forsworn, and the theological, or poetic journey toward an encounter with a God of known terms is "blanked" out. The "columnar," or stationary stance of vision gives way to a terrible surrender.

Chief among gifts surrendered is the poet's vision. Why is blindness "lighter"? Because, to employ the terms established above, spiritual sight is optical illusion. Sight is seeing in God the self, its terms, and so its own finity. And this, after all, is the essence of an old idolatry, the doubling of God through mediant image. We remember the odd equivalence of "Time" and "Eternity" in #765, where God "constituted" time while the speaker "deemed" Eternity. A similar equivalence, one explicating the speaker's preference for "blindness," occurs in the poem to follow. There an exchange of the human and divine, a falsification of God's ontology by man's epistemology, again results from the poet's reaching beyond circumference. Language, however rarefied, still interposes itself as that duplicitous membrane, that means by which the multiple defrauds the One. Antinomy, at the very moment it is transcended, parodies itself. God's unity is again yielded to a poet's double vision. Accordingly, #800 begins:

Two – were immortal twice –
The privilege of few –
Eternity – obtained – in Time –
Reversed Divinity –

What is this reversed "Divinity" but God in the "convex mirror" – as Ashbery might put it – of human perception? "Eternity," only accessible through "Time," must "reverse" itself in order to disclose itself. This reversal, this disclosure based on multiplication and so on falsification, is the inevitable process of human vision. As the poem goes on:

That our ignoble eyes
The quality conceive
Of Paradise superlative –
Through their Comparative.

Although Paradise may indeed be "superlative," our instruments of superlative – the comparison, the hierarchilization according to human scale – "reverse" it. The old Emersonian confidence that identifies the eye with the "I" as they converge in a transparent paradise or Poirier's "world elsewhere," is here destabilized just as "Eternity" was in #765.[14] The poet's cherished "superlatives," like her "Eternity," are optical illusions glimpsed by the eye that diminishes by doubling: In "comparative" image or metaphor, the poet sees God not as through Emerson's "transparent eyeball" but as through a telescope backward.

These poems tell us it is better to be blind than, by the compass of our narrow hands, to "deify." In blindness, in the groping unchartered poem that forgoes not only the "centre" but also the "circumference," not only the Romantic persona but also the "Pentateuchal robes" that would salvage that persona as martyr, divinity avails itself as "possibility," albeit a possibility never to be claimed in stable image or expression. One might think here of Mallarmé and of his blank page. Yet it is here that European experimentalism and the American disclose their real difference.[15] In the European pursuit of "blankness" there is the search for a rarefied, sacral language to write the artist's secular exile as a poem. This is quite different from the American experiments, their involutions not so much surreal as scholastic, evolving not from theological malaise but from a probing, deepening, and problematizing of constructs long vexing the Puritan mind. This American blankness seems rather to consist in poems *unwriting* themselves as poems, the better in their blindness to glimpse God. Looking to find a view unobstructed by human idol, to find a poetry of faith that will transcend fallen language and the fallen reifications – Christology, Demonic imitation, idolatry – such poetry goes blank, goes blind. The exiled Moses or poet, in this American tradition, must cut out from under his own feet the verities that support the traditional encounter with God; the movement is one of negation. "Possibility" turned inside out, becomes the absurd faith; hope reveals itself in a fallen world as dread. Doubt replaces compensation:

> A Doubt if it be Us
> Assists the staggering Mind
> In an extremer Anguish
> Until it footing find.

> An Unreality is lent,
> A merciful Mirage
> That makes the living possible
> While it suspends the lives.   (859)

This doubt, this poignantly human disorientation, is what Dickinson's most mature theological inquiry arrives at. The "ends" are invisible, or, in the terms of #761, "Indefinite disclosed." The poet gains not an ideal or transcendental "reality" but an "unreality," not a vision of Paradise, but a "mirage" in the desert. Transcendental "possibility" and Emersonian struggle are alike ceded to a precarious and existential "living" that purges itself of both the certainty of center and circumference. Always risking the Devil's transgressions, his imitations of God from the vantage point of circumference, the poet escapes virtual heresy in moments of recognition, or blind revelation, when she cancels her own terms, seeing those terms for idolatry, or worse, for the parody that is the Devil's only recourse. Nevertheless, the poetic and theological movement that risks this heresy by circumnavigating the unknown, finds beyond circumference, in doubt and in the forms doubt vacates, piety. Only doubt, in these hard terms, holds promise of "footing"; only the "mirage," toward which the poet wanders as if "lost" in Machado's "world of objects," promises "The stupendous / Vision / Of his Diameters." It is worth noting that Dickinson's theology recapitulates her much discussed psychology of loss or privation.[16] She is a poet who theologically, as well as psychologically, lives on very little:

> God gave a Loaf to every Bird –
> But just a Crumb – to Me –
> I dare not eat it – tho' I starve –
> My poignant luxury –

Yet we should note that to renounce the specific object is, in a way, to possess all. The structure of loss replicates the structure of desire which is loss's "mirage"; doubt and desire share one interstitial form, both making available possession of that kingdom "impregnable of eye." Although blind, such a theology ensures for itself a richness of "possibility," and a wellspring of regeneracy, the poem draws on and replenishes.

It might be Famine – all around –
I could not miss an Ear –
Such Plenty smiles upon my Board –
My Garner shows so fair –

I wonder how the Rich – may feel –
An Indiaman – An Earl –
I deem that I – with but a Crumb –
Am sovereign of them all –   (791)

6

Hand of Fire: Crane

More than any other poet since Taylor, Hart Crane is the American poet of Awe. As such, he is the twentieth-century American poet Emerson least prepares us to understand. Emerson had urged the poet to retune the thoughts of minor men in a major key, to reflect for the sinner his own Godlike image. Crane's God is all too different from us to oblige the likeness, and Crane's typical speaker, all too pressed by acuteness of seeing to totalize himself or his vision. Crane's accustomed key is minor; his contribution and gift, the lyrical representation of sin's affective states.

Crane's typical speaker navigates the same vertiginous world that Edwards described and that Taylor gave form to in his lyric meditations. The ground he walks is a "slippery" covering; the moments of transport afforded him are fundamentally surprising. He can prepare to receive, though not precisely to work toward, the Word he seeks: He is what Kierkegaard called a knight of faith. Thus, characteristically projecting his voice through personae singled out by vision, and lending lyric after lyric a tone of startled surmise, Crane is the poet not embarking but struck, not instructing but called, not empowered but shaken. Self-taught in general and unschooled in any religious tradition but his mother's eccentric brand of Christian Science, Crane's poetry is nevertheless informed by a trepidation before Mystery and a belief in the soul's singularity that makes him not only Dickinson's greatest heir, but also Whitman's best, though least noticed, interlocutor. The twentieth century's most important student of Edwardsean uncertitude or, as Yvor Winters put it, of "the Way and the End" (Winters, 598), Crane is also the poet who, living with the Way and the End in consciousness always, understands their power in life and not merely their power for death. Inasmuch as they restore to suffering its edge, retrieving it from the cosmos to visit it anew on the solitary one – on the speaker as sinner – Crane's poems render audible a feature of the poem that Whitman himself, in all his "comprehensiveness," mutes. This feature is voice.

184

Crane may indeed be described as the extreme case of the poet whose lyrics are sustained by little more than voice. Recall that it was voice, as I showed in Chapter 2, that the poems of Emerson signally lacked. The descent into voice – in "Days," in "The Snow-storm," and in the first part of "Hamatreya" – tended materially to benefit Emerson's poems, at the expense, however, of his poetics. With Emerson, one first entertains the thought that perhaps totality itself is anathema to the poem. With Crane, the thought ripens to the conviction, admittedly strange, that poems can thrive in linguistic systems incapable of articulating the conditions of their power. The poem can thrive absurdly on voice alone, as it cannot live on the logic of its own necessity. It can support, or "bridge," propositions rationally unassimilable. It can exist unsupported by anything but its own faith.

The example of such faith as Crane's lyrics possess makes Crane important not only for the way he interrogates Emersonian system. His work also illuminates, as no other poet's quite does, the likelihood of a necessary discontinuity between totality and revelation, or "comprehensive" vision and poetic seeing. Formal affinities between poets as far-flung as Whitman and Eliot are thereby revealed by Crane's hard discovery that wideness of vision may itself structure and perpetuate a sense of spiritual vacuity; that singular seeing can best ease the soul's pain.

Eliot and Pound, to take up the obvious instances for just a moment, may resoundingly reject Whitman's shagginess, but both accede in complex and crucial ways to his comprehensiveness. Like Whitman, both Eliot and Pound make a poetic virtue of inclusion. As Whitman allays the agonies of his beautiful gigantic swimmer through aggregation, Eliot creates as dramatis personae deputies who suffer archetypically the indignities of their wasted times. Pound's speakers (with the possible exception of the Pisan singer) ventriloquize the various voices of the paedeumae from which they come. Eliot may, in his essay on Baudelaire, elegize the extinction of the great saint or sinner in the "ennui of modern life," and yet, in Whitmanian fashion, he craves "absorption." Finally Eliot's consummate gesture of faith is to "kneel where prayer has been valid." Crane stands apart from this, answering Whitman's birds-eye sanctification of high and low with a stern conviction of human suffering; Whitman's disavowal of the one for the many with his rededication to the one; and Whitman's poetics of camaraderie with an insistence on "the world that comes to each of us alone."

Apposite to the Whitmanian fellowship, this immutable aloneness is Crane's theological signature and my starting point for a reading of Crane which allows the fundamental privacy – and, yes, obscurity – of his vision, but makes of that privacy a context giving to obscurity purpose. For if we are accustomed to using private as a polite adjective for garbled, we are less used to using it as Taylor must have seen it. Like Taylor's, Crane's poems reveal a faith – the very faith Whitman gainsaid – in the solitary soul as the fundamental spiritual and poetic medium, in a poetry uttered by the individual voice, implicated, and answering like Abraham, "Here I am." Such a poetry, taking for granted a Being necessarily concealed – and thus a Being that illuminating universals must defraud – is based on interstitial, unparaphrasable moments of apprehension. Precisely as Crane claims of his "logic of metaphor," the poem produces an "experience which may for a time engross the total faculties of the spectator . . . , [and] that gains our unquestioning assent" (219). Not in the least arbitrary, as Harriet Monroe suspected and posterity has more or less granted, Crane's "logic" needs nothing so little as reason; reason is anathema to a poet seeking such assent.

Rather, when Crane's images do hold, it is as though grace meets faith, and we, like the speaker, believe what we do not necessarily understand. With their repertoire of supplicant and groping tones, of vistas narrowing to pin holes – crabbed and blind – Crane's poems may commit everything to the act of song, but they place no bets on what that song might secure. As religious structures, they find analogue in that lonely Church of one member Luther imagined when he wrote, "If I were the only one in the entire world to adhere to the Word, I alone would be the church" (Pelikan, 174). Alternatively, and closer to home, they seem modern glosses on such American texts as Thomas Hooker's "Application for Redemption," based on an Augustinian suspicion of any faith not derived introspectively.

> [T]here is no greater hindrance to be found on earth to holy meditation than frothy company and companions; while a man is in the crowd among such wretches there is no possibility in reason that one should search his own heart and examine his own way. (Heimert and Delbanco, 176)

Andrew Delbanco has recently written that "classic American literature . . . is characteristically committed to the restoration of what the Puritans had lost: a powerful, but privative, sense of sin" (*The Puritan Ordeal*, 235). Perhaps for this reason Crane's work survives the skepticism of his many detractors, survives even wholesale misinterpretation of its central aims. Forswearing the sanctuary of abstraction, the boon of the valid, the solace of understanding, Crane's typical speaker has the expectant sound of a soul on trial, awaiting a revelation not his own to produce, but pushing words to the breaking point for its dear sake. No wonder that Crane's plangent rhetoric is inevitably found wanting in theories that would push a constitutional tenuousness further than it can go. Epic, pilgrimage, chronicle, and myth – these are some of the generic tags that have been attached to Crane's *oeuvre* over the years. Such forms, however, fulfilling themselves only to the extent that they are comprehensive, tend to presume an integration and a security Crane does not prejudge and so cannot attain. I want to argue that such integration is not only not available to Crane's lyric speaker, it is not afforded by the world he wanders, a world as insubstantial of outline as his speaker is of knowledge. Just as he wanders on an errand whose satisfaction is nowhere assured, the errand takes him through a wilderness equally obscure of landmark and purpose. Where he lives is where his soul finds its ordeal. Indeed, the reader of Crane's poetry is not only pressed to "dwell," as Allen Grossman puts it, "in the bewilderment of Crane's style" (Bloom, *Hart Crane,* 223) but in an America that, for all its subways and tugboats, seems yet undiscovered, yet unredeemed, still incipient, shadowy, wild.

Crane's poems go beyond taking on those personal risks characteristic of the Reformed sensibility that Perry Miller called an "externalization of the subjective mood." Call Crane a poet who literally subjectivizes the external mood, introjecting a vision of America not yet rounded off in realization. When Crane writes in "General Aims and Theories," "I am concerned with the future of America . . . because I feel persuaded that here are destined to be discovered certain as yet undefined spiritual qualities, perhaps a new hierarchy of faith not to be developed so completely elsewhere" (Weber, 219), and suggests further, "In this process I like to see myself as a potential factor," the dynamic he suggests between a self groping purblind and clumsy for place and an America of undecided fate is precisely that which early Americans called *covenantal.* Believing, as he puts it, that "new kinds of vision may be discovered in new forms," Crane may be said to propose a faith in the regenerative American locale analogous to that proposed by those who saw in the American landscape a spiritual topos: a Kingdom of God in America. Like them, he writes a poetry shadowed by the brokenness and exile only our good oaths can forestall: only the Word will ensure the promise of the Promised Land. Poet of Adamic exile and American wandering, Crane brings to bear on the American locale a pressure that has the fervency of the Puritans', of Winthrop or Mather. Without the bridge of language, what Crane calls the "Incognizable Word," all is lost, not only the poet, but his Israel too, and the holy precincts of his City on the Hill.

For Crane, personhood and nationhood both hang on the slenderest of inflections, the most hairthin of towlines. For perhaps no other American poet is the will to believe more crucial because more freighted with disbelief, more undermined, more thwarted. Crane's verse rediscovers that human condition whose remediation such notions as faith and covenant are addressed to: the condition of sin. Just so, he reintroduces us to the bearer of that sin: the articulate sinner, heir to Augustine, to Ignatius, to Baxter, to Taylor. Where, Crane's work impels us to ask with a start, have all the sinners gone?

As I have already shown, the question of sin was one Emersonian liberalism and transcontinental Romanticism had effectively mooted. Those not reprieved by Unitarian humanism had gone – albeit in style – to the Devil. But if the general pardon issued sinners by the ascendancy of liberalism in America obviated the function of the eloquent sinner, with, as I argued in Chapter 2, some baleful effects on the fortunes of the poem, this is not to say that eloquence was dead. It simply got a more magnificent mouthpiece in a febrile, if vital, figure – Byron's Cain, Wagner's Tristan, Nietzsche's Ubermensch – whose Satanic activism better complemented liberal nineteenth-century notions of human grandeur than the Adamic sinner, cowering and passive in the hands of an angry God. Emerson's own affection for continental Romanticism, for Goethe and magnificos in general, ironically exemplifies the hospitality liberalism could offer Lucifer while it sent the sinner packing. The Romantic poetics which made Milton's Satan not only a better poet than his sinners, but really – as scorched Orphist – the only poet, shifted the spotlight from the ordinary to the extraordinary sinner: from supplication to sublimity, from waiting and wondering to subversion and resistance. Whether or not this sublimity is a fundamental or simply a decorative element of the national religion Emerson codified, there can be no doubt that it is the Orphist in which the critical tradition has rested its faith. From Hyatt Waggoner through Harold Bloom, the attractiveness of this antinomian or Orphic model of the poet has been nearly unshakable.

Nowhere is this clearer than in the critical consensus about Crane. Indeed, in the misunderstanding of Crane, two critical generations elsewhere at loggerheads have joined forces. Crane's prewar New Critical mentors and friends mourned him as an inevitable casualty to Eliot, as a poet of that very "split religion" Eliot's magisterial anti-Romanticism swept off the literary deck. In this perspective Crane could not be other than a casualty to Eliot's stringencies. In the aftermath of the New Criticism, the rediscovery of Emerson as thinker of "antithetical power" once more shows Crane to his accustomed niche in a redefined but still Romantic tradition Emerson is now credited with founding. The new understanding of Emerson as "agonist" gives new cachet to a strain of thought to which the literary establishment has long been predisposed.

Thus, Crane has for more than fifty years been our young Werther, paragon of sublime self-destruction and the transcendence that a vivid infernalism wins. The son of a Cleveland candy manufacturer who acted the industrial demigod, Crane, the legend goes, was too thin-skinned to captain his father's dark satanic mills, and, at the same time, too gifted not to mind his virtual disinheritance. Like Satan chafed by his own marginality, Crane, born fifty years after Emerson's death, "inherited," writes Allen Tate, "a jungle of machines and disintegrating values which he could not control . . . and which soon destroyed him" (Weber, 270). As Romantic poet, however, he has a longevity beyond his years: the poet posthumous given his second chance. If America could not sustain Crane in life, he is preserved in death as a Byronic hyperbole.[1]

To this view early resistance was slight, and it came from isolated places. Taking exception to Philip Horton's view, one shared by Crane's friends, that "had [Crane] led a better life he would have been a worse poet," Delmore Schwartz tried to disable the mechanism which was already turning Crane to legend just three years after his death. As he cautioned Horton in 1937, "literary legends are generally vicious" (Schwartz, 36). Less skittish than prescient (Schwartz himself is now incarcerated in Crane's own unhappy legend), Schwartz knew that once "the legions accept the Romantic idea of the poet," the poetry is already moribund. Schwartz's worst predictions swiftly came to pass. In the years after Crane's death, his poetic contribution was truncated in his swan dive into the sea. This last gesture served as epigraph to a career in Romantic circularity, the poet rendering a world as the reflection of his own soul, his need for love magnified in its sublime brokenness. As Allen Tate famously wrote:

> His world had no center and his thrust into sensations is responsible for the fragmentary quality of his most ambitious work. . . . Crane could only assert a quality of will against the world, and at each successive failure of the will he turned against himself. In the failure of understanding, the Romantic poet of the age of science attempts to impose his will upon experience and to possess the world. (291)

Tate's influential summing-up clips Crane to a tautology: On the one hand Tate attributes Crane's lack of grip to a "machine age" which cannot provide minimum Romantic requirements; the mirror of Nature no longer reflects the poet's soul. He sees instead pistons and fragments, girders and industrial noise. On the other hand, still vitally invested in the idea of the monumental Romantic ego, Tate laments Crane's insufficient supply of "thrust."[2] Either way, though, whether Crane had no center, leaving his poetry fragmentary, or whether his world was fragmentary and so he had no center, he fails. His drunken and promiscuous life and his suicide close the argument, ensconcing him among Satan, Faust, Marlowe, and Byron, reducing his poems to overtures to the great act of Liebestod. Indeed, the suicide completes the poems' more cryptic gestures, proving that what Crane sought all along was ecstasy, to lose himself.

Departing from this, Crane's most readable act, critics have been able
to forge a case out of all the configurations of Crane's failure, to see his
"thrust" consistently vitiated by the undertow of victimhood. Thus Joseph Riddel, in "Hart Crane's Poetics of Failure," formulated a view of
"The Bridge" that synthesizes the opinion of fifty years:

> Crane had to create a persona (of the poet-quester) who could be in-
> volved in both time and eternity, or who, in other words, was both per-
> sonal and archetypal. Circumscribed by history, this persona was
> nonetheless cognate with the poet-hero victim of all time, archetypes of
> the poet in the guise of mythical or historical anti-heroes: with Faust,
> with Columbus, with Whitman and Poe and Emily Dickinson (Fellow
> victims in the same sequence of history). . . . The archetype of the
> poet-quester becomes the archetype of visionary victim, Dionysus-
> Christ. (Mazzaro, 279)

Leaving aside for the moment whether Whitman and Dickinson can,
with any accuracy, be called "victims," it is easy to follow Riddel's premises: The anti-hero departs from the finite in search of the infinite, moves
from "time" to "eternity," or from misunderstood martyrdom to nothing less than the grace that comprehends all history, all particular suffering. Such a victim owes his spirit to that Satan whose motto hangs
over "The Bridge": "From going to and fro in the earth, and from walking up and down in it." The route he follows is a mirror image of the
Christian "journey of the Spirit," and the Romantic ethos which transfers the center of the world from God to self elides the poet and his work
as Christ and his teachings. Just as the Satanic suffering (parody of
Christ's) is more important than those teachings, Crane's death becomes
the crown of his *oeuvre,* and the formidably difficult poems are simply
footnoted to the higher clarity of an act that makes Crane's corpse the
most perfect Romantic poem in his corpus.

In a certain way, and as I have demonstrated in treating Whitman and
Dickinson's common understanding of sublimity's costs, the difference
between angels and devils can be negligible. The Emersonian strain of
Romanticism gives highest honors to a hypertrophied resistance without
distinguishing or weighing out too carefully power's intentions. As the
preceding chapters detailed, Whitman and Dickinson both evince considerable wariness before any creative power that trades human scale for
the sake of superhuman reach. Voice reaching-beyond-itself can yield to
giantism or Faustianism which shows up in the poem as a quality of
bombast, or insincerity. Hence, both of Crane's most important precursors, Dickinson and, to a more limited extent, Whitman, guard the integrity of the individual in history, while they subject to hard and
skeptical pressure the transpersonal or transtemporal aspirations of the

angel/giant. They do so because they share an understanding that devils and angels become indistinguishable in their quest for what Schlegel called "an eternally living and moving activity which begets under itself, under constantly altering forms and shapes, an infiniteness and manifoldness" (Abrams, 503). When the pursuit of such "infiniteness and manifoldness" is given ultimate latitude and prestige, then differences of psychology, point of view, spiritual timbre, or what I am calling simply, voice are swiftly effaced by a magnificence of purpose that imbues the speaker, angel or devil, with a certain nobility, uniting contraries. Then, this Orphic or Dionysian figure (as beautiful gigantic swimmer, or female pugilist, or simply as Promethean poet) marries good and evil, transmuting them into "power." But the power achieved, inasmuch as it marks the transcendence of language beyond the speaker's particular need for speech, nullifies, or makes irrelevant, such speech. Poetic voicing is a casualty of poetic power.

Thus the poem that strives to meet an Orphic agenda easily exceeds its human mandate, and so its good faith. In the case of Crane, critical assumptions about the Romantic underpinnings of the poetry have put his hewing to voice in an even more unflattering light. Understood to pursue an agenda of fusion with the All, Crane is readily glimpsed as falling short of that All. He seems an Icarus, pathetic. He seems stranded, or arrested, along a power trajectory. He is readily diagnosed as a hyper-Romantic, but with weak nerves. Unable, the argument goes, to transcend where he would transcend, to discharge himself into his language (except, say, in such Shelleyan successes as the "Atlantis" section of "The Bridge"), Crane allows ego to encase pure intention, history to make sluggish the flow through time. Thus Crane's Dionysus seems to bloat: Sublime loneliness deflected through self-reliance becomes grandiose; the solitary in echoing space becomes egoist or giant. In Emerson's terms, Crane cannot but fail, and especially when he takes resistance personally, recording impediment in the affect of his lines and internalizing fate as an appurtenance of the will. He fails when he writes as if ignorant of the notion that "transition" must purify travail as *langue* redeems *parole*. And he fails when he writes without irony, as if he did not know that only the long view, divinely schooled, will preserve the poet's power; that otherwise this power leaks to a trickle, and he writes mere "days."

Exactly so. Crane's "days," his poetic inventory of keen, discontinuous states of soul, are all that justify his poetic importance. And when this spiritual soreness – the soul's ache in the instep arch – is repackaged as rejuvenative "power," Crane becomes less and less worth reading. Only with that Augustinian pain, that ultimate powerlessness, brought to the fore, can Crane's reputation long survive.

I think it should, of course, if for no other reason than that the salient difference between the Romantic, ineffable transcendence – secured through power – and the Calvinist's Unknowable God is clarified in Crane's work as it is nowhere else. In Crane's poems, as in Taylor's, voice marks the limits of the knowable and, accordingly, the humanness of the poem. This gets at a problem my analysis has deferred until now. Obviously enough, one is hardly justified in distinguishing a Calvinist from an Emersonian language simply on the grounds of "context" or "attitude": That is, "vastness" when it appears in the poem of a signed-up Christian must mean inscrutable divinity, whereas in the poem of a post-Christian Romantic, it means imaginative power. This would give language a merely executive function, and make poetry a kind of advance publicity, or late notice, for preexisting faith commitments. Crane's spiritual dualism, inferred from language, is therefore doubly instructive, inasmuch as it seems untied to any but the most tenuous understanding of, or commitment to, Protestant practice.

What Crane's poetry reveals is how the very structure of language, the distance between word and thing, language and world, can become a converting ordinance. The gap between word and thing is identical in a Romantic – or Emersonian – and a "regenerate" – or anti-Emersonian – poem, but what differs is the direction and quality of the poet's passage through the dualist aperture. The distinction finally devolves on the speaker and on voice. A Romantic sense of that vast presence behind the screen of natural facts ultimately frees the poet from his voice. He becomes "one with the perfect whole" and the perfect poem he speaks is a silence (Mallarmé is thus the poet who finally fulfills what is implicit in Holderlein).

The withdrawn presence of a Calvinist universe, by contrast, concentrates the speaker in himself, in his own volume and particularity. The language of the poem registers this difference by, if you will, speaking the speaker. The difference is not secured by biography – that is, a poet of Calvinist predisposition writes poems that "reflect" his sense of a world resisting human understanding. Rather, the ineluctability of his own presence, and the urge to preserve that presence, are learned in a language never free of that presence. The hovering opacity of language itself is the poet's instructor in the Fall; the poem provides a route of spiritual access to one whom no mere doctrine could persuade. The Romantic subject comes into himself through attempts to pierce the screen and enter, become coextensive with, a certain vastness. For it is this vastness of the object that is his true measure. The regenerate subject uses this (now recalcitrant vastness) to discover his own limitations.

A use of language as an aid to humility, a sense of the vast beyond as register of the poet's smallness and limitation – these are typical of

Crane. In the very disjunctive, balked, dualism of Crane's language we can discover the lineaments of his faith.[3] I begin, then, with these lines from "Voyages":

> The bay estuaries fleck the hard sky limits.
> – As if too brittle or too clear to touch!
> The cables of our sleep so swiftly filed,
> Already hang, shred ends from remembered stars.
> One frozen trackless smile . . . What words
> Can strangle this deaf moonlight? For we
> Are overtaken. Now no cry, no sword
> Can fasten or deflect this tidal wedge,
> Slow tyranny of moonlight, moonlight loved
> And changed . . .   (Weber, 39)[4]

One chooses this passage from "Voyages" because of the questions it raises about the Romantic or transcendental "thrust" of Crane's work. Note that the very first line transports us to the traditional site of transcendence where earth meets sky, and yet there is no egress.[5] The "hard sky limits" form an ineluctable barrier. In fact, the very idea the lines pursue is the incapacity of the will to transcend limits. Crane's concern here is the very inadequacy of Romantic subjectivity. This philosophical problem stands in metaphorical relationship with the poem's emotional subject: the elusiveness of complete erotic union. He writes the dual problem – the agony of individual perception, the separateness of the lovers – in a kind of invisible ink, employing negative language to suggest positive desire.[6] Precisely what the speaker wants or fears is only hinted at in questions that obscurely indicate what he cannot say – "There's nothing like this in the world" – and – "And never to quite understand!" Like *what*? to understand *what*? we puzzle.

Further, corresponding to this negative language are images of a landscape whose focal points regress, eluding our perceptual grasp. Thus the "merciless white blade" of the horizon and the "shred ends of our sleep" are visually articulate places which stand for what we do not know, what does not exist, or what flees consciousness. These images cast a double beam on the problem of describing a desire resisting all possession: "What words / Can strangle this deaf moonlight?"

Crane is prying apart the semantic bridges to unity. Denotation itself unravels, showing "shred ends," as the poet severs the knit of vehicle from stabilizing tenor. In the line above it is not clear what strangles what, or how. Although it is not difficult to imagine deafness strangling words, what does it mean to say that words strangle deafness? Were the phrase "mute moonlight" we might have an easier time. Crane might then be arguing that the imposition of language can strike beauty mute. The post-Kantian advance beyond phenomena can become a kind of suffocation, the thrust a kind of rape. With the word "deaf," however, Crane implies a moonlight inarticulate even to itself, and the synesthesia that couples "moonlight" and "deaf" decouples them too. The modifier bristles, repelling its object. The world held together by language comes unjoined in the shred ends of the lines. In their broken-off and arrested cadences they seem just to hang there.

Further still, while the objects of perception elude us, we shrink back as well (as, for instance, dreams elude consciousness, leaving only "shred ends," as muteness becomes deafness). The cat and mouse of the lovers' dialogue allegorizes the cat and mouse of self and world, perceiver and perceived. As our perception threatens to "strangle" deaf moonlight, the "tidal wedge" of stimuli presses on us in an urgent advance we can neither "fasten or deflect." A lexicon of active and passive serves here – as in Whitman's poetry – to analogize and in a certain way psychologize the endemic rupture severing lover and perceiver, beloved and perceived. But there is no consummation, only the "tyranny" of desire, that incompleteness that lets us know we are fallen.[7] The horizon does not close. "And never to quite understand?" asks the speaker's interlocutor, only to be answered, "No." For what is loved, like moonlight, is also "changed." The only possession is "piracy."

The final horizon of Crane's language not only mimics – it also virtualizes – the rent world. Tenor and vehicle, rather than meeting fingertip to fingertip, instead strain toward, just passing, each other. Just as "deaf moonlight" gropes for a place in consciousness we did not know we had, finally claiming a place uncannily new, literally "trackless," it is similarly impossible to track whether this is a love poem that uses images of an evasive perception or a poem about perception whose enabling trope is sexual passion. The poem puts off its arrival at any enclosing category, any prior or organizing "archetype," such as would give its metaphoric play a resting place.

What these lines evince is a poet much more self-conscious about the problem of release or union than Romantic categories allow. Such a tortuous and exacting meditation as these lines enact is obscured by such descriptions as "Orphic," "transcendental," or even "Emersonian." The poet is after something more – or something less – than that "thrust" of self-reliance that makes the poem its own world and the poet's new home. In the lines above the poet may be justly described as thrusting in air.

The gesture has more than its quotient of foolishness. And this foolishness, a clownish striving that takes no refuge in irony, but rather lingers in the absurd, is key; it will absorb me in the pages to come. For the time being I want simply to observe that foolishness is not the same as failure. Like Dickinson's swinging out beyond the "Dip of Bell," it is only Crane's ungrounded aspiration, his resolute casting off, that holds promise of spiritual success. This is because, like Dickinson, Crane seeks not his completion but his limit; or, in older terms – Taylor's terms – not a sanctification but a justification. He seeks that experience of the Infinite that only a soul cast off, strung-out, supported solely by faith, can receive. Thus, although the dialectic five decades of criticism have described is about right – Crane's poems do travel between union and the broken world – there is some question about the relationship of background to foreground. We need to ask whether Crane's poems are violated by, or predicated on, that "broken world."

For the images above do not fail to achieve – rather, they renounce – that release that would redeem their struggle in the rising power of the poem. Turning away from worlds elsewhere, they refuse the new start of Whitmanian autogenesis and the transparent access to All of the Emersonian eyeball. Obsessed as they are with the mediate and obscure nature of all perception, they disintegrate at the summing up. At close range their richness detonates; subjected to abstract analysis they grow tenuous. In "General Aims and Theories," Crane describes the poem as emerging from sources less linguistic than purely ontological. "Essentialized" from experience, the poem for Crane is a kind of enigmatic artifact, testifying to a Being whose mystery it husbands. There is no language outside the poem more adequate than its language. In the terms I have used before, it repels the theoretical:

> It is my hope to . . . give the poem as a whole an orbit or predetermined direction of its own. . . . Its evocation will not be toward decoration or amusement, but rather toward a state of consciousness, or "innocence" or absolute beauty. In this condition there may be discoverable under new forms certain spiritual illuminations, shining with a morality essentialized from experience directly and not from previous precepts or preconceptions. (Weber, 221)

The paradox Crane points to should be familiar by now. As Whitman sought purity in the very bowels of contaminate experience, Crane seeks a "spiritual illumination" or "innocence" in the imperfect and eclectic experience that Platonic, or ideal, categories sift and purify. It is to err, then, to overstate the relation of this innocence with the various neo-Platonic idealisms. Crane's innocence is precisely a state that sustains itself without the oxygenization of the ideal, without the prop of an abstract general category.[8] It is best able to find itself, its "orbit," once alone and before that Being which, precisely resisting all taxonomy, defies human organization with its "I am that I am." When, in a letter to Gorham Munson, Crane spurns the comforts of Plato's "classic serenity" – "Plato doesn't live today because of the intrinsic 'truth' of his statements; their only living truth consists of their harmonious relationship to each other in the context of his organization of them" (Weber, 226) – it is to distinguish categorical from poetic thinking. Eschewing a poetry of "organization," Crane goes on:

> [M]y poetry – insofar as it was truly poetic – would avoid the employment of abstract tags, formulations of experience etc., it would necessarily express its concepts in more direct terms of physical-psychic experience. If not, it must by so much lose its impact and become simply categorical. (Weber, 227)

If the general direction of Crane criticism is to call this aim chimerical, only reading more of his poems will indicate whether his work is "simply categorical," centrally occupied with devising archetypes of vision and sacrifice that secrete particular flawed poems. If not, we will require new terms closer to Crane's own to describe his poetry of "innocence," terms that show just where Crane diverges from Emerson's American religion, to what extent his "innocence" differs from that of his Dionysian or Orphic precursors.

"Innocence" is Blake's word, and like Blake, Crane is deeply concerned with the breach of subject and object, desire and desired, language and world, that is a central problem for the Romantics, not excluding Emerson. Yet his solution to this problem may be said to diverge from Blake's inasmuch as Blake totalizes the tension between contraries, so that union is constituted by a state of pure mediation. As Donald Pease explains in a discussion distinguishing Blake's "contraries" from Derrida's "difference," for Blake "it is repetition, not difference, that is original, and this original repetition functions through the power of the imagination" (Bloom, *Hart Crane*, 204).[9] Rather than find a pellucid transcendence, Blake's "Perfect Unity," Crane "enters the broken world / To trace the visionary company of love." I want to suggest, therefore, that it is a Kierkegaardian limit more than a Blakean juncture, or, to recur to the terms of Chapter 4, a Pauline and Edwardsean gate more than a Whitmanian valve, that Crane fronts.

For Crane, the cleft of the Fall is a wound that gapes and burns, not, as it is for Whitman, a passage that soothes and gives succor. Crane never closes the distance between us and the world of objects, never surmounts the divisiveness of language. Rather, his poems take that division as axiomatic. And if the voice through which they speak knows nothing more original than its own division, that division is neither naturalized, as in Blake, nor, in Whitman's terms, made "sane and sacred," warrant for "peace." Sign manifest of the human condition, division is for Crane the structure of understanding, and the sinner, the Adam, God's chosen poet. For Crane, it is our division and remoteness from anything like transcendence that opens space for the soul's perambulatory progress. Without such division, without, as it were, chasms to "bridge," then hope, then dread, then faith – all our spiritual moods – would lie dormant and humans remain unfree. Untaxed, yes, but also unfree, because freedom for Crane, as for Kierkegaard, is not thought wresting loose from limitation – to lose limitation is to lose the self – but thought coming into limitation and so into itself.

As in my last chapter, Kierkegaard – himself in self-conscious revolt against the Hegelian, and by extension, Romantic, syntheses – lends me terms for the quality of "spiritual illumination" Crane is after. Recall that Kierkegaard describes an illumination as not transcendent but humanly implicated, formally paradoxical. The systematic Idea, writes Kierkegaard, "is the identity of subject and object, the unity of thought and being. Existence, on the other hand is their separation" (Bretali, 205). In Crane's view the task is to seek spiritual illumination without defrauding the conditions of one's own existence, without positing the particulars of an absolute realm we do not actually know. Emerson's "perfect whole" is out of bounds. Kierkegaard, arguing in *Concluding Unscientific Postscript* that "System and Finality correspond to one another, but existence is precisely the opposite of finality" (Bretali, 201), thus deems "leaping . . . the accomplishment of being essentially earthly, of one who respects the earth's gravitational force, since the leaping is only momentary" (Bretali, 206). Unlike Emerson's poet freed from the Fall, but very much like Kierkegaard's dancer, whose "accomplishment is essentially earthly," Crane's images spring, showing tendon and line, without ever shearing the silken cords that bind the poem to the earthly.[10]

Crane's language is a medium in which finite existence composes a mode of self-consciousness. Its lyricism is made out of division. "Poetry," Crane writes in the letter to Munson,

> is simply the concrete evidence of the experience of a recognition. . . . When you attempt to ask more of poetry you will get as variant terms from the abstract terminology of philosophy . . . whereas poetry may well give you the "sign manifest" on which rests the assumption of a godhead. (Weber, 225)

Crane's confidence in poetry as more properly spiritual than systematic philosophy links his work more firmly still to Kierkegaard's lyric brand of Protestantism. When, in the Preface to *Fear and Trembling*, Kierkegaard rejects Hegelian system building – "The present writer is nothing of a Philosopher, he has not understood the System, does not know whether it actually exists" (24) – it is in order to call his own work a "dialectical lyric," so preparing the reader for the moment-by-moment immediacy of his "Meditations" on Abraham's travail. Kierkegaard's choice of the word "lyric" points to that same antiidealism Crane advances when he says that his work "insofar as it was truly poetic – avoids abstract tags and formulations."

In these terms, it is not that Crane conceives a "visionary" project his lyrics cannot sustain. Better to say that his conception of the lyric redefines vision. Writing from the particular, abjuring in nearly orthodox fashion the balm of taxonomic sanction – or sanctification – his practice of poetry proceeds from an acceptance of limitation that closely resembles Dickinson's, and, from a resignation of any proof of divinity save what can be experienced by an individual. Vision is apprehended not in any discharging of finite subject into infinite world, but in an igniting together of finite subject and finite object: "Poetry," Crane explains,

> can give you a ratio of fact and experience, and in this sense it is both
> a perception and the thing perceived, according as it approaches a
> significant articulation or not. This is its reality, its fact, its being.
> (Weber, 225)

To arrive at such a definition of "being" may be to call language not the shadow of the real but its crystallization,[11] but it is also to allow the severe limitation of a consciousness formally irreducible beyond "perceiver" and "thing perceived": It is to allow, as Dickinson does, the ultimate inaccessibility of a total knowledge.

Now to an illustration perhaps overdue. When I say that Crane's is a poetry of the subject/object fracture, of the "broken world," and of our essential disjunction from our experience, I am calling him a poet of the Fall. For such a poet the founding experience is this:

> So he drove out the man and he placed at the east of the garden of Eden
> Cherubims and a flaming sword which turned every which way, to
> keep the way of the tree of life. (Genesis 3:24)

This flaming sword, emblem of our division from the unity that was, appears in the "Ave Maria" and "Tunnel" sections of "The Bridge" as the "Hand of Fire." The image, synthesizing the cherub's sword, Christ's, and the Fiery Hand of the Edwardsean God, is one that Crane worked and reworked in his many drafts of the "Bridge." As Dickinson traces round her enterprise the frontier of circumference, Crane discerns a razor-edged boundary of human limitation on which death, desire, and the need to know all vibrate. The sword is "kiss of our agony," sign of the labor and covenant of living after the Fall. As a trope of division, the "Hand of Fire" functions as dark twin and impetus for Crane's chief emblem, the "bridge." As I shall show, "The Bridge," even as it seeks a fusion of subject and object, only retraces their separation. Even as it

achieves moments of vision, its language remains oblique, its speaker
stranded, cut off, by his ignorance. Complete knowledge is unavailable
except to the Being whose limitlessness defines our finitude, whose
knowledge in repose reveals the more our frantic ignorance. Dickinson
named the back side, the visible side, of God's knowledge "Reversed Divinity" (Dickinson, 800). Crane points to a similar reflexivity of absolute knowledge, an opacity of the Divine that is as if thickened by our
efforts to penetrate it. In "Ave Maria," Columbus apostrophizes:

> O Thou who sleepest on Thyself, apart
> Like ocean athwart lanes of death and birth,
> And all the eddying breath between doth search
> Cruelly with love thy parable of man, –   (Weber, 51)

Writing a poetry of "eddying breath between," a poetry whose
"bridges" only trace the fault line of a broken world, Crane seeks not
transcendence but a "parable of man," a form as chastened by existence
as Christ's parables were. His poetry resists even as it unveils those categories that such critics as Bloom and Riddel describe, resisting especially the snares of the "sacrificial" savior or "visionary victim." Without
further delay I want to turn to the greatest "visionary victim" in Crane's
work, to the Faust speaker of "The Marriage of Faustus and Helen." I
begin my exposition with two questions: Who is Crane's Helen? And
who is his Faust?

Discussing "The Marriage of Faustus and Helen" in "General Aims and
Theories," Crane complains, "The name of Helen, for instance, has become an all too easily employed crutch for evocation whenever a poet
felt a stitch in his side" (Weber, 217). In order to give new vigor to a
"mythology that has been obscured rather than illumined by the frequency of poetic allusions made to it," the opening lines of "The Marriage of Faustus and Helen" indict allusion itself, decrying the conventional habits of mind which lend themselves to universal application:

> The mind has shown itself at times
> Too much the baked and labeled dough
> Divided by accepted multitudes.   (Weber, 27)

In these lines Crane's poetic apprenticeship ends and his preparations for
"The Bridge" begin. Significantly, the lines resist a certain Roman ur-
banity, a Philistinism, or, perhaps closer to home, the complacency of a
Visible Sainthood that would routinize the sacramental precisely by so-
cializing it, by making the sacred normative. Specifically, not only do
these lines reject the Platonic "organization" to which Crane objected
in his letter to Munson, but they indict the aridity that will blight any

experience made consumable by "multitudes." The generalization of the sacred can only yield spiritual ennui: The true spirit will always seem arcane, even outré. Thus against the stolid sing-song of the opening three lines, the Marlovian epigraph seems precisely exotic: dark but comely at the tent flap of the normal. For in this epigraph, the poet points to another kind of knowledge, the "alchemical" knowledge of "Talmud Skill / and profane Greek," which yields a wisdom not mass- or archetypically produced, but acutely individuated. As we shall see, it is this more esoteric cast of mind that will live compatibly, companionably, with the world equivocal, the "world dimensional" where the speaker meets his Helen.

No surprise, then, that Crane's tactic is sharply to individualize Helen, stripping her of those archetypal associations which "bake" and "label" her. Forgetting the "fare and transfer," the speaker is dislocated, stripped of expectation, when he finds his Helen on the subway, eyes "Half-riant before the jerky window frame." Snatched from the elevated niche of the mythological, she is now framed by the smudged window of a subway car. The bordello light suffusing Faust's traditional "paramour" (or Poe's synthetic amalgam of a Helen with her "agate lamp") is corrected by the more exact light of "pink and green advertisements." Neither degraded nor ironized by her context, Helen's beauty is intensified by the particular circumstances in which the poet finds her.

Section II of the poem makes short work of the ideal or archetypal rape of Helen. There, Crane shrewdly collapses the deep time of the archetype rather as Whitman collapsed the deep time of his "beautiful gigantic swimmer" in Part 4 of "The Sleepers." To render the desired woman wholly contemporary, he stylizes the rape of Helen, pushing the event onto a flattened plane that seems as glossy as a photo ad. The consummation of love is set not in some roseate Olympus but on the "incandescent wax" of a roof garden, "Among slim skaters of the gardened skies." His very metrical decisions brush back the nap of expectation. The insistently trochaic opening lines

> Brazen hypnotics glitter here;
> Glee shifts from foot to foot,   (Weber, 30)

already drive the poem into a jazz rhythm at odds with, say, Wagnerian orchestrations of high tragedy. His use of synesthesia further baffles archetypal identifications. "Hypnotics" may be visual or aural – it is hard to tell which – and the "brazen . . . ricochet" from roof to roof describes both the glancing light and the jittery blare of brass instruments. Imprecision only swells the richness of the scene; this is the ambience of temptation disseminated in films or songs or perfume advertisements.

Crane is less after an interpretation of the rape of Helen than a brutal stylization, or send-up, that deflates the ideal as the rhythms of jazz, or comic opera, send up cathartic musical forms.[12] The events of this section simply do not bear the weight of the archetype. The consummation of the love of Faustus and Helen comes accompanied by cornets, as a "fall downstairs." This short drop, a "tumble," clips the much deeper Fall of Faustus and his "paramour," the blare of cornets aping the derisive laughter of Mephistopheles. The very culture that Faustus and his flapper profane is overseen neither by the pantheon of envious gods who brought war as punishment for the rape of Helen, nor by the one God who tolerates no blasphemy. Rather, theirs is a culture slumped in comfortable dotage: "relatives serene and cool, / Sit rocked in patent armchairs." Helen's fall is no violation with cosmic repercussions but preamble to a "marriage."

Indeed, what describes the singularity of this poem best is that it orchestrates a marriage. Marriage is the supremely nontranscendent state. It is the life cycle arrangement left out of tragedy, and yielding comedy. Marriage is that condition – unlike desire or actual death – that fully occupies human time. Crane's Helen does not become Faustus's paramour, ensuring his damnation; she becomes his wife, and so cuts his work loose from the transcendent possibilities of tragedy. Set in what Northrop Frye calls a low mimetic mode (*Anatomy of Criticism,* 51), Part II of "The Marriage of Faustus and Helen" returns us to a flattened comic world which substitutes simple indiscretion for a sin of infinite knowledge, promising heaven, punishable in hell.

No great wonder then that the poem would deprive the Faustian anti-hero, or invert Christ, of his archetypal depth. Crane's Faustus becomes a figure who reverses the Faustian bargain. Instead of gaining the absolute at the price of his soul, he sells the absolute in order to love a particular woman.

> And now, before its arteries turn back
> I would have you meet his bartered blood.
> Imminent in his dream, none better knows
> The white wafer cheek of love, or offers words
> Lightly as moonlight on the eaves meets snow.   (Weber, 28)

If the symbolic details, coded red and white, promise a more sublime and traditional union – a movement from blood to pure snow, body to spirit – the lines do not release the speaker into any such rarefied purity. The moment of union is one seized "before its arteries turn dark" – in some interstice of human time. The love exchanged needs the sacrament of words, the "white wafer cheek" of love. Speech itself is reduced but not dissolved; the moonlight on the eaves touches snow in an imperceptible white on white, a metaphor degree zero, that does not efface but rather traces the point of meeting. And if, as the poem goes on, Faust finds in Helen's body "Reflective conversion of all things" – a transubstantiation – then the love she promises chastens aspirations to the transcendent:

> . . . the body of the world
> Weeps in inventive dust for the hiatus
> That winks above it, bluet in your breasts.   (Weber, 28)

"Bluet" disciplines the azure sky. Incarnated in cornflowers, the "hiatus," or long pause, of heaven is domesticated, lent human scale just as the Helen of the archetype is repatriated to the realm of the human.

When Kierkegaard devotes a section of *The Concept of Dread* to detailing what constitutes an inauthentic relationship to the infinite and unknown, the pact of the traditional Faust is his example. This Faust, an aspirant who would sacrifice all for the beauty of infinity, wills the absolute without living in what Crane calls the "imminent." Aspiring to such infinity, he seeks the infinite outside the resources of the self. Shrugging off the pain of being Faust, he forces – even rapes – the absolute rather than suffering its unrequital; he would find some higher life outside the tarnished world by imitating an absolute state not legitimately available to human beings. Such a person, described by Kierkegaard in *The Sickness Unto Death,* "is not willing to attire himself in himself, to see his task in the self given him; by the aid of being the infinite form, he will construct it himself" (Bretali, 366).

Crane's Faustus, by contrast, not unlike Whitman's early Lincoln, "attires [himself] in [himself]." To a Helen who fulfills none of the conditions for beauty "divided by accepted multitudes," he addresses his "inconspicuous glowing orb of praise." Never escaping the equivocal, in the very act of lifting his arms

> . . . it is to bend
> To you who turn away once, Helen, knowing
> The press of troubled hands, too alternate
> With steel and soil to hold you endlessly.
> I meet you, therefore, in that eventual flame
> You found in final chains, no captive then –
> Beyond their million, brittle bloodshot eyes,
> White, though white cities passed on to assume
> The world which comes to each of us alone.   (Weber, 28)

That last line seals the poem's resistance to transcendence. If it was the sin of trading his own soul and peculiar circumstances that damns the tra-

ditional Faust, Crane's Faustus accedes to "the world that comes to each
of us alone." The contemporary detailing ironizes "eternity": There is no
archetypal woman to hold "endlessly." Turning her back, the Helen of
mythology is all printed with the "press of troubled hands." But only
when chained to this world is she released from the violation of the archetype; to love her is to sustain the punishment of this world for her, to
see her violated by "their million brittle, bloodshot eyes." Suffering a
world relentlessly brushed by "smutty wings" and mired in "equivoca-
tions," Helen and Faustus earn not the "tragic" outcome that comes to
archetypes, but the comic outcome of "marriage." If as archetypes they
were "visionary victims," it is the work of the poem to restore them to
life as vulnerable souls. Bloom's Orphic Faust – who loses Eurydice to
make his loss art – is ousted. Crane's Faust, no visionary victim, is rather
one sentenced to live in a world of particulars unrelieved by any transcendent noumenality.

The first two parts of "The Marriage of Faustus and Helen" thus
effect a virtual transformation of Faustus and Helen from archetypal
ciphers to implicated mortal agents. Of a particular time, suffering
particular pangs, they do not pierce but are rather pierced by history.
Section III of the poem establishes the same particularity, rescuing
the "religious gunman," a World War I bomber, from the archetype
that would absorb him. No mere type of a Trojan hero, this gunman
shares with the speaker the giddy memories of "the tensile boughs,
the nimble blue plateaus, / The mounted, yielding cities of the air."
Rather than act the generic warrior, the gunman has a history that
comes to him alone. Crane's very images of flight seem to simulate
the saddleless sensation of the human body suspended for the first time
and alone in air: the surmise of the impossible, the stomach just poised
to drop. As such, they are less archetypal than documentary, valuable
for correcting such "three winged and gold-shod prophecies of heaven"
as myth provides with a flyer's thumbed log and testimony. The technique is that same which let the green and pink advertisements correct
the bordello kitsch of legend. And like Helen, who, enduring in the pedestrian setting of the interurban, renounces the mystique of transcendent unapproachability, Crane's flyers, rather than die as visionary
victims, as sublime Orpheuses, "Have survived, / And will persist to
speak again."

The poem ends with a praise of a human time wrenching itself free of
the sacrificial time:

> Distinctly praise the years, whose volatile
> Blamed bleeding hands extend and thresh the height
> The imagination spans beyond despair,
> Outpacing bargain, vocable and prayer.   (Weber, 33)

Observe that it is not time contracted or absorbed by the blamed, bleeding hands of a sacrificed type. The passion is in time, in "years" praised "distinctly." Like Whitman, Crane manipulates Christology to his own ends. Where Whitman's savior of "drooping eyes" showed himself not a pure but a transgressive savior, Crane's "blamed, bleeding hands" bind the imaginative process not to *kairos* but to *chronos,* to the "years" with no escape route into the infinite. Thus the imagination "outpaces" all verbal gestures at a beyond which would vault immediate human consequence, surpassing "bargain, vocable and prayer."

A closing word on the stylistic instruments Crane deploys in "The Marriage of Faustus and Helen." Corresponding to a metaphysic that collapses archetypal depth in immediacy, this style records images with a precision that exhausts them. As though beauty itself had no tenure, the images reach consummation and disintegration almost simultaneously:

> White shadows slip across the floor
> Splayed like cards from a loose hand

The couplet is of a complexity both enigmatic and overdetermined. Tenor and vehicle meet obliquely, if at all, in some interstice of meaning whose domain Dickinson called that of the "riddle." In "White shadows slip," for example, notice how whiteness is all but canceled by the duskiness of "shadow." Yet "shadow" enriches and complicates the image, preparing us for that "slip." Slip, as a verb, connotes both stealth and grace. But, rewelded to "white" through the agency of "shadow," we glimpse as well the lingerie worn by a Helen whirling toward her "fall downstairs." This fall is presaged both by the "loose hand" and the "cards" which evoke the risk "shadowing" Helen and shadowing the whole poem with subtext of the Faustian bargain. If these lines record an arrested, even hallucinatory moment, packing both abandon and a nascent eroticism into the words "splayed" and "loose," there is no "category" of poetic reference to which the reader can appeal, no archetype connecting the whirl of skirts to cards. The "innocence," the sheer originality of the image, is too acute to sustain more general ideas. As Crane explains in "General Aims and Theories":

> It is as though a poem gave the reader as he left it a single new *word,* never before spoken and impossible to actually enunciate, but self-evident as an active principle in the reader's consciousness henceforward . . . the entire construction of the poem is raised on the organic principle of a "logic of metaphor" which antedates our so-called pure logic. (Weber, 221)

If for other American writers style can erect what Richard Poirier calls "a world elsewhere," Crane charges his style with the task of rendering a world nowhere but here. Illumination is produced rather than simply reflected by the image. There is no semantic guarantee to secure meaning: Only faith secures it. Working without the safety net of general categories, Crane employs a language of "innocence" that typically risks unintelligibility; his willingness to engage the unpredictable or the unknown leaves his language, like Dickinson's, vibrant but double exposed. The poetry proceeds from those premises Kierkegaard describes in *Philosophical Fragments* when he writes of

> The paradoxical passion of the Reason [which] comes repeatedly into collision with the unknown, which does indeed exist, but is unknown, and insofar does not exist.

He goes on, "The reason cannot advance beyond this point, and yet it cannot refrain in its paradoxicalness from arriving at this limit and occupying itself therewith" (35).

Crane's most ambitious and interesting poem, "The Bridge," is stretched across precisely this limit. The poem's literal subject is the Brooklyn Bridge, link between Brooklyn and Manhattan, rural and urban America, preindustrial and technological culture. But stretching as well between the poet, his poetic forebears, and a mass culture that makes poetic invention problematic, the bridge is an image of art dislocated from the sanctum of art, of art released to history. Most of all, the bridge is a self-reflexive figure. With its delicately fretted cables, humming and tight-strung, the "Bridge" is, all at once, the poet's harp, the subject of his song, and the language in which he sings that song. At the same time subject, object, and instrument of the desire to unify them, the bridge is an image of dualism, of disjunction, and of the urge to join that only articulates our severedness. That is why to see it simply as a metaphor for various kinds of union, or release, is to reduce it to a cliché – and Crane to a hack, overliteral: a pallid Shelley. It is instead the impossibility of union that Crane takes for granted. The trajectory his bridge traces is the "exile's," its course, the way of Adam left to range over a world he has played his part in spoiling. Monument to the inarticulateness into which all poetry resolves, to the ignorance that drives knowledge, and to the "eddying breath between" that interrupts immortality with the mortal, the Bridge is "sign manifest" of our fallenness and of that limit which torments all passion, all knowledge.

To move on from the discrete lyrics of *White Buildings* to "Proem: To Brooklyn Bridge" we find the opening lines of this poem poised on just such a limit, laying open to question the very conditions of our understanding. Throwing into crisis the simplest act of seeing – the tourist's gape at the Brooklyn Bridge – these lines point directly to the transformational effect of the Unknown on the urgent Reason as the two meet on an edge vibrantly paradoxical:[13]

> How many dawns, chill from his rippling rest
> The seagull's wings shall dip and pivot him,
> Shedding white rings of tumult, building high
> Over the chained bay waters Liberty –
>
> Then with inviolate curve, forsake our eyes
> As apparitional as sails that cross
> Some page of figures to be filled away;
> – Till elevators drop us from our day.

The crucial definition of this edge, or limit, comes at the syntactic mid-point of the first lyric sentence. There, "forsake our eyes / As apparitional as sails that cross / Some page" grounds wings in sails and then folds sails in pages. The seagull as a figure of ascending spirit yields to a flutter of documents, finally losing lift in the plummet of the "elevator." Which, then, is the subject of "apparitional as sails"? Is the seagull, in whom we have invested shedding, or metamorphic, powers, a mere illusion, "apparitional"? Or are our "eyes" themselves "apparitional" – not really there – and so, in following the flight of the seagull, not really seeing him? Like Dickinson employing a bewildered syntax to express uncertainty as to where our vision ends and God's Being begins, Crane reaches in these lines a nexus of the unknown. The smaller increments only reinforce this ambiguity – "inviolate" is both pure and stained with "violet"; the "bay waters Liberty" is chained; the "seagull" may "gull" our seeing. Read vertically – that is, down the column of closing rhymes – the second stanza hints at a thwarting, a mis-signaling and a failure of optical competence in "eyes" / "cross" / "away" / "day": Poetic sight is a strabismus that sideswipes light. The passion of the subject to know the object is thwarted by a poetic diction that raises questions about the act of cognition itself, about perception. The subjectivity of what Dickinson calls "our ignoble Eyes" (800) is always thrown back on itself, on the Eyes' "Comparative."

The lines exact closer attention still, for in themselves they substantially belie such claims as that Crane asserted a "quality of will against the world" and at each "failure of the will he turned against himself." Whatever Crane's personal response to the frustration of his ambitions, these lines describe a more thoughtful and flexible relation of poet to world than dumb "thrust" or yowling disappointment. What we see here and throughout "The Bridge" is a poetry that intrepidly releases will into the very experience of the unknown that baffled the will. The poems cultivate a certain Edwardsean attentiveness to the crosswinds of power outside the self. Such attentiveness is fundamentally different from the agonism of Emerson, which gains lift in fronting adverse currents. One should be careful as well to distinguish Crane's kind of attentive resignation, or Awe, from Dionysian ecstasy, not to confuse Crane's letting go with that Dionysian release that rescues self from self for the sake of a larger wholeness. There is no wholeness to be so attained. Crane's letting go, his abdication of the logical control which blocks the union of self and other in song, is always played out on that "limit . . . which is a torment for passion," a limit not to be overleaped. Division is the condition of Crane's writing. When brokenness cedes itself to wholeness, the release is momentary.

Look, for example, at a stretch of this "Proem" where the speaker addresses the bridge in a long apostrophe. Much more than an architectural marvel, the bridge is now "harp and altar of the fury fused"; it is "terrific threshold of the prophet's pledge." It is so beautiful that the poet asks, "How could mere toil align thy choiring strings?" Surely some apprehension of the infinite is at hand as he goes on to praise "unfractioned idiom, immaculate sigh of stars." The "idiom" yearns toward some language unbroken by subject and object, the "sigh" toward a virgin purity; the moment of union or ecstasy is at hand. And when union finally comes in the lovely breakthrough line

And we have seen night lifted in thy arms

the incipient associations building in the foregoing lines cohere: The Bridge is now a woman, a Muse or madonna, cradling the tender night in her arms. In language like a gift, after long preparation, grace comes. The sinner's, or dualist's patience, yields the experience all sinners crave: vision.

Yet the moment is necessarily short-lived. The "idiom" falls into fraction. The figure who appeared like a holograph now dissolves into a kind of dot-to-dot, into the "traffic lights which skim," now brokenly buttressing the arc of the bridge. The passionate moment of breakthrough – the leap – is necessarily ceded to another moment, a dimmer moment: "Under thy shadow by the piers I waited / Only in darkness is thy shadow clear."

The lines return us to a logical syntax of subject and object, to consciousness homesick, as Lukacs might put it, for the moment of union. That "harp and altar of the Fury fused," is now nothing more sacred than a technological accomplishment, a structure welded out of plain metal. Timelessness resumes its mundane increments in the "iron year" and the speaker for whom experience and consciousness were fused in one "incognizable word" is now returned to a pedestrian reporting under the bridge. The paradoxical but ecstatic moment of engagement with limit recedes for him into a history he can only witness.

Such oscillation between release and constraint, innocence and experience, will typify Crane's procedure in "The Bridge." When Kierkegaard writes "Innocence . . . only comes into existence by the very fact that it is annulled, comes into existence as that which was before it was annulled" (*Concept*, 32), he might be reflecting on the annulments of "The Bridge." There, moments of epiphany, of the absolute, are always brought to earth. Like moonlight meeting snow on the eaves, the world may go transparent. But, caught as we are between earth and heaven, we never transcend the paradox of aspiring to the Word in human words, seeking the infinite by finite means. Let me backtrack to the "Proem" to supply a last example of this disciplining of transcendental consciousness that is the vernacular of "The Bridge":

> And Thee, across the harbor, silver paced,
> As though the sun took step of thee, yet left
> Some motion ever unspent in thy stride, –
> Implicitly thy freedom staying thee!

Addressing the bridge here, the poet finds in it a redemptive emblem of the grace he seeks. Yet the evocation of sunlight on the bridge requires the closest attention; the paradoxical tension it posits measures a *relation* between the buoyancy and incandescence of grace and the gravity of the earthly.

The images begin modestly enough. The sun, climbing the struts of the bridge, imparts not only its light but also its principle of motion to the mechanism which, by the grace of that light, now has a "stride." Yet only because of the bridge's fretwork – static and frozen – is the "stride" of the light perceptible. In the final line, the paradox is manifest: "Implicitly thy freedom staying thee." While the bridge gains its stable form by the glancing play of light, the sun gains its freedom in the form that restrains it. The bridge is stabilized by aspiration and gravity; its form results from their counterpull. These lines set a pattern for "innocence" or for the quality of illumination available in "The Bridge," a pattern of form arrested in expression, of retinal impressions lending expression to spiritual states through a language that is both their means of release and their limitation. As the "Proem" ends

> Unto us lowliest sometimes sweep, descend
> And of the curveship lend a myth to God.

Through this myth, this innocent language, we "lend to God" – an inversion of the myth of Christ "lent" to man – we realize our innocence. The tessellated fractioning of the "curve" attests to our brokenness, and the changeable voice of its speaker – now charged with prophetic clarity, now fallen into unintelligibility and chaos – testifies to all that in our fallenness we cannot "bridge."

To this speaker I shall now turn. For what we have not yet characterized is what Kierkegaard would call the "psychology" of that individual who makes his way by "tracing the broken world." As my analysis of "The Marriage of Faustus and Helen" suggests, this individual, far from fitting a general description of "visionary victim," is instead charged with the essentially ethical task of discovering the shape of his own existence: with inhabiting "the world that comes to each of us alone." I want to take this idea further by suggesting that "The Bridge" frames such a psychology of belief, an ethics, by establishing a set of evocative spiritual profiles and, moreover, by plotting a spiritual catalogue of responses to the fact of the Unknown. It is worth noting that such a psychology is nowhere really essayed in American poetry before Crane, not even in the work of Whitman and Dickinson. For Whitman writes not a psychology but a policy and a law of transgression and Dickinson's theology of anonymity ingests psychology as a rite of faith. On the other hand, in a certain way, Crane gives us in "The Bridge" a *Concept of Dread* in verse, a *bildungsroman* of spiritual pilgrimage that educates the singer – through possibility and dread – to a just understanding of the "world that comes to [him] alone." The poem draws a trajectory of alternatives, articulates a set of spiritual types. Among these must the one who seeks vision choose.

One such type, as I have already said, is the "visionary victim," the Romantic self-immolator readers typically assume governs Crane's work. It is no use denying, nor do I mean to deny, that from the outset – from the very epigraph introducing the Satan of Job "going to and fro in the earth walking up and down" – this figure haunts the poem. But in the course of explicating how Crane incarnates this lost soul as Poe, I would go some distance toward showing the limited power such a figure possesses. If his power is that of arch-tempter – Satan to Job, snake to Adam – his enemy is faith, and his nemesis, the poetic survivalist: the singer as Adam.

To be sure, rather than sell his soul outright to the Devil, to Poe as poet maudit, the speaker of "The Bridge" celebrates the "patience that is armor and that shields love from despair" ("Quaker Hill"), imputing this patience to a range of Joblike figures, whose survival counterpoints the demise of Poe and whose prototype is the clown of "Chaplinesque" from *White Buildings*. Chaplin and Poe will serve as useful endpoints for the discussion to follow inasmuch as they are stationed at the two spiritual poles "The Bridge" touches. In Crane's Joblike Chaplin we can read the possibility a fallen and implicated language affords; in Poe, the risk it entails. My point will be to suggest how the wide-ranging flexibility of Chaplin harbors within it the derangement of Poe; how Chaplin's adaptability contains Poe's Satanic Byronism: this, in order to emphasize the ambiguity of the innocence Crane champions. For innocence is Janusfaced: on one side a clown, on the other a gargoyle. Acting as a corrective to Poe, Chaplin also promises to correct the critical view of an overextended, hyperromantic Orphism, or an Emersonian agonism, as Crane's singular contribution to our literary history.

"Chaplinesque," inspired by Chaplin's "The Kid" and written in 1921, is the first poem of Crane's maturity. Calling Chaplin "the greatest living actor, and the prime interpreter of the soul imposed upon by modern civilization" (Weber, *Letters*, 85), Crane writes a poem that imitates Chaplin's art by assuming a stance nimble yet engaged with the world. Crane learns from Chaplin how a certain agile and vigilant artfulness can transform the unbearable, can "lend" epiphanies to degraded circumstance. Implicit in the poem is the idea that the failure of such art will leave the subject helpless, abject, and dehumanized *because* silent.

Chaplin's particular brilliance illuminates Crane's enterprise. To watch a Chaplin film is to be struck by his gift for putting the formidable limitation of his art form – its silence – to use. The flicker of silence and gesture have an almost allegorical power in Chaplin's work. Silence is the domain of sad anomie; in bits of film not animated by gesture we see the pallor, the soul's emaciation, the vulnerability of the little tramp, as through gesture and gesticulation the tramp engages the world, flicking his cane to show us he is alive, that he can even be happy.

From Chaplin Crane gets this stripped yet elegant lexicon of silence and balletic gesture. Nonspeech or degraded speech or speech that would be *more* than human gives access to that despair, or to that "shutupness" Kierkegaard calls the trademark of the demoniacal. The gesture of an engaged art, on the other hand, preserves the subject and redeems contact with the world. Such an art can achieve the "lyric" grace which, for Kierkegaard, provides the ground for faith.

Crane and Kierkegaard are here, as elsewhere, mutually illuminating as twinned figures of the Protestant lyricist in his role as the psyche's anatomist. Kierkegaard, master of a dizzying array of fictions, masks and poses, purveys mediate forms for the sake of "the responsibility a man has before God for the reflection bestowed upon him" (*The Point of View for My Work as an Author*, 91). The "reflection" he describes corresponds to the "spiritual illuminations . . . discoverable under new forms" in Crane. If Kierkegaard, the soul's poet, does his apprenticeship to faith by toiling in the duplicities of art, Crane relieves a toiling world through a faith in duplicity. For both Crane and Kierkegaard the quality

of spiritual experience is tested by the *lyricism of its expression*. Kierkegaard here recalls for us the bankruptcy of theory and the richness of the
lyric that Emersonianism discovers in spite of itself in "Days." Not only
does the lyric thrive in the throes of a spiritual experience, even as it lan-
guished in the precincts of philosophy. But more, lyricism becomes the
touchstone of spiritual authenticity. Precisely at the point where Kierkegaard's lyric "reflection" is occluded by system building, Crane's lyric
sustains that human "responsibility before God" to the "reflection bestowed." Discursivity, that offers the total view as opposed to the partial
ray, is revealed in both bodies of work to be drastically limited. Discursivity, and the efficacy of theory itself as a totalized system of language,
are brought up short before the penetration of a single lyric beam.

Let us look back from "The Bridge" to "Chaplinesque" and to a description of the kind of innocence, or faith, that an absurd art makes
available. Innocence and faith begin in a common soil, in an acceptance of
the finite condition of existence, in the inescapability of limitation Kierkegaard calls "infinite resignation." We might be struck by the extraordinary resemblance between the resignation Kierkegaard describes:

> The infinite resignation is that shirt we read about in the old fable. The
> thread is spun under tears, the cloth bleached with tears, the shirt sewn
> with tears; but then too it is a better protection than iron and steel. (*Fear
> and Trembling*, 56)

and Crane's arresting sketch of a human being stripped to an attribute of
vulnerability. Crane's clown is less a person than a scarecrow personification of shelter and shelterlessness, an abstract of nesting, collapsible
boxes.[14]

> We make our meek adjustments
> Contented with such random consolations
> As the wind deposits
> In slithered and too ample pockets
>
> For we can still love the world, who find
> A famished kitten on the step, and know
> Recesses for it from the fury of the street
> Or warm torn elbow coverts.

In both passages there is the sense that existence, if it is to yield meaning,
must use the materials that come to hand, must "wear the shirt sewn
with tears" or "love the world, who find / A famished kitten on the
step." Existence capable of this is ready for what Kierkegaard calls faith,
and Crane "innocence" – the state which might be described as experience conscious of itself, yet purged, momentarily, of the anguish of being
itself. Note, though, the way in which Kierkegaard defines "resignation,"

by discursively framing, theorizing a paradox which Crane allows his language simply to dramatize. Unglossed, Crane's lines displace the down-and-out lot of the figure buffeted by wind onto the "kitten" protected by "too ample pockets."

The crossing over into "faith" in *Fear and Trembling* and into "innocence" in "Chaplinesque" marks a crucial juncture. For it is here that Kierkegaard, author of a "dialectical lyric," yields the lyric to the dialectic, or poetry to philosophy, and it is here that Crane yields up the program of "General Aims and Methods" to a poetry that must explain itself. The impetus to these divergent movements is an identical apprehension of the absurdity of infinite resignation. The discontinuity to be bridged, the sheer length of the leap between infinite resignation and faith, is unimaginable. The faith an Abraham requires to sacrifice his son remains utterly outside the comprehension of the one who is infinitely resigned. "Innocence" which recognizes the "fury of the street" is hard put to remain innocent. Having gone so far as to isolate the moment of "resignation" as the "last stage prior to faith"; having, in fact, prepared us for the breakthrough into faith and for the speaker's triumphant shedding of the ironic pseudonymous voice of Johannes Silentio, the masked Kierkegaard writes:

> I can well describe the movements of faith but I cannot make them. When one would learn to make the motions of swimming one can let oneself be hung by a swimming belt from the ceiling, but this no swimming . . . in that way I can describe the movements of faith. (*Fear*, 48)

This is exiled and prosaic language. The lyricist, close kin here to the Emersonian dilettante who realizes theory's limits in "Days," has reached the limits of his control. He indicates that what will follow is discursive speculation and not the risk of poetic announcement. If we expect the breakthrough of a lyric speaker in whose altered tones we will trace the passage from infinite resignation to faith; if we expect that the voice of the artful dodger Silentio will deepen or break, revealing the passage to faith in apostrophe, confession, aria, we are to be disappointed. Rather, Silentio makes for the exits, fleeing the lyric bind, the cul-de-sac of implication, his lyricism giving way to a more systematic language. Where there was paradox there is now personification allegory. The intrapersonal hierarchy of states toward grace within the individual subject gives way to a hierarchy of knights whose talents correspond not to stages along life's way, ambiguously overlapping, but to a stratified hierarchy of souls. And if Kierkegaard's philosophical relay between these two knights has the virtue of rhetorical clarity, it cannot express that paradoxical moment when one yields to the other. The very category of the absurd that permits decorous discussion forecloses evocation of the experience itself. The knight who is, above all, individual, in order to show himself, splits himself; in order to communicate, sacrifices lyric grace. His "All" occludes his "Each."

This fission sheds light on both the theoretical clarity Crane sacrifices and the lyric grace he gains, that grace which, as Lukacs puts it, can "create a protean mythology of the substantial subjectivity out of the strength of its own ignorance" (*Theory,* 63). Living without the wisdom of an overarching understanding, such grace – won of ignorance – is achieved in the "sidestep" of the clown:

> We will sidestep, and to the final smirk
> Dally the doom of the inevitable thumb
> That slowly chafes its puckered index toward us,
> Facing the dull squint with what innocence
> And what surprise!
>
> And yet these fine collapses are not lies
> More than the pirouettes of any pliant cane;
> Our obsequies are, in a way, no enterprise.
> We can evade you, and all else but the heart;
> What blame to us if the heart live on.

To be fair, the clown's "fine collapses" are lies. To "dally" death, the "inevitable thumb" of experience, is to gain an innocence belied by experience. To upstage the pain of the world by putting on the motley of the clown is not to defer its impaling "dull squint." The clown figure – turning his pirouettes, proffering his "obsequies" – stands in the space of the absurd, asserting precisely what is not so. Withal, the choreography of his "pliant cane" can yield a beauty that is "innocent," that forges, at least for a moment, a genuine regeneracy. Refusing irony, the poem goes on:

> The game enforces smirks; but we have seen
> The moon in lonely alleys make
> A grail of laughter in an empty ashcan,

This is the epiphany available to a clown. This great "lyric moment" is one of those, again Lukacs', when "sudden flashes of substance become like lost original manuscripts suddenly made legible" (63). The image scavenges illumination in the garbage. While the moment of vision lasts, the confrontation of vulnerable subject and punishing world is ameliorated. "Innocence" is achieved, but an innocence unprotected by sentiment, an innocence with a price.

The price is that the "grail of laughter" is utterly consumed. The ash remaining shows the condition of our loneliness harshened. In the Kierkegaardian terms employed earlier, this is the return of the dancer to earth, the descent attending the ascent to faith. The "grail of laughter," the spiritually irradiated moment, echoes, and what we hear in the second wave of sound is not celestial music but the common, curled cry of a "kitten in the wilderness." In this kitten we see the speaker's brave pronoun "we" shaved to a mewing "I." The stabilizing power of an absolute experience was illusory, the representativeness of the clown who redeems all our finite suffering defeated. If there is a Christ who suffers for us all, our faith is proven best by living without his abiding comforts. In the "world that comes to each of us alone" each of us is a clown, or, to borrow a phrase from "The River," a child on a "loose perch" and there is no higher logic to release us from our isolation. We may "dally the doom of that inevitable thumb" only so long before the thumb has the final word, before the vulnerability of individual existence reasserts itself.

It would perhaps be wise at this juncture to distinguish Chaplin's "innocence" from what in Romantic parlance is called "sincerity" – Wordsworth's "spontaneous overflow of powerful feelings." Crane's Chaplin is no urban Noble Savage whose utterance transcends the pretense of representation, no solitary reaper whose song shucks off artifice. He is a dissimulator, a lying poet, so worldly that he can live in the world as though it will not flatten him. In sallying forward, tramping on, he is *performing*. His art is the sign of his assent to finite existence; it describes the mediate nature of all that the soul attains. Such an art is Chaplin's stock in trade. When in a famous scene the tramp dines on a stewed boot, the gesture is suffused with the absurd; the innocence is in the pretense, in making the motions. Kierkegaard described how making the motions of faith – like the motions of swimming – are requisite to faith. Crane's Chaplin makes such motions and so serves as guardian – even guardian angel – for a poetry that finds not a traditional innocence, not that innocence seized beneath the divided, fallen world and a dividing fallen language, but an innocence achieved, to quote a later poem, in "hell's despite." The "grail of laughter in an empty ashcan" that ends the poem is not a vision of transcendence but of submission made art.

Chaplin's anonymous persona is also crucial. Hardly a Prometheus, his identity is borrowed like his clothes. His wandering confederates him with the down and out, with what, for the sake of convenience, we currently call the marginal. His physical appearance is, in a way, a refusal of the Satanic or Orphic consistency. Looking like a child or a woman in man's clothing, Chaplin wears the immigrant's mustache in an era of the clean jaw. His comrades are criminals, black men, outcasts in the Yukon. He is nothing like the Emersonian strong poet coursing with a rounded and unique coherence. Chaplin's defining feature is his ephemerality; his very selfhood is vagrant, defined extemporaneously, ad-libbed.

Chaplin is the prototype for other wanderers in Crane, figures on the circumference of American life, the "pliant cane" of whose language can secure an innocence, but an innocence paradoxical, chastened by life on earth. The "black man in the cellar" in "Black Tambourine" is one of these; his tambourine is the sign of an art that mediates absurdly between the world where "gnats toss in the shadow of a bottle" and "Aesop, driven to pondering, found / Heaven with the Tortoise and the Hare."

This determination, despite the high style, to write a poetry of the cursed and ignored, the impure and the improvident, is what connects Crane's poetic project most firmly to Whitman's. Crane's salient contribution is to return to Whitman's blessed citizens their mortal souls. By treating life lived on the dim side of the tambourine, Crane advances the aims of the poet who wrote: "Through me long dumb voices, / Voices of the interminable generations of slaves, / Voices of prostitutes and deformed persons, / Voices of the diseased and despairing, of thieves and dwarfs." In "The River," perhaps the finest section of "The Bridge," Crane rewrites "Song of the Open Road," but in it he addresses a problem Whitman skirts: the imperative to know the "world that comes to each of us alone." For what the communalized self of "Song of Myself" or the transgressive savior in "The Sleepers" never allows is the travail of those discrete individuals blessed, as a matter of policy, *en masse*. Whether Whitman "stops somewhere waiting for you" or enfolds the ennuyée, the lover, the slave in his arms, his broad gestures of inclusion eclipse what it feels like to be "you," a "lover," or a "slave."[15] Striving for a chant democratic, he overeconomizes on "the world that comes to each of us alone."

It is Crane's triumph in "The River" to release individual experience back into the democratic poem, but to do so in such a way as will preserve the feel of diminished existence. Crane gives us a poetry that lives inside, under the skin of, forsaken souls left to wander the terrain of their anonymity. Or better, lives inside their words. Working at that juncture where frail and pauperous souls redeem themselves in their speech – living fully in language if nowhere else – Crane unearths a linguistic medium that dignifies its subjects by individualizing them. Crane resurveys the human vista Whitman swept with his yawp, going silent to render audible the speech of others. If Whitman sometimes blessed before he listened, overanxious to extend his fiat of approval, Crane hangs back. The poem listens:

> Stick your patent name on a signboard
> brother – all over – going west – young man
> Tintex – japalac – Certain-teed Overalls ads
> and lands sakes! under the new playbill ripped

in the guaranteed corner – see Bert Williams what?
Minstrels when you steal a chicken just
save me the wing for if it isn't
Erie it ain't for miles around a
Mazda – and a telegraphic night coming on Thomas

This is Whitman's turnpike, only what we hear on the wires is speech unredeemed by prophetic utterance. No nursing poet binds up this fragmented language, rounding out its cadences. The cadences stand on their own and their cacophony says as much about American loneliness as about American collectivity. Consciousness registers as the blurred view one might have watching billboards pass from a boxcar, or stuck between cities, picking up vagrant radio waves. The "young man" on the road absorbs his culture as a kind of static to which he adds his voice. If this evocation of American life lacks the shape Whitman can give, nevertheless it permits us to hear the individual voices freed from the poet's smothering approbation. It allows another variety of what Crane calls "innocence." Controlled neither by the solicitude of the poet nor by "preconception," the mouth of the river sets loose an American music:

> *My Old Kentucky Home* and *Casey Jones,*
> *Some Sunny Day,* I heard a Road gang chanting so.
> And afterwards, who had colt's eyes – one said,
> "Jesus! Oh I remember watermelon days!" And sped
> High in a cloud of merriment, recalled
> " – And when my Aunt Sally Simpson smiled," he
>   drawled –
> "It was almost Louisiana, long ago."
> "There's no place like Booneville though, Buddy."
> One said, excising a last burr from his vest,
> " – For early trouting."

These accents fall from the mouths of figures who dignify their lives with the pliant gesture of their language. Yet, like the clown of "Chaplinesque" and like the youth of "The Sleepers," whose vulnerability we glimpse too briefly ("O hot cheeked and blushing"), they are terribly exposed, easily engulfed by silence and sadness, by being nobody:

> Behind
> My father's cannery works I used to see
> Rail-squatters ranged in nomad raillery,
> The ancient men – wifeless or runaway
> Hobo-trekkers that forever search
> An empire wilderness of freight and rails
>
> Each seemed a child, like me, on a loose perch,
> Holding to childhood like some termless play.
> . . .

> – Memphis to Tallahassee – riding the rods,
> Blind fists of nothing, humpty-dumpty clods.

Like the little tramp, Crane's hobo trekkers are desperately fragile, children with mustaches or clods always risking a fall off the wall. The paragon of this American fragility is the black man, or "minstrel." Precisely as his song is absorbed, taken up into American culture, he drowns:

> The River, spreading, flows – and spends your dream.
> What are you, lost within this tideless spell?
> You are your father's father, and the stream –
> A liquid theme that floating niggers swell.

The River, even as it sings its "hosannas," is striated with the cruelty of history – It is "a liquid theme that floating niggers swell." Writing a poem of deep engagement with the world, Crane, in "The River," promises nothing like the transcendent release of the "Orphist," and, curiously, nothing really like Whitman's general balm. What he offers instead is what he called "Voyages," calls "infinite consanguinity"; or, what Kierkegaard calls more simply a "purely human" engagement with history. We see this in the compression of Crane's language. In the lines above – "rail-squatters ranged in nomad raillery" – observe how the "rails" resolve into "raillery"; the relationship is reciprocal. The rails wandering over the American landscape figure a wide ranging language, a democratic articulation absorbing mass culture. Cohering out of the "facts" of American experience, the lines derive their "innocence" from a poetic technique that will not force unity, or felicity, on material whose innocence is the innocence of the broken.

By now another problem this poem engages should be manifest. That is the problem of poetic language in a culture increasingly given over to advertising, radio, to the proliferation of "billboards." When a poem begins "Stick your patent name on a signboard," the line between a human expression accommodating itself to the facts of experience and the appropriation of that expression by the banal twitter of mass culture is quite fine. On this line two other lyrics from "The Bridge" are poised.

In these two lyrics leading up to the "The Tunnel," Crane intimates the threat mass culture poses to individual expression. These are poems tainted by trash language, a language auguring the "shutupness" in store in "The Tunnel." Thus, in "Cutty Sark," the name of both a ship and a liquor which uses seafaring adventure as a selling point, we see Melville's sailors gone flabby. Corrupted by commerce and a new strain of Ishmael's "hypos," they speak a language strained to the fraying point. The ennui of hawking afflicts the once hearty:

> "I ran a donkey engine down there on the Canal
> in Panama – got tired of that –

> then Yucatan selling kitchenware – beads –
> have you seen Popocatepetl – birdless mouth
> with ashes sifting down – ?
>   and then the coast again . . .

Threading the whole poem is the percussive chord "the nickel in the slot piano jogged." The song the piano plays, "weaving somebody's nickel," evokes "skeletons of cities – / amid galleries, galleries of watergutted lava / snarling stone." The Melvillean sea argot of a democratic and inventive community descends to this commercial cacophony;[16] the watery frontier which offered Ishmael refuge from the landlocked hypos is degraded in cheap trade routes. Melville's visionary sees through the "green glasses" of bar lights. The only visions are those drink summons: "the rum was Plato in our heads." Hallucination supplants imagination.

Only the bridge can redeem such tainted vision. Rising out of South Street, arched over the River, the bridge is reformed, a detoxified version of that language dragging its belly along the wharves, that language reduced to a bad dream of Romantic dissipation. The last lines of the poem, enunciating an epic catalogue of ships, show the speaker born again into his linguistic competence, reconnecting him with an authentic maritime language that seems to purify, freshen the poem:

> Bright skysails ticketing the Line, wink round the
>   Horn
> To Frisco, Melbourne . . .
>   Pennants, parabolas –
> clipper dreams indelible and ranging,
> baronial white on lucky blue!
> Perennial-*Cutty*-Trophied-*Sark*!

This last line effects a return to what Crane calls elsewhere the "genetic basis of all speech." Anatomizing, parsing the dead phrase "Cutty . . . Sark," the poet restores to it its spring and resiliency. Lingering thus over sea talk, the poet plies the fiber of a spiritual rebirth. The tension of the poem stretches between a jargon spinning drunkenly under the automatic arm of mass culture and an expressive and volitional language of engaged self-expression. As we move closer to "The Tunnel," mirror image and parody of "The Bridge," this dichotomy grows more extreme. The contrast between a speech still pirouetting, inventing, absurdly innocent, and a speech martyred to mass inertia is the difference between survival and visionary victimhood. Thus "Quaker Hill" is introduced by Dickinson's "The gentian weaves her fringes / The maple's loom is red," an epigraph that insists on that "consanguinity" of innocence with the earthly that has informed the poem all along.

This is by no means to apologize for "Quaker Hill," clearly among the weakest of Crane's poems. Trading the quickened hearing of "The River" 's listener for tone-deaf exhortation, Crane sermonizes. Dickinson's own caustic term for such talk was "narcotic." Unhinged from the earthly, when Crane lets forth, his "strong Hallelujahs roll" grandiloquent and hollow:

> This was the Promised Land, and still it is
> To the persuasive suburban land agent
> In bootleg roadhouses where the gin fizz
> Bubbles in time to Hollywood's new love-nest pageant
> Fresh from the radio in the old Meeting House.

There can be no question of the badness of these lines. Note, however, how short the leap between "Cutty Sark" and them. The difference is in the degree of good faith, or of innocence, that the speaker brings to his subject. "Chaplinesque" coins a phrase for such bad faith: "the game enforces smirks." The precise problem with "Quaker Hill" is that it smirks, cowers behind irony, rerouting images that might otherwise sustain "innocence" through certain preformulated prejudices. By the end of the poem Crane rallies, however. The lines before the final descent to the "Tunnel" recapture innocence, bidding us consecrate painful existence through actual communion with it. The very experience that severs us from what we love is all our protection. The lines are "infinitely resigned":

> Listen, transmuting silence with that stilly note
>
> Of pain that Emily, that Isadora knew!
> While high from dim elm-chancels hung with dew,
> That triple-noted clause of moonlight –
> Yes whip-poor-will, unhusks the heart of fright
> Breaks us and saves us, yes, breaks the heart, yet yields
> That patience that is armour and that shields
> Love from despair – when love foresees the end –
> Leaf after autumnal leaf
>   break off,
>   descend –
>   descend –

It is the very pain we suffer, that pain not only "Emily [and] Isadora knew" but that, as Crane puns, "breaks the heart" [Hart] and "whips the will" – this very pain is our armor. The paradox Crane describes here fulfills the conditions for a Kierkegaardian dread, or an Augustinian self-consciousness, that state receptive to innocence yet cognizant of its fallenness. "Dread is," as Kierkegaard puts it, "a sympathetic antipathy and an antipathetic sympathy" (*Concept*, 38). A corresponding pair of phrases from "Voyages" expresses the same ambiguous state poised between breakthrough and descent.

Earlier, I spoke of one member of this pair, the "infinite consanguinity" that corresponds to "sympathetic antipathy." Dark coeval to that state of redemptive engagement, however, is the "silken skilled transmemberment of song." "Transmemberment" is a word that gestures two ways: to heaven and to hell, or toward the Bridge and then toward the Tunnel. It points first to transubstantiation, the vital and religious exchange of Word and flesh, the alleviation of silence by gesture that enables, in Crane's pun on his own name, "the heart to live on." But transmemberment contains also dismemberment, a decoupling of self from self, a severing of language from will, that resolves into silence, noise, or empty abstraction.

If Chaplin's value for Crane, to recap briefly, is that he represents a poetry that makes of its circumstances innocence, a world where the gesture of art is equivalent to faith, in the absence of this gesture there is the vacuity of silence. And silence, Kierkegaard writes, "is the snare of the demon." Already, the "Proem" anticipated the slip into silence that transformed Chaplin to Poe. Silhouetted against the swanlike curve of the Bridge, "harp and altar of the Fury fused," is the sickening trajectory of the leaping "bedlamite," diving deathward.

> Out of some subway scuttle, cell or loft
> A bedlamite speeds to thy parapets
> Tilting there momently, shrill shirt ballooning,
> A jest falls from the speechless caravan.

If the mute, desperate bedlamite, his shirt clownishly "ballooning," remotely echoes the pierrot of "Chaplinesque," the linguistic constriction under which this figure labors impels the collapse of clown into gargoyle. For Kierkegaard, such constriction is a sure sign of the "demoniacal." As he puts it, the demoniacal is *shutupness*, "unfreely revealed . . . the shut up is precisely the mute . . . and it has to express itself. . . . this must come about against its will" (*Concept*, 109–10).

The bedlamite's leap off the bridge in the "Proem" reveals just such an "unfree" eruption of shutupness. The displacement of "shrill" from the bedlamite to his "shirt"; of "jest" from a speaker deflecting irony to one weighted by irony as by two stones in the pockets – here is a portrait of Poe hoist on his own best effects.

By the time Poe appears in the Tunnel, he is shrouded with all the attributes of the "shut up" and "demoniacal." He is, first of all, closely associated with degraded language. One need only read ten lines or so into the "The Tunnel" to recognize it as the domain of expressionless expression. Dim and repetitive, "The Tunnel" exposes a photographic

negative of "The Bridge" – a Satanic imitation. The balletic resignation
of a Chaplin is parodied in the figure adjured to "be minimum" to "[pre-
pare] penguin flexions of the arms." Thus diminished, the subject no
longer governs his engagement with his world by wielding a pliant art;
rather, he is governed by the vacuous babble of the culture now possess-
ing him. It is his "shrill shirt." He is empty inside.

> Our tongues recant like beaten weather vanes.
> This answer lives like verdigris, like hair
> Beyond extinction, surcease of the bone;
> And repetition freezes –

These lines provide a kind of sound track of that "speechless caravan"
Kierkegaard calls "vacuous." The language here is moribund, already
covered with "verdigris," horribly growing postmortem. This linguistic
petrification stands for a static culture babbling inanities:

> "what do you want? getting weak on the links?
> fandaddle Daddy don't ask for change – IS THIS
> FOURTEENTH? its half past six she said – "

Of such speech Kierkegaard notes:

> The continuity which corresponds to the sudden is what one might call
> extinction. . . . Tediousness, the impression of being extinct is in fact a
> continuity of nothingness. . . . The comical effect can be easily pro-
> duced in exactly the same way. In fact, when all ethical determinants are
> put to one side and one employs only the metaphysical determinants of
> emptiness, we have the trivial, from which can easily derive a comic
> effect. (*Concept*, 118)

Precisely as Crane's language grows more empty, it becomes comic:

>   if
> you don't like my gate why did you
> swing on it, why *didja*
> swing on it
> anyhow –"
>   And somehow anyhow swing –

Heed how plain sound takes over this poem. Sense survives, like verdigris, in sound's default. Language has been released into a mass culture
where it languishes or maddens; it has been turned over to what Poe describes in the "Philosophy of Composition" as an "effect." Such vacuity
of speech, cut off from any agent, urges the poem toward some moment
of purgation. Thus Kierkegaard describes how from the vacuous bursts
"the sudden":

> The continuity which close reserve may have can be compared with the vertigo we may suppose a top must feel as it revolves perpetually upon its pivot. In case the close reserve does not carry the thing so far as to become completely insane, insanity being the pitiful perpetuum mobile of monotonous indifference, the individuality will still retain a certain continuity with the rest of human life. Against this foil of this continuity, that apparent continuity will display itself as the sudden. . . . Depending upon the content of close reserve, the sudden may signify the terrible. . . . This bound within the leap, recalling the plunge of the bird of prey and the bound of the wild beast, which are doubly terrifying because they break forth from complete immobility, produces therefore an infinite impression. (*Concept*, 116–17)

Into this atmosphere of linguistic "immobility" Poe bursts as a kind of human mausoleum to the power of expression. Amputated from any legitimating selfhood, the fearful constriction of such a self admits no expression but a *deconstriction* that is sudden, uncanny, dismembering, that all of a sudden detaches the subject from his repertoire of human gestures.

> And why do I often meet your visage here,
> Your eyes like agate lanterns – on and on
> Below the toothpaste and the dandruff ads?
> – And did their riding eyes right through your side
> And did their eyes like unwashed platters ride?
> And death, aloft, – gigantically down
> Probing through you – toward me, O evermore!
> And when they dragged your retching flesh,
> Your trembling hands that night through Baltimore –
> That last night on the ballot rounds, did you,
> Shaking, did you deny the ticket, Poe?

No more transubstantiation. We are now in the domain of dismemberment. The self is a twitch or function governed by remote control, dangling like a footnote from the world into which it has released itself. The animate and inanimate cross: the strap is "swollen" like some horrible body part,[17] while the eyes of the poet, dehumanized, are like "agate lanterns." Crucified by eyes "right through your side" Poe is situated at the junction of Christian pity and the vampirism that borrows Christian forms. Like Whitman's late lurid Lincolns, as a sacrificed figure he is a Christ clone whose death would offer a Romantic poem its cathartic escape route. But as an imitation Christ, as another Faust, he is monstrous.

This vision of Poe educates the speaker of "The Bridge," "through dread," as Kierkegaard might say, to the consequences of visionary victimhood. The end of a hyper-Romantic self annihilation, an Orphism, is not release but an atrophied blasphemy. In this moment of recognition the wanderer who was Chaplin apprehends his double in the Poe dragged through Baltimore, a figure whose soul, whose will, like Poe's vote, has been purchased. After these lines Poe is ruthlessly eclipsed.

> For Gravesend Manor change at Chambers Street
> The platform hurries along to a dead stop.

The wittily Gothic "graves end" is only a point of transfer; likewise the "dead stop" is a mere screeching of gears on the local. And this relativizing of Poe – parallel to Whitman's relativizing of the "beautiful gigantic swimmer" – is only reinforced by the lines that follow. Shrugging out of Poe's death embrace they reconfederate the poet with homelier, less memorable models; not archetypes, but the clownish, cloddish riders of the interurban. The poet asks plaintively: "And does the Daemon take you home also / Wop washerwoman with the bandaged hair?" Riding with the insignificant, with poor sinners ground under heel "like pennies beneath soot and steam," the speaker earns the epiphanic moment of ascent:

> Kiss of our agony thou gatherest;
> Condensed, thou takes all – shrill ganglia
> Impassioned with some song we fail to keep.
> And yet, like Lazarus, to feel the slope,
> The sod and billow breaking, – lifting ground,
> – A sound of waters bending astride the sky
> Unceasing with some Word that will not die

Again, some transcendence seems at hand, yet just as this speaker is allowed no death pact with the Devil Poe, neither is he permitted a resurrection that cancels his bond from the world. For the "Word that will not die" dies, in fact, on the speaker's lips. A "song we fail to keep," it is drowned out, degraded by plain industrial noise; "A tugboat wheezing wreaths of steam, / lunged past, with one galvanic blare strove up the River." Not a Satan or a Christ, but an Adam or a Job, the speaker lives, and gains such visions as he can inside the world "dimensional," the world conditional. There is no deliverance that lasts, no release from the existence that tests faith again and again.

Crane's fidelity to such conditions is true. At the moment the "infinite" form, the archetypal compact, is seized, it is as quickly released. The lovely rhetoric of "Sod and billow breaking – lifting ground" – that incandescent moment – is resigned to the blare of the tugboat. In his most ambitious poem, "The Bridge," Crane makes the kind of Kierkegaardian leaps responsible to their essential earthliness, bearing as an ethical duty engagement with the broken world.[18] Out of responsibility to that "broken world" Crane ends the section with an apostrophe to the

"Hand of Fire," revision and metonymy of the angel with the flaming sword that is emblem of our violent separation from the infinite. Literally "kiss of our agony," the Hand sanctifies the innocence which takes that "limit . . . which is a torment for the Passion" as condition of its realization. Such an innocence is enjoyed by the one to whom glory is revealed, if only fleetingly. This knight of faith

> knows the bliss of the infinite. He senses the pain of renouncing everything, the dearest thing he possesses in the world, and yet finiteness tastes to him just as good as to one who has never known anything higher. It is supposed to be the most difficult task for a dancer to leap into a definite posture in such a way that there is not a single second when he is grasping after that posture, but in leap itself he stands fixed in that posture. Perhaps no dancer can do it – that is what this knight does. To be able to fall in such a way that at the same second it looks as though one were standing and walking, to transform the leap of life into a walk, absolutely to express the sublime in the pedestrian – that only the knight of faith can do. (Kierkegaard, *Fear and Trembling*, 51–2)

Crane's project in "The Bridge" is to express through application of faith the salvific richness of personal experience, of individualized moments of transport. From linguistic degradation comes beauty; from the Fall, human grace. If the descent into Hell, climaxing in the crucifixion of the bedlamite as Poe, defines a kind of leaping pulse in "The Bridge," this pulse is not its essential rhythm. The "visionary-victim" who finds transcendence in a "leap" off the Bridge is part of the speaker's spiritual education in hyperbole. Counterpointing this hyperbole is the more chastened, the more inward turning mood struck in lyrics whose speakers query: "What blame to us if the heart live on?"

Crane's hobo trekkers who "have survived, / And will persist to speak again" endure a spiritual pressure and an Adamic exile that redeems their language even as it diminishes them. Denied access to agonistic power or to the transcendent release tendered Romantic victims, they describe a broken world in a broken language. They recall us to the lyric's reservoir of sin and limitation, and so, to a regeneracy poetically richer than Emerson's "original relation." The clown of "Chaplinesque," the hoboes and "humpty-dumpty clods" of the "The River," the wop washerwoman of "The Tunnel" are sinners whose language snags them, strands them between earth and heaven. Fracturing prophetic utterance and fuzzying philosophical categories, Crane's poetry of the Fall speaks for a severed human community searching "Cruelly with love thy parable of man."

Epilogue. The Regenerate Lyric: Lowell and Frost

In his 1958 acceptance speech of the Ralph Waldo Emerson Award, Robert Frost pencil-sketched a portrait of the Unitarian Emerson that is as revealing for its white spaces as for its bold lines. As if summing up a whole tradition's vexed relationship to that question, "Why should we not enjoy an original relation to the universe," Frost queried Emerson's faith in any originality independent of theology's strictures. Even as his words, tailored to the occasion, maintain a tone of exaggerated politeness and circumspection; even as they render Emerson his tribute and due, inexorably they question that due. Indeed, just as the assurance with which Frost ends – "If Emerson left us nothing else he would be remembered longer than the Washington Monument for the monument at Concord" – is patently arguable, any conviction Frost might hold as to the superordinate power of Emersonianism is hedged about with questions. What Harold Bloom calls the "American religion" misses a convert in Robert Frost. Frost's acceptance speech of the Ralph Waldo Emerson Award contains the following disclaimer:

> Emerson was a Unitarian because he was too rational to be superstitious and too little a storyteller and lover of stories to like gossip and pretty scandal. Nothing very religious can be done for people lacking in superstition. They usually end up abominable agnostics. It takes superstition and the prettiest scandal story to make a good Trinitarian. It is the first step to the descent of the spirit in the material-human at the expense of the spirit. ("On Emerson," 718)

What compliments this encomium might be said to offer Emerson are backhanded at best. Leaving aside Frost's own many and affectionate poetic portraits of "storytellers," and how centrally both "pretty scandal" and "superstition" figure in his own work, it is hard not to take literally his dismissive joke that "nothing much can be done for people lacking in superstition." One is also hard put to wish away what is surely disdain for "abominable agnostics." Frost was honored in Emerson's name, but his resistance to standing in Emerson's long shadow is nonetheless palpable, and not only for reasons Bloom would call Oedipal: His trouble is not so much with Emerson's gigantic presence as with the legerdemain to which Emerson subjects Presence itself.

This is most clear at the end of the passage where Frost's elliptical "It is the first step" allows the wishful skeptic to believe it is superstition he maligns as a "descent" or "risk" of spirit. Here as elsewhere, though, Frost relies on the perspicacious to recognize in his admonitory phrase quite the opposite. If, perhaps, it is an exaggeration to call a certain kind of Christian occultism one of Frost's changes of clothes, still, superstition is for Frost as rich with the marrow of our existence as rationalism is numb at the extremities. His caution echoes that of Andrews Norton, who came close to his orthodox opponent Moses Stuart when he called Emerson's religion a "halfway house to infidelity." Norton's fretful predictions about the descent of spirit a theology so compensated as Emerson's would incur are clinched by Frost. But, as I hope I have shown, Frost was hardly the first to worry about the loss of the sacred and of sin. Frost's leeriness with respect to a religion so "material-human" as Emerson's has abundant precedent in the work of a century of poets whose chief response to the Emersonian religion was to recant their liberalism. The poet who began his essay with the not entirely gentle complaint that Emerson "quotes Burns as speaking to the devil as if he could mend his ways" now makes epigrams out of the American poet's long-standing demurral before the Emersonian deferral of Ends. Frost's very humor is tinged with a patience that has long bided its time.

Such patience at last was reaping its reward. By the year of Frost's speech, the American poem was no longer fidelity's only sanctuary. After long dormancy theology had enjoyed a renaissance in Richard and Rheinhold Niebuhr's works of the 1930s and 1940s, in the recovery of Kierkegaard, and in the transformation of Early American studies by Perry Miller. Richard Niebuhr's *The Kingdom of God in America*, the seminal work of the Neo-Orthodoxy and a history of American religion from a non-Emersonian point of view, had raised a theology of finality and Ends back above the cultural subfloor. The respect for crisis manifest in Whitman's engagement with Christology, in Dickinson's scourge of idols, in Crane's poetry of dread and limitation was now codified in Niebuhr's critique of liberalism:

> The coming kingdom was robbed of its dialectical element. It was all fulfillment of promise without the judgment. It was thought to be growing out of the present so that no great crisis needed to intervene between the order of grace and the order of glory. In its one sided view

of progress which saw the growth of the wheat but not of the tares, the
gathering of the grain but not the burning of the chaff, this liberalism
was indeed naively optimistic. (193)

Niebuhr's famous summary judgment of liberalism's flaccid mandate,
"A God without wrath brought men without sin into a kingdom without
judgment through the ministrations of Christ without a cross," recalls
the judgments of the poets who anticipated him, who preserved in their
language a "dialectical element" that Taylor and Edwards knew. Wrath,
sin, judgment, and suffering, Frost's "superstition" and the "prettiest
scandal story" – whatever their ultimate truth or falsehood – are terms
out of a lexicon which our major American poets, Emerson notwithstanding, will not do without. The redemption of the poem often depends, as Taylor's praxis shows, on the crisis it hazards. The American
poetic voice is often only as true as its sense of the Fall.

In the foregoing chapters I have argued that the classic American poem
cannot be relied on to shore up Emerson's reputation as inventor of the
definitive set of American poetic norms. His power to inspire is culturally secure. Indeed, the sheer exhilaration delivered by his vagrant prose
style amply earns him the attention he gets as proto-postmodernist. Nor
are any of the major poets – not Dickinson, not Whitman, not Crane –
wholly unsusceptible to the lures of the sublime. Yet Stevens took Emersonianism to its limits over fifty years ago, and beyond those limits is
Ashbery, whose orthodox indecideability foils choice, and so the voice
itself. Ashbery's poems are not voiced at all. They are brilliantly spliced,
their occasions not crises but transitional moods; their homelessness el-
egizing, though wryly, the lyrical impulse. With Ashbery, the debate
with Emerson becomes simply moot. Thus Emerson's last great antag-
onists are two poets whose productive careers crested, not accidentally,
during the ascendant years of the neo-Orthodoxy. Robert Lowell is a
poet who rediscovers Taylor and Edwards' Protestantism of crisis by
overshooting, by becoming Frost's "good Trinitarian." Frost himself, a
self-described "Presbyterian-Unitarian," remolds his Emerson to a poet's requirements. In these last pages I want to read briefly in the work
of these poets who bring the mandates of Taylor and Emerson into the
twentieth century.

If Frost is perhaps best understood as the poet Emerson's poetics necessitated by default, Lowell is a poet, like Taylor, of sin. Making a career of
Adamic self-consciousness, Lowell's use of the poem as the soul's rotis-
serie makes him Taylor's meditative brother; his most famous poem,
"Skunk Hour" adumbrates Taylor's sense of a human burden and stink
poetic language must share.

A poem that reexperiences the Fall as a portent of apocalypse, "Skunk Hour" predicts the poem with which this book began – "Shifting Colors" – rather as the Edwards of "Sinners in the Hands of an Angry God" predicts the chastened Emerson of "Days." The unwritten epigraph of "Skunk Hour" might be "I stink therefore I am," for it describes that dynamic by which Cartesianism educated to sin becomes Reformation theology, by which dualism becomes alienation becomes a regenerative self-consciousness. What the poem discovers is that there is no Fall the self does not originate anew, and no form of contemplation more steeped in the Fall's corruptions than critical – or theoretical – distance.

Opening in dualism's own season, Fall, "Skunk Hour" begins in a detached, almost clinical analysis of the New England Way now fallen on "sick" times. The "hermit heiress who buys properties only to let them Fall," the "summer millionaire" slumming in garb out of the "L. L. Bean Catalogue," and the "fairy decorator who brightens his shop for fall" are all figures of the Puritan self-consciousness declined in coy inversion, just as the poem's site – an Island – and its autumnal season recall the decline of Visible Sainthood in coy attention-getting. Reclusiveness, pretensions to rustic self-effacement, tourist trade kitsch – all share a common origin in self-regard, the very self-regard the speaker would profess to abjure but instead imposes on all he surveys.

Fleeing this campy jack-o'-lantern hell, the speaker longs for a sight of something pure, a pleasure untainted by self-reflection, by knowledge. But like Milton's Satan who, as Frank Kermode puts it, "actualizes the human contrast between innocence and experience," "Skunk Hour" 's speaker cannot escape himself. No transparent eyeball, he is rather an aching one, his very sight opaque with tension, clenched with consciousness. Climbing the "hill's skull" in his "Tudor Ford," his view of young love is the voyeur's view. Hiding is as close as he comes to transcendence. He cannot see, but can only "spy on love cars": "Lights turned down, they lay together hull to hull, / where the graveyard shelves on the town."

At this twilight zone of exteriority the speaker gets no further than Satan who reached "utmost orb of this frail world," God's vantage point, only to distort. In Satan's eye, Adam and Eve's love is turned to pornographic sport. Just so, Lowell's speaker realizes, "My mind's not right," and "I myself am hell," as he peers through eyes made mechanical by dualism. Literally "love machines," the bodies of cars lying "hull to hull" parody the erotic concourse of lovers, and what's more, these cars, perched where "the graveyard shelves on the town" and "bleating careless love" from their radios, are grotesque emblems of the human mechanism. So, goatlike, we discharge our reckless lives only to be junked, so all human love is necrophilia enjoyed amid waste, on a death's head. This queasy fusion of desire and horror is consonant with the poem's already blasphemous design. The speaker's "hour" is an hour of ersatz suffering, where Fall and Apocalypse converge on Passion. Ghoulish, he converts Christ's travail to the Devil's pained thrill, the dark night of the soul to Halloween.

Like New England poems of three hundred years before, "Skunk Hour" ends with the speaker's apprehension that it is his own self-division that pollutes the atmosphere. He is Edward Taylor's "bag of botches, lump of loathesomeness." And so the closing lines of the poem follow a troop of skunks, fallen pilgrims in their black and white, now made grotesquely comic metonyms of man's dividedness. The impulse for a vision unimpassioned by the body resolves back into a fetid physicality. Like the skunk in his stripes, like the Devil who is himself hell, man cannot escape his own stench.

Is there no egress from that circuit defined by the Devil's watching and Adam's guilty self-knowledge? Is there no expressive being that guilty knowledge does not peep at? The animals in Lowell's "Shifting Colors" have it; they coin metaphor out of pure being, not reflecting on the world, but reflected by it, existing in a unity of resemblances at which the poet can only marvel: "Ducks splash deceptively like fish; / fish break water with the wings of a bird to escape." The "deceptively" is the speaker's: It is his imposition on a pure resemblance without intention. Struggling to subtract himself he tries again – "The single cuckoo gifted with a pregnant word / shifts like the sun from wood to wood." Here the portentousness of the "pregnant word" would lose itself in an echo of "wood to wood," as the sun, fitful, loses itself among branches. Nature displays itself not as imitation, not as vision, but as a kind of pure expression the poet defrauds even as he writes it down. It is this unwritten art, this antic power of expressive conversion unaided by the converting eye, that Lowell must mean when he ends the poem wishing with Mallarmé that he might find a style to make writing impossible.

Closer to home than Mallarmé, though, he might have found a kindred seeker of this style in the poet who said that "Adam in Eden was the father of Descartes." We have already seen the results of Stevens' literalization of Emersonian originality: a poetry whose most radically Emersonian moments have a theoretical power that does not compensate for a certain human weightlessness. Such poems as Stevens' "Metamorphosis" do all language can to purge the human stink, to escape the voyeurism of subjectivity. Eliminating the vantage point outside, language uses the poet to enter the world of objects. Thus Stevens outdoes Lowell who could only watch the animals' artful transformations, wishing for a more astringent abstraction.

The problem, as we saw in Chapter 3 with Stevens' "Metamorphosis," is that even as the poem escapes the landscapist's subjectivity, his fishing, it is humanly unutterable. Unviolated by any interposed human voice, evading that dualism which gives consciousness its arms and legs, its mortal extent, Stevens' poem attains an abstract unfallenness at the price of the fallen. In its comprehensiveness rather like Emerson's "Each and All," it lacks the urgent decision of a poem by Taylor, or the weight of the significant Frost's poems must bear, that weight Frost must have had in mind when he complained that Stevens' poems were so much bric-a-brac. Self-contained, even original, "Metamorphosis" is also sterile. And sterile, Lowell knows, "Shifting Colors" is not. Taking in "horse and meadow, duck and pond" in his fractured way, reflecting crudely, "transcribing" verbatim, the fallen poet may offer mere "description without significance" and yet this "description without significance" is "universal" and "consolatory." However unoriginal, however generic the dualist's vision, the artist's distance from what he sees is duplicated, mirrored, in the act of reading, and so a human intercourse springs up. Words make visible more than the subject's distance from the object; they make visible as well the lines of that mutuality on which all versions of the Fortunate Fall depend. They trace out love.

No coincidence, then, that these last poems in Lowell's book, dedicated to a new wife, form a marriage suite, a rewriting of Milton's marriage suite that ends with Adam and Eve who "hand in hand with wandering steps and slow / through Eden took their solitary way."

The longing for a diction free of human affect, uncolored by shame and projection, exceeds the human day. And so, when, in the last poem of his last book, Day by Day, the speaker drifts into musing on "something imagined, not recalled," he catches, corrects himself. The lines chide: "the painter's vision is not a lens / It trembles to caress the light." What the dualist in his travail called "voyeurism" is finally rehabilitated as love. Ending in this Miltonic key, renouncing the "style that made writing impossible" for the vision that "trembles to caress the light," the landscapist resigns himself to project his "shifting colors." Such is the burden of the fallen poet: to witness and reflect, not stinting to record the desire that draws subjects back to love's birth in a garden.

In a critical age that grounds the value of language in its capacity to suspend both origin and telos, alpha and omega, the open question enjoys considerable prestige, and no one asks better open questions than Emerson. Thus in recent years, and as I have detailed in the last six chapters, there has been a renaissance of attention to Emerson by critics who find in his writing, and especially in his open questions, a mandate for a contemporary "poetics" more capacious than any poem. We have seen how Emerson's post-Unitarian impatience with dogma has made him the most natural of honorary poststructuralists. Delivering us beyond the Logos and the forms that secure it, Emerson's sentences are now studied as the American fossil prints of *langue* itself – dilating and self-reflexively open, nowhere more so than in such questions as these: "Why should we not enjoy an original relation to the universe?" ("Nature"). Or, "Where now sounds the persuasion, that by its very melody imparadises my heart, and so affirms its own origin in heaven?" ("Divinity School Address"). Or, "Yet what are those millions who read and behold but incipient writers and sculptors?" ("Experience"). Studiously unknotting all absolutes, dissolving his own presuppositions by making contradiction the rule and not the exception, Emerson asks rhetorical questions – no longer merely tolerated as the necessary. . . . dot . . . dot . . . preceding the fade-out to transcendent All – that are now read as demonstrations of that necessary deferral he understands to be language's modus vivendi.

If such openness is consonant with the goals of a poetics – by which I mean a theoretical description of what can be said (what *langue* and not *parole* says) – the open question is a poor mandate for the poem, as Emerson himself discovered. Despite Emerson, if not in response to him, many of the classic American poems are made not of linguistic possibility but of linguistic decision. Honed things, things that end, these poems are vessels of choice. This word and not that. Not "why should we not" but "we could but for." Not "where is," but "there is." For this poem, *parole* is what the deep breath of *langue* is drawn in for. These are not uttered to defer, or, as Whitman puts it, to pass the time while one waits for a bus. The poem is, to return to Robert Frost's words, the impossible undertaking we undertake.

Frost, not accidentally, is the closest we have ever come to that figure at the center Emerson described. Better than Whitman and better than Stevens, he knew how to make himself the poet America could affectionately absorb. Committed, as Emerson was, to the expressive possibility of the landscape, Frost wrote many poems that read like new and improved versions of Emerson's. Try matching "The Onset" to "The Snow-storm." Compare "Tree at my Window" to "The Rhodora." Moreover, Frost's cultivated persona of representative curmudgeon is a variant on Emerson's image as stump sage; both men were in certain ways recluses who happened to live in public. For all the surface similarities, however, Frost's perspective on Emerson, and especially on the Emersonian indeterminacies, is filled with shadow and obliquity. The rhetoric of the open question gets no better critique than Frost's. His coy comparison of Emerson to the Washington Monument is only the last super-subtlety in a speech that begins "Naturally on this proud occasion

I should like to make myself as much an Emersonian as I can. Let me see if I can't go a long way." Frost's journey is too craftily evasive to do justice to in these last pages, except to note with emphasis his correction of his mentor's chief image of openness: the image of the circle.

Citing Emerson's poetic dictum of transition, or flow, "Unit and universe are round," Frost qualifies,

> Another poem could be made from that, to the effect that ideally only in thought is a circle round. In practice, in nature, the circle becomes an oval. As a circle it has one center – good. As an oval it has two centers – good and evil. Thence monism versus dualism.

Make no mistake, this qualifying gloss on his teacher is not only a critique of transcendental aspirations, not only a critique of perfection or of that unity we now consider déclassé. It is also a critique of the illusion of indeterminacy that circles describe. For if the circle is the geometric representation of openness, the oval's asymmetry makes it a shape of adaptation rather than perfect freedom, and so a proper analogue to the poetic language with which Frost counters Emerson.

When Frost says that poetry is the impossible undertaking we undertake, and when he corrects Emerson's poetic circle with his oval, figure of the "only soundness," a "melancholy dualism," he draws the poem back into those very regions of ineluctable choice from which Emerson rescued it. Death or life. Saved or damned. Man or God. Poems for Frost are forms less of openness – premise dissolving into premise – than of faith pledged in the face of hazard. Or to invoke Emerson's other single best critic and a thinker from whom Frost himself learned much, William James, call them forms of the "will to believe." What James sees missing in Emerson is exactly what Frost sees: the credibility that a belief in something lends to the power of believing; what is difficult about faith, after all, is that it may be wrong, and so the open question is only as compelling as the foreclosures it fronts.

At the close I want to read a poem I take to be representative of Frost's answer to the master of the circles, a poem ovoid in shape and pledged to an impossible undertaking. One of Frost's many answers to the poetics of Emerson, "Rose Pogonias" is a relatively early poem, anticipating as an *ars poetica* does, such late, great works as "The Silken Tent." The perfect equipoise and unstrained accommodation of that latter poem to the sonnet form – emblemized in the image of a tent squared off yet still supple, swollen with breeze but nevertheless secured – is presaged in "Rose Pogonias" which stakes its tent, as it were, in the closing image of the simple prayer. This prayer, like the tent of the later poem, gives freedom, consciousness, and the restless movement of language with its many branching routes, the good faith of one road taken.

As in many poems by Frost, the pastoral, even picniclike atmosphere of "Rose Pogonias" introduces the poem's seriousness. The meadow setting suggests not bucolic pleasures casually enjoyed but the urgent and serious "need of being versed in country things." Country things, country poems: Both verse us in dying and how to fill the interval before we go. As Richard Poirier's exemplary reading of the poem suggests, the grass amid which the speaker picks orchids is scriptural grass. We are like grass and we, like the stalks in this meadow, will fall before the general mower. Thus the hallucinatory, almost migrainal intensity of the opening lines is an intensity gathered in against blankness, a yes marshaled against the mower's (reaper's) final no. The lines read:

> A saturated meadow
> Sun shaped and jewel small
> A circle scarcely wider
> Than the trees around were tall
> Where winds were quite excluded
> And the air was stifling sweet
> With the breath of many flowers
> A temple of the heat

The light-drenched vision of these first lines recalls that intensity of transcendence to which Emerson's "I am nothing; I see all" is caption. Just so Moses turned aside to see in the burning bush what he could not see. Indeed, sun and jewel both seem to burn here unconsumed by the predications that would cup or set them. The sun resists the specifications of shape, and the jewel, the constraints of size. Each image holds the other in its depths, so that we see, like a penumbra or summer's lingering imprint on the eyelids, the sun as a faceted, lapidary thing, the jewel husbanding solar glory. Dazzle seems an insufficient term for such intensity we cannot look on; its proper name is Revelation, with the jewel, the sun, deployed to mimic the radiance of the End promised in the Revelation of John and, as tradition has it, prefigured in Moses' vision. The "circle scarcely wider than the trees around were tall" mimics the precincts of the burning bush and God's jeweled and symmetrical city that "lies foursquare, its length the same as its breadth." Here, we might feel tempted to conclude, is Emerson's new revelation, the poem now the space of holy transport superannuating the old revelation.

And yet shrewd readers of Frost will note his qualification of Emersonian confidence. If the meadow is like the city of God, it is also different. "Wider" than the trees around were tall, the meadow is in fact asymmetrical, imperfect, and like the circle which is, in "practice or nature," ovoid, jewels too are measured against a finally theoretical model of perfection, even as the typological emblem of the sun (s-u-n) is mere simulacrum to that Son (S-o-n) whose glory no one can look on for long. The images in the stanza are compromised versions of the real Revelation.

Or, in Frost's terms, they are what mortal practice and nature can make. The closest we come to the Son is sun; to circles is ovals; to Revelation's perfect glory the meadow's small jewel. Not incidentally, it is not light but "heat" that fills the temple, with heat suggesting light transferred from idea to practice, refracted through body: given mass. Or, simply: fallen. As the next stanza picks up:

> There we bowed us in the burning
> As the sun's right worship is
> To pick where none could miss them
> A thousand orchises
> For though the grass was scattered
> Yet every second spear
> Seemed tipped with wings of color
> That tinged the atmosphere

The "tinged" of the last line sums up much about the second stanza of the poem. Although this "tinge" may evoke, say, the luminist's brush stroke – which, thickening downward, going feathery near the frame, shows God's mediating, ubiquitous presence – "tinge" is more compromised than mediating. Tinge is tint with a taint, and the lines of the stanza are suffused, saturated even, with this taint. The explicitly sacramental, nearly Miltonic admonition to right worship is nevertheless unsuccessful at keeping the object of worship in focus. God's Son blurs into sun-God. Worse, all this bowing and burning in the heat invokes practices more animal and direct, more cultic and infernal, than kneeling before Him to Whom all praise is due. Not only off-center, the stanza is both literally and figuratively off-color.

And for a reason. Interposed between the eye and its Revelation is: the Fall. Thus the meadow is only a mirage of the holy city, or better, a palimpsest of another place no winds crossed over, the jewellike Eden which, in its ruined beauty, was the first "temple of the heat," its horizon not luminous, but, as in Masaccio's painting of the Expulsion, luridly burning. In Eden, heat is of the blood. The Son's revelatory Logos descends in a flush of carnal warmth that thickens the scene. Christ's martial glory that released us from Adamic flesh is now backed up in those phallic spears tipped with color, every other one unsheathed, like the unsheathed phallic spear of Adam, the first.

Picking where "none could miss them" a thousand orchises, the speaker links himself definitively to that Adam whose theft brought sex into the world, and, along with it, the uneven contest between man and nature. For although the meadow is full of the breath of flowers, the speaker finds the air "stifling sweet." In this sixteen-line tour de force Frost strings the tension of our ovoid world where pleasure comes most fully into its own by hefting itself against the gravity, the counterpull, of death. The congested eroticism of the landscape is almost suffocating. The hazy surfeit of the first stanza distends in the virtual engorgement of the second, but the paradoxical yield of both is a poetic harvest more exquisitely replete, and more sensuously intoxicating than any mere openness would afford. Jewels, like sexual excitation, are products of a certain pressure from without, a certain closure. Thus in this virtual psalm to the good fortune of Ends, to the Fortunate Fall, Frost corrects the Psalmist's image of supernal bliss: the cup running over. As in "Birches," where Frost describes the formal poise of a boy "climbing careful, / With the same pains you use to fill a cup / Up to the brim and even above the brim," the limitation pressed to the utmost is exquisite. The shivering of fluid above the brim is the miracle of the impossible undertaking we undertake. As we follow the boy's climb in "Birches" to learn the poise that great beauty and good sex share with the making of poems, here images of jewels and flowers tipped with color suggest delight seized in the face of numb annihilation, blessing wrung out of curse. The honing, or stroking, gesture of jeweler, of lover, of poet, is interrogatory, true. But not open. It knows false moves from true. There is little to be gained from indeterminacy but dull stone, disappointment, or doggerel. To lay bare the nerve, or the stanza faceted with nuance, is a matter of choice to its smallest increments, querying but directed, standing to lose all and so requiring commitment. The difference between the Emersonian deferral Frost eschewed and the patience he revered is made explicit in all these images of decision, of questions raised above the rhetorical.

The poem's first two stanzas give us forms of human making flattened with practice, elliptically wheeling around the circle's unattainable perfection. And so the revelation that yielded the imperfect jewel, the mere sun, and the fallen figure of Adam is itself enclosed in a sacramental question:

> We raised a simple prayer
> Before we left the spot
> That in the general mowing
> The place might be forgot:
> Or if not all so favored,
> Obtain such grace of hours
> That none should mow the grass there
> While so confused with flowers

Prayer is a form that lifts questions above idleness. Prayers may be described as lapidary questions, not open but urgent. They play for what Frost elsewhere calls "mortal stakes." In "raising" such a prayer, suing for "grace" of hours, the point is neither that Frost, like Eliot or the deathbed Stevens, is a closet pietist, nor that poetry is his modern religion. Read here neither a strict religiocentrism nor a secularizing modernism. The point is rather that poems, like forms of religious utterance, come into their own behind Ends. Not openness to the indeterminate, but commitment to the unknown is the mandate that sustains them, with the difference between these the same that obtains between poetics and poem.

I am aware at the close that I could hardly have chosen a work whose images of the poem were less palatable to current tastes than the images of jewel, penis, and prayer that structure "Rose Pogonias." Respectively implicated in literature's safe depositing for the delectation of idle elite (jewel), in the historical spoilage of women and continents (penis), and in the subjugation of a brave language to the illegitimate demands of a Logos (prayer), such terms currently bear a stigma whose tenure may lapse about the same time as that of the untested prestige of poetic indeterminancy. When rhapsodies to the open grow tireder than they now are, we may discover in such poems as Frost's "Rose Pogonias" useful emblems of the choice that not only art's good faith but also political good faith requires. In politics as in art, "openness" is a term finally unmoored from practice. Open questions, like the poet's final vision of the field "confused with flowers" await confusion's resolution in images; await some localization of "the pleasure of the text" in acts of choosing. Thus, the subjunctive question with which the poem ends – "That none should mow the grass there / While so confused with flowers" – modifies the Emersonian dream of deathlessness or indeterminacy – "The place might be forgot" – for a more chastened hope: a simple surcease of destruction. Time enough for a poem. "Grace of hours" evokes both that interval and "our" collective and responsible knowledge of its proper use. "Rose Pogonias," like many another American answer to Emerson, corrects the poetics of circles yielding ever more interrogatory circles with a lyric. Ovoid and limited by time's foreclosures, this lyric finds in limitation its retaining wall, and in Ends the beginning of all its regenerate inceptions.

Notes

1. "Embarrassed figuration" is Barthes' characteristically gnomic statement of the self-consciousness that attaches to all acts of mimetic representation. And the distinction he makes between representation, or embarrassed figuration, and figuration elaborates on the primary distinction governing *The Pleasure of the Text:* that obtaining between "readable" texts which offer *plaisir* and writable texts which offer *jouissance.* Characteristic of the representational *plaisir* is a mimetic framing which always stands outside. Barthes writes "Here is a text of pure representation. . . . 'She stands upright very perpendicularly posed. By posture and by movement we know the chaste woman; wantons droop, languish and lean, always about to fall.' Note in passing that the representative undertaking has managed to engender an art (the classical novel) as well as a science . . . and that it is consequently fair, without any sophistry, to call it immediately ideological." This proclivity to frame makes pornography, for Barthes, a "representational" form structurally identical with the "ideological" work he describes above. As he writes, "the text of pleasure is not necessarily the text that recounts pleasures; the text of bliss is never the text that recounts the kind of bliss afforded literally by an ejaculation . . . pornography is not sure." Lowell's poem, tracing out distinctions between pornographic vision and a "language to make writing impossible" seems hospitable to Barthes' distinctions. Yet it is different from Barthes in the quality of its suffering. In Barthes this "representation," associated with monogamy and institutional stability, is the bourgeois remnant which his own linguistic revolution is happy to dislodge. For Lowell, representation is the product of sin, and much more intransigent. When Whitman seeks *jouissance,* as I shall show in Chapter 4, he never forgets the Fall that denied him *jouissance.* This vigilance of memory distinguishes the American poets studied here; their crossing of the linguistic impasse is never made manageable as a philosophical or theoretical undertaking, but is always compelled either by Awe, or apostasy.

2. Freud suggests that "Man has not been able to acquire even his oldest and simplest conceptions otherwise than in contrast with their opposite . . . he

237

only gradually learnt to separate the two sides of the antithesis and think of the one without the conscious comparison of the other" (Freud, *On Creativity*, 58). As Frank Kermode has shown ("Freud and Interpretation" in the *International Review of Psychoanalysis*), whereas "The Primal Meaning of Antithetical Words" shows Freud in basic sympathy with linguistics, the synchronic implications of his material escape him. Kermode writes, "The formula ontogeny recapitulates phylogeny thus provides Freud with the means to extend indefinitely the past of the individual, and so create space for historical explanations." In this essay ("The Primal Meaning") coming only three years before *Totem and Taboo,* Freud is more interested in establishing a prehistorical origin – the feminist would say, authority – for the binariness of language, than in noticing, as Saussure does, the arbitrariness of that binariness.

This very act of notice, which waited for Lacan, has engendered both the determination among feminist revisionists of Lacan to overthrow a system so literally conventional, and the realization that to do so is to sacrifice certain structures which give culture coherence. This is the problem of the "language of the patriarchy," whose best, if clearly makeshift, solution thus far is Kristeva's celebration of the anarchic language of the Mother. The feminist revolt against Freud, though mainly focused on his phallocentrism, is no doubt also triggered by his nostalgia for cosmic kinds of explanations historically authorized, by the way in which his psychoanalysis put prehistorical accounts of origin we would call religious under the protection of History.

3. In the Jewish tradition, for example, these matters are the purview of the Kabbalah which devotes itself to describing, or describing how to describe, the *Ein Sof,* roughly translated: that without end. The paradox of Creation, problems of time, extension, and mediation, are all worked out in terms different from, but not unrelated in mystical tenor to those of Taylor. When Heidegger takes up the same questions he is, in a certain way, disabled for eschewing the radiant, if anthropomorphic, language of religious mystics, and is thrown on the mercy of such terms as "isness."

4. This is by no means to deny, but rather to augment, the arguments of Barbara Lewalski (*Protestant Poetics and the Seventeenth Century Religious Lyric*) who takes exception to Perry Miller's doubts about the possibility of a freestanding Puritan poetics. By and large Miller lets the Bay Psalmist's sober renunciation of ornament – "God's Altar Needs not our Polishing" – serve as *ars poetica* for the Puritan age, though his thinking veers sharply in the pioneer essay, "From Edwards to Emerson." Lewalski argues that through a "doctrine of accommodation," the Puritan poet, modeling his word on the mediating model of Scripture, found religious warrant for much more expansive poetic license than Miller credits as possible. If God was wordless, His text provided a model for sanctioned mediation. Writing, in these terms, becomes a form of reading, of parsing revelation. In this connection, see also Peter White's excellent analysis of the Lewalski/Miller debate in his *Puritan Poets and Poetics*.

What Lewalski's argument is perhaps leery of admitting is fully acknowledged in Robert Daly's *God's Altar* and overstated in Karl Keller's *The Example of Edward Taylor:* the efficacy of a debased sense of language in the
process of conversion, or the way in which the Puritan makes language an
organ of salvation, working overtime. See, in particular, Daly's *God's Altar,*
which has much informed my own views.

5. The phenomenon I am describing is roughly reminiscent of Freud's polymorphous perversity, but should not be reduced to such. Hugged by time
and space, by a repleteness of experience sufficient to jar the self from for-
getfulness, this state Heidegger calls the *dasein,* whose nature it is to be
"thrown" into language, into "thereness." For Heidegger, the detheologiza-
tion of this "throwing" makes language not a falling away from, but the
coming into immanence of Being. And yet when Heidegger's theory would
account for an inauthenticity of *dasein,* it reverts to an older terminology –
inauthetic *dasein* suffers *Verfall,* a cadence into decline. As Steiner suggests,
"Again and preeminently, the tonality is theological. It was as if Heidegger's
whole diagnosis of inauthenticity amounted to a quasi secular version of the
doctrine of the Fall of man"(Steiner, *Heidegger,* 97).

CHAPTER 2

1. Calling Emerson the founder of "the American religion," Bloom adopts a
tone characteristically vatic – "his truest achievement was to invent the
American religion. . . . Starting from Emerson we come to where we are,
and from that impasse, which he prophesied, we will go by a path that most
likely he marked also" – but his argument is canny as well. Among such du-
tifully cited but dubiously qualified contenders as "Ellen Harmon White of
the Seventh Day Adventists, Joseph Smith of the Mormons, Alexander
Campbell of the Disciples of Christ, Mary Baker Eddy of Christian Science,
and Charles Taze Russell of Jehovah's Witnesses," Emerson indisputably
earns the title as founder of "the" rather than "an" American religion. Here,
as elsewhere, though, Bloom's preoccupation with discerning the "strongest" among poets diverts attention from matters ultimately more interesting than Emerson's preeminence. Namely, the complex way in which
American religion has institutionalized precisely by deinstitutionalizing itself, "stirring successive aspirations of the American dream, aspirations
which when transformed into achievements belonged no longer to the saints
but to the citizenry" (Clebsch, 2). This phenomenon, the implicit subject of
Perry Miller's work, and, in the next generation, of Sacvan Bercovitch's, is
placed historically in William A. Clebsch's *From Sacred to Profane America:
The Role of Religion in American History.*

2. A parallel might be noted between the contemporary preference for *langue*
over *parole* and Emerson's invention of a spacious prose poetics not bound to
stabilize itself, or come to rest, in a poem. It is perhaps important to recall
that Emerson's development of a poetic theory of linguistic crosstides and
fastnesses (too swift for the small craft of the poem) flows out of a Unitarian

faith become too enlightened for the violation of any such merely religious notion as Christ. But if Emerson's freedom from the constraints of a limiting Word both authorizes and predicts the contemporary poetics become, in the interests of the text, too free for the encumbrance of the mere "work," his was also a freedom whose costs hindsight gives us the luxury of surveying.

Clearly, it is too soon to judge just how much satisfaction the updated Emersonian freedom will give the next generation's students of literature, too soon to have tested the staying power of "indeterminacy" and "power" as arch-tropes. We can predict, though, that the same questions the Emersonian poetics fronted will be asked again. In time we will know how different is our current theory from what in mid-nineteenth-century America was simply called liberalism, our "human sciences," with their focus on excavation, from that "scientific" Christianity with its own deference to "archaeology." All that is now certain is that the contemporary protest against New Critical pieties was not without parallel in Emerson's day. The intellectual revolution Sydney Ahlstrom has called the "American Reformation," its last charge spearheaded by Emerson, was also aimed at battering myth and myth's oligarchic caretakers. To identify with Emerson's buoyant oppositionalism thus ultimately exacts consideration of his fate. Like Emerson's post-Unitarianism, the current poststructuralism may already be coming to seem the self-confuting movement of an educated elite against the very forms securing its own authority: resourceful in opposition, but necessarily weak in sustaining a rhetoric of self-continuance.

For some representative examples of the narrativizing of the poem see, for example, Adrienne Rich's essays on poets Bradstreet and Dickinson in *Lies, Secrets and Silences,* Calvin Bedient's Bakhtinian treatment of Eliot, *He Do the Police in Voices,* and Joseph Riddel's discussion of Williams as a poet of "decentering" in *The Inverted Bell.* Bedient's book, quirky and dense, is the most engrossing study of "The Waste Land" I know, and this despite the fact that by page 15 it has already sacrificed the poem's lyricism: "Lyricism is not the dominant tonality of 'The Waste Land,' and for a reason; lyricism is itself a disease." Similarly, the first sentence of Riddel's book is "This is a study in 'poetics' as distinguished from a book of poetry" (xi.).

3. The notion of play is useful to an understanding of the "regenerate lyrics" this book treats insofar as it recalls us to an understanding of poetic closure as neither necessarily exclusive nor fetishistic but rather delineated by Kierkegaardian choice. As Gadamer writes in "Play as the Clue to Ontological Explanation" (*Truth and Method,* 91–119), play "has a special quality which the player 'chooses.' He first of all separates off his playing behavior from his other behavior by wanting to play. But even within the confines of his readiness to play he makes a choice. He chooses this game and not that. It accords with this that the movement of the game in not simply the free area in which one plays oneself out, but is one that is specially marked out for the movement of the game" (Gadamer, 96). This notion of play may, in addition, help us to find an attitude more consonant with the study of art than a ritual suspicion of its "self-mystification" and thus a determination to reveal the "serious" or "material" reality its surface felicities would conceal. Play's

relationship to the "serious," as Gadamer argues, is not that of illusion to reality, but rather that defined by a "seriousness" that maintains and, in fact, constitutes the game as game. "It is not that relation of seriousness which direct us away from play, but only seriousness in playing makes the game wholly play. . . . The mode of being of play does not allow the player to behave towards play as if it were an object. The player knows very well what play is, and that what he is doing is 'only a game': but he does not know exactly what he knows in knowing that" (92). Reminding us that "one who does not take the game seriously is a spoilsport," Gadamer provides an acute, and disarming, critique of the contemporary hermeneutics of suspicion.

His point is not that art trifles with truth by claiming to corner it, so covering the traces of its own constructedness, but that this constructedness, or as Gadamer puts it, the "transformation into structure," is a means of Being:

> [T]ransformation means that something is suddenly and as a whole something else, that this other transformed thing that it has become is its true being . . . what represents itself in the act of play . . . is what is lasting and true." (100)

Rather than describe the good faith of the art work as dependent on its skepticism before essentials and ontology, Gadamer offers "play the clue to ontological explanation." Such a view complements that of William James which, pitched against skepticism, champions a will to believe that brings into being what was hitherto impossible but now is. Anticipating both James and Gadamer, Bushnell wrote "poetry is play, as opposed to prose which is work" (32), and the poet, "a free lyric in his own living person, the most animated and divinest embodiment of play" (*Work and Play*, 34).

One wonders what would happen if, before looking to the New Critics who derived their oligarchic notions of closure from Eliot, we looked to Bushnell and James whose convictions as to the Emersonian transport poems afforded necessarily tie this transport to a specific faith commitment. Minus the hyperbole, Bushnell formulates just what American poets find to be true: "Christian love is demonstrably the only true ground of a perfect aesthetic culture." More equably, and more theoretically, James in effect makes the same commitment his bottom line: "Our passional nature not only lawfully may, but must, decide an option between propositions, whenever it is a genuine option that cannot be decided on intellectual grounds; for to say, under such circumstances, 'Do not decide but leave the question open,' is itself a passional decision – just like deciding yes or no – and is attended with the same risk of losing the truth" (*Faith and Morals*, 42). Finally, this ethos of choice, this dictum of ultimate decidability, is all crystallized in the work of Kierkegaard who, in the work of the Neo-Orthodox theologians as in the present study, becomes a kind of honorary American, arch-interpreter of Edwards, theorist of an art that is faith's proving ground. The thinking of Kierkegaard, especially his notions of choice (exfoliated in *Either/or* and, less diffusely, in *The Sickness Unto Death*) inspires many of my assertions about lyric choice.

4. "Here I am" say Adam, Noah, Abraham, Moses. This statement of singular relationship to and responsibility before the Infinite is Kierkegaard's point of

departure in the "dialectical lyric" of *Fear and Trembling*, and this same sense of the ultimately mysterious disjunction of man and God the Neo-Orthodox theologians discern, with the help of Kierkegaard, to be Jonathan Edwards' salutary and most American contribution to Christian history. My claims about the Kierkegaardian quality of American poems imply that the theological chain connecting Edwards to the Niebuhrs is not broken in the century between Emerson and Stevens but rather strengthened in the poetic tradition that sublimates in order to preserve the very either/ors that Unitarianism discarded. Particularly useful texts in understanding Neo-Orthodoxy are Sydney Ahlstrom's *A Religious History of the American People* (Chapter 55); H. Richard Niebuhr's classic *The Kingdom of God in America*, and Joseph Haroutunian's brilliant, if tendentiously structured, interpretation of American religious history, *Piety versus Moralism: The Passing of the New England Theology*.

5. For a well selected sample of responses to Emerson's address, see Burkholder and Myerson's *Critical Essays on Ralph Waldo Emerson*, pp. 33–66.

6. On the Unitarian Controversy, its backgrounds and issues, see Jerry Wayne Brown's *The Rise of Biblical Criticism in America 1800–1850*, and the classic work by Sydney Ahlstrom, *A Religious History of the American People*, Earl Morse Wilbur, *A History of Unitarianism in Transylvania, England and America*, and Conrad Wright's *Unitarianism in America*. Two works concerned more specifically with the controversy and its major players are Ahlstrom's *An American Reformation: A Documentary History of Unitarian Christianity* and Andrew Delbanco's *William Ellery Channing*.

   Wright's work is especially illuminating on the ways in which challenges from popular movements spawned by the Great Awakening both necessitated and bred distaste for techniques of Christian outreach. Delbanco's book treats Channing as an exemplary figure of a New England tradition pressed by time and circumstances to adopt some of the very techniques of "self interest"– honed by evangelicals and part of the new Jacksonian *Weltenshaung* – which he reviled.

7. Ann Douglas's important study, *The Feminization of American Culture* has much enriched my thinking in these matters. Although the debate over the feminist implications of Douglas's work has both energized and clarified critical discussion of sentimentalism, this debate has also eclipsed some of Douglas's more compelling claims about theological vitiation and reaction to such by writers surfeited on liberalism.

8. Delbanco points out (*Channing*, 95–7) that Channing's opponent in matters of mystery was Moses Stuart, who cannily defended Christian mystery on the grounds that "modern science tolerates – indeed depends upon – exactly the same imprecision that religion demands." He goes on to argue from this that "Stuart is asking that man consent to live with metaphor" (96). The question this argument raises is whether metaphor is a mode of disjunctive mystery – trope of the veil ever interposed between a thing and its origin – or a mode enabling identities. Stuart and Taylor would no doubt argue the former; Channing, Emerson, and Bushnell the latter. The collective verdict of the poets this book treats seems by and large to accord with Stuart and

Taylor's; it is as though metaphor stripped of mystery is unworthy of the name, platitudinous, and better left to preachers. In a paradoxical way, it is this very disjunction that Stevens, surfeited on a theology given over to genteel likeness, craves when he writes "Is there no change of death in paradise? / Does ripe fruit never fall? Or do the boughs / Hang always heavy in that perfect sky, / Unchanging, yet so like our perishing earth, / With rivers like our own that seek for seas / They never find, the same receding shores / That never touch with inarticulate pang?" It is this same sameness that Huck Finn finds so tedious. All *Huckleberry Finn* is a search for an old sense of Awe not utterly appropriated by some sect making violence an ersatz substitute for religion. The secularism of both Stevens and Twain is much exaggerated. Both figures may be said to crave Revelation, to write works showing Revelation thwarted by religion made genteel hoax.

9. Chapter 4 will take up this matter of divine violence and human identification more fully. For a lucid account of debates surrounding the Atonement in America see Haroutuntian's chapter "Wrath of God and Cross of Christ" and Ahlstrom's Introduction to *The American Reformation*. To trace the waning of the Atonement as a theological idea among European thinkers see Karl Barth's great work *Protestant Thought from Rousseau to Ritschl* and, for general background in the theology of the Cross, Jaroslav Pelikan's magisterial *The Reformation of Church and Dogma: 1300–1700*. For a discussion of the way changing ideas of the Atonement bred a twentieth-century tolerance for the consumption of violence see Douglas' discussion in "The Loss of Theology" (*Feminization*, 143–96).

10. The dangers of poststructuralist praxis have long been recognized. Derrida's own writing can be credited with hardly ever leaving to "indeterminacy" what the critic is too lazy or inept to determine; Derrida holds "free play" to the most rigorous and exacting of standards. And yet the freeness of play as a theoretical maxim, its eschewal of choice, can not only cover a host of critical disingenuities, but also raise questions about the final disposition of *différance*. Ten years ago Maria Ruegg was one of many to sound the alarm in an article in *Criticism*, "The End(s) of French Style" where she probed why

> Derrida gives us two reasons for not choosing between the structuralist's "ethic of nostalgia for origins" and the Nietzschean affirmation of a loss of center; first, he says, because today "the category of choice seems particularly trivial"; and secondly, "because we must first try to conceive of the common ground, and the differance of this irreduceable difference."

Ruegg goes on to wonder,

> But if the category of choice seems "trivial" to Derrida, it is precisely because he sees the difference(s) between Levi-Strauss and Nietzsche, between structuralism and deconstruction . . . in terms of what he calls "differANCE." And to see two elements in terms of their differance is to see them in terms of a relation according to which the one (say structuralism) merely defers, or puts off, the other (say, deconstruction) – another which is already there, within it. . . . it is to see differences all maintaining their difference, as the same; it is to see, with the addition of a temporal framework (in order to keep – artificially – the difference between the two poles, in order to prevent the dissolution of their differences) what bears more than an uncanny resemblance to the old identity of opposites.

Ruegg's discussion of what Derrida himself admits is a certain "sterility" in his theory is illuminating for the student of Emerson who would discern the difference between, say, the transcendental and the de-transcendentalized Emerson. Both Emersons risk falling prey to the same "sterility" inasmuch as Emerson's "or" – like Derrida's sterile eschewal of choice – may prove an escape hatch out of that crisis Time necessarily brings on when not diverted by deferral. Like Derrida, whose dismissal of dualist choice is necessary, but not sufficient, cause for the ascendancy of deferred critical English (coherence is always just around the bend!) Emerson lays himself open to Frost's complaint that he is one for whom "evil does not exist, or if it does exist, needn't last forever." As Ruegg complains that Derrida's contrivance of a time lag in "deferral" eludes inevitable conclusions about the identity of *différance*, Frost complains that "Emerson quotes Burns as speaking to the Devil as if he could mend his ways" ("On Emerson," 713).

11. My arguments against the ultimate usefulness to students of the American poem of the Emersonian poetics would by no means dismiss the high distinction of recent studies on Emerson. Indeed, to the strength of these works in describing just what the Emersonian poetics *does* I owe many of my own conclusions about what it doesn't do. The remarkable consensus uniting Emerson scholars of sometimes very different methodological dispositions is that Emerson renounced finality, pledging himself rather to the hazards of experience. It is generally agreed that this eschewal is responsible for a poetic prose of superordinate skepticism, a prose learning from language itself that power comes from encounter with an antithetical force, with contradiction. Virtually all the best recent work on Emerson – Poirier's *The Renewal of Literature*, Packer's *Emerson's Fall*, Cheyfitz's *The Trans-parent: Sexual Politics in the Language of Emerson*, Ellison's *Emerson's Romantic Style* – concurs with Bloom in celebrating Emerson the agonist rather than Emerson the unifier, or in Lawrence Buell's summary phrase, an Emerson who is a "struggler rather than an affirmer." A convenient selection of this criticism can be found in the Modern Critical Views volume *Emerson*, edited by Harold Bloom, while Michael Lopez's "Detranscendentalizing Emerson" (*ESQ: A Journal of the American Renaissance* 34) offers an intelligent interpretive survey of the latest offerings of the Emerson industry. If I had to choose one book, Poirier's aphoristic, sometimes elliptical, but brilliant *The Renewal of Literature* would be it.

In addition to the general agreement about rupture, most of the current critics take the problem of time in Emerson to be central. Everyone wonders just how successfully Emerson's typical mode of "detachment" (in Ellison's terms) or restless "self-awareness" (in Packer's) serves his ends. Calling Emerson a poet who lives by "transition," Ellison takes Emerson at his word in averring that it is arrest that makes language inert and movement that gives it life. Packer, too, finds Emerson's power gathering in his restless, if sometimes grim, struggle out of being into becoming. Nevertheless, she follows Emerson, troubled, through to the realization that "Life is not intellectual or critical, but sturdy. . . . To fill the hour – that is happiness." In "Experience," argues Barbara Packer, Emerson tries for the first time in his career to describe life as it looks from the standpoint of the "hyphens rather than the heights" (Bloom, *Emerson*, 129), with the result, as Packer quotes Maurice Gonnaud as having observed, that "the greatness of an essay like 'Experience' lies . . . in our sense of the author's being engaged in a pursuit of truth which has all the characters of faith except its faculty of radiating happiness" (Packer, 168). Packer and I agree in the failure of "transition" to provide something Emerson craved, not only in his life but in his writing. In a work of theory such a paradox as Gonnaud reveals may indeed be greatness of a sort. Theory does not lose but rather gains from being ingested by ironies its next sentence outwits. But a poem of "faith" removed from its "faculty of radiating happiness" is – unless, perhaps, it is a poem about bad faith – simply a bad poem, lapsed from itself. That poetics has its blind spot, and that this blind spot matters, is signally illustrated, as Richard Poirier notes, by the power of a rhetoric of transition to ingest almost anything. Poirier writes: "Emerson . . . at times could treat even the birth and the death, at age five, of his firstborn son, as a transitional event, part of a creative mythology, forgetting how much he doted on his own and his wife Lidian's little boy" (42).

12. Altieri predicted this softening in "The Hermeneutics of Literary Indeterminacy: A Dissent from the New Orthodoxy," a 1978 essay in *NLH*. Twelve years later the new orthodoxy shows signs of aging, one sign being the proliferation of jeremiads by hitherto temperate critics who have had enough. I think in particular of Robert Alter and his *Pleasure of Reading in an Ideological Age* which, overcompensating for the critical abuse of indeterminacy, locks subtle and invariably elegant readings into rearguard polemicizing.

13. A most useful study of Ashbery and the poetry of the post-Emersonian universe is Marjorie Perloff's *The Poetics of Indeterminacy*.

14. To restore an idea of individual human work and human will to the poem is inevitably to raise questions about "humanism" itself. Just so, to make reference to the Kierkegaardian individual is to lend credence to the "subject" of such late disrepute. But only a wholly secularized ethos needs to disabuse this subject of his various props, needs to tell us that the human hero is a chimera, constructed differentially out of position and not essence. The religious subject, or the subject inhabiting a religious universe, knows nothing so completely as his own utter, drastic powerlessness. This knowledge, however, yields not to determinism and accounts of the forces that impinge, but rather to a lyric experientialism, a pursuit of the very ontology he must believe in to be at all. Again, the difference is all in timing. Put it this way: Religious writing summons up a survival instinct that theorists of the long view can afford to leave dormant. One thinks of the new humanism, for example, in the AIDS community. The devotion to lyricism, to memorializing, to the person himself – these arrive, perhaps, after theories of power run out of time.

15. David Porter, in his excellent study of Emerson's poetry, *Emerson and Literary Change*, observes this same gratuitousness of Emerson's poetry. Where Porter and I differ is that he draws salutary conclusions, stating positively

what I have stated, perhaps, negatively: that Emerson's less than successful experiments with the lyric are redeemed in his "Breakthrough into spaciousness," or into prose. As Porter argues, "The poetics of his prose sanctioned texts with the special movement – self-discovering, seemingly spontaneous – of his own intelligence acting in the reality about him," whereas, as the bulk of his book shows, the poems are formula-driven, vaulting into Platonic ideality before ever establishing themselves on earth. Porter's book, for all its intelligence, takes for granted that the loss of poetry to poetics is a salutary "change" without discernible cost. If Emerson saw, and grieved for, this cost, Porter acts in a way as his literary therapist, tracing out with satisfaction Emerson's final, hard won reconciliation with himself and his true metier, "a self promoted prosaicism" (214).

16. For instance, from *The Prelude*:

> That very day
> From a bare ridge we also first beheld
> Unveiled the summit of Mont Blanc, and grieved
> To have a soulless image on the eye
> That had usurped upon a living thought
> That never more could be. The wondrous Vale
> Of Chaumony stretched far below, and soon
> With its dumb cataracts and streams of ice,
> A motionless array of mighty waves,
> Five rivers broad and vast, made rich amends,
> And reconciled us to realities . . .
> Whate'er in this wide circuit we beheld,
> Or heard, was fitted to our unripe state
> Of intellect and heart. With such a book
> Before our eyes, we could not choose but read
> Lessons of genuine brotherhood, the plain
> And universal reason of mankind,
> The truths of young and old. Nor, side by side,
> Pacing, two social pilgrims, or alone,
> Each with his humour, could we fail to abound
> In dreams and fiction pensively composed.

17. It is worth considering how much the current schism separating poets from academicians and "creative writing" from criticism is related to the declined prestige of voice among academics and the concomitant devotion to voice among poetic practitioners. I once heard a live interview with Frank Bidart, a poet of highly distinctive voice, in which he answered a question about his own "productivity" by disparaging the notion of poetic output. Yes, Bidart admitted, one can always "look out of the window" and produce a poem, but somehow, he says, "this isn't what one's soul wants art to be." Bidart, like many other contemporary poets nearly unknown among academics, takes for granted that poems emerge from the interior space of the poet, are wrested out of that space rather simply from a vagrant *langue* the poet rides like a bus. If such "essentialism" is passé among critics, so too, though, is the poem.

18. See David Leverenz's *Manhood and the American Renaissance* for an illuminating discussion of gender value in Emerson's language.

CHAPTER 3

1. Vendler is a fine critic of Stevens, but her affection for his work leads her to overhistoricize, plumbing Stevens' "secrecies" to unearth what she calls "submerged autobiography," and frequently overstating Stevens' sense of responsibility to the past by too closely identifying his "necessary angel" with the figure of the "Man on The Dump." The Stevens she describes puts one in mind of that "angel" from the ninth section of Walter Benjamin's "Theses on the Philosophy of History":

   > A Klee painting named "Angelus Novus" shows an angel looking as though he is about to move away from something his is fixedly contemplating. His eyes are staring, his mouth is open, his wings are spread. This is how one pictures the angel of history. His face is turned toward the past. Where we perceive a chain of events, he sees one single catastrophe which keeps piling wreckage upon wreckage and hurls it in front of his feet. The angel would like to stay, awaken the dead, and make whole what has been smashed. But a storm is blowing from Paradise; it has got caught in his wings with such violence that the angel can no longer close them. The storm irresistibly propels him into the future to which his back is turned, while the pile of debris before him grows skyward. This storm is what we call progress. (Benjamin, 257)

2. Two books that pay a great deal of attention to these "gaudy" poems, though for vastly different reasons than my own, are Daniel Fuchs's *The Comic Spirit of Wallace Stevens* and Alan Filreis's recently published *Wallace Stevens and the Actual World*.

3. Michel Benamou's "Wallace Stevens and the Symbolist Imagination" (in Pearce and Miller) is an invaluable resource to the study of nakedness and savagery in Stevens. Providing a table which charts the accretion of the terms "nude," "naked," "bare," "pure," "nothingness," and "abstraction" through the course of Stevens' career, Benamou calls *Parts of a World* the book of "heroic nakedness." His discussion of the epistemological ramifications of these words is brilliant.

4. For a more complete discussion of Dickinson's early antinomianism see Chapter 5, "Beyond Circumference."

5. Stevens' use of typology here makes sense since the typological mode is "prospective" as well as retrospective, not only forging links with the founding Biblical text but looking forward eschatologically to that renewal at the end of days. Yet this is the problem with the typological mode. Stevens' linear projection of a figure "not as a god but as a god might be" runs head on into the figure who rises on the Sunday Morning at the end of days. The poet is, as it were, outflanked by Christian history.

6. M. H. Abrams writes

   > Behind many Romantic versions of the internal circuitous quest we can recognize the chief prototype of the circular variant of the ancient Christian perigrinatio, that is, the parable of the Prodigal Son interpreted as the type of the journey of all mankind out of and back toward its original home; and in Romantic as in Christian literature, this parable is frequently conflated with the apocalyptic marriage that signalized the restoration of Eden in the Book of Revelation. (*Natural Supernaturalism*, 194)

7. *Tristes Tropiques* offers the sobering education of a Romantic, an account of one who went into the tropics to "discover" and instead "imposed" exactly as the Neo-Kantians claimed. Earlier in this chapter Levi-Strauss derisively describes the "young man who isolates himself for a few weeks or months from the group and exposes himself to an extreme situation of any kind." This young man, identical with the "amputated" figure earlier described, is Levi-Strauss himself. *Tristes Tropiques,* like Crispin's travels, is the tale of his tragicomic initiation into a post-Romantic thinking.

8. See Jeffrey Mehlman's article "The Floating Signifier from Levi-Strauss to Lacan" for a discussion of desire and subject/object relations analogous to Helen Vendler's discussion of desire in *Words Chosen Out of Desire.*

9. Frank Kermode described Stevens' commonsensical rhetoric as it frames nonsensical diction in a Columbia University graduate seminar on Stevens in the Spring of 1985. See Helen Vendler's chapter, "Stevens's Secrecies," for a discussion of Stevens' hypothetical titles.

10. See Roy Harvey Pearce's "Toward Decreation" in Doggett and Buttel. Dedicated to the memory of Michel Benamou, Pearce's essay develops Benamou's comments on nakedness into a theory about Stevens' late work. Note that "decreation" is different from the defoliation or the state of "winter" described in such essays as Richard Macksey's "The Climates of Wallace Stevens" (in Doggett and Buttel) and elsewhere. Stevens' "winter" awaits the remetaphorization of Spring. It is the "base" or "reality" on which he builds "imaginative" poems like "Notes Toward a Supreme Fiction." Decreation, by contrast, points to an abstract state outside the passage of seasons, outside God's nature.

11. In Chapter 6 we will see these determinants give "The Bridge" its ethical structure. It is precisely Crane's interest in the irreducibility of the individual, his human makeup, himself, that Stevens subtracts.

12. See Chapter 4 for a discussion of a parallel exposure in Whitman's "The Sleepers."

13. Emerson's "Divinity School Address" sets the man of spirit the same monumental task. Depriving his auditors of the common terms (of dogma), Emerson sues for a spiritual experience that paradoxically atomizes rather than binds his community.

CHAPTER 4

1. It has long been recognized that Whitman's cadences and perhaps even his use of parallelism are grounded in his reading of Scripture. Increasingly, though, we are coming to understand that Whitman learned more than his metrics from his Bible reading. For all the grandiloquence of the claim, Whitman's intention to write "a New American Bible" was grounded in considerable knowledge and familiarity with the texts his own would superannuate. With a mother of pious Dutch Reformed background, not only was he, in Stovall's words, "under the usual influences of a Protestant Christian home" (84), but he apparently also made it his business to know the Scrip-

tures. As a young man he "went over thoroughly the New and Old Testaments" (Stovall, 117). Moreover, not only did Whitman have "varied experience in Brooklyn Sunday schools," but coming of age in the feverish evangelical climate of the Second Great Awakening, he was exposed to the most charismatic preachers of the day: as a boy to the Quaker Elias Hicks; later, to Father Taylor and other itinerant Brooklyn-based ministers. Such experience, in combination with his reading, gave him that native understanding of fallenness and its tropes hard for the modern reader to fathom but entirely explicable in a culture that still taught its children the ABCs with the primer verse "from Adam's Fall we Sinned All." Whitman's notebooks are full of early ruminations on the "reformation" he planned. The best systematic account of the theological foreground to *Leaves of Grass* is Floyd Stovall's *The Foreground to Leaves of Grass*. See also David Reynolds, *Beneath the American Renaissance* (15–27) for a fascinating insight into the religious milieu of antebellum New York, and John Irwin's *American Hieroglyphics* (26–40) for an illuminating explication of Adam and the Fall in "Song of Myself." By and large, Gay Wilson Allen's view that even though Whitman was moved by the rhetoric of evangelists he "could never stomach Calvinism" needs rethinking. As I hope to show, Whitman does not so much reject as ingest Calvinism, swallowing it whole.

2. Lewis's classic case for an Emersonian Whitman, made in *The American Adam,* is criticism so authoritative and persuasive one can hardly imagine seeing it improved on, much less disproved. In the last ten years Lewis's case has been taken up, if radically metamorphosed, by Harold Bloom, who sees Whitman as the key disseminator of that "American Sublime" that Emerson invented. In Bloom's own idiom:

> Walt is indeed Emerson's New Adam, American and Nietzschean, who can live as if it were morning, but though he is *as* the Biblical and Miltonic Adam, that "as" is one of Stevens's "intricate evasions of as." Old Adam was not a savior, except in certain Gnostic traditions of Primal Man: the new, Whitmanian Adam is indeed Whitman himself, more like Christ than like Adam, and more like the Whitmanian Christ of Lawrence's "The Man who Died" than like the Jesus of the Gospels. (*American Poetry Through 1914,* 303)

Bloom's sentence delivers us finally at some distance from where it begins: from an account of Emersonian *power* in Whitman to a suggestion of Whitman's retrieval of the very Christ the Emersonian Adam does not need: the Christ who lends power when Adam fails through his suffering.

Here, as elsewhere, Bloom has his case all ways: When Whitman is poet of New Morning he is Emersonian, and when Whitman takes up material Emerson reviled he is Emersonian, too. In fact, he is then more Emersonian (and thus more himself!) since his strength as poet depends precisely on links to the precursor he is closest to when differing from! Bloom's Freudian model of struggle obscures the question of Whitman's relationship to Emerson inasmuch as his readings are tautologically premised on such a relationship. Critics for whom the question remains live are Buell, whose *Literary Transcendentalism* calls Whitman's book both "the culmination and the epitaph of literary transcendentalism" (326) and Stovall, whose chapter "Emerson and Whitman" in *The Foreground of Leaves of Grass* ends with a concise inventory of the ways in which Whitman diverges from his teacher. Rather than absorb, as Bloom does, Whitman's dissent from Whitman into a trope of Oedipal struggle where difference *is* attachment, we do best to let the power of Emerson for American poets prove, and complicate, itself. Lewis's argument thus stands to retain its authority better than Bloom's since it husbands a prerogative of interrogatory doubt Bloom cannot afford. Lewis is very close to Buell when he writes "Adam had moments of sorrow too. But the emotion had nothing to do with tragic insight; it did not spring from any perception of a genuine hostility in nature or to the drama of colliding forces. Whitman was wistful, not tragic. We might almost say he was wistful because he was not tragic" (48). The "wistful" and the "tragic" are a false dichotomy; the alternative to tragic consciousness for Whitman is not wistfulness but an imaginative commitment to loss. Still, Lewis's qualified language allows for such revision whereas Bloom's does not.

3. For a discussion of Whitman's negotiations with Emerson over the 1860 version of *Leaves of Grass* see Kaplan 248–50 and Zweig 320–2.

4. My point about Emerson's prose style as a rhetoric of flight substantially echoes Steven Whicher's still persuasive case that Emerson was a poet whose freedoms were always contravened by fates, with the latter dominating the late essays and the former the early. As Chapter 2 documents, recent work (by Barbara Packer and Richard Poirier especially) has restored tension to the early essays, showing how sentence by sentence Emerson's rhetoric may be observed to wrest movement out of inertia, transition out of "adamantine limitations," how he reinterprets struggle as part and parcel of the good. It needs to be said, though, that the glory of such sentences is also their limitation. If Emerson's prose does not rest because it identifies movement with life, this insomnia must nevertheless sacrifice the rendering of extent, the snugness of things, as Whitman puts it, "in their place." The experiential *dasein* of body conscious and at home with itself cannot be represented in a style whose raison d'être is "transition." Thus, the transformation of fate to power necessarily yields a certain homelessness contradicted in the American poet's love of the *local:* from Whitman born of "this soil" to Williams of this highway, this interstate, this junction; from Bradstreet who "here in Ipswich lies" to Frost crushing his body "to earthward."

5. Packer writes wittily of the Emersonian tendency to make the "*essays similar* and the *paragraphs diverse.*" Bemusedly she confesses that

> while his paragraphs are extraordinarily easy to remember word for word, they can be almost impossible to locate. Anything can be anyplace. The most time consuming feature of being a student of Emerson is the necessity it places one under of repeatedly rereading half the collected *Works* and *Journals* in the maddening pursuit of some paragraph one can remember but not find. (155)

Whitman's insistence on things "in their place" seems less cryptic against this Emersonian background.

6. Harold Aspiz compares a similar section of "Song of Myself" to a "hauntingly proto-Roethkean harrowing of hell." Whitman recounts in his old age that he read of many such harrowings: in Homer, in Virgil, and Dante, not to mention *Paradise Lost,* a book he famously disliked. It is more than likely,

though, that the "haunting" quality he gave his descent to the Land of the Dead in "The Sleepers" borrows from a revivalist tradition which, since Edwards, had deployed hair-raising techniques to portray the strangeness of hell, the vertigo of falling, the shock of unpreparedness, the regurgitation of the dead. Standing on the lip of the underworld had been, since Edwards, almost a mnemonic act. The precipice offers both a vantage point over the sufferers and a jarring reminder. The instability of the perch is an incitement to renewed wakefulness and purification.

7. From Wigglesworth:

> Still was the night, serene and bright,
>   when all men sleeping lay;
> Calm was the season, and carnal reason
>   thought so t'would last for aye.
>
> Soul, take thine ease, let sorrow cease,
>   much good thou hast in store:
> This was their song, their cups among,
>   the evening before.

8. For this formulation I am indebted to Phyllis Trible. She suggested that it is properly the *Creation itself* and not just the Fall that Whitman unwrites in these lines. I should also credit Jonathan Arac here for insisting over several years that I consider Emersonian originality in the light of aboriginality.

The point here is not simply that Whitman unwrites the Emersonian Fall, but that he goes beyond Emerson in rewriting Creation itself, mooting by *preempting* the Fall. In so doing he embraces the very ab-originality Emerson can't quite commit himself to but which is, in fact, implicit in the Emersonian "original relation."

9. Peter M. Sacks's excellent book, *The English Elegy,* gives a psychoanalytic explanation for the production of the elegy and can thus be paired with works like John Cody's *After Great Pain* on Dickinson, or even John Irwin's *Doubling and Incest* on Faulkner. Religious ideas like fallenness, division, and sin can be treated as externalizations of intrapsychic processes (hence, the Fall, for example, mythologizes the universal individual experience of separation from the mother), but this should not distract us from their power *as religious ideas* for the figures in question. More useful to my purposes have been studies informed, but not so explicitly governed, by psychoanalytic knowledge, for example, René Girard's *Violence and the Sacred.* Girard's central argument is that sacrifice (which for Sacks is the ritual act of castration that permits vegetative rebirth) functions in a culture to put a brake on untamed reciprocal violence. Hence, Girard will argue that the Levitical taboo on menstrual blood derives from fear of the violence any blood represents. It is interesting to compare Kristeva's *Powers of Horror* (99–103) view (derived from Mary Douglas's) that the fear of menstrual blood is, rather, a fear of a female principle of cyclicality – of life yielding inevitably to death. For Kristeva, fear of violence is a by-product of fear of the Female. Despite disagreements, Kristeva and Girard's common debt – and Michel Foucault's – is to Georges Bataille whose nearly shamanistic work, *Death and Sensuality,* traces out the whole constellation of relations their arguments introduce to

scholarly debate. Whitman's poem, with its interest in death as the female antidote to violence, bears closest affinity to the work of Bataille, for it does not "argue" but rather disseminates its dynamic of sacrifice, sexuality, and law in a poetic rhetoric transfixed. It trades denotative accuracy for affective power.

10. George T. Wright explains of such verbs, "The poet's pageant, his presentation, profits from the sense we have of prolongation. He makes us feel that the interlude taking place is not only timeless but somehow enduring; it is outside of time but it has duration" (566). Whitman's use here of verbs in the simple present frames the incident of the beautiful gigantic swimmer as "something that deserves to be held, fixed, memorialized . . . the material of myth" (Wright, 573). Such timelessness as these verbs secure is that of the *kairos,* chronometricals. The beautiful gigantic swimmer is a typological figure, and so his demise marks an end to typological history as such. My own understanding of typology has been much enriched by reading Bercovitch, Brumm, and Lowance. See also Edward Taylor's lucid exploration of typology in Milton, *Milton's Poetry,* especially "The Tempestivity of Time" (123–47).

11. Whitman describes this subjectivity by contrasting it with the traditional "objectivity" he calls "epic." "*Leaves of Grass* must be called not *objective* but altogether subjective – 'I know' runs through them as a perpetual refrain. Yet the great Greek poems, also the Teutonic poems, also Shakespeare and all the great masters have been objective, epic" (*Notes,* 43). The effect of the "subjective" use of "I" in this passage is only to aggravate the subject/object anguish other modes would meliorate through various closural devices, those devices Whitman calls "objective."

12. If such passages have the sound of idle boast, even of self-persuasion, we must note that they complement Whitman's grass roots, on-the-street efforts to answer sectarianism with his own brand of easy, if omnivorous, ecumenicism. Thus in a letter to his mother of 1857 he reports: "A minister Rev. Mr. Porter, was introduced to me this morning, a Dutch Reformed Minister and editor of *The Christian Intelligencer,* NY. Would you believe it, he had been reading *Leaves of Grass* and wanted *more.* He said he hoped I retained the true Reformed Faith which I must have inherited from my mother's Dutch ancestry. I not only assured him of my retaining faith in that sect, but that I had perfect faith in all the sects, and was not inclined to reject one single one" (*The Correspondence,* I, 43).

13. See Mary Douglas's chapter on Levitical taxonomy for a complete explanation of how categories of holy and profane, and specifically of pollution and purity, maintain communal order and the covenant with God. Douglas describes how the disorder signified by "wandering" symbolizes both "danger and power." She gives the example of the Andaman Islander who "leaves his band and wanders in the forest like a madman. When he returns to his senses and to human society, he has gained the occult power of healing." This is precisely Whitman's danger and his power. Mary Douglas's important work *Purity and Danger* is indispensable for the student who would understand Bib-

lical taboo. Of particular usefulness to my understanding of Whitman is Douglas's spatialization of danger.

14. Despite its somewhat dated insistence on "alienation" as the chief outcome of monotheism, Herbert Schneidau's provocative, often brilliant, work on Hebrew Scripture and Near Eastern myth, *Sacred Discontent,* is a rich source-book for an understanding of the biblical proscriptions against mixing. See especially the chapter entitled "The Hebrews Against the High Cultures."

15. Two watershed texts that treat God as arch-patriarch are Mary Daly, *Beyond God the Father,* and Margaret Homans, *Women Writers and Poetic Identity.* For some discussion of the French feminist take on this God see Note 20.

16. Whitman may be borrowing here from Job, a poem similarly concerned with the equalizing power of death: "There the wicked cease from troubling; / And there the weary are at rest. / There the prisoners are at ease together; / They hear not the voice of the taskmaster. / The small and great are alike; And the servant is free from his master" (Job 3:17–19).

17. In characterizing Whitman's task in "The Sleepers" as a radiant transmogri-fication of Christian doctrine, my interpretation allies itself and invites com-parison with earlier work by such critics as James E. Miller who called "The Sleepers" a "traditional mystical experience" and "an exploration of the world of spirituality," and, especially with the work of Roger Asselineau who begins his work *The Evolution of Walt Whitman* with a chapter arguing for a "mystical" wellspring to Whitman's evolution. That Whitman's jour-ney in "The Sleepers" could be called "mystical" seems to me perfectly just: My question is *which* mysticism, or whose? My argument is that the mys-tical transports the speaker enjoys in the poem are not in the least generic, but are rather seized in Christianity's despite. Thus, the gates through which the mystic readily passes are related to the straight gate admitting only the elect; the "sleep" he enjoys is precisely the state Christian wakefulness would combat; the corpse he becomes is precisely the corpse from which Christian sacrifice would protect him. Mysticism is rarely a free-floating entity, but rather comes adjoined to a system whose hedged promises its transports ex-pedite. Whitman's mysticism is of this kind: It is the mysticism pleasuring itself in the interstices of a specifically Calvinist either/or with yes/and.

18. See John Irwin's fine essay on Whitman's use of opera to obviate subject/ object, and in turn, poem/world distinctions. Irwin suggests that inasmuch as music is *of the body,* of the vocal chords and breath, it is an art form acting *in* rather than reflecting *on* the world. Whitman's use of music is hence one way to collapse distinctions, to write a poetry in *contact* with the world. A most illuminating essay on this same issue of music and song in Whitman, and a model of what "formalism" did best is Leo Spitzer's 1949 "Explication du Texte" (*English Literary History,* 16).

19. The image functions similarly in Poe's *Eureka* where the poet, spinning on his heel, loses his sense of the difference between the true and the beautiful. He writes: "Only by a rapid whirling on his heel could he hope to compre-hend oneness. . . . We require a mental gyration on the heel" (187). In both cases it is through physical vertigo that mental unity is achieved.

20. That the abandonment of the binary yields to "mysticism" and "metaphysics" has become even clearer in the work of such French feminist theorists as Irigaray whose "essentialism," again, is not a contradiction but the natural outcome of her theoretical enterprises. In *The Speculum of the Other Woman* Irigaray seeks indeed to recuperate the mystical alternative by decrying, in Toril Moi's words, "the theologization of mysticism" – as though mystical traditions were not, as a matter of course, adjoined to theologies. One might wonder if the real blind spot of the poststructural enterprise isn't finally its utopian craving for a metaphysical release from skepticism. The mystique surrounding a French feminism that habitually chooses the incantatory over the analytic, not to mention the sociology of discipleship this feminism has spawned, recalls similar, though in some ways more self-aware, moments in American literary history: the swing to Gurdjieff in the 1930s, the interest in Buddhism in the 1960s. Despite coming of age in the atmosphere of Paris in 1968, the theories of the French feminists bear only the most attenuated of relationships to what can legitimately be called politics, or even revolutionary rhetoric. Gifted hermeticists, they practice a species of altered consciousness, freeing, as such disciplines do, but also, as such disciplines are, liable to obscurantism.

21. These lines miniaturize the whole structure of "Out of the Cradle Endlessly Rocking": the landscape features are identical, the sea, the land, the wave rubbing out their distinctness, the wakening poetic powers borne to the ears of the boy as an erotic music come in both poems through the agency of death, a song the sea sings.

22. Whitman's relationship to the Christ figure is easily oversimplified, especially since his early resistance to Christ's centrality is slowly eroded over the years between the 1855 and 1891 versions of *Leaves of Grass*. Thus, even though Whitman writes approvingly in the 1870s of Ingersol and Huxley whose theories might (perhaps better than his own?) "unhorse the Christian giant" (Asselineau, 46), Thomas Crawley will assure us that "the religion of *Leaves of Grass* has at its center a single personality strikingly like the Christ of the Hebrew Bible" (68). Erkkila argues more recently that "Christ's lesson of regenerative potency – signified by the blossoms in his hat – is transformed into the political base of the American republic and the moral base of a new democratic religion" (113).

    Although the presence of the Christ figure is unmistakable, it is fallacious to interpret this presence as affirmation of the poet's faith in the salvific power of a Christ metaphor. By the end of his career, as Erkkila points out in a note and as I argue in pages to come, Whitman's resistance slackens sufficiently that he can write, rhapsodically, in *Goodbye my Fancy:* "how refreshing to know that the same founts of consolation at which we drink, have been tasted by the now dead and past ages, and still by thousands every day" (Erkkila, 335). Christ's function here reflects Whitman's own late sense of the poet's vocation: He is a figure "absorbed" by the people. The early work, though, is much more vigilant. There Whitman gives the Christ of the Atonement – both his appeal and his perils – more scholastic and rigorous examination than was expended by theologians proper. These lines are key nodes in that examination.

23. A useful source for an understanding of the Calvinist Christology Whitman sought to topple is Joseph Haroutunian's *Piety Versus Moralism: The Passing of the New England Theology*, especially Chapter 7, "The Wrath of God and the Cross of Christ." See also Conrad Wright's *The Beginnings of Unitarianism in America* and *American Unitarianism*, Barth's *Protestant Thought from Rousseau to Ritschl*, and Ann Douglas's discussion of the Atonement and Bushnell in *The Feminization of American Culture*. For a useful introduction to Christology in general: John O'Grady's *Models of Jesus*. My treatment of these passages also benefits from some illuminating conversations with Geoffrey Sharpless.

24. For a large-scale treatment of the homosexual theme in Whitman see Robert Martin, *The Homosexual Tradition in American Poetry*.

25. In a certain way it is Poe and not Emerson who converts Calvinism to a durable literary form, for Poe takes the Calvinist Awe and makes of it Gothic thrill, the scene of Agony, and reveals its sadistic content. Giants and dwarfs, pits and churchyards, mediatorial agents of half-spirit half-flesh, spectacles of torture and narratives of feverish confession – these are Poe's stock in trade, all parodic templates of Calvinist forms. Whitman, the only American poet to attend Poe's funeral, had, one might hazard, a unique understanding of Poe's importance. His own Gothic moments recall Poe's.

26. The mythic event unifies type and antitype. See especially Ursula Brumm's *American Thought and Religious Typology*.

27. Allen Grossman's article, "The Poetics of Union in Whitman and Lincoln: An Inquiry toward the Relationship of Art and Policy," has much fertilized my thinking on these matters. But well before I read the article, Allen Grossman was helping me to shape the right questions. The beginning of this whole chapter was his remark, made over a decade ago, that the "beautiful gigantic swimmer" was a Lycidas figure.

28. In a chapter entitled "George Washington, Commander in Chief," from his *A History of the United States of America*, Vol. 7. Bancroft gives Washington precisely that hyperbolic classic grandeur of outline Whitman resists:

> Courage was so natural to him that it was hardly spoke of; no one ever at any moment of his life discovered the least shrinking in danger; and he had a hardiness of daring which escaped notice, because it was enveloped by calmness and wisdom (207). . . . [H]is qualities were so faultlessly proportioned that the whole people chose him as their choicest representative, the most complete expression of its attainments and aspirations. (209)

CHAPTER 5

1. Dickinson criticism, pretty much run as a cottage industry until the late 1960s, is now burgeoning at an amazing rate. This is hardly to be regretted, since Dickinson earns all the attention she gets. Feminist readings of Dickinson as a poet resisting patriarchy were given a crucial push by Adrienne Rich's "Vesuvius at Home" which, placing Dickinson's use of the word "freedom" in skeptical inverted quotes, laid the groundwork for Gilbert and Gubar's reading of Dickinson as Gothic prisoner and woman in white. The eighties have seen a spate of follow-up studies. A partial list would include

Barbara Antonia Clarke Mosberg's study of Dickinson's incarceration within a patriarchal family, *Emily Dickinson: When A Writer is a Daughter;* Vivian Pollak's study of linguistic convention, *Dickinson: The Anxiety of Gender;* Sharon Leder and Andrea Abbot's *The Language of Exclusion;* Joanne Dobson's *Dickinson and the Strategies of Reticence,* and Wendy Barker's *Lunacy of Light.* As is often the case, the best of these studies were also the first. Margaret Homans' *Women Writers and Poetic Identity* makes most persuasive use of feminist theory to understand Dickinson's "subversive" gestures, and Suzanne Juhasz's *Feminist Critics Read Emily Dickinson* offers a fine compendium of feminist perspectives.

The popularity of the incarceration theory has, however, deflected attention from valuable studies of the uses to which Dickinson put her much contested poetic freedom. See, then, Emily Miller Budick's admirable *Emily Dickinson and the Life of Language.* Budick's chapter "The Fraud that Cannot Cheat the Bee: The Dangers of Sacramental Symbolism" is a fine investigation of what I call "columnar" thought, and Shira Wolosky's two-page discussion of Christian paradox (*Emily Dickinson: A Voice of War*), especially her argument with Sharon Cameron's premium of Dickinson's center, redeems some of her more arguable conclusions about Dickinson and war. For Christian paradox is precisely a kind of semantic warfare, the face-off of mutually opposed terms mimicking the soul's battle with what Barbara Packer calls, in her book on Emerson, "adamantine limitation." Other studies I have found illuminating are Robert Weisbuch's *Emily Dickinson's Poetry,* Allen Tate's still trenchant essay "Emily Dickinson," Christanne Miller's excellent *Emily Dickinson: A Poet's Grammar,* and especially Lawrence Buell's readings of Dickinson in *New England Literary Culture.* Buell's work, to my mind the most disinterested, brilliant, and informative study of nineteenth-century literary culture published in the last decade, only came to my attention as this book was being completed. Thus, although I did not read it early enough to have benefited from the instruction and support its argument about New England "religiocentrism" might have afforded me, it is altogether gratifying to discover oneself toiling in such rich vineyards as Buell cultivates.

2. In Frost's parallel poetic manifesto, "Two Tramps at Mudtime," the poet declares, "My object in living is to unite / My avocation and my vocation / As my two eyes make one in sight."

3. For a focused discussion of the Puritan problem with images and how it was circumvented in Taylor's poetry, see Daly's *God's Altar* and Barbara Lewalski's *Protestant Poetics and the Seventeenth Century Religious Lyric.*

4. See Geoffrey Hartman's "Purification and Danger: 1" in his *Criticism in the Wilderness* for a provocative and interesting discussion of purity and metaphors of purity in American poetry.

5. Harold Bloom suggests the struggle between Jacob and the angel in Genesis as a paradigm for the struggle for poetic originality. The paradigm is particularly apt as applied to American poets, not only to Dickinson but to Crane as well, and also to Stevens in whose work angels – as figures of the power of the poet seized out of the hands of God – are ubiquitous.

6. Denis Donoghue stands out among critics who argue that, for Dickinson, the Romantic transfer of "centre" from God's garden to the walled garden of the poet's soul may be taken for granted: "We can think of Emily Dickinson as primarily a poet who valued her own work, who believed that the poet's soul is the center of the universe. . . . Without this belief her exaltation of 'Circumference' would be meaningless." Donoghue goes on "this belief once granted, she moved with considerable grace among the world of objects (113). . . . Emily Dickinson carried very little theological freight" (115). Donoghue's claim must base itself on a very select corpus of poems. Those treated here bear considerable "theological freight."

7. Dickinson's use of various diminutives has been thoroughly explicated by feminist critics who see the personae of "bird," "child," and so forth as metaphoric representations of Dickinson's diminished stature as a woman in Victorian America. See, for instance, Barbara Antonina Clarke Mossberg, "Emily Dickinson's Nursery Rhymes" in Juhasz. For a more general, but concise, treatment of Dickinson's language as defense against patriarchy and specifically the male God, see Joanna Feit Diehl, "Ransom in a Voice," in Juhasz's *Feminist Critics*.

8. Sewall, arguing along the same lines as Donoghue, identifies Dickinson's "columnar self" with her sense of herself as poet. He thus writes "Not until about 1863 could she write the poem . . . that came close to reconciling the two disparate states of her being: her love of the God of her fathers and her belief in herself" (390). The tension between these two surely governs the poem, but there is an ironizing of the "columnar self" here that I believe Sewall simply misses.

9. For a discussion of Dickinson's love of the sentimental novel, see Sewall, "Books and Reading" (*The Life* 672–3), and for the best treatment of Dickinson steeped in her culture, that of nineteenth-century Victorianism, see Barton Levi St. Armand's excellent *Emily Dickinson and her Culture*. See also Ann Douglas's groundbreaking treatment of the "domestication of death" in nineteenth-century American sentimental fiction (240–72).

10. I am thinking especially of Whitman's sacrificed "beautiful gigantic swimmer" in "The Sleepers" and the Christological characterization of Lincoln in "When Lilacs Last in the Dooryard Bloom'd." See Chapter 4 for a discussion of Whitman's struggle against such sacrifice and the relationship of Christology to his speaker's transgressive perambulation among the dead.

11. George Poulet points out that the "isolation" we identify as "modern" or "existential" began, in fact, in the seventeenth century when "separated from the duration of things, and even from that of the modes of its existence, the human consciousness finds itself reduced to existence without duration" (13). Such consciousness drives home the precariousness of a human life in which "God's succor is always momentary . . . the supernatural preservation of existence no longer lays any foundation for permanence" (17). These observations about the seventeenth century are framed by the observation that "such is the essential experience of modern man" and they are qualified by the provision that Calvinist thought – with its emphasis on Providence – proves the exception to the seventeenth-century rule. It is worth noting that

Dickinson's very distance from Calvinist thought may be said to predict her experiments with techniques we call modern, but that perhaps an older resistance to the relativism such isolation has inspired in later literature leaves in her poems a religious rigor twentieth-century poems have largely jettisoned.

12. Sewall relates (347–8) that Revelation was Dickinson's favorite book in the Bible and what she called the "Gem Chapter," (Sewall, 21) her favorite there. It is precisely the visual splendor of this chapter, its feast for the eye, that Dickinson forgoes in the poems of theological "blindness" to follow. Another informative investigation of Dickinson's use of jewels is Rebecca Patterson's chapter on jewels and gems in *Emily Dickinson's Imagery*. See also Joanna Feit Diehl's discussion (*Dickinson and the Romantic Imagination*) of Dickinson as a poet who takes Emerson's skepticism before illusion (in "Experience") to its logical conclusion – a renunciation of the "eye." Diehl writes that Dickinson "defines negatively the positive values Emerson had praised. . . . She cannot believe that 'a flash of his eye burns up the veil.' " Finally, see Evan Carton's essay, "Dickinson and the Divine," which claims quite rightly that "images of blindness or thwarted vision . . . usually signify achievement or its potential, rather than frustration" (*ESQ: A Journal of the American Renaissance* 28:243). Carton and I share a point of departure. We both see that Dickinson poetics makes Emerson's "original relation" to the universe problematic, and we agree that blindness is in Dickinson a sought after state. But it is misleading to claim that frustration is not equally sought. Indeed frustration is another name for that "limit" which may be "a torment for the passion," but is, at the same time, God's frontier. Frustration is a mood of Protestant *engagement*.

13. In his lectures on Milton given at Columbia University 1983–84 Stanley Fish made a similar point about the contest between Christ and the Archangel in *Paradise Regained*. Christ's steadfast refusal of the Devil's terms, Fish argues, is a refusal of the fallen language that would reduce all utterance to equivalent idolatries.

14. Poirier, who holds that American style is powered by a rejection of the reality in favor of *A World Elsewhere,* offers the best reading there is of the endurance of Emersonian idealism in American literature. Dickinson's "world elsewhere," like the "worlds elsewhere" of the several poets Poirier's work does not treat, is simply a world still owned, at least in part, by a God not absorbed into the transcendental self.

15. David Porter's study (*Dickinson: The Modern Idiom*) gives Dickinson's stylistic difficulty, and this difficulty as it might make Dickinson "modern," thorough and focused treatment. Whereas, for instance, Kenneth Stocks (*Emily Dickinson and the Modern Consciousness*) vaguely gestures at a certain "existential" mood present in Dickinson and characteristic of "modern consciousness," Porter engages more fruitfully with the particulars of this consciousness. Thus he is at his best in the chapter, "The Curse of Spontaneity" where he makes the crucial point that for Dickinson "death is the summoner of style," catching the way negation is Dickinson's poetic engine, as the "banquet of abstemiousness" is goad to her desire. To my mind, however,

the chapter entitled "Dickinson and American Modernism" makes the mistake of arguing backward from an a priori, largely Europe-based, conception of modernism to Dickinson, rather than forward from Dickinson to an investigation of what an *American* experimentalism might be. More interesting to me than the ways in which Dickinson uncannily predicts the anomie of a figure like, say, Eliot, is how her poetics – and the tradition it heads – ineluctably separates itself from the Eliotic modernism. To say that she predicts the modern is to beg questions about which modern? Is Frost "modern" in the same way that Eliot is? Is Crane? That neither is is the argument of this study. With Crane and Frost Dickinson belongs to a tradition characterized by latter-day Calvinist faith rather than by a postreligious defeat.

16. The encroachment of Christian structures bears striking resemblance to the psychological strictures critics like John Cody (*After Great Pain*) have noted as governing Dickinson's work. Rebellion against a theological system locates Dickinson helplessly within the system as sinner, as, for example, Dickinson's praise of what she does not have, her "sumptuous destitution," might figure in a psychological system as denial. See, in addition, Gilbert and Gubar for a discussion of self-annihilation and anorexia in Dickinson's work.

CHAPTER 6

1. It is ironic that the classic criticism penned by those who knew and loved Crane best has least sustained his literary reputation, although feeding the legend. See, for example, Allen Tate's essay in *Man of Letters in the Modern World* (293), R. P. Blackmur's "New Thresholds, New Anatomies" in *Form and Value in Modern Poetry*, Waldo Frank's retrospective of Crane in Brom Weber's edition of Crane's poems and letters, or Malcolm Cowley's "Roaring Boy" in *Exile's Return*. On this foundation has been constructed the following generation's view of Crane, summed up most concisely in John Unterecker's 1969 biography, *Voyager*, which adumbrates Tate's view in allowing, despite manifold influences bearing on Crane, that

> he found in Nietzsche's Appolonian-Dionysian dichotomy a satisfactory explanation for the nature of man, and particularly for the nature of the artist. Feeling his own orientation to be Dionysian, Crane came increasingly to believe he had been destined for the role of wine inspired prophet poet. (109)

Harold Bloom's view of Crane as "a prophet of American Orphism, of the Emersonian and Whitmanian Native Strain in our national literature" conforms to the pattern set by earlier critics both in its specification of the Sublime as Crane's terrain and in its dismissal of other factors. Thus when Bloom writes that he is concerned with Crane's "religion *as a poet*," he hastens to qualify, "(not as man, since that seems an inchoate version of Christian Science background, an immersion in Ouspensky, and an all but Catholic yearning)" (*Hart Crane*, 200).

The significance of Crane's Christian Science is not so easily dismissed as was, say, Norman Vincent Peale's in Bloom's essay on Emerson. Just as the inspirationalists that Bloom shunts off in a list may justly be said to be card-carrying popularizers of the Emersonian religion, Mary Baker Eddy's "harmonial religion" (Sydney Ahlstrom's term) and even Ouspensky's brand of theosophy have strong links to Emersonianism. The emphasis on the will, and on self-reliance, not to mention the fact that Eddy and Emerson shared a supporter and sounding board in Bronson Alcott, make the Christian Science that Crane's poetics explicitly challenge little more than a front for the Emersonian. Crane's exasperation with his mother's Christian Science cannot be dissociated from his disenchantment with Emerson's technology of optimism.

As both Unterecker and more recently Warner Berthoff point out, Crane's adolescent devotion to the Christian Science of his mother and his brief flirtation with Gurdjieff followed the same trajectory: into disillusionment. Why what Bloom calls his Emersonian "Orphism" should have held its arc any better is not clear to me, since the Emersonian optimism, for all its greater intellectual dignity, may – without stretching – be called a fair copy from which templates of Christian Science and theosophy are fashioned. For a pithy discussion of Christian Science and theosophy as part of an Emersonian umbrella coalition, see Ahlstrom. See also Berthoff's balanced evaluation of the relative impact of Crane's Christian Science and the Calvinism it displaced in *Hart Crane: A Re-introduction*. Berthoff is undoubtedly right in arguing that it is a "futile" exercise that seeks to match, say, Crane's sense of the "Word" with the "logos or the Fourth Gospel or Gnostic transumption" (Berthoff, 43): Crane is neither a dogmatic nor even a learned, religious thinker. This ineluctable and inconvenient fact, one might hazard, drives Bloom into even more than ordinarily compulsive capitalizations of the Emersonian zeitgeist, and hampers such intelligent scholars as Alfred Hanley whose *Hart Crane's Holy Vision: White Buildings* must circumspectly stop short of capitalizing anything (scriptural, psalmic, visionary, holy). In claiming that Crane is a poet of the Augustinian, or Kierkegaardian, sensibility, poet of a voice defined by the Fall, I want to name the "religion" both Hanley and Bloom in their separate ways leave obscure. It is an essentialized, experientially based Protestantism.

2. Note how Crane's sexual extravagance invades Tate's usually chaste New Critical rhetoric, forcing him to submerge biography in critical metaphor. For an interesting, more recent study of "thrust" see Thomas Yingling's groundbreaking *Hart Crane and the Homosexual Text*.

3. The best work to date on Crane (like, in certain ways, the best work on Dickinson) resists the Manichean antinomizing of Satan/God, mortal/immortal, industry/beauty to dwell on the "bewilderment" of Crane's style. I have learned much from the fine and thought-provoking recent analyses of Crane collected in Alan Trachtenberg's introduction to his collection, *Hart Crane*, in Eric Sundquist's "Bringing Home the Word: Magic Lies and Silences in Hart Crane" (*English Literary History* 44, 2, 1977), Donald Pease's "The Poetics of Pure Possibility," and especially Allen Grossman's "Crane's Intense Poetics," the last two in Harold Bloom's collection, *Hart Crane*. Writing on Crane as on other American poets, Grossman is unique among critics for insisting that "Poetry as discourse was for Crane, as for

us all, an instance of persons in relationship." Grossman's emphasis on the burden and privilege of personhood, exfoliated more fully in the theoretical work *The Sighted Singer,* conditions my own interest in Crane as sinner and sorely tried soul. I did not read this particular essay until my own was well launched, but Grossman's humanism has been a salient influence on my work. Although I assign a Protestant lexicon and emphasis to Crane's urgencies, I am in complete accord with Grossman's characterizations of Crane as a "mariner in the course of an unsurvivable voyage" (Bloom, 225) and thus as a poet who hazarded the "imprudence of refusing irony" (Bloom, 223).

Though there has been, to my mind, an immoderate critical susceptibility to Romantic cliché when it comes to locating Crane and assessing his importance, he is a poet whose work has benefited greatly from the New Critical dexterity. The rule seems to be that the closest readings are the best ones: it is the long view that is perilous. R. W. B. Lewis's *The Poetry of Hart Crane* is abundantly readable and admirably illuminating. Herbert A. Liebowitz's *Hart Crane, An Introduction to the Poetry* provides the reader useful points of access to Crane's formidable difficulties, although his Neo-Platonic frame is exceptionable. More recently Sherman Paul's work of old fashioned appreciation, *Hart's Bridge,* is, though flat-footed at times, excellent at demystifying Crane's style but more important, at defining the function of his multitudinous allusions. Lee Edelman's *Transmemberment of Song* and Yingling's *Hart Crane and the Homosexual Text* accommodate Crane's work to the current theoretical interest in rhetoric and power in interesting ways, but not without encumbering an already overfreighted poet with Greek and Latinisms he could surely do without. A poet who already uses words like "corymbulous" is in no great need of critics fond of "chiasmas" and "catachresis." My favorite 1980s book-length studies of Crane are Paul Giles's fresh and inventive *Hart Crane: The Contexts of "The Bridge,"* and Edward Brunner's deservedly acclaimed *Splendid Failure.*

4. Unless noted otherwise, all selections from Crane's work are from Brom Weber's *Hart Crane: The Complete Poems and Selected Letters and Prose,* still the best one-book source for the student of Hart Crane.

5. This horizon is, like Dickinson's "circumference," an image of the limit traced by the Fall.

6. Lee Edelman, writing on the "disjunctive" quality of "Voyages" in Bloom's *Hart Crane* (255–91), rightly claims that in "Voyages" Crane "embraces negativity in the hope of using it as an 'anchor,' a means of stability."

7. Crane eroticizes subject/object duality in the stead of his mentor, Whitman, for whom the truest knowledge is carnal. See Chapter 4 for a discussion of knowing and intimacy in Whitman.

8. For a representative view of Crane as "neo-Platonic" see Herbert A. Liebowitz's *Hart Crane.*

9. My understanding of Blake and romantic poetics in general is informed by – J. Hillis Miller's critique notwithstanding (see *The Linguistic Moment*) – M. H. Abrams' still superb *Natural Supernaturalism.* Writing of Blake's contraries, Abram states:

> Blake's redemption is figured as a circling back of divided man to his original wholeness; he breaks out of his ceaseless wandering in what Blake calls 'the circle of destiny' . . . into a Resurrection to Unity which is the full and final closure of the Christian design of history. The dynamic of this process is the energy generated by the division of unity into separate, quasi sexual contraries which strive for closure. (260)

10. One thinks in this connection of that American pragmatism that controls Frost's "Silken Tent" which "strictly held by none, is loosely bound / By countless silken ties of love and thought / To everything on earth the compass round."

11. Or, as Heidegger puts it, "Words and language are not wrappings in which things are packed for the commerce of those who write and speak. It is in words and language that things first come into being and are" (Steiner, 37).

12. A useful parallel to consider is Brecht's epic theater (Brecht, 281–2) that opposes the big bang of tragic catharsis, the manipulation that makes us munch the "dough / Divided by accepted multitudes."

13. Among its other notable contributions to understanding Crane, Paul Giles's *The Contexts of "The Bridge"* anatomizes this "Proem" in a separate index. There Giles enumerates a multitude of puns and ambiguous phrases that function to complicate the idea of "bridging." He writes "the smaller units of the poem are 'bridgings' which are synechdoches mirroring the larger design." To give a typical example from this rich book, Giles notes that the opening phrase of the "Proem" – "How many" – is a pun on the "harmony" to which "the Bridge" as whole aspires.

14. Gaston Bachelard's *The Poetics of Space* meditates on such structures in provocative ways.

15. "In place of fixed identity," writes Donald Pease of Whitman, "he created what might be called an 'inter-subject,' a subjectivity reducible to neither self nor other and not even equivalent to intersubjectivity, but rather a consciousness of the never ending collocution between self and other. . . . Whitman's persona in *Leaves of Grass*...is not a separate person but a personification of the 'common place' between persons" (Bloom, *Hart Crane*, 210). Ann Douglas has pointed out that "As I Ebbed with the Ocean of Life," "Tears, Tears, Tears," and "Dalliance of Eagles" are poems that confine Whitman in a smaller, more vulnerable self.

16. I am thinking of the function of such language in, say, *Redburn,* where the hero enters democracy, and his maturity, by learning a language of labor – an equitable currency. When language is degraded in Melville, it is the medium of "confidence men" who use it to buy us; in its more "innocent" guise, it can function as the scrip of equality.

17. These images offer a very definition of the "uncanny" as Freud describes it. The uncanny is evoked by "doubts whether an apparently animate thing is really alive; or conversely, whether a lifeless object might not in fact be animate" (*On Creativity*, 132). For a fascinating account of the uncanny and doubling in "The Bridge" see John T. Irwin's "Freud and Crane" in Bloom's *Hart Crane* (155–88).

18. The "Atlantis" section of "The Bridge," cut free of this responsibility, is not treated in this essay. I am aware that this is a section of considerable Romantic appeal and that to centralize it is to see the entire poem struggling toward the emergence of poetry itself as hero. Indeed, on the basis of what he calls the synthesis of "Atlantis" R. W. B. Lewis writes that "*The Bridge* belongs to . . . the well established tradition of the modern and Romantic epic. The hero is poetic imagination personified, and the context is a welter of contemporary activity." Lewis continues, "the plot of *The Bridge* is the gradual permeation of an entire culture by the power of poetic vision – by that ever pursuing, periodically defeated but always self renewing visionary imagination which . . . is the true hero of the Romantic epic."

If one believes that "Atlantis" is a good poem, then its placement at the end of "The Bridge" might suggest that final triumph of vision over brokenness, of hero over circumstance. Remember, however, that "Atlantis," though placed at the end of the poem, was the first section written. I judge it a poem substantially lacking the vigor of sections written later which Crane held responsible to an engagement with modern life. Reading less like a poem than like a catalogue of obliquely reflexive tropes, "Atlantis" offers synthesis raised to a metalevel that only makes it inert. I hold with Alan Trachtenberg (Bloom, *Hart Crane,* 64) that "the original tension, between the poet-hero and history, seems to be replaced by an unformulated struggle within the poet, a struggle to maintain a pitch of language unsupported by concrete action. . . . the bridge achieves its final transmutation into a floating and lonely abstraction.

Works Cited

Abrams, M. H. *Natural Supernaturalism: Tradition and Revolution in Romantic Literature*. New York: W. W. Norton, 1971.

Ahlstrom, Sydney. *A Religious History of the American People*. New Haven and London: Yale University Press, 1972.

Ahlstrom, Sydney, and Carey, Jonathan S. *American Reformation: A Documentary History*. Scranton: Wesleyan University Press, 1985.

Allen, Gay Wilson. *The Solitary Singer*. New York: Macmillan, 1955.

Alter, Robert. *Defenses of the Imagination*. Philadelphia: Jewish Publication Society of America, 1977.

The Pleasure of Reading: in an Ideological Age. New York: Simon & Schuster, 1989.

Altieri, Charles. "The Hermeneutics of Literary Indeterminancy: A Dissent from the New Orthodoxy," in *New Literary History* 10 (Autumn 1978).

Aspiz, Harold. *Walt Whitman and the Body Beautiful*. Urbana: University of Illinois Press, 1980.

Asselineau, Roger. *The Evolution of Walt Whitman: The Creation of a Book*. Cambridge: Harvard University Press, 1962.

Bachelard, Gaston. *The Poetics of Space*. Translated by Maria Jolas. Foreword by Etienne Gilson. Boston: Beacon Press, 1969.

Bancroft, George. "George Washington Commander in Chief," in Vol. 7 of *A History of the United States of America*. New York and London: D. Appleton and Co., 1912.

Barker, Wendy. *Lunacy of Light: Emily Dickinson and the Experience of Metaphor*. Carbondale: Southern Illinois University Press, 1987.

Barth, Karl. *Protestant Thought from Rousseau to Ritschl*. New York: Harper and Row, 1959.

Barthes, Roland. *The Pleasure of the Text*. Translated by Richard Miller. New York: Hill and Wang, 1975.

Bataille, Georges. *Death and Sensuality: A Study of Eroticism and Taboo*. New York: Walker and Co., 1977.

Bedient, Calvin. *He Do the Police in Voices.* Chicago: University of Chicago Press, 1986.

Benjamin, Walter. *Illuminations.* Translated by Harry Zohn. Introduction by Hannah Arendt. New York: Harcourt, Brace, 1968.

Bercovitch, Sacvan. *The Puritan Origins of the American Self.* New Haven: Yale University Press, 1975.

  Typology and Early American Literature. Amherst: University of Massachusetts Press, 1972.

Berthoff, Warner. *Hart Crane: A Re-introduction.* Minneapolis: University of Minnesota Press, 1989.

Blackmur, Richard P. "New Thresholds: New Anatomies," *Form and Value in Modern Poetry.* Garden City: Doubleday, 1957.

Bloom, Harold. "Wrestling Sigmund: Three Paradigms for Poetic Originality," *The Breaking of the Vessels.* Chicago: University of Chicago Press, 1982.

  editor. *Ralph Waldo Emerson. Modern Critical Views.* New York: Chelsea House, 1985.

  editor. *Hart Crane. Modern Critical Views.* New York: Chelsea House, 1986.

  editor. *American Poetry to 1914.* New York: Chelsea House, 1987.

Brecht, Bertolt. "Notes to the Rise and Fall of Mahagonny," in *Collected Plays, Volume II.* Edited by Ralph Manheim and John Willett. New York: Vintage, 1964.

Bretali, Robert. *A Kierkegaard Anthology.* New York: Random House, 1946.

Brown, Jerry Wayne. *The Rise of Biblical Criticism in America 1800–1870: The New England Scholars.* Middletown: Wesleyan, 1969.

Brumm, Ursula. *American Thought and Religious Typology.* Translated by John Hoaglund. New Brunswick: Rutgers, 1970.

Brunner, Edward. *Splendid Failure.* Urbana: University of Illinois Press, 1895.

Buckminster, Joseph. *The Works of Joseph Stevens Buckminster with Memoirs of His Life.* Boston: James Monroe and Co., 1839.

Budick, Emily Miller. *Emily Dickinson and the Life of Language.* Baton Rouge and London: Louisiana State University Press, 1985.

Buell, Lawrence. *Literary Transcendentalism.* Ithaca: Cornell University Press, 1973.

  New England Literary Culture. Cambridge: Cambridge University Press, 1986.

Burkholder, Robert E., and Myerson, Joel. *Critical Essays on Ralph Waldo Emerson.* Boston: G. K. Hall, 1983.

Bushnell, Horace. *Work and Play.* New York: Scribners, 1903.

Cameron, Sharon. *The Corporeal Self.* Baltimore and London: Johns Hopkins University Press, 1981.

  Lyric Time: Dickinson and the Limits of Genre. Baltimore and London: Johns Hopkins University Press, 1979.

Carton, Evan. "Dickinson and the Divine." *ESQ: A Journal of the American Renaissance* 28 (1974), pp. 242–52.

Cassuto, Umberto. *From Adam to Noah: A Commentary on the Book of Genesis.* Translated by Israel Abrahams. Jerusalem: Magnes Press, 1972.

Channing, William Ellery. *The Works of William Ellery Channing.* Boston: American Unitarian Association, 1892.

"Sermon Delivered at the Ordination of Jared Sparks May 5, 1819." Liverpool: F. B. Wright, 1821.

Cheyfitz, Eric. *The Trans-parent: Sexual Politics in the Language of Emerson.* Baltimore and London: Johns Hopkins University Press, 1981.

Clark, David, editor. *Critical Essays on Hart Crane.* G. K. Hall, 1981.

Clebsch, William A. *From Sacred to Profane America: The Role of Religion in American History.* New York: Harper and Row, 1968.

Cody, John. *After Great Pain.* Cambridge: The Belknap Press of Harvard University, 1971.

Cowley, Malcolm. *Exile's Return.* New York: Viking, 1951.

Crane, Hart. *The Complete Poems and Selected Letters and Prose of Hart Crane.* Edited by Brom Weber. Garden City: Doubleday and Co., 1966.

Crawley, Thomas Edward. *The Structure of Leaves of Grass.* Austin and London: University of Texas Press, 1970.

Daly, Mary. *Beyond God the Father.* Boston: Beacon Press, 1973.

Daly, Robert. *God's Altar: The Word and Flesh in Puritan Poetry.* Berkeley: University of California Press, 1978.

Damrosch, David. "Leviticus," *Harvard Guide to the Bible.* Edited by Robert Alter and Frank Kermode. Cambridge: Harvard University Press, 1986.

Delbanco, Andrew. *William Ellery Channing.* Cambridge: Harvard University Press, 1980.

The Puritan Ordeal. Cambridge: Harvard University Press, 1989.

Derrida, Jacques. *Of Grammatology.* Translated and Introduction by Gayatri Spivak. Baltimore and London: Johns Hopkins University Press, 1974.

Dickinson, Emily. *The Complete Poems of Emily Dickinson.* Edited by Thomas Johnson. Toronto: Little, Brown, and Co., 1955.

Diehl, Joanna. *Dickinson and the Romantic Imagination.* Princeton: Princeton University Press, 1981.

Dobson, Joanne. *Dickinson and the Strategies of Reticence.* Bloomington: University of Indiana Press, 1982.

Doggett, Frank, and Buttel, Robert. *Wallace Stevens: A Celebration.* Princeton: Princeton University Press, 1980.

Donoghue, Denis. *Connoisseurs of Chaos: Ideas of Order in Modern American Poetry.* Second edition. New York: Columbia University Press, 1984.

Douglas, Ann. *The Feminizaiton of American Culture.* New York: Knopf, 1977.

Seminars on Theology in American Poetry. Columbia University. New York. Fall 1984.

Douglas, Mary. *Purity and Danger.* New York and Washington: Frederick Praeger, 1966.

Eagleton, Terry. *Criticism and Ideology: A Study in Marxist Literary Theory.* London: Verso, 1975.

Edelman, Lee. *Transmemberment of Song. Hart Crane's Anatomies of Rhetoric and Desire.* Stanford: Stanford University Press, 1987.

Ellison, Julie. *Emerson's Romantic Style.* Princeton: Princeton University Press, 1984.

Emerson, Ralph Waldo. *Selections from Ralph Waldo Emerson.* Edited by Stephen E. Whicher. Boston: Houghton Mifflin, 1960.

Erkkila, Betsy. *Whitman the Political Poet.* New York and Oxford: Oxford University Press, 1989.

Filreis, Alan. *Wallace Stevens and the Actual World.* Princeton: Princeton University Press, 1991.

Fish, Stanley. Graduate Lectures on Milton. Columbia University. Fall 1983.

Self Consuming Artifacts. Berkeley: University of California Press, 1972.

Foucault, Michel. "A Preface to Transgression," *Language, Countermemory, Practice: Selected Essays and Interviews.* Edited and Introduction by Donald F. Bouchard and Sherry Simon. Ithaca: Cornell University Press, 1977.

Frei, Hans. *The Eclipse of the Biblical Narrative.* New Haven: Yale University Press, 1974.

Freud, Sigmund. *On Creativity and the Unconscious: Papers on the Psychology of Art, Literature, Love, Religion.* Selected, introduced, and annotated by Benjamin Nelson. New York: Harper and Row, 1958.

Frost, Robert. *The Poetry of Robert Frost.* New York: Holt, Rinehart, and Winston, 1972.

"On Emerson," *Daedalus* 88 (Fall 1959), 712–18.

Frye, Northrop. *Anatomy of Criticism.* Princeton: Princeton University Press, 1957.

Fuchs, Daniel. *The Comic Spirit of Wallace Stevens.* Durham: Duke University Press, 1963.

Gadamer, Hans Georg. *Truth and Method.* New York: Crossroad, 1986

Gelpi, Albert. *Emily Dickinson: The Mind of the Poet.* Cambridge: Harvard University Press, 1965.

Gilbert, Sandra, and Gubar, Susan. "A Woman – White: Emily Dickinson's Yarn of Pearl," *Madwoman in the Attic.* New Haven: Yale University Press, 1979.

Giles, Paul. *The Contexts of "The Bridge."* Cambridge: Cambridge University Press, 1986.

Girard, René. *Violence and the Sacred.* Translated by Patrick Gregory. Baltimore and London: Johns Hopkins University Press, 1977.

Grossman, Allen. "The Poetics of Union in Whitman and Lincoln: An Inquiry Toward the Relationship of Art and Policy," *Essays of the English Institute* (1983): 183–209.

Grossman, Allen, and Halliday, Mark. *The Sighted Singer: Two Works on Poetry for Readers and Writers.* Baltimore: Johns Hopkins University Press, 1992.

Hall, Arethusa. *Life and Character of the Reverend Sylvester Judd.* Boston: Crosby, Nichols and Co., 1854.

Hanley, Alfred. *Hart Crane's Holy Vision: White Buildings.* Pittsburgh: Duquesne University Press, 1981.

Haroutunian, Joseph. *Piety Versus Moralism: The Passing of the New England Theology.* New York: Harper and Row, 1960.

Hartman, Geoffrey. *Criticism in the Wilderness.* Baltimore: Johns Hopkins University Press, 1980.

Hartman, Geoffrey, and Budick, Sanford. *Midrash and Literature.* New Haven: Yale University Press, 1986.

Heimert, Alan, and Delbanco, Andrew, editors. *The Puritans in America*. Cambridge: Harvard University Press, 1985.

Homans, Margaret. *Women Writers and Poetic Identity*. Princeton: Princeton University Press, 1980.

Irigaray, Luce. *The Speculum of the Other Woman*. Ithaca: Cornell University Press, 1985.

Irwin, John. *American Hieroglyphics*. New Haven: Yale University Press, 1980.

Doubling and Incest: Repetition and Revenge. Baltimore: Johns Hopkins University Press, 1975.

"Self Evidence and Self Reference: Nietzsche and Tragedy, Whitman and Opera," *New Literary History* 11:1 (1979): 177–92.

James, William. *Faith and Morals*. Cleveland: World Publishing Company, 1962.

Juhasz, Suzanne. *Feminist Critics Read Emily Dickinson*. Bloomington: Indiana University Press, 1983.

Kaplan, Justin. *Walt Whitman: A Life*. New York: Simon & Schuster, 1980.

Keller, Karl. *The Example of Edward Taylor*. Amherst: University of Massachusetts, 1975.

Kermode, Frank. "Adams Unparadised," *The Living Milton*. London: Routledge and Kegan Paul, 1960.

"Freud and Interpretation," *International Review of Psychoanalysis* (1985) 12.

The Genesis of Secrecy. Cambridge, London: Harvard University Press, 1979.

Kierkegaard, Soren. *The Concept of Dread*. Translated, Introduction, and notes by Walter Lowrie. Princeton: Princeton University Press, 1941.

Fear and Trembling and the Sickness Unto Death. Translated and Introducton by Walter Lowrie. Princeton: Princeton University Press, 1941.

Philosophical Fragments. Translated and Introduction by David Swensen. Princeton: Princeton University Press, 1936.

The Point of View for My Work as an Author. Translated by Walter Lowrie. London and New York: Oxford University Press, 1939.

Kristeva, Julia. *Powers of Horror: An Essay on Abjection*. Translated by Leon S. Roudiez. New York: Columbia University Press, 1968.

Leder, Sharon, and Abbot, Andrea. *The Language of Exclusion*. New York: Greenwood Press, 1987.

Leverenz, David. *Manhood and the American Renaissance*. Ithaca: Cornell University Press, 1989.

Lévi-Strauss, Claude. *Tristes Tropiques: An Anthropological Study of Primitive Societies in Brazil*. Translated by John Russell. New York: Atheneum, 1969.

Lewalski, Barbara. *Protestant Poetics and the Seventeenth Century Religious Lyric*. Princeton: Princeton University Press, 1979.

Lewis, R. W. B. *The Poetry of Hart Crane: A Critical Study*. Princeton: Princeton University Press, 1967.

The American Adam: Innocence, Tragedy, and Tradition in the 19th Century. Chicago and London: University of Chicago Press, 1955.

Liebowitz, Herbert. *Hart Crane: An Introduction to the Poetry*. New York: Columbia University Press, 1968.

Lopez, Michael, "De-transcendentalizing Emerson," *ESQ: A Journal of the American Renaissance* 34 (1988), 77–139.

Lowance, Mason. *The Language of Canaan: Metaphor and Symbol in New England from the Puritans to the Transcendentalists.* Cambridge: Harvard University Press, 1980.

Lowell, Robert. *Day by Day.* New York: Farrar, Straus & Giroux, 1977.

Lukacs, Georg. *The Theory of the Novel.* Translated by Anna Bostock. Cambridge: MIT Press, 1971.

Martin, Robert. *The Homosexual Tradition in American Poetry.* Austin: University of Texas Press, 1979.

Matthiessen, F. O. *American Renaissance: Art and Expression in the Age of Emerson and Whitman.* London, New York: Oxford, 1941.

Mazzaro, Jerome. *Modern American Poetry.* New York: David McKay, 1970.

Mehlman, Jeffery. "The Floating Signifier from Lévi-Strauss to Lacan," *Yale French Studies* (48) 1972: 5–26.

Miller, Christanne. *Emily Dickinson: A Poet's Grammar.* Cambridge: Harvard University Press, 1987.

Miller, Edwin Haviland. *Walt Whitman's "Song of Myself": A Mosaic of Interpretations.* Iowa City: University of Iowa Press, 1989.

Miller, J. Hillis. *The Linguistic Moment: From Wordsworth to Stevens.* Princeton: Princeton University Press, 1985.

Miller, James E. *A Critical Guide to Leaves of Grass.* Chicago: University of Chicago Press, 1957.

Miller, Perry. *American Puritans, Their Prose and Poetry.* New York: Anchor, 1956.

Miller, Perry, and Johnson, Thomas. *The Puritans.* New York: American Book Company, 1938.

Moi, Toril. *Sexual/Textual Politics.* New York: Methuen, 1985.

Mossberg, Barbara Antonina Clarke. *Emily Dickinson: When a Writer Is a Daughter.* Bloomington: Indiana University Press, 1982.

New, Elisa. "Reconsidering Delmore Schwartz," *Prooftexts* 5 (1985): 245–62.

Niebuhr, H. Richard. *The Kingdom of God in America.* New York: Harper and Row, 1959.

Norris, Christopher. *The Deconstructive Turn.* London: Methuen, 1983.

O'Grady, John. *Models of Jesus.* New York: Image Books, 1982.

Packer, Barbara. *Emerson's Fall: A New Interpretation of the Major Essays.* New York: Continuum, 1982.

"Origin and Authority," *Reconstructing American Literary History.* Edited by Sacvan Bercovitch. Cambridge, London: Harvard English Studies 13, 1986.

Patterson, Rebecca. *Emily Dickinson's Imagery.* Amherst: University of Massachusetts Press, 1979.

Paul, Sherman. *Hart's Bridge.* Urbana: University of Illinois Press, 1972.

Pearce, Roy Harvey, *The Continuity of American Poetry.* Princeton: Princeton University Press, 1961.

Pearce, Roy Harvey, and Miller, J. Hillis. *The Act of the Mind: Essays on the Poetry of Wallace Stevens.* Baltimore: Johns Hopkins University Press, 1965.

Pelikan, Jaroslav. *Reformation of Church and Dogma (1300–1700).* Chicago: University of Chicago Press, 1984.

Perloff, Marjorie. *The Poetics of Indeterminacy.* Princeton: Princeton University Press, 1981.

Poe, Edgar Allan. *Eureka.* Vol. 16 of *The Complete Works of Edgar Allan Poe.* Edited by James A. Harrison. New York: AMS Press Inc., 1965.

Poirier, Richard. *A World Elsewhere: The Place of Style in American Literature.* New York: Oxford University Press, 1966.

    The Renewal of Literature: Emersonian Reflections. New York: Random House, 1987.

Pollak, Vivian. *Dickinson: The Anxiety of Gender.* Ithaca and London: Cornell University Press, 1984.

Porter, David. *Emerson and Literary Change.* Cambridge and London: Harvard University Press, 1979.

    Dickinson, The Modern Idiom. Cambridge: Harvard University Press, 1981.

Poulet, George. *Studies in Human Time.* Translated by Elliot Coleman. Baltimore: Johns Hopkins University Press, 1956.

Reynolds, David. *Beneath the American Renaissance: The Subversive Imagination in the Age of Emerson and Melville.* New York: Alfred A. Knopf, 1988.

Rich, Adrienne. "Vesuvius at Home: The Power of Emily Dickinson," in *On Lies, Secrets, and Silence.* New York: W. W. Norton, 1979.

Riddel, Joseph. *Modernism and the Counterpoetics.* Baton Rouge: Louisiana State University Press, 1974.

Ruegg, Maria. "The End(s) of the French Style," in *Criticism* 21 (Summer 1979), pp. 89–216.

Sacks, Peter M. *The English Elegy.* Baltimore and London: Johns Hopkins University Press, 1985.

Schneidau, Herbert. *Sacred Discontent: The Bible and Western Tradition.* Baton Rouge: Louisiana State University Press, 1976.

Schwartz, Delmore. *Letters of Delmore Schwartz.* Selected and edited by Robert Phillips. Princeton: Ontario Review Press, 1984.

Sewall, Richard B. *The Life of Emily Dickinson.* New York: Farrar, Straus & Giroux, 1974.

Spitzer, Leo. "Explication du Texte," *English Literary History* 16 (1949).

St. Armand, Barton Levi. *Emily Dickinson and Her Culture.* Cambridge: Cambridge University Press, 1984.

Steiner, George. *Martin Heidegger: Penguin Modern Masters.* Edited by Frank Kermode. Middlesex: Penguin, 1982.

Stevens, Wallace. *The Collected Poems of Wallace Stevens.* New York: Vintage, 1982.

    The Necessary Angel: Essays on Reality and the Imagination. New York: Vintage, 1952.

    Opus Posthumous. Edited by Samuel French Morse. New York: Alfred A. Knopf, 1951.

    The Man of Letters in the Modern World. New York: Meridian Books, 1955.

Stocks, Kenneth. *Emily Dickinson and the Modern Consciousness: A Poet of Our Time.* New York: St. Martin's Press, 1988.

Stovall, Floyd. *The Foreground to Leaves of Grass.* Charlottesville: University of Virginia Press, 1974.

Sundquist, Eric. "Bringing Home the Word: Magic Lies and Silences in Hart Crane," in *English Literary History* 44 (1975).

Tate, Allen. "Emily Dickinson," *Essays of Four Decades.* Chicago: Swallow Press, 1968.

    The Man of Letters in the Modern World: Selected Essays, 1928–1955. New York: Meridien Books, 1955.

Taylor, Edward. *Milton's Poetry: Its Development in Time*. Pittsburgh: Duquesne University Press, 1979.

Taylor, Edward, *The Poems of Edward Taylor*. Edited by Donald E. Stanford. New Haven: Yale University Press, 1960.

Trachtenberg, Alan. *Hart Crane: A Collection of Critical Essays*. Englewood Cliffs: Prentice-Hall, 1982.

Twain, Mark. *The Mysterious Stranger and Other Stories*. Foreword by Edmund Reiss. New York: New American Library, 1962.

Unterecker, John. *Voyager: A Life of Hart Crane*. New York: Farrar, Straus & Giroux, 1969.

Vendler, Helen. *On Extended Wings: Wallace Stevens' Longer Poems*. Cambridge: Harvard University Press, 1969.

Words Chosen Out of Desire. Knoxville: University of Tennessee Press, 1984.

Waggoner, Hyatt. *American Poets, From the Puritans to the Present*. Boston: Houghton Mifflin, 1968.

Waskow, Howard J. *Whitman: Explorations in Form*. Chicago: University of Chicago Press, 1966.

Weber, Brom. *The Letters of Hart Crane*. Berkeley: University of California Press, 1965.

Weisbuch, Robert. *Emily Dickinson's Poetry*. Chicago: University of Chicago Press, 1975.

Whicher, Steven. *Freedom and Fate*. Philadelphia: University of Pennsylvania Press, 1953.

White, Peter. *Puritan Poets and Poetics: Seventeenth Century American Poetry in Theory and Practice*. State College: Pennsylvania State Press, 1983.

Whitman, Walt. *The Complete Prose Works of Walt Whitman*. Philadelphia: David McKay, 1897.

The Correspondence 1842–1867. Edited by Edwin Haviland Miller. New York: New York University Press, 1961.

Leaves of Grass. Edited by Harold W. Blodgett and Sculley Bradley. New York: W. W. Norton, 1965.

Leaves of Grass: A Facsimile of the First Edition. Introduction notes, and bibliography by Richard Bridgeman. San Francisco: Chandler, 1968.

Notes and Fragments Left by Walt Whitman. Edited by Richard Maurice Bucke. London and Ontario: A. Talbot and Co., 1899.

Wilbur, Earl Morse. *A History of Unitarianism in Transylvania, England and America*. Cambridge: Harvard University Press, 1952.

Winters, Yvor. *In Defense of Reason*. New York: William Morrow, 1947.

Wolosky, Shira. *Emily Dickinson: A Voice of War*. New Haven: Yale University Press, 1984.

Wright, Conrad E. *American Unitarianism*. Boston: Mass. Historical Society and Northeastern University Press, 1989.

The Beginnings of Unitarianism in America. Boston: Beacon Press, 1955.

Wright, George T. "The Lyric Present: Simple Present Verbs in English Poems," *PMLA* 69 (May 1974).

Yingling, Thomas. *Hart Crane and the Homosexual Text: New Thresholds, New Anatomies*. Chicago: University of Chicago Press, 1990.

Zweig, Paul. *Walt Whitman: The Making of the Poet*. New York: Basic Books, 1984.

Index

Continued from the front of the book